THE
VOLGA
TATARS

STUDIES OF NATIONALITIES IN THE USSR
Wayne S. Vucinich, Editor

THE VOLGA TATARS

A Profile in
National
Resilience

Azade-Ayşe Rorlich

HOOVER INSTITUTION PRESS
Stanford University
Stanford, California

Hoover Press Publication 339

Copyright 1986 by the Board of Trustees of the
    Leland Stanford Junior University

First printing, 1986

Manufactured in the United States of America

90 89 88   9 8 7 6 5 4 3 2

Library of Congress Cataloging in Publication Data

Rorlich, Azade-Ayşe.
    The Volga Tatars.

    (Studies of nationalities in the USSR)
    Bibliography: p.
    Includes index.
    1. Tatars—Russian S.F.S.R.—Tatarskaia A.S.S.R.—
History. 2. Tatarskaia A.S.S.R. (R.S.F.S.R.)—History.
I. Title. II. Series.
DK511.T17R67 1986   947'.83   86-18631
ISBN 0-8179-8391-0 (alk. paper)
ISBN 0-8179-8392-9 (pbk.: alk. paper)

Design by P. Kelley Baker

To the memory of my father

To my mother

With deepest gratitude
for their unselfish love

Contents

Foreword

Azade-Ayşe Rorlich is eminently qualified to write this, the second in the Hoover Institution Press's "Studies of Nationalities in the USSR." She has spent many years investigating the history of the Volga Tatars and of the Turkic and Muslim peoples of the Soviet Union. Professor Rorlich received her Ph.D. from the University of Wisconsin and is today a member of the Department of History at the University of Southern California. She is proficient in the Turkic languages of the Soviet Union as well as Russian, and uses major European languages with ease. The excellence and thoroughness of her work is reflected by her extensive bibliography, the most complete available on Tatar history and culture, which includes sources in several languages and scripts. Although other studies have been published on various aspects of the Tatar past and present, none is so comprehensive and all-encompassing as this first Western-language study of Tatar history.

Professor Rorlich begins with the early history of the Tatars, discussing the controversies regarding their ethnogenesis, their adoption of Islam, the characteristics of their settled way of life, and the emergence and evolution of their first political entity—the Bulgar khanate. She addresses the issue of the contacts of the Bulgar khanate with the Russian principalities and comments on the nature of their relationship in the years before the Mongol conquest. Professor Rorlich's discussion of the Mongol conquest, the demise of the Bulgar khanate and emergence of its heirs, and the nature of the Kazan principality and Kazan khanate is crucial to an understanding of the roots of Tatar national resilience. She proceeds to discuss Ivan the Terrible's conquest of the Kazan khanate (1552) and the incorporation of its territory and population into the Muscovite state. The policies of russification and forced conversion to Christianity are described, and attention is given to the different means Russian rulers employed between the sixteenth and twentieth centuries to achieve the unchanging goal of russification. The Tatars' response to these policies was translated into an even deeper commitment to their religion, language, and culture.

The fundamental changes brought about by the emancipation of the serfs in 1861 unleashed a multifaceted process of modernization and growth in Russia, widening the gap between Russian and Tatar society and thus prompting the Tatars to cast a critical eye on the reasons for their economic backwardness and stagnation. The period between 1861 and 1917 saw a revival within Tatar society precipitated by the twin stimuli of developments in Russia and the Muslim world. Professor Rorlich provides a sophisticated analysis of the evolution of the reform movement from its beginnings as a challenge to religious dogma to later stages, when the most important goals became secular education and political action. All these issues, and their relationship to the evolution of Tatar identity, Professor Rorlich analyzes with exactitude, thoroughness, and expertise.

Professor Rorlich also discusses the impact of the 1917 revolutions and civil war on the Volga Tatars, their hopes for the establishment of an Idil-Ural state, and the emergence of the Tatar autonomous republic from the broken Bolshevik promises for a Tatar-Bashkir republic (which would have encompassed virtually all the territory of the former Kazan khanate). She carefully traces the roots of national communism in Tatarstan and gives an especially fine treatment to Sultangaliev's analysis of the relationship between Islam and communism, which played an important role in the evolution of Tatar identity in the Soviet period. Tatar responses to Soviet nationality policy, and the commitment of the Tatars not only to retrieving their distinguished national heritage but also to enriching and furthering it, represent some of the major topics that Professor Rorlich addresses in her analysis of the manifestations of Tatar national resilience in the post–World War II years.

This superb work is the kind that every library will want to have on its shelf. It will have an enduring value as the principal study of the Tatars of the Volga region.

WAYNE S. VUCINICH

Preface

Terminology and transliteration posed a variety of challenges for the present study. The purpose here is to identify not only the challenges but also the criteria that determined this author's use of terminology and transliteration throughout this work.

This book deals with the history of the Volga-Ural Tatars. In keeping with an already established tradition, the terms *Volga Tatars* and *Kazan Tatars* are used synonymously throughout.

The use of the term *inorodets* raised special problems. The word has no equivalent in English; etymologically it designates a person with other ethnic origin. Until 1917, Russian sources applied the term to all non-Slavs, regardless of their religious affiliation. *Inorodtsy* were mainly the Eastern peoples of the Russian empire who lived beyond the Ural Mountains and the Volga River. Soviet scholars have carefully avoided the term *inorodets*, employing instead such terms as *nerusskie* (non-Russians), *natsional'nosti* (nationalities), or *natsional'nye menshinstva* (national minorities), which apply to all non-Russians— Ukrainian, Belorussian, Baltic, and Eastern peoples alike. This study has used in transliteration the original Russian term *inorodets* because, despite its awkwardness, the term still designates most concisely the miscellaneous Eastern peoples of the Russian empire.

It was a common practice in Russia to add either the suffixes *ii*, *ov*, *ev*, or the suffix *in* to Muslim names; the onomastic change probably aimed at providing the Russians with a means of distinguishing Muslim family names from first names. The suffixes were not a sign of russification, and the Tatars themselves displayed a marked freedom in spelling them. Consequently, suffixes *ov* and *ev* often became *uv*, *ev*, and even *if*.

As a general rule, the present study has used Muslim names in their russianized form, the form in which they appeared most frequently in both Tatar and Russian sources. To avoid ambiguity and confusion, spelling variants have been disregarded. When there existed a choice between russianized forms of Muslim names and their Turkic counterparts, the Turkic were chosen in such cases as Gasprali (rather than Gasprinskii), Ishaki (Ishakov), and Akchura (Akchurin) when the incidence of the Turkic form in the sources was higher than that of the russianized.

This study rendered Russian names, terminology, notes, and bibliographical entries according to the Library of Congress system of transliteration of modern Russian, which omits diacritical signs. It adopted modern Turkish orthography in the case of Turkish names and sources.

The modern edition of H. A. R. Gibb, ed., *Encyclopaedia of Islam* (Leiden and London, 1960–) was the source of reference for Arabic names as well as for terminology connected with Islamic thought and institutions.

F. R. Unat's *Hicri tarihleri miladi tarihe çevirme kılavuzu* (Ankara, 1959) provided the table for converting the Islamic dates into their equivalents in the Gregorian calendar.

For Tatar materials in the Arabic script, the transliteration system found in E. Allworth's *Nationalities of the Soviet East: Publications and Writing Systems* (New York, 1971) was used; other materials published after the adoption of the Latin alphabet in 1926 were rendered in the official Latin transliteration. The discrepancies that still exist, however, do not represent the whim of this author. They reflect spelling innovations of individual authors as much as they indicate some of the problems inherent in the use of three different alphabets and their corresponding systems of transliteration.

Introduction

The emergence of a Soviet Russia at the end of World War I meant the unexpected triumph of an eminently Western ideology in the easternmost frontiers of Europe; the emergence of a Communist China in the middle of this century marked the beginning of a trend in which Asia was to increasingly challenge Europe's central place in world communism. The shift of the center of gravity from Europe to Asia was generally associated with Mao Tse Tung because of his role in the victory of the Chinese revolution. Yet in the early 1920s, long before Mao's emergence to power, there existed among the Muslim Communists of Russia doubting Thomases who challenged the validity of European Marxist doctrines for the peasant societies of Asia. Their names are little known; most often it is oblivion that awaits the defeated.

The theoretician of the Asiocentric doctrine of communism in Russia was Mirsaid Sultangaliev, a Volga Tatar by nationality, a *jadid* (reformist) teacher by training, and after his appointment by Stalin in 1918, a member of the Commissariat of Nationalities. Sultangaliev went so far as to advocate a secession from the Third Communist International in order to organize a Colonial International of the Peoples of the East. Party discipline prevailed over a creative interpretation of the Marxist doctrine, however, and in 1923, at the Twelfth Party Congress, he was purged as an exponent of national communism.

The overwhelming majority of the Muslim national Communists in Russia were Volga Tatars, and almost without exception, they represented the extreme products of the movement for Islamic revival. At the end of the nineteenth and beginning of the twentieth centuries, in Russia as well as in the Middle East and

India, Muslims strove to efface the gap between the development of the West and the stagnation of the Islamic world by accepting the imperative of change and renewal. The position of leadership the Volga Tatars occupied among Russian Muslims during the 1920s was hardly a post-1917 development. Instead, it both represented a continuation of the outstanding role they had played within the movement of reform that had affected the entire Islamic community of believers in Russia and signaled the resilience and dynamism that has characterized Tatar culture throughout the Soviet period.

The results of the 1979 census showed the existence of 6,317,000 Tatars in the Union of Soviet Socialist Republics (USSR), but Soviet statistics and official documents make no distinction between Crimean Tatars, Volga Tatars, and Siberian Tatars. It is believed that there are more than 400,000 Crimean Tatars living in the USSR, with perhaps as many Siberian Tatars living in the towns and cities of Western Siberia. This being the case, it can be assumed that there are more than 5,000,000 Volga Tatars in the USSR, the overwhelming majority of whom live in the Tatar and Bashkir autonomous republics of the Russian Soviet Federated Socialist Republic (RSFSR), although some live in the Chuvash, Komi, Mordvinian, and Udmurt autonomous republics and in the large cities of the RSFSR proper.[1]

Until recently, the study of Russian Muslims has been neglected by both the historians of Europe and the scholars of Islam, whose interests focused mainly upon the non-Russian Muslim world. During the last two decades, however, the centrifugal force of nationalism in the countries of the developing world has forced a reassessment of the effect that similar forces might have had on the durability of the multinational fabric of Soviet society. As part of this new interest, Western historians and social scientists, alike, have undertaken the task of analyzing the composite cultures of the Soviet Union. Yet compared with the Jews or the Slavic or Baltic nationalities, the Muslims are still of peripheral interest to the Western historian, although they are increasingly becoming the subject of investigation in the works of social scientists. Nonetheless, the student of Russian Islam has benefited greatly from the studies of E. Allworth, A. Bennigsen, H. Carrère d'Encausse, Ch. Quelquejay, T. Rakowska-Harmstone, M. Rywkin, S. E. Wimbush, and S. Zenkovsky, all of which offer analyses of the Russian Islamic community in its unity and diversity.[2] A. W. Fisher's pioneering book on the Crimean Tatars is the first study dedicated to the history of one Muslim nationality.[3] Such studies may yet become a trend in Western historiography.

Soviet scholarship has given greater attention to the history of Muslim nationalities, on both all-union and republican levels. But its forces have concentrated primarily on producing either general histories or monographs of the revolutionary movement among a given nationality. In the case of the Volga Tatars, the past two decades have been marked by a renaissance of archaeology, historical inquiry, and scholarship. Sailing the unpredictable, and often turbulent, seas of ideological imperatives and taboos, Tatar archaeologists and historians, such as A. Kh. Khalikov, R. G. Fakhrutdinov, G. V. Iusupov, S. Kh. Alishev, A. G. Karimullin, Ia. G. Abdullin, and Kh. Kh. Khasanov, have gradually reclaimed crucial components of the Volga Tatars' early (as well as more recent) history, reassessing in the process the relationship of the Tatars with the Russian state.[4] Particularly outstanding among these are A. Kh. Karimullin and Ia. G. Abdullin's studies of the Tatar reform movement and cultural awakening, with their respective emphases on the history of book publishing and the emergence of secular thought.

The main goal of this first Western-language study of the history of the Volga Tatars is to consider the most important themes of their social, economic, cultural, and political life since the tenth century A.D. The study is divided into three parts.

Part One addresses the issue of the origins of the Volga Tatars and the controversies surrounding their ethnogenesis.[5] It also focuses on the emergence of the Bulgar state, reviewing its major socioeconomic, cultural, and political coordinates before the Mongol conquest. It then examines the Mongol conquest and its impact on the Bulgar khanate and finally considers the Kazan khanate and its relationship to the Bulgar state, its links with Moscovy, and the major characteristics of its society, economy, and culture.

Part Two is concerned with the impacts of both the Russian conquest of the Kazan khanate in 1552 and the subsequent incorporation of the khanate into the Russian state. The policies of the Russian state aimed at russifying the Tatars are identified, as are the Tatar responses to those policies, the most spectacular and complex of which was the emergence of a reform movement aimed at re-evaluating the traditional Volga Tatar culture and values in their relationship to the Russian state. The roots, dimensions, and evolution of that reform movement, from a re-evaluation of religious thought to acceptance of secularization and political organization, represent other major concerns of Part Two.

Part Three addresses the impact on the Volga Tatars of the transformations ushered in by the revolutions of 1917. The degrees to which these transformations affected the national identity and consciousness of the Tatars are noted, with an eye to identification of the major characteristics of Tatar cultural resilience and national identity in the post–World War II period.

Addressing these themes of Tatar history, I also trace the evolution of the identity of the Tatars since the turn of this century and investigate the impact that the renewed Islamic identity, with its strong emphasis on national consciousness and secular values, has had on their life in the twentieth century, both as subjects of the last Russian tsar and as citizens of Soviet Russia.

It is my pleasant duty to express my indebtedness and gratitude to the many persons and institutions who have helped in one way or another in the various stages of the preparation of this study.

A grant from the International Research and Exchange Board made possible the completion of essential research during the early stages of this project, and a University of Southern California Haynes Fellowship enabled me to revise the manuscript in its final stages; I am thankful for both.

My greatest debt of gratitude belongs to professors Alexandre Bennigsen and Alfred E. Senn. I am fortunate not only to have studied with them but also to have benefited from their discerning and generous guidance whenever I sought help.

I am thankful to my American and European colleagues who at various stages of the project read the manuscript and offered their criticisms. Special thanks are due Professor Edward Lazzerini for his detailed criticism and suggestions.

I also owe a debt of gratitude to Noel Diaz, who prepared the maps; to Alexander Rolich, the Slavic bibliographer at the University of Wisconsin Memorial Library in Madison, for his expert advice throughout my association with the University of Wisconsin and, even more so, for answering promptly my many long-distance calls for assistance. Thanks are also due the staffs of the Hoover Library on War, Revolution and Peace, Stanford, California; the Doheny and Von Kleinsmid Libraries, University of Southern California, Los Angeles; the Research Library of the University of California at Los Angeles; the Western Illinois University Library, Macomb; the Columbia University Library, New York; the New York Public Library; the Helsinki University Library; the Royal Library, Stockholm; the Uppsala University Library, Uppsala; Centre Russe, Sorbonne, Paris; Centre de Documentation, Nanterre; Türkiyat Enstitüsü, Istanbul; and Milli Kütüphane, Ankara.

I am indebted to Mrs. Clara Harada, Mrs. Sharon Mather, and Ms. Martha Rothermel for typing the manuscript and to Ms. Marla Knutsen for her editorial advice, and I am thankful to all of them for their patience and ability to cope in good humor with the bewildering collection of foreign names, words, and transliteration systems used in this study.

I would also like to express my special thanks to the Tatar communities of Finland, Turkey, Germany, and the United States for sharing with me family archives and collections and for providing valuable advice and moral support at various stages of this project. Last, but not least, my thanks to Hari for his understanding, unqualified support, and energizing faith.

To conclude, I would like to add that, of course, I alone take responsibility for any errors of fact, judgment, or translation contained herein.

EARLY HISTORY

PART ONE

1 The Origins of the Volga Tatars

Tatar or Turk?

Tatarmï, torekmä?

(G. Gubaidullin)

The Volga Tatars are the westernmost of all Turkic nationalities living in the Soviet Union. Among them, there are two major groups—the Kazan Tatars and the Mishars; although each is characterized by linguistic and ethnogenetic particularities, their differences have not hindered the emergence and development of a common language and culture.[1]

THE ETHNONYM *TATAR*

As late as the second half of the nineteenth century, Volga Tatars preferred to identify themselves, and to be identified by others, as Muslims. In addition to this, however, they used such ethnonyms as *Kazanis* (Kazanli), *Bulgars*, and *Mishars*, as well as *Tatars*, and were identified as such by Russians and other peoples. Preference for ethnonyms other than *Tatar* may have represented a reaction to the popular, as well as scholarly and official, identification of the Volga Tatars with the Mongol Tatars of the thirteenth century.

At the end of the nineteenth century, enlightened Tatar thinkers, such as Kayyum Nasiri and Shihabeddin Merjani, played a major role in the rehabilitation of the ethnonym *Tatar*. Merjani urged the Kazanis not to be ashamed to call themselves Tatars. He noted that, because Russians employed the name *Tatar* as a curse, "some have regarded being a Tatar a shortcoming, hated it, and insisted 'we are not Tatars, we are Muslims' . . . If you are not a Tatar, an Arab, Tajik, Nogay, Chinese, Russian, French . . . then, who are you?" challenged Merjani.[2]

Apparently, the guilt and shame the Russians inspired in the Tatars in connection with their identity has endured to this day among some. Giuzel' Amalrik recalls in her memoirs: "I was ashamed of my nationality, even though I did not want to be Russian either, but I was ashamed of what seemed to me Tatar primitivism and lack of culture." Particularly relevant to this discussion are the remarks the father of a friend made to the thirteen-year-old Giuzel': "You tormented us 300 years, Tatar-mator, yes, and now repeat, how many years you tormented us."[3]

What is the origin of the ethnonym *Tatar*? Although there is no consensus on this issue among scholars, little has changed in their positions since the nineteenth century, which makes the task of identifying the basic theses less forbidding than the task of determining the ethnogenesis itself. Two theses stand out: the Mongol and the Turkic.

Proponents of the first accept the etymology of *Tatar* as deriving from the Chinese *Ta-Tan* or *Da-Dan* (a term of contempt applied to the Mongols by the Chinese) and believe that it refers to one group of Mongol tribes subdued by Ginghis Khan.[4] According to V. Thomsen, V. Bartol'd, and others, the name *Tatar* in the Orkhon Inscriptions refers to these tribes.[5]

The Mongol Tatars lived amidst Turkic tribes that had survived the demise of the seminomadic Turkic kaganate of the sixth and seventh centuries A.D. After their conquest by Ginghis Khan at the beginning of the thirteenth century (1202–1208), the Mongol Tatars, as well as the Turkic tribes of the southern Siberian plains and Central Asia, were included in the army headed by Ginghis Khan's grandson, Batu. In 1236, Batu, in the company of his sons Chagatai, Ogotai, and Tului, set out to conquer the eastern European *ulus* (lands) bequeathed to him at the 1235 *kurultai* (council).[6] Conquering the lands beyond the Ural mountains and the Aral and Caspian seas, the Mongols came into contact with the Turkic Kypchaks, who had reached the zenith of their political power in the eleventh and twelfth centuries A.D. as rulers of Dasht-i Kypchak, the huge territory between the Irtysh and Danube rivers.[7]

The Mongols and the Mongol Tatars, who were minorities in Batu Khan's army and even smaller minorities among the peoples of the "Golden Horde" that had emerged after Batu's conquest of the ulus beyond the Urals, underwent a process of assimilation by the Turkic peoples among whom they settled. This assimilation was both biological and cultural, as Al-Omari commented in his fourteenth-century account:

In the old times this state [the Golden Horde] was the country of Kypchaks [Cumans], but when the Tatars [Mongols] conquered them, the Kypchaks became their subjects. Later, they [the Tatars] mixed with them [Kypchaks], and the land had priority over their racial and natural qualities and they [the Tatars] became like Kypchaks, as they were of the same origin with them, because the Tatars settled on their lands, married them, and remained to live on their lands.[8]

The unification of all Mongol tribes under Ginghis Khan would not have been possible without eliminating the resistance of the Mongol Tatar tribes. A lasting sign of this victory emerged in Ginghis Khan's 1206 order that all conquered peoples be called Tatars, where *Tatar* is synonymous with *conquered*. Gradually, however, the Mongol conquerors were assimilated by the peoples they had conquered, and in 1246, Plano Carpini, an Italian traveler, noted that "even the Mongols themselves, especially since they have been cut off from their homeland, have come to be called 'Tatars.' Thus, the name *Tatar* has become synonymous with Mongol."[9] It seems that most of the peoples of the Golden Horde accepted their new ethnonym without significant resistance, yet the ancestors of the Volga Tatars were still reluctant to embrace the name in the sixteenth century.[10]

The Turkic thesis, which is not as widely accepted as the Mongol thesis, was advanced by scholars who rely heavily on the *Diwan-i Lugat-it-Turk*, a dictionary of the Turkic languages compiled by Mahmud al-Kashgari during the period 1072 to 1074.[11] In this book, al-Kashgari mentions that west of the Irtysh river there existed a Tatar branch of the Turkic languages. Ahmet Temir interprets this information as a testimony to the existence of a Turkic people called *Tatars* long before the Mongol conquest bestowed the name on the peoples of the Golden Horde. Broadening his interpretation of the information provided by the dictionary, Temir also suggests that the name could apply independently and equally to two different peoples: the Mongol tribe of Tatars and a Turkic tribe that inhabited a territory west of the Ural mountains.[12]

It is more likely, however, that in his dictionary al-Kashgari was referring to the language of the Mongol Tatar tribe, a tribe that, as a result of its territorial and cultural contiguity with the heirs of the Turkic kaganate of the sixth and seventh centuries A.D., might have spoken a Turkic language.

ETHNOGENESIS

The issue of the origins of the Volga Tatars is still being debated among scholars, both inside and beyond the borders of the USSR. However, even if the opinions of scholars seem still to be divided on the issue of the origins of the

Kazan Tatars, there is no disagreement over the fact that, by the sixteenth century, the Kazan Tatars were living in an area that included the northern lands of the former Bulgar state, which despite the fact that western European maps of the period still identified these lands as *Bulgaria Magna*, practically coincided with the territory of the Kazan khanate. Although the Kazan khanate could hardly claim firm borders, the 700 settlements mentioned in the *pistsovye knigi* (population registers and tax records) make it possible to identify the homeland of the Kazan Tatars with reasonable accuracy (see Map 1). They lived in an area bounded on the north by the Ilet and Viatka river basins. On the east, the Viatka provided a natural border beyond which, however, they did have villages along the Izh and Toima rivers. The southern and southwestern limits of their territory were marked by the Malaia Cheremsha, Utka, Maina, and Sviaga rivers. The Sviaga river basin was the most densely populated, with 150 villages recorded in the pistsovye knigi.[13]

The existence of a densely populated rural and urban network might be interpreted as a measure of the degree of economic and cultural continuity the settled Kazan Tatars enjoyed, distinguishing them from their nomadic and seminomadic neighbors to the east. The issues of territorial, economic, and cultural continuity have played a significant role in the discussions on ethnogenesis, but no single argument has carried enough weight to mold a universally accepted thesis.

The two main lines of thought that have emerged concerning the origins of the Kazan Tatars have found expression in the Kypchak and Bulgar theses; other theories exist, but they are either variations of one of these theses or a combination of both.[14] Proponents of the Kypchak thesis argue that the Kazan Tatars are direct descendants of the Tatars of the Golden Horde. This idea has been advanced by Russian historians, such as S. M. Solov'ev, G. I. Peretiatkovich, and N. I. Ashmarin, as well as by Tatar nationalist and émigré historians, such as A. Z. Velidi-Togan, and A. Battal-Taymas.[15]

The Bulgar thesis traces the ancestors of the Kazan Tatars to the Bulgars—a Turkic people who penetrated the Middle Volga and lower Kama region during the first half of the eighth century after being displaced from the Azov steppes by frequent Arab campaigns.[16] At the heart of this thesis is the idea that, when the lands of the Bulgars were conquered by the Mongol Tatars in 1236 and 1237, their culture survived the demise of the political entity and provided a foundation for the emergence of the Kazan Tatars. What characterizes this thesis is its intransigent rejection of the concept of acculturation and its predilection for absolute categories. Such instransigence has not deprived the thesis of supporters, however. N. Karamzin, I. Berezin, V. Grigoriev, N. Chernov, and M. Aitov carried its banner during the prerevolutionary period, and A. Kh. Khalikov, Kh. G. Gimadi, A. B. Bulatov, N. F. Kalinin, and F. Kh. Valeev are probably its most loyal Soviet disciples.[17]

MAP 1.   THE KAZAN KHANATE: 1437–1552

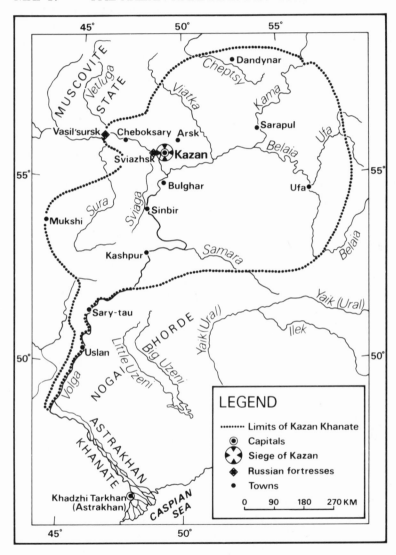

Each of these unilinear theses has generated discussion, and in the process, new theories have been born. In response to the Kypchak thesis, G. N. Akhmarov has advanced the theory of the Bulgar-Tatar heritage, which emphasizes the contribution of the Bulgar element to the ethnoculture synthesis triggered by the Mongol conquest. Sh. Merjani, on the other hand, has qualified his acceptance of the Bulgar thesis by a recognition of the significant role the Kypchak elements played in the culture of the Kazan Tatars.[18] During the 1920s, N. N. Firsov and M. G. Khudiakov were among the first Soviet scholars to recognize the existence of a Kypchak component in the Tatar ethnogenesis, but they contended that its impact was not strong enough to alter the Bulgar essence of the Tatar ethnos.[19]

In 1928, G. S. Gubaidullin articulated a different interpretation of the Kypchak thesis. According to him, the ethnogenesis of the Kazan Tatars had been completed during the fifteenth and sixteenth centuries, when they emerged as descendants of the Bulgars and the turkicized local Finno-Ugric tribes that were assimilated by the Golden Horde Tatars—carriers of a new language and a new ethnonym. These Golden Horde Tatars discussed by Gubaidullin were no other than the Kypchaks of the lower Volga, who had assimilated the Mongol Tatars of the thirteenth century.[20]

Gubaidullin was not alone in his adherence to the modified Kypchak thesis. His views have been shared by V. F. Smolin, A. Rakhim, Sh. F. Mokhammad'iarov, and others.[21] Although far from being universally accepted, this thesis has endured the ideological campaign aimed at eradicating the memory of the Golden Horde heritage.

In 1944, the Central Committee of the Communist Party of the Soviet Union condemned the idealization of the Golden Horde by Tatar historians and deemed the scientific investigation of Tatar history a task of utmost urgency. The response of the scholarly community to this political imperative was the April 1946 Moscow conference sponsored by the Academy of Sciences. The list of participants matched the scope of the task: archeologists A. P. Smirnov, N. F. Kalinin, and S. P. Tolstov; linguists L. Z. Zaliai and N. K. Dmitriev; ethnographer N. I. Vorob'ev; anthropologist T. A. Trofimova; and historians M. N. Tikhomirov, R. M. Raimov, A. B. Bulatov, and Kh. G. Gimadi. The conference broke no new ground; instead, it led to a regrouping of the participants around existing theories. Kh. G. Gimadi and N. F. Kalinin emerged as the strongest proponents of the Bulgar thesis, claiming once more that the Bulgars of the Volga-Kama were the sole ancestors of the Volga Tatars. On the basis of evidence provided by their respective disciplines, A. P. Smirnov, N. I. Vorob'ev, T. A. Trofimova, and L. Z. Zaliai defended the Bulgar-Kypchak thesis.[22]

Four decades have passed since the Moscow conference, but the issue of Tatar ethnogenesis is far from settled. If anything, it has gained in *aktual'nost'* and has brought into the discussion an impressive number of scholars.

Today, A. Kh. Khalikov, F. Kh. Valeev, and Ia. Abdullin are among the most ardent disciples of the Bulgar school.[23] Since the mid-1970s, however, the number of those who view the Bulgar and Kypchak contributions to Tatar ethnogenesis as a symbiotic, rather than antagonistic, relationship seems to have increased. M. Gosmanov is highly critical of F. Kh. Valeev's approach to the study of the art of the Bulgars. In response to the latter's claim that "the steppe art of the Kypchaks could influence neither the highly sophisticated art of the Bulgars, nor their culture as a whole, in any substantial way," Gosmanov argues that Valeev conducted the analysis in such a fashion as to suggest that his sole purpose was to provide an answer to the question "Who were our ancestors?" Gosmanov's own conclusion is that the Kazan Tatars cannot claim either the Bulgars or the Kypchaks as only their ancestors because both Bulgars and Kypchaks also played a role in the ethnogenesis of other peoples who inhabited the Volga-Ural region.[24]

Gosmanov's voice of moderation is reinforced by M. Z. Zäkiev and V. Khakov, who argue that neither the Bulgars nor their language disappeared after the Mongol conquest—that, on the contrary, the Bulgars enjoyed a remarkable degree of autonomy. When the Golden Horde was organized, however, the new set of political and socioeconomic conditions determined changes in the functions of the languages spoken in the area under the rule of its khans. Kypchak emerged as the official language, and it was in this capacity that it had an impact on the evolution of the Bulgar language. Zäkiev's and Khakov's adherence to the Bulgar-Kypchak thesis is restricted to the sphere of language; they contend that, from the anthropological viewpoint, the Volga Tatars are direct descendants of the Bulgars.[25]

There is little reason to believe that the final chapter on Tatar ethnogenesis will be written soon. There is sufficient reason to believe, however, that the Kypchak-Bulgar thesis may best endure the test of time and the scrutiny of scholarly inquiry.

2   The Bulgar State

Layers upon layers of history
Sleep divided into centuries...
Tear drops after tear drops
Speak of the sufferings of people.

Katlam-katlam tarikh iata
Gasïrlarga bulenep...
Khalïklar ah-zari kaita
Kus iashena elenep.

> (Asiya Minhajeva, *Bolgarda Uilanular*
> *[Meditation at Bulgar].*)

At the end of the ninth and the beginning of the tenth centuries, the process of
territorial, tribal, and political consolidation the peoples of the Middle Volga
had been undergoing for more than a century culminated in the emergence
of a political entity founded by the descendants of those Bulgar tribes whom
Batbay had led out of the Azov steppes during the first quarter of the eighth
century A.D.[1]

Arab travelers who visited the Middle Volga region during the tenth century
identified the territory of the Bulgar state as the geographic area between the
rivers Cheremshan (on the south), Sviaga (on the west), Kama (on the north)
and Sheshma (on the east). Ibn-Fadlan enumerated most of the rivers he and his
embassy had to cross during their trip to the khan of the Bulgars in A.D. 922:
"And we left the country of [these people] Bashkirs and crossed the river

Dzharamsan [Cheremshan], then the river Uran [Uren], then the river Uram [Urem], then the Bainakh [Maina], then the river Vatyg [Utka], then the river Niiasna [Neiaslovka], and then the river Dzhavshyz [Gausherma]."[2]

By the eleventh and twelfth centuries, the Bulgar state had augmented its territory: in the east, its borders reached the river Zai, and in the south, they extended to the Samara. The bulk of the population belonged to five tribes: the Bulgars proper, the Suvars (Savan), the Esegel (Askl), the Bersula, and the Barandzhar. Despite the tribal diversity, the basins of the Volga and the Kama seem to have been characterized by an impressive unity of material culture, as testified by the pottery unearthed since the 1960s in the areas along the upper Sura, Moksha, and Vada rivers.[3]

Yet the very nature of the fabric of the Bulgar state—a tribal and ethnic conglomerate—was a source of grievous complications during the period of consolidation and centralization. The struggle for supremacy was fueled by tribal rivalries, and travelers noted the rebelliousness of some of the tribes, who submitted only reluctantly to Bulgar rule. During the tenth century, the Suvars and the Bulgars had emerged as the most serious contenders for supremacy, and this polarization had led to the emergence of two political centers: Biliar-Bulgar and Suvar. Each represented the nucleus of a political entity sophisticated enough to have its own ruler, court, and coins. Also during the tenth century, Biliar-Bulgar emerged as the center around which the gathering of the Bulgar lands was completed, once the sovereignty of Suvar was liquidated.[4]

Almush (Almas), the son of the Bulgar prince Shilki, became the *yltyvar* (ruler) of the Bulgar state, and his decision to adopt Islam had a catalytic effect on the process of consolidation and centralization in his lands. In the spring of 921, Abdallah ibn-Bashtu arrived in Baghdad as the envoy of Almush, the ruler of the peoples of the north, to Caliph Ja'far al-Muktadir. He carried three letters conveying Almush's desire to be instructed in the religion of Islam, for which he was requesting assistance.[5] It was in response to this request that, in the same year, al-Muktadir sent Ibn-Fadlan's embassy to the land of the Bulgars. The result was that, in 922, the people of the Bulgar state joined the Islamic *umma* (community of believers). (To be accurate, however, it should be noted that this was the year Islam became the official religion of the Bulgar state, and that even before Ibn-Fadlan's arrival, Islam had become the religion of the people who lived along the shores of the Volga and Kama.) Caliph al-Muktadir's embassy met some "5,000 souls—men and women—[who] had already accepted Islam. They are known under the name Barandzhar."[6] Another visitor to the area at the beginning of the tenth century was the Arab geographer Abu-Ali Ibn-Rusta, who remarked that "most of them adhere to Islam; they have mosques and elementary schools in their villages."[7]

Almush stood at the head of a social hierarchy comprised of clearly distinguishable groups: tribal heads and lesser princes were subordinated directly to him; these, in turn, controlled the craftsmen and the semifree peasantry.[8] The yltyvar of the Bulgars seems to have put a great value on ceremony and symbolism to underline his position, and he also seems to have indulged in some of the trappings of power even before the victory of the Russian prince Sviatoslav over the Khazars in 965 ended the Bulgars' vassalage to the Khazar khan.[9] Ibn-Fadlan recorded some of these trappings: "the princes were seated to his right, and he asked us to sit to his left; his sons were seated in front of him, and he alone sat on a throne covered with Byzantine brocade."[10] It seems that Almush had become so elevated in his status that the very perception of his relationship to God had been distorted. Ibn-Fadlan was shocked by the audacity of Almush, who allowed a sermon that read: "O, Allah! Preserve the well-being of the Lord yltyvar, the Lord of the Bulgars."[11] Ibn-Fadlan reprimanded the ruler of the Bulgars and lectured him on some basic dogmas in Islam: "Truly, the Lord is Allah and nobody but He, the Great and the Almighty, can be addressed in this manner from the *minbar* [pulpit]."[12]

One of the true measures of the emancipation of the Bulgar state from Khazar vassalage was the ability of its rulers to establish diplomatic ties and conclude treaties with their neighbors, as well as with the rulers of more distant lands. In 984, for instance, the Bulgars signed their first treaty with Kiev. When that treaty was renewed in 1006, it included trade privileges for the Bulgar and Russian merchants. During 1024 and 1025, the Bulgar ruler Ibrahim sent an embassy to Khorasan; its main purpose was to provide for the cities of Sebzevar and Khosrovdzher, assistance in building mosques and other edifices.[13] The relationship of the Bulgar state with neighboring Russian principalities was neither smooth nor free of tension. In fact, throughout the twelfth and thirteenth centuries, they clashed frequently. The Russian campaigns against the Bulgars unfolded over an entire century, with the most notable ones taking place in 1120, 1160, 1164, 1172, 1183, 1186, and 1220—at which times Russian armies devastated the right bank of the Volga, destroying the city of Oshel'. The Bulgars, in turn, penetrated the Russian lands in 1201 and 1219, and it was only the imminent Mongol danger in 1223 that brought the hostilities to an end and led to conclusion of a peace treaty.[14]

Despite tension and frequent clashes, the relationship between the Bulgar state and the Russian principalities was not solely one of hostilities. Trade and commercial ties were as important for the Bulgars as they were for the Russian principalities, and the economic life of the Bulgar state, although disrupted by hostilities, never came to a halt because of them. Agriculture, crafts, cattle breeding, hunting, fishing, and trade represented the backbone of Bulgar economy.

The Volga-Kama region, with its rich black soil, was suitable for agriculture. The two-field system that was used was particularly suitable for the cultivation of virgin lands. The basic implements were the heavy metal plow with a single share *(saban)*, which was effective for the virgin, black-earth soils, and the light wooden plow with two iron shares used for podzol soils. The climate, more than the soil or agricultural technology, determined the types of crops the Bulgars cultivated. Barley, wheat, and millet seem to have been the traditional crops because most travelers noted their presence in the Volga-Kama region. Ibn-Fadlan commented: "They met us carrying bread, meat, and millet. . . their food consists of millet and horsemeat but they have also wheat and barley in abundance, and every one of them who planted this harvests it for himself. The ruler does not have any right to this, except for the fact that they all pay him every year one sable pelt per household."[15]

Ibn-Fadlan's comments are informative not only for reconstructing the profile of Bulgar agriculture but also for shedding light on their tax system. Because no taxes were levied on agriculture, the bulk of the revenues seems to have come from taxes on trade—one-tenth of the goods traded by both Bulgar and foreign merchants was relinquished to the treasury. In addition to the annual sable pelt tax, there were taxes on weddings and on booty taken during military campaigns, even if the ruler had not participated in them.[16]

Plentiful harvests enabled Bulgars both to satisfy their own needs and to trade the excess. Russian chronicles mention the fact that, when famine ravaged the land of Suzdal in 1026, the population could survive only because food was brought in from Bulgar ("privezosha zhito i tako ozhishsha").[17] Fruits were also plentiful in the Bulgar lands, and travelers were impressed by the orchards, walnut groves, and even melons they saw in those northern lands. Abu Hamid al-Garnati, the twelfth-century Arab geographer who traveled twice to Bulgar noted: "They have so many kinds of fruits that it is impossible to find more than this elsewhere. There is an extremely tasty melon that can be preserved during the winter."[18]

Crafts were highly developed in Bulgar state, where skilled potters, blacksmiths, coppersmiths, carpenters, stonemasons, jewelers, and tanners could be found not only in the towns but also in villages, where they fashioned goods of outstanding quality, indistinguishable from similar items produced in urban centers.[19] Bulgar craftsmen became experts in processing the hides and the pelts that were plentiful in an economy in which cattle breeding and hunting played a significant role. In fact, they became such experts in processing leather and fashioning such leather goods as boots, coats, belts, and trunks that their fame extended beyond the Urals, and a certain type of leather came to be known as Bulgari.[20] The Russians who encountered the Bulgars on the battlefields were impressed that they were all wearing boots ("sut' vse v sapozekh").[21]

Bulgar potters developed a technology and style of their own, which has made it possible to identify easily the yellow-reddish earthenware found at various archaeological sites. Most of the bowls, pitchers, pots, cauldrons, cups, and saucers these potters fashioned featured a glazed strip and were often decorated with original motifs.[22]

The gold and silver jewelry produced by Bulgar craftsmen is particularly interesting: Rings often feature a waterfowl motif, as do the silver and copper twisted bracelets, pendants, and bronze mirrors. The fascination with waterfowl was, in fact, a fascination with ducks, for they were the symbol of life in Bulgar mythology. Particularly relevant to this issue is a legend that has endured among Siberian Tatars to this day, and according to which Earth was born when the duck dived to the bottom of the primeval sea and brought up a piece of mud that it placed afloat on the surface of the water.[23]

Bulgar stonemasons and carpenters acquired recognition at home, as well as in such faraway places as Central Asia or Vladimir-Suzdal, where they were invited to erect palaces, mosques, and public edifices. At home, they probably erected most of the buildings in a typical Bulgar town: the official buildings, mosques, caravanserais (inns), warehouses, workshops, and houses. Wood was the principal building material, although bricks and stone were also used for public edifices and homes of the well-to-do. Some of the stone buildings were even equipped with a system of central heating. Most dwellings, however, were wooden structures that rose well above the ground and had chimneys through which the smoke from their stoves was evacuated.[24] Objects of household use and tools came from the forges of blacksmiths, who produced everything from knives, stirrups, cauldron chains, and locks to axes, scythes, and sickles.[25]

Craftsmen in general, and carpenters and stonemasons in particular, were probably in high demand in the Bulgar lands, which were densely populated. Archaeologists have identified approximately 2,000 villages and 150 towns. Of these, by far the largest and most impressive town was probably Biliar, which was located on Malaia Cheremshan, where it occupied more than 7 million square meters. Only half of its territory has been excavated, but some 1,000 wooden and several dozen brick and stone structures have already been revealed. Among the latter are the ruins of the palace, the caravanserai, and several houses. Smaller than Biliar, but no less prominent, were the cities of Bulgar (on the Volga), Oshel (on the Tetiush), and Kashan (on the Kama), each of which occupied an area of 1 million square meters. Al-Garnati noted, "Bulgar is a big city; its walls are made of oak and the houses in it of pine."[26] Bulgar and the other cities, however, also had many brick and stone structures. Most numerous in the Bulgar state were the small fortress towns—residences of feudal lords that were protected by two or three rows of earthen ramparts and were also surrounded by unfortified villages.[27]

Trade constituted a most important branch of the Bulgar economy. Bulgar merchants engaged in both domestic and foreign trade, but they monopolized the transit trade, utilizing the advantages of their land, which was richly endowed with a network of navigable rivers and located at a crossroads between

Asia and Northern Europe.[28] From the Caucasus, Central Asia, and Iran came spices, precious stones, rugs, gold, silver, and other luxury items. The Russian principalities sent furs, weapons, and glass ornaments; and European merchants brought cloth, Frankish sabers, and amber. The Bulgars sold grains, honey, beeswax, felt, leather goods (Bulgari), and furs. Slaves were also an important Bulgar trade commodity; as such, they were subject to the tax levied on all traded goods, thus supplying additional revenue for the treasury of the Bulgar ruler.[29]

It was the intense trade activity that was responsible for the emergence of fairs and marketplaces throughout the territory of the Bulgar state. Aga-Bazar on the Volga was perhaps the most famous, but there were fairs and markets in the cities and the countryside alike. The economic function of the cities—their emergence as trade centers—had a tangible impact on their physical development: caravanserais, which catered to the needs of the eastern merchants, became fixtures in Bulgar towns. The main function of the caravanserai was that of an inn, but most often it doubled as a combination inn, warehouse, and cultural center that provided merchants with food and shelter, storage facilities for their goods, and mosques where Muslims could perform the ritual prayers required by their religion. Christian merchants lived on the outskirts of towns in segregated colonies probably not too different from the *nemetskaia sloboda* (foreigners' quarters) of medieval Moscow. Eastern coins were used exclusively in trade transactions until the tenth century, when the Bulgars began minting their own. In addition to coins, pelts seem always to have fulfilled the function of units of exchange rather successfully, as suggested by the etymology of the Tatar word *tien* (squirrel), which stands for the monetary subdivision of a kopek.[30]

Islam became the nucleus around which the spiritual life of the Bulgar state developed after the tenth century. The Arabic script that accompanied the adoption of Islam became not only the vehicle for disseminating a new religion but also the key to learning and opening the door to the cultural heritage of the Muslim East. It should be noted, however, that the Bulgar lands were hardly a cultural wasteland at the time of their adoption of Islam. On the contrary, they had a rich written culture based on the Turkic runes of the Orkhon type. Writing had developed and spread largely as a means of coping efficiently with economic (taxes, trade), legal, and political matters. Records were kept on wood and salt plaques until the tenth century when paper was introduced from Khorezm in Central Asia. The only reminder of this practice today is the Tatar proverb "Tuzga yazmagannï soiläme," or in liberal translation:

> What is not written on salt
> Just to mention is a fault.

With the adoption of Islam, Arabic script replaced the Bulgar runes, and two styles of calligraphy—Qufi and Thuluth—became particularly popular. The literary Bulgar language that emerged during the twelfth century became the vehicle of communication for the new written culture. The ethnic and cultural kinship enjoyed by the Turkic tribes living on the territory of the Bulgar state, along with the increasing centralization, made possible the emergence of such a language, which rendered the existing dialectal differences less significant even if it could not erase them entirely.

The existence of a literary language had a profound effect on education, and in turn, that language was enriched by the fruits of education. The Muslim Bulgars had schools where secular subjects received as much attention as the teaching of the religious dogma. In addition to training future *ulama* (Islamic scholars) and government bureaucrats, these schools provided at least basic literacy for the majority of the population.[31]

Many Bulgar scholars of the twelfth and thirteenth centuries gained fame and recognition beyond the shores of the Volga and Kama. Al-Garnati was impressed by the work of historian Yakub ibn-Noman, who wrote a history of the Bulgars in 1112. Ibn-Noman was not unique; Burhaneddin Ibrahim ibn-Yusuf had become famous with his books on rhetoric, medicine, and religious commentaries; and no less prominent were the ulama and scholars such as Hamid ibn-Idris, Ahmed al-Bulghari, Muhammed Sadr ibn-Alaeddin, Hasan ibn-Omer, and Muhammed al-Bulgari.[32]

Unfortunately, history has preserved the name of just one Bulgar poet of this period: Kul Gali. His poem "Kyssa-i Yusuf" has been of interest to literary historians and linguists alike as an outstanding example of the spiritual legacy of thirteenth-century Bulgar society.[33]

The legacy of the Bulgars endured and, in the nineteenth century, was so tangible that Russian historian S. M. Solov'ev reflected:

> For a long time Asia, Muslim Asia built here a home; a home not for nomadic hordes but for its civilization; for a long time, a commercial and industrial people, the Bulgars had been established here. When the Bulgar was already listening to the Qur'an on the shores of the Volga and the Kama, the Russian Slav had not yet started to build Christian churches on the Oka and had not yet conquered these places in the name of European civilization.[34]

3 The Mongol Conquest

We are gone. Others will come.

Bez kittek. Bashkalar kiler.

(From the inscriptions in the Kazan fortress.)

One of the decisions of the Mongols kurultai of 1228 was to launch a campaign against the Bulgars of the Middle Volga. A year later, Batu reached the shores of Iaik (Ural), where he was successful in defeating the Bulgar outpost detachments. Despite this victory, he chose to interrupt the campaign, only to renew it in 1232, at which time he failed to bring the Bulgar lands under Mongol control.

The outcome of these military operations prompted the kurultai of 1235 to decide on a general campaign aimed at conquering not merely the Bulgar territories but the entirety of Batu's ulus. In the spring of 1236, after careful preparations, Batu's 150,000-man army set forth for the Eastern European campaign. His forces were joined by those of other Ginghisids (some 450,000 men), whose participation in the campaign had been made mandatory by the kurultai.[1]

Earlier encounters with the Mongols had awakened the Bulgars to the reality of the restless giant to the east. In response, they had improved the defense of their cities to the degree that Bulgar alone boasted a defense force of 50,000 men. The Bulgars, however, were no match for Batu's formidable army, which in 1236, conquered and devastated their lands. The charred buildings and bones unearthed by archaeologists in 1969 and 1970 on the territory of the former Bulgar state have provided time-capsule evidence of the magnitude of the destruction.[2]

After conquering the Bulgar lands, Batu's armies swept through Russia west of Moscow and, in the winter of 1240, reached Kiev, the seat of the grand prince and the Metropolitan See of Rus'. On December 6, abandoned by its grand prince, Michael of Chernigov, Kiev fell. Batu's armies continued their victorious march through Eastern Europe. The northern army moved forward through Podolia, Volynia, Galicia, Central Poland, Moravia, and Silesia; the southern army, through the central and southern Carpathians to Hungary, where they defeated King Bela IV on April 11, 1241.

The Hungarian plains, with their excellent grazing ground, prompted Batu to begin to settle down and even mint coins there. As soon as the news of the great khan's death on December 11, 1241, reached him, however, Batu abandoned his Hungarian conquests, pushed through the Danubian plains into the steppes on the northern shore of the Black Sea, and moved north along the Volga to Bulgar, where he could observe more closely the issue of the succession to the great khan.[3]

At the same time, he embarked on the task of organizing the conquered lands and setting up the blueprints of his rule over the sociopolitical entity that came to be known as Orduyu Muazzam (Great Horde) or the Golden Horde.[4] Batu chose Bulgar as his temporary capital. There the first coins of the Golden Horde were minted and vassal rulers of the conquered lands came to receive their *yarlyks* (charters).[5] Batu built himself a new capital, Saray, on the lower Volga, and as soon as it was completed, he moved there and the political center of the Golden Horde shifted to the south.

The immediate impact of Batu's conquest of the Bulgar state was massive population dislocation. Most of the survivors moved north, to the lands beyond the Kama. Some made their homes on the shores of Kazanka, a tributary of the Volga; others, in the Moksha river basin or along the Ika and Belaia rivers; still others went to the Bashkir lands.[6] Some, however, chose to settle among the Udmurts, thus contributing to what Khalikov calls "the Bulgarization and Islamization of the local Turkic tribes." Khalikov also claims that in settling on the lands to the north, the Bulgars were returning to the homeland of their ancestors, thus making possible the preservation of their anthropological purity.[7]

The demographic shift to the north, northeast, and northwest was partly responsible for the emergence of new cities that developed as economic centers rather than military outposts and fortifications. By the end of the thirteenth and the beginning of the fourteenth centuries, these urban centers had become the nuclei around which the principalities of Kazan, Shongut, Narovchat, Zhukotin (Zhuketau), and Kashan emerged; in addition, Bulgar revived.[8] Of

TABLE 1
RULES OF THE PRINCIPALITY
OF KAZAN (1297–1437)

Hasan	1376	Abdullah	
Muhammed Sultan	1376	Altyn Bek	
Tetiak (Entiak)	1394	Ali (Gali) Bek	1429–1445
Talych	1411		

NOTE: Based on the documents that I have consulted, I have compiled this table. Where years are supplied, the number has been mentioned in the document.

the principalities that emerged in the Kazanka river basin, the rulers (emirs) of the Kazan principality (Table 1) belonged to the former Bulgar dynasty, a fact attested to by the epitaph dated September 27, 1297, on the tombstone of Princess Altyn Berke, the niece of Emir Mahmud.[9]

Not all the inhabitants of the Bulgar state moved north after the destruction of their homes. Many stayed and even chose to revolt against their alien conquerors. Batu Khan sent one of his fiercest commanders, Subudai, to quell a revolt led by Jiku and Baian in 1238 and 1239, and Mengu Temir himself went to the Middle Volga to put down a revolt of the local population in 1261.[10]

Soon, however, as the political and administrative structure of the Golden Horde took shape and the people of the former Bulgar state began rebuilding their lives in the new principalities that had emerged as the result of the fragmentation that followed the Mongol conquest, revolts became the exception rather than the rule. There may have been two major reasons for this acceptance. First, despite their vassal status, and although their emirs could not rule without receiving a yarlyk from the khan in Saray, the Bulgars enjoyed a considerable degree of autonomy, which at times even enabled them to exhibit a certain independence in foreign policy.[11] Second, after the adoption of Islam by Khan Berke (1256–1266)—and even more so under Khan Ozbek (1313–1341), who made Islam the official religion of the Golden Horde—the Bulgars may have acquired a sense of belonging to the political entity, which they probably perceived as an Islamic commonwealth.

The khans of the Golden Horde (Table 2) never aimed at molding the conquered lands in accordance with a Mongol Weltanschauung. The goals of their administration were of a more pragmatic nature: They sought efficient support of the complex state bureaucracy and the army through taxes and replacement of military losses. It would be erroneous, however, to regard the Golden Horde as merely a steppe empire and ignore its unique nature, which combined in one sociopolitical entity the characteristics of the nomadic as well as settled societies over which the Mongol khans were beginning to rule. There

TABLE 2
GOLDEN HORDE KHANS—1256–1502

Batu	d. 1255	Conqueror of the Ulus.
Berke	1256–1266	Adopted Islam.
Mangu Temir	1267–1280	The Golden Horde became independent from the great khan.
Tuda Mangu	1280–1287	
Tele Buga	1287–1291	
Tokhta	1291–1313	
Ozbek	1313–1341	Islam became the official religion. Arabic became the language of politics and diplomacy.
Tinibeg	1341–1372	
Yanibek	1342–1357	
Berdibek	1357–1359	
Khaidar	1360–1362	
Murid	1362–1364	Weakening and fragmentation of the Golden Horde begins.
Toktamysh	1376–1391	Attempted to reunite the horde. Beginning of final disintegration of the Golden Horde and emergence of its successor khanates: Kazan—1437; Crimea—1443; Astrakhan—1466; Sibir—1483.
Kuchuk Mehmed	1435–1465	
Ahmed	1465–1481	1480, grand duke of Moscow stops tribute payment.
Seyid Ahmed	1481–1502	

were at least 25 major cities in the Golden Horde. Saray, its capital, was not a tent city. By the time of Khan Ozbek's rule, it had grown into a sophisticated urban entity with a complex water supply system and a physiognomy that was distinctly Eastern and was shaped by the mosques, medreses (Muslim schools of higher learning), caravanserais, and baths. Furthermore, the architecture of Saray was not a pale copy of Bulgar architecture but had a character of its own.[12]

The ethnic and cultural diversity, the differences in the socioeconomic development, and the political and administrative practices that Batu and his successors encountered in the Golden Horde determined their approach to the conquered lands and shaped their administration. For the Bulgar lands, for instance, Mongol administration amounted to indirect rule. In the southwest, the Mongols displaced the Russian princes and ruled directly; in the northeast, they retained the local hierarchy and princes, who became the intermediary (but

crucial) links responsible for the implementation of the economic and administrative policies of the khan.[13] However, a system of tax collection and drafting
of military recruits, which emerged as the backbone of Mongol administration,
was applied throughout.

To assess the potential tax and recruit contributions of the population and
also ensure the efficient collection of the taxes, Berke Khan ordered a series of
population censuses between 1251 and 1262 and appointed tax officials who
were responsible for supervision of tax collection and recruitment of soldiers.
Although there are no specific data regarding the Bulgar lands, it can be
assumed that their census took place between 1253 and 1257, because it was at
this time that the Iranian territories and the lands of the western ulus were being
registered in census reports.[14]

In keeping with the tradition of the Mongol-Turkic states, the Golden
Horde deemed the collection of taxes and duties its main administrative function.[15] Consequently, Batu's ulus was divided into distinct administrative units.
The Russian lands, the Caucasus, and the northern Black Sea shore were
divided into several smaller administrative units, and the principalities that were
emerging in the Middle Volga were organized as the Bashkir (or Bulgar or
Moksha) ulus.

In addition to taxes to the local emirs and feudal lords, the population of
the former Bulgar state was subject to a series of duties, obligations, and taxes
that were paid to the Golden Horde khan; these included tithe, storage tax,
road and river tax, contribution of recruits for the army, and support of the state
bureaucracy.[16] To ensure fulfillment of this administrative function of the state,
the Mongols devised an intricate bureaucracy based on the functions of two
types of administrators: *baskaks* (tax officials who, as military representatives
of the central rule, had security obligations in addition to supervision of tax and
duty collection) and *darugas* (civil representatives who supervised tax collection
and also acted as provincial governors).[17] Although documents do not confirm
the existence of either baskaks or darugas in the Bulgar lands, such administrators (at least darugas) were probably known in the Middle Volga during the
Golden Horde period because these terms were known at the time of the Kazan
khanate, where, however, they designated provinces rather than tax officials.[18]

In addition to Mongol tax officials, a category of tax collectors *(tamghachï)*
and service people *(soiurghal)* from among the local population added to the
number of those charged with the operation of the Mongol administrative
system.[19] Only one social group was exempt from taxes: the *tarkhan*, a privileged nobility who held hereditary land grants given to them by the khan, most
likely in return for some type of military service.[20]

It would be erroneous to contend that Mongol rule affected equally the
political life, economic patterns, social structure, and culture of the principalities in the Middle Volga. The principle of indirect rule, which occupied a

significant place in the sociopolitical system of the Golden Horde, was responsible for the preservation of the ruling class and local dynasties until 1445.

The Mongol tax system was indirectly responsible for an increased stratification of the population in the Middle Volga area. The landed aristocracy had always represented the upper level of the former Bulgar state. It continued to enjoy that position under the Mongol khans, but it was no longer a homogeneous class. The emergence of soiurghals and tarkhans contributed to the stratification of the aristocracy while also being responsible for significant differences that emerged among the peasantry; this was because tarkhans owned peasants who were de facto serfs or had lost their freedom at least partially.

In addition to the emergence of a category of dependent peasants, the deterioration of the economic status of the free peasantry represented one of the important developments that affected the rural population of the Middle Volga under Mongol rule. The obligations of the peasants increased as *kalan* (the land tax paid in kind), and *urtak* (the land rent paid in services) were increased. The craftsmen and merchants continued to occupy an important place in the social structure of the principalities of the Middle Volga, but they, too, underwent a process of gradual stratification.[21]

The Bulgar lands recovered gradually from the destruction and disruption of economic life that accompanied their conquest. Agriculture, cattle breeding, crafts, and trade still represented the backbone of the economy. During the period immediately following the conquest, however, the exodus of the population to the north seriously affected agriculture and rendered a blow to urban life. Cities were deprived of skilled craftsmen, who were taken prisoner and sent to the south to build and beautify the cities of Golden Horde.

Some cities, such as Biliar, never recovered from the Mongol conquest. By the late thirteeth and early fourteenth centuries, however, Bulgar, Suvar, and other old centers experienced a revival. Bulgar, in particular, boasted a dynamic urban life during the fourteenth century: A city of 50,000, it was, above all, a trade center that attracted merchants from Russia as well as the Muslim East and became known as the Golden Throne *(Altyn Taht)* of the Mongol khans. In addition, new cities, such as Kashan, Kazan, and Kremenchug emerged, and they represented the main catalysts in the economic recovery; this is attested to by the resumption of coin minting, a clear sign of market revival.[22]

The process of recovery, however, was hindered by the instability that accompanied the weakening and fragmentation of the Golden Horde and ultimately caused its disintegration. The Bulgar lands absorbed successive waves of shocks: They became the theater of confrontation between Bulat Timur and Toktamysh, who in 1391 and 1395 clashed in their struggle for supremacy and control of Batu's disintegrating ulus. Then, in 1395, the neighboring Russian princes attacked and devastated the entire area. Drought and plague, which ravaged the Middle Volga between 1428 and 1430, added to the devastation and triggered still another wave of migration. The Bulgars once again moved to the north, northwest, and northeast and settled on lands along the Kazanka and Kama, thus contributing to the process of ethnic consolidation around Kazan, or Bulgar-al-jadid (the new Bulgar). Gradually, Kazan gained in prominence, and although it never enjoyed the right to mint coins stamped with the names of its rulers, the throne of the principality was occupied by emirs from the old Bulgar dynasty until 1445, when the throne was taken over by Mahmud, son of Ulu Muhammed, who was the ousted khan of the Golden Horde and the grandson of Toktamysh.[23] Having taken over the throne of the Kazan principality, Mahmud became the founder of the Kazan khanates, which along with the Crimean and Astrakhan khanates the kingdom of Sibir, and the Nogai Horde became one of the successors of the Golden Horde.

The disintegration of the Golden Horde eliminated many of the common denominators that had held together the heterogenous political and socio-economic entity forged by Batu Khan. The many lands that had made up the fabric of the Golden Horde embarked on paths of development that grew increasingly distinct, but they all carried the legacy of Mongol rule.

For the Bulgars of the Middle Volga, the most enduring impact of their incorporation into the Golden Horde was the reinforcement of their Islamic identity and culture under the catalytic stimuli of an environment that had become an Islamic-Turkic commonwealth with its beginnings in the fourteenth century. When the ruling dynasty and the court of the Golden Horde adopted Islam under Berke Khan, it also adopted the urban culture of the Muslim East, and Saray became a Muslim city. The intensification of the ties with the Muslim East, and the increased interaction between the Turkic peoples of the Golden Horde, must have enhanced the Bulgars' awareness of belonging to an umma that had a distinctly Turkic cultural profile. The decision of Khan Ozbek to eliminate Mongol as the language of politics and diplomacy and replace it with Arabic, as well as his decision to make Turki the official language of the Golden Horde, intensified the process of acculturation. Despite the contentions of the Bulgar-theory purists, the Golden Horde became to a great extent the melting pot in which the ethnic and cultural syntheses that shaped the future history of the heirs to the Bulgar state took place.

4 The Kazan Khanate

To make my future bright
I reach for the fire of the past.

Kilächägem nurlï bulsïn öchen
Utkännärdän härchak ut alam.

(Mökhärräm Kaiumov, Kazanïmda shundïy chatlar bar
[The crossroads of my Kazan].)

Ali (Gali) Bek (1429–1445) was the last ruler of the principality of Kazan—an entity that had emerged in 1297 as one of the most dynamic heirs to the Bulgar state. His ouster by the Ginghisids of the Golden Horde brought about the political demise of the local dynasty and marked a turning point in the metamorphosis of the principality into a khanate. If the prestige of the Ginghisid dynasty as the crucial element in that metamorphosis leaves little room for controversy, the same does not hold true for the date of the foundation of the khanate, which continues to remain a subject of debate.[1]

The flight of the ousted Golden Horde khan, Ulu Muhammed, from Saray in 1437 and his migration toward a new ulus on the Middle Volga are viewed by many historians as the turning point in the history of the principality. But others regard 1445 as the first year of the Kazan khanate because it was then that Ulu Muhammed's son, Mahmud, took over the throne of Kazan, thus adding a dynastic dimension to the political disintegration of the Golden Horde.[2] (Rulers of the Kazan khanate are listed in Table 3.)

TABLE 3
RULERS OF THE
KAZAN KHANATE (1437–1552)

Ulu Muhammed	1437–1445	Sahib Giray	1521–1524
Mahmud (Mahmutek)	1445–1462	Safa Giray	1524–1531
Halil	1462–1467	Jan Ali	1531–1533
Ibrahim	1467–1479	Safa Giray	
Ali	1479–1484	(second rule)	1533–1546
Muhammed Emin	1484–1485	Shah Ali	
Ali (second rule)	1485–1487	(second rule)	1546
Muhammed Emin		Safa Giray	
(second rule)	1487–1495	(third rule)	1546–1549
Mamuk	1495–1496	Utemish (regent	
Abdullah Latif	1496–1502	of Suyumbike)	1549–1551
Muhammed Emin		Shah Ali	
(third rule)	1502–1518	(third rule)	1551–1552
Shah Ali	1518–1521	Yadigar Muhammed	1552

Ulu Muhammed's other two sons, Iakub and Kasim, went to Moscow and entered Vasilii II's service. It was not unusual for Tatar princes to be invited to the Muscovite court or to seek refuge there in the aftermath of dynastic clashes and domestic turmoil. The grand princes and the tsars of Muscovy (Table 4) endowed such princes with domains and towns and fully exploited a situation that enabled the rulers of the Muscovite state to interfere in the domestic crises of the Kazan khanate by intervening, directly or indirectly, on behalf of their protégés.

Vasilii II endowed Kasim with the small town of Meshchera on the Oka, which soon thereafter came to be known as Kasimov. Of towns such as Serpukhov, Zvenigorod, Kashira, Iur'ev, and Surozhik, only Kasimov became the nucleus of a khanate because, compared with the others, its population was non-Russian: Tatar and Fino-Ugric peoples had settled there long before it became the endowed domain of the Tatar princes.[3]

The fact that accident, rather than design, was the major force in the emergence of the Kasimov khanate left a mark on its internal affairs and organization. It differed from the other khanates that emerged after the disintegration of the Golden Horde because it lacked a ruling dynasty of its own. Instead, its rulers were selected by the Muscovite grand princes and the tsars, who were guided in their choices by the interests of the Muscovite state.[4] As a result, the khanate of Kasimov emerged as a client of Muscovy and often served as a waiting station for ousted khans of Kazan or new candidates to its throne.

TABLE 4
RULERS OF THE MUSCOVITE STATE
FOR THE PERIOD 1437–1552

Vasilii II	1425–1462	Vasilii III	1505–1533
Ivan III (The Great)	1462–1505	Ivan IV (The Terrible)	1533–1584

Thus the year 1445 marked the emergence of not one, but two, Tatar khanates. In the case of Kazan, however, dynastic changes alone would not stand as a sufficiently convincing argument for selecting that year as the date of establishment of the khanate were it not for the fact that it also marked the beginning of intercourse between the Muscovite state and the khanate and for the fact of Kazan's political daring and military superiority vis-à-vis Moscow.

For the most part of its 107-year existence, the khanate of Kazan was independent.[5] Despite the contention of many Russian historians who regard the year 1487 as the beginning of Kazan's vassalage vis-à-vis Moscow, Muscovite-Kazani relationships should be viewed within the context of Kazani history, which is marked by relatively extended periods of formal independence (1505–1516, 1521–1532, 1535–1546, and 1546–1551) alternating with spans of Muscovite protectorate status (1516–1521, 1532–35, and 1546) and direct interference in the domestic affairs of Kazan.[6] Furthermore, a black-and-white interpretation of the Muscovite-Kazani relationship does not do justice to the complexity of the relations Muscovy maintained with Kazan, and such a view may perpetuate the misconception of the uninterrupted and undiluted hostility said to have guided their behavior toward each other.[7]

In the mid-1450s, Muscovy launched an expansionist policy in the northeast, and the clashes that occurred between Moscow and Kazan had nothing to do with an a priori Tatar hostility toward the Russians. Rather, they resulted from Muscovite interference in Kazani domestic strife and also stemmed from Muscovite expansionist moves into the northeast, which fell within Kazan's sphere of influence.[8]

The full debut of Russian interference in Kazani domestic affairs took place in 1467, when Ivan III, the first grand prince to forge an active policy with regard to Kazan, chose to take an active part in the dynastic struggle of the khanate. Upon Mahmud's death in 1467, the throne of Kazan was contested by his son Ibrahim and his brother Kasim, who had been in Muscovite service since 1445 and had served the grand prince loyally as appanage prince of Meshchera.[9]

When Mahmud's widow traveled to Moscow to marry Kasim, she may have done so in compliance with Islamic tradition, which requires a man to marry the widow of his brother; in doing so, however, she may also have provided an added measure of legitimacy to Kasim's claims to the throne of Kazan and at the same time increased the hopes of the Kazani faction that supported Kasim's candidacy.[10] Ivan III backed Kasim in his bid for the throne of Kazan, but despite Muscovite blessing and military support, Kasim was not successful in ousting Ibrahim.[11] Ibrahim's death in 1479 and the dynastic conflict that ensued were skillfully exploited by Ivan III, who successfully backed the candidacy of another Tatar prince, Muhammed Emin, and as a result, was able to interfere freely in the domestic affairs of the khanate throughout Muhammed Emin's first rule (1484-1485).[12]

Muhammed Emin's death in 1518 brought about the extinction of Ulu Muhammed's line and prompted Crimea to join Muscovy in openly disputing the issue of Kazani succession. In 1521, Sahip Giray, the Crimean candidate for the throne of the khanate, went to Kazan at the invitation of the local princes and nobility, and thus the first step was taken toward attracting Kazan into the orbit of the Crimean political and economic interests.[13] Kazan's Crimean orientation facilitated its participation with Muscovy and Crimea in a tripartite alliance aimed at reducing and even annihilating the threat the Great Horde posed to the commercial interests of the three partners.[14]

If Muscovy's expansionism and interference in Kazani dynastic struggles resulted in hostility and clashes between the two polities, Muscovite commercial interests in the northeast, south, and southeast were responsible for the adoption of a policy that, by the end of the fifteenth century, was aimed at maximizing the advantages derived from peaceful relations with Kazan. The khanate of Kazan was more than the heir to the commercial traditions and contacts of the old Bulgar; it had expanded those contacts considerably and built a market that included Muscovy, the Siberian khanate, the Caucasus, Persia, and Central Asia.[15]

Muscovy benefited greatly from its trade with Kazan. As the volume of trade between the two partners expanded, Muscovy's dependence on it grew as well, rendering its commercial interests increasingly vulnerable to changes in the political climate between the two polities.[16]

Muscovy's interest in forging peaceful relations with Kazan, and its emphasis on commercial relations with the khanate, were organically linked with its Crimean alliance. Consequently, any change in Muscovite-Crimean relations also affected Muscovy's behavior toward Kazan. The demise of the Muscovite-Crimean alliance in 1521 may not have brought about a sudden turn to hostility toward Kazan on the part of the Muscovite state, but signs of change were evident as early as the period 1512 to 1515, when the deterioration of Muscovite-Crimean relations was paralleled by gradual changes toward Kazan as well. At the core of these changes was Muscovy's perception of the Kazani political scene in terms of its bearing on the relationship with the Crimean khanate. As a result, counteracting Crimean interests in Kazan became the primary goal of Muscovite policies toward the Middle Volga khanate.[17]

For more than two decades after the collapse of the Muscovite-Crimean alliance, the Kazan khanate became the theater in which the former allies tested each other's influence over Kazani politics and sought to confine that khanate to an exclusive partnership with one or the other. The pro-Muscovite and pro-Crimean khans who occupied the throne of Kazan after 1518 succeeded each other in a pattern that both reflects this rivalry and suggests an increased eagerness on the part of Muscovy to bring Kazan under its absolute control.

Ivan IV's coronation as tsar in 1547 marked the beginning of an overtly hostile policy toward Kazan that would culminate in its conquest on October 2/15, 1552. This shift to unredeeming hostility toward Kazan was largely determined by the role militant orthodox ideology played in encouraging the expansionist and annexationist policies of the autocratic Muscovite state.[18]

Although it is difficult to define the precise boundaries of the Kazan khanate during this period, its core area can be identified as the territory located in the Middle Volga basin around the confluence of the Volga and Kama rivers, an area that roughly corresponds to the territory of the Tatar Autonomous Soviet Socialist Republic (TASSR) and to the north-central lands of the Bulgar state.[19]

Kazan's economic and political influence transcended the borders of the khanate, however, and extended over an area flanked by Sura to the west and upper Kama and Belaia to the east. The khanate was a multinational state: Within its boundaries lived not only Tatars but also Bashkirs, Cheremises, Chuvashes, and Votiaks (the ancestors of today's Udmurts). This ethnographic mosaic was captured in the description of the 1524 encounter between the Muscovites and the Tatars: "And the generals shot the *mïrzas* [hereditary Tatar nobles], the Tatars, and the Cheremises, and the Chuvashes, and took as prisoners several princes and several mïrzas."[20]

The binding element in the conglomerate that composed the Kazan khanate was provided by the office of the khan, in which alone, the sovereignty of the state was vested.[21] The khan had, at least in theory, unlimited power; in reality, his power was checked by the nobility, who controlled the political institutions of the khanate. The most important institution was that of the *karachi* (the overseers), which was a sui generis royal council comprised of four members of the aristocracy led by the *ulu karachi* (the great, main overseers). The hereditary nature of the office of karachi is a measure of the power wielded by the Kazani aristocracy. Many of the karachi belonged to Crimean princely families, such as Shirin, Baryn, Argyn, and Kypchak, which testifies to the considerable influence the Crimean khanate exerted over Kazani policies.[22]

Another institution of significance was the Assembly of the Land, probably a local adaptation of the Mongol-Turkic kurultai, which was comprised of representatives of the landed aristocracy, the military, and the ecclesiastical establishments. Its principal function was to decide matters of succession and foreign policy.[23]

The Tatar princes; the mïrzas, emirs, and begs; and the princes of the Chuvash, Cheremis, and other peoples were the most prominent members of the landed aristocracy, followed by the Kazakhs and the hereditary tarkhan (nobility who enjoyed exemption from *yasak* [tithe] and kalan [tax on cultivated land]).[24]

The most prestigious members of the military establishment were the *ulan*s, who were probably commanders of cavalry units who at times performed diplomatic as well as military services. Afash ulan led the Kazani army that marched against Astrakhan in 1491, and Allaberdei ulan was Kazan's envoy to Moscow in 1546.[25] The ulans were endowed with land holdings in return for their services.[26] The *ichki* were probably a "praetorian guard" of Kazan, since the term means "insiders" and most likely refers to the military stationed in the fortress proper.[27]

The *seyit*, the leading religious authority, stood at the head of the ecclesiastical establishment. According to Islamic tradition, he had to belong to the house of the prophet. Next in importance were the *sheikh*s (senior Islamic scholars) and the *imam*s and *mullah*s (congregation leaders and teachers). The entire ecclesiastical establishment seems to have been an important land owning element in Kazani society because village names, such as Seitovo, Kulseitovo, Khodiashevo, and Derbyshki, suggest that their owners were persons who had religious titles.[28]

Merchants and artisans comprised the bulk of the free urban population of the khanate, and the Tatar, Bashkir, and various Fino-Ugric peasants were their free counterpart in the villages. At the very bottom of Kazani society stood the serfs and the slaves. Because they represented one of the main trade commodities of Kazan, the number of the slaves was impressive. In view of this reality, references to Kazan as a warehouse for slaves should be viewed not as metaphors but as reasonably accurate statements of fact.[29]

The Kazan khanate was true to the Mongol-Turkic heritage in the manner in which it approached its most important administrative function: collection of taxes and duties. The yarlyk of the Sahip Giray (1523) makes it possible to reconstruct in reasonable detail the administrative hierarchy of the khanate. It lists titles of officials who performed an impressive variety of services—as judges and as postal, customs, and tax officials. The yarlyk also contains a reference to city administration that suggests that, despite the dominant role that agriculture played in Kazan's economy, the physiognomy of the khanate was not eminently rural.[30] The important role of agriculture is underlined by the tax structure of the khanate, where *yasak, kalan, yer khablasï* (tax imposed on the sale of land), and *tütün sanï* (household tax) were the major taxes imposed upon the population.[31]

The existence of a sedentary agricultural economy with roots in the Bulgar past of the khanate is not indicated by the structure of the tax system alone; it is reinforced by linguistic evidence and by the folk traditions of the Tatars.[32] Sabantui, the Tatar festival of the plow, is perhaps the most enduring cultural legacy of the pre-Islamic traditions of the Bulgars and stands today as a living testimony to the sedentary agricultural life of the ancestors of the Kazan Tatars.[33]

The economic structure of the Kazan khanate retained the principal features of the Bulgar state; agriculture, crafts, and trade were its chief components. The land tenure system maintained the privileged positions of the khan, the nobility, and the *waqf*s (pious foundations) as the biggest landowners. On nobles' lands, the three-field technique was widespread and was combined with gardening and cattle breeding. On smaller plots tilled by the tributary peasants (*yasachnye*), agriculture was much more primitive and yielded poorer results. Hunting provided a major supplement for the livelihood of the peasants; furs were one of the principal items of trade. In the crafts, the Bulgar traditions continued; leatherwork, shoemaking, jewelry, and pottery remained important.

Kazan remained a center of transit trade where the daily markets, as well as the annual fair, enabled the Tatar, Russian, Armenian, Central Asian, Persian, and other merchants, to exchange their goods.[34] Direct participation in trade that was based on goods produced by the local economy grew throughout the history of the khanate and contributed to the emergence of Kazan as the most important commercial center of the Volga basin. Kazan merchants sold leatherwork, furs, fish, and slaves (who were purchased mainly by the Crimeans), and in the fifteenth and sixteenth centuries, the city emerged as a center vital to the Muscovite fur trade with Asia in general and with the Ottoman empire in particular.[35]

Kazan grew into a wealthy, prosperous state on the basis of trade and trade taxes and enjoyed a flourishing cultural life. Education and literature developed in the spirit of Islamic religion. *Mekteb*s and *medrese*s—elementary and secondary Muslim schools, respectively—enjoyed the support of the khans and pious foundations. It is believed that Suyumbike, the mother of Utemish Khan, founded libraries and archives and, following a court tradition, probably also encouraged the literary efforts of contemporary poets.[36]

The period of the Kazan khanate is also the time in Tatar history when the ethnogenesis of the Kazan Tatars entered its final stages and when their language took shape as a distinct branch of the Turkic languages. The yarlyks of the khans, the tombstone inscriptions, and the religious commentaries, as well as the poetry of the period, represent the earliest monuments of the Kazan Tatar language. The diplomatic yarlyks of khans Ulu Muhammed (1428), Mahmud (1466), and Ibrahim (1477), written to the Ottoman sultans Murad II and

Mehmet II, and the tarkhan yarlyk of Sahip Giray (1523) are important not only as valuable historical sources but also as monuments of early Kazan Tatar language.[37] The more than 75 tombstone inscriptions studied by Sh. Merjani, K. Nasiri, and G. Rakhim have preserved a language that, although Turkic in its general characteristics, was already exhibiting differences that would, in time, shape Kazan Tatar as a distinct language, the language of the Volga Tatars.[38] Commentaries to the Qur'an, such as the Tafsir of 1513, are a testimony to Kazan's role as a center of Islamic scholarship and learning. There were five stone mosques and probably as many medreses in the fortress of Kazan alone; the Kul Sheref and Nur Ali mosques seem to have been quite impressive. The Kul Sheref mosque, adorned by its eight minarets, was the largest and in all likelihood served as the cathedral mosque.[39]

Muhammediar Mahmut-ogly is the best known of the poets of the khanate period. His poems, "Tuhfai-Mardan" (1539) and "Nur-i Sudur" (1542), provide insight into the values of Kazani society in the sixteenth century, while also revealing the richness of the literary life of the khanate. There were so many poets in Kazan that "there was no room left; child and venerable old man alike aspired to be poets."[40] Most of these poets who apparently crowded the Kazani literary scene have remained anonymous. Some names—such as those of Garifbek, Emmikamal, and Muhammed Sheref, the author of *Zafername-i vilayet-i Kazan* (1550)—have been preserved.[41]

Even a brief review of the socioeconomic and cultural coordinates of the Kazan khanate during the sixteenth century leads to the conclusion that Kazan exhibited dynamism and vitality. Therefore, the demise of the polity in the fall of 1552 can be understood only if it is viewed in terms of the failure of the political system to adjust to the needs of an increasingly sedentary domestic milieu and to the imperatives of an international environment in which the amorphous political conglomerate of Kazan proved to be no match against the forces of centralization, autocracy, and expansion.[42]

The conquest of Kazan projected Muscovite Russia, still in its infancy as a centralized national state, into the orbit of multinational empires. At the same time, it added to the fabric of Russian society its first non-Slavic and non-Christian population, while also bringing about the acquisition of a socioeconomic and political entity that had developed its own political institutions, social system, economic practices, and religious and cultural values.[43] (See maps 2 and 3 for Muscovy's expansion during the sixteenth century.)

MAP 2.   TERRITORIAL EXPANSION OF RUSSIA: 1550–1905

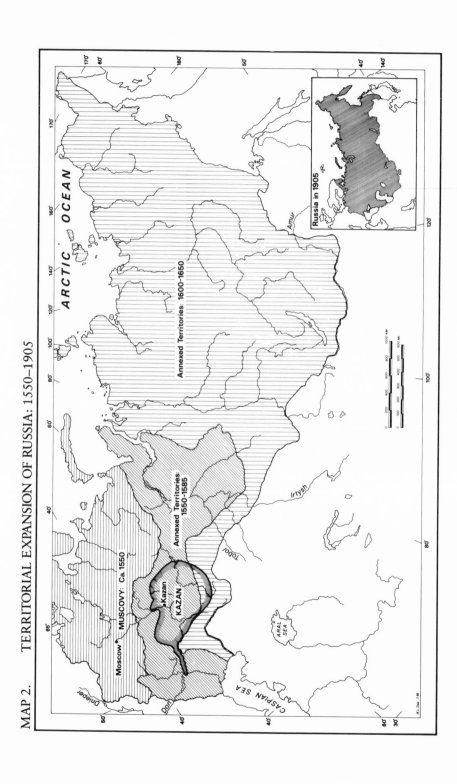

MAP 3. IVAN IV'S KAZAN CAMPAIGN OF 1552

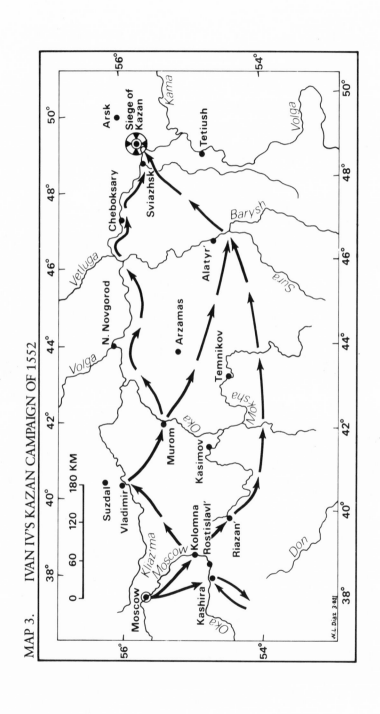

THE VOLGA TATARS AND THE RUSSIAN STATE

PART TWO

5 Annexation of the Kazan Khanate and Russian Policies Toward the Tatars

Victorious ruler.
People bow.
Their foreheads touch the earth.
Bondage ravages the land.

Patsha jingän
Khalïk bashïn igän
Chal manggae jirgä tigän
Ireksezlek kamap algan böten yäktan.

(Sh. Mannur, Sabïr töbe [At the end of patience].)

When, in 1552, Kazan was conquered and destroyed by the armies of Ivan IV, the very existence of its people as a different national, cultural, and religious entity was in danger. This danger was nowhere better illustrated than by Ivan IV's own statement: "Let the unbelievers receive the True God, the new subjects of Russia, and let them with us praise the Holy Trinity for ages unto ages."[1]

Ivan's attitude fit perfectly into the context of the religious ideology of his time. A sense of mission permeated the historical, dynastic, and national justifications of the conquest of Kazan. The Muscovite political elite and the leadership of the Russian Orthodox Church were to a great extent motivated by religious beliefs in their political and military actions against the Kazan khanate. After the conquest, their policies vis-à-vis the population of the khanate in general, and the Tatars in particular, were shaped by a perception that placed the Tatars and the Russians at antipodes; as can be seen in the following comparison:[2]

Russians: Believers, religious, Christians, pious, pure, peaceful, and good

Tatars: Nonbelievers, godless, pagans, impious, unclean, warlike, and bad

Throughout the centuries, the Russian state pursued a policy of national integration that meant conversion to Christianity and cultural assimilation. The new subjects of Muscovy were inorodtsy: Muslim Tatars, animist Chuvash, Mordvinians, Cheremis, Votiaks, and others. The most urgent task confronting the Russians was the absorption of these new elements into the fabric of their own society. Religious, legal, educational, and economic policies were designed and enforced in a concerted effort to transform the inorodtsy into better Russian subjects by making them Christians first.

Missionary activities represented one of the major channels through which the Russian state exercised religious pressure upon its inorodtsy. Although the goal of the Russian missionaries remained unchanged until the Revolution, the scope of their activities and the methods they employed between the sixteenth and early twentieth centuries varied.

Between 1552 and 1917, Russian missionary policies experienced six major shifts as represented by (1) the time of Archbishop Gurii, (2) the seventeenth and eighteenth centuries until the reign of Empress Anna Ivanovna, (3) the period of the Kontora Novokreshchenskikh Del (Office for the Affairs of the New Converts), (4) the reign of Catherine II, (5) the nineteenth-century policies until Il'minskii, and (6) the Il'minskii era.

The first period began on February 7, 1555, when Gurii was appointed archbishop of Kazan. The importance attached to Kazan as an outpost of Christianity was reflected by the special pomp and splendor with which Gurii was honored upon his departure for Kazan on July 26, 1555: All church bells rang in Moscow, and the service was performed by the metropolitan Makarii.[3]

Gurii's arrival in Kazan inaugurated the first wave of mass conversions, a campaign that extended from 1555 to 1576. To facilitate conversion, the tsar had invested Archbishop Gurii with special authority. The *jus asyli* provided him with the power of giving refuge to and protecting any non-Christian in conflict with the Russian authorities. The archbishop also stood above the civil officials of the local hierarchy, thereby ensuring his ability to override any of their decisions.

Although Ivan IV was anxious to see "the unbelievers receive the True God," he advised Gurii to approach the Tatars tactfully, suggesting that well-to-do Tatars be baptized in their homes and poorer ones be sent to the newly built monasteries for baptism.[4]

When this mild approach brought no results, the Tatars were forcibly converted to Christianity, a move that created the oldest Tatar Christian group, the starokreshchennye. The Tatars, who resented forced conversion fully as much as they resented Russian settlers, rebelled in 1556. Their revolt was suppressed, and those Tatars who still refused to become Christians were forbidden to live within the walls of the city. They moved outside the fortress and founded a new district, which came to be known as Staraia Tatarskaia Sloboda (the old Tatar quarter).[5]

Despite the pressures and punitive actions against the Tatars and animist inorodtsy, pagan apostasy and return to Islam were a chronic problem after the death of Gurii.[6] In a letter to Tsar Fedor Ivanovich, Metropolitan Hermogen complained that some of the baptized Tatars had returned completely to their former beliefs and others were only nominal Christians. The tsar responded with an *ukaz* providing that newly baptized Tatars be settled among the Russians and given pasture lands belonging either to Muslim Tatars or to the imperial domain.[7] These measures, too, proved futile, and missionary activity yielded no significant results during the ensuing decades.

During the Time of Troubles, missionary activity ceased. Instead, civil measures, such as economic coercion and granting of privileges (which coexisted during the seventeenth century), became the means of subduing the inorodtsy, chiefly the Muslim Tatars, in an effort to attract them to Christianity. The *ulozhenie* (law code) of 1649, however, addressed the Muslim issue in a special section where it was made clear that all Muslims found guilty of proselytizing would be burned at the stake. The provisions of the ulozhenie were to some extent softened by a law issued by Tsar Alexei Mikhailovich in 1654; it provided that any inorodets who agreed to become Christian was to receive 15 rubles. Chapter XVI, Article 42, of the same law provided that Tatar princes who became Christians could maintain their holdings but no Tatars could rent land from Russians. There was a further stipulation that, upon the death of a Muslim Tatar, that individual's wealth was to be transferred to any Christian relative, no matter how distant, despite the claims of more immediate Muslim heirs.[8]

Neither punitive nor conciliatory measures did much to increase the number of Tatar converts. On the contrary, these measures against Islam only increased the discontent of the Tatars, making them prone to open rebellion. Their participation in the great revolt of Stepan Razin in 1669 and 1670 illustrates this point.[9] These conversion policies likewise prompted the beginning of an exodus of the Volga Tatars toward Bukhara, the Kazakh steppes, and Central Asia. Many, finding themselves expelled from the fortress cities, had no other choice. Their best lands, situated in the river valleys or meadows, were confiscated and distributed among the Russian nobility or given to the monasteries or to the peasants arriving from central Russia to escape serfdom. This situation naturally aroused the antagonism of the Tatars against the Russians and fostered in them distrust of the official state policies.[10]

Peter the Great brought about the renewal of missionary activities in the Volga area. He subordinated missionary activities to the needs of the state and wanted the missionary priests to play an active role in the educational system he was structuring at the time. Consequently, education emerged as a new means of conversion to Christianity. The role of education was to increase, especially during the nineteenth century, when it came to be regarded as the only feasible means of conversion.[11]

The new mission with which education was endowed by the state was clearly reflected in the ethnic profile of the Theological Academy of Kazan, which in addition to its 36 Russian students, had, in 1723, 14 novokreshchen-nye (eighteenth-century converts) Tatar students.[12] These students were meant to form the nucleus of a future native orthodox priesthood who would be much more competent in dealing with inorodtsy in general and with Tatars in particular. It is not known how many of these students actually graduated and became priests, but those who did represented too small a group to cause any real changes in the attitude of the Tatars toward Christianity and conversion.

Peter the Great was more successful in his use of economic coercion and reward for missionary purposes. In his November 1713 report to the senate, he indicated that the Muslims of the Kazan and Azov regions should be given no more than six months to convert to Christianity if they wished to retain their holdings. It is known that a considerable number of Tatar mïrzas who were unwilling to give up their wealth submitted to this pressure, and for the first time since Archbishop Gurii, missionary activities registered some success. It is believed that by 1725 some 40,000 inorodtsy had been baptized. The laws of September 1, 1720, August 23, 1721, July 17, 1772, and April 13, 1791, provided further advantages for those who converted to Christianity, including tax exemption for three years, with taxes to be collected instead from those Tatars who remained Muslims, and exemption from military service.

In terms of moral commitment, this wave of conversions was no different from the previous ones; although numerous, the new converts were only nominal Christians. Dissatisfaction with this superficial conversion was expressed in a letter written by Metropolitan Sylvester to the Holy Synod on January 16, 1730.[13]

The anti-Muslim policies of Peter the Great were only a prelude to harsher activities of the mid-eighteenth century, during the reigns of the empresses Anna Ivanovna and Elizaveta Petrovna. On September 11, 1740, Empress Anna Invanovna issued an ukaz for the organization of the Kontora Novo-kreshchenskikh Del, which was to succeed the commission that had existed during the previous decade. The missionary activities of this office developed in three directions: physical attacks on Islam, economic coercion, and educational policies.

The Novokreshchenskaia Kontora Novokreshchenskikh Del had jurisdiction over the Kazan, Astrakhan, N. Novgorod, and Voronezh regions and received an annual subsidy of 10,000 rubles. It was headed by the archbishop of Kazan, Luka Konashevich.[14] Funds were granted to this office to provide both financial assistance for the missionary schools and rewards for new converts. Apparently not many Tatars were enticed by these material advantages, because the counselor Iartsev complained, in a letter dated June 25, 1742, that Muslim Tatars were not coming forward voluntarily to ask to be baptized and that rewards did not attract them ("ne l'stiatsia ni na kakiia za to sebe dachi").[15]

Physical attacks on Islam began in 1740, when an ukaz issued by the empress provided that all newly built mosques be destroyed and the construction of new ones prohibited. Between 1740 and 1743, 418 of the 536 existing mosques in the Volga area were destroyed. The destruction intensified in 1743, when Luka Konashevich was informed that 293 animist Chuvash had accepted Islam instead of Christianity, and as a result, more punitive actions were taken against the Tatars.

These actions failed to intimidate the Tatars, who in the spring of 1744, petitioned the government for permission to rebuild their mosques. It was perhaps fear of violent resistance that, in April 1744, prompted the senate to allow them to build two mosques in Kazan and one mosque for every 200 to 300 people living in the Kazan region.[16]

However, to further intimidate the Tatars, Luka Konashevich built churches in Tatar districts, organized religious processions with icons accompanied by church bells and choirs, and literally abducted Tatar children for enrollment in the missionary schools.

To crown these abuses, a new law was issued providing that no mosque could exist in the vicinity of a church and that Tatars could not reside in any area where a church stood. The August 8, 1750, ukaz of the senate ordered the Tatars to leave Staraia Tatarskaia Sloboda, the district they had established after being ousted from the fortress of Kazan in 1552. They were given land that had once belonged to the Spassko-Preobrazhenskii monastery near Kazan, where they founded a new settlement called Novaia Tatarskaia Sloboda (the new Tatar quarter). In 1759, this new settlement had 128 households comprising some 800 people. On September 23 of that year, a senate ukaz allowed them to erect two mosques in this new district.[17]

Economic coercion consisted chiefly of heavy taxes and obligations to which Muslim and animist inorodtsy were subjected. They had to pay the taxes, and provide the recruits, for those members of their communities who had been freed of these obligations after converting to Christianity. In 1747, the

Muslim Tatars of the Sviazhsk province complained about the burden of their taxes. They agreed to pay taxes for the Muslims who had converted but refused to share the taxes for the animists who, because they had become Christians, had been freed from their financial obligations toward the state.[18]

Educational policies in the schools for new converts (Novokreshchenskie Shkoly) organized by Luka Konashevich were aimed at bringing up a whole generation of true inorodtsy Christians who could, in turn, be more successful in converting the still-numerous Muslims and animists.[19] There was a special emphasis on cultivating the native languages, which had come to be regarded as one of the most important means of achieving missionary success. The schools for the new converts were also designed to train a generation of Christian inorodtsy teachers who could, in time, replace the mullahs, the Muslim teachers whom Luka Konashevich held particularly responsible for the stubbornness of the Tatars. Konashevich's accusations against the mullahs could be explained by the fact that, owing to the strong commitment of the Tatars to Islam, their mullahs—who served as clergymen, teachers, judges, and even doctors— wielded considerable authority and served as a unifying force, thereby hindering missionary activities.

By 1750, as a result of Luka Konashevich's repressive policies, Kazan was in a state of near revolt. To avoid the possibility of an open confrontation, Konaschevich was transferred in December 1755, and on February 2, 1764, the Kontora Novokreshchenskikh Del was closed. At that point, the persecution of the Muslim Tatars came to a temporary halt.

The reign of Catherine II has often been called the golden age of the Muslim Tatars. This contention is only partially true because she still approved funds for missionary activities, although on a much more limited scale than had her predecessors. Catherine did not share the contempt of her predecessors for the Muslim Tatars; moreover, she believed that Tatars could play a civilizing role among the animist peoples of the Russian empire. Catherine's own correspondence with Voltaire indicated that she harbored no hostility toward the Tatars, regarding them with a certain warmth, childlike curiosity, and understanding.[20] It is conceivable that her admiration for Islam was influenced by Voltaire, who considered it an enlightened religion.[21]

It would be inaccurate, however, to see only the enlightened despot in Catherine II. She was not only the friend and admirer of the French Encyclopedists but also a shrewd and pragmatic ruler. The golden age of the Tatars should be considered bearing in mind that Catherine's expansionist policies toward the east could succeed only if the persecution of Muslims stopped.[22] Tatar merchants could facilitate Russian trade with the Muslim khanates of Central Asia and with the Kazakh steppes. The laws issued by Catherine in 1763 and 1776 reflect her understanding of this reality: Tatars were allowed to engage in trade and to organize commercial enterprises. As a result, many

TABLE 5

MUSLIM AND CHRISTIAN MERCHANTS
IN THE VOLGA-URAL REGION IN 1851

Province	Christians	Muslims	Total	Muslims as Percentage of Total
Penza	1,439	189	1,628	11.6
Samara	5,084	608	5,692	12
Viatka	1,959	123	2,084	.6
Kazan	1,455	762	2,216	34
Orenburg	1,314	1,752	3,066	57
Tobolsk	834	87	922	9

SOURCE: A. J. Rieber, *Merchants and Entrepreneurs in Imperial Russia* (Chapel Hill, 1982), p. 73.

Tatars moved to the Kazakh steppes, where they founded commercial outposts for trade with Central Asia and established new Muslim settlements. They also sent their children to the famous Bukhara medreses to receive higher education.

Tatars who remained in Kazan were able to accumulate wealth and thus contribute to the formation of a rich commercial bourgeoisie in the nineteenth century (see Table 5).[23] Moreover, in 1773, the Holy Synod issued its Toleration of All Faiths edict, granting freedom of worship to all religious beliefs. This should not be regarded as being inspired by Catherine's affection for Tatars, however; rather, it was inspired by her fear of the rapidly spreading Pugachev revolt, in which a great many inorodtsy, including Tatars, were participating.

Perhaps the greatest legacy of Catherine II's "golden age" was the establishment in 1789 of the *muftiat* (Muslim Ecclesiastical Council), which was invested with authority in all purely religious matters affecting Muslims.[24] Its organization had a catalytic effect on the Tatars, even though the real authority of the *mufti* vis-à-vis the Muslims could be questioned on the basis of the fact that the *Shariat* (Muslim law) requirement that a mufti be elected by the believers themselves and not nominated by an outside power was not observed.[25] This catalytic effect was less a function of the real power invested in the muftiat than one of the symbolism connected with its creation. Establishment of the muftiat meant recognition of the Muslims as a separate religious entity and contributed significantly to their sense of unity and self-confidence.

The breathing space, the period of relatively peaceful coexistence between the Russian state and its inorodtsy subjects, did not last long. Missionary activity resumed with the reign of Nicholas I (1825–1855), as the ideals of the French Enlightenment and its universalism began gradually to give way to an ideology that valued only specifically Russian institutions.[26] This time, however, there was a shift toward a disguised missionary activity: Physical assaults on Islam were halted, economic rewards were augmented, and education was increasingly viewed as an effective vehicle of russification.

During the first half of the nineteenth century, the educational policies continued some of the traditions of the novokreshchenskie schools. The emphasis on native languages in general, and on Tatar in particular, as a means of facilitating missionary activity found further expression in the laws and regulations passed by the Ministry of Education and in the attention given to translations of Christian religious materials into Tatar. The first translation of a catechism into Tatar was published in 1803, and the first major Tatar grammar and a dictionary were compiled between 1816 and 1826 by A. Troianovskii, a teacher of Tatar at the Kazan Theological Academy. This stress on native languages as a means of russification was also embodied in a proposal for a project to create a Tatar newspaper, submitted by M. Nikol'skii to M. N. Musin Pushkin on February 3, 1834. That project, however, never materialized.[27]

Economic rewards for converts were increased during the nineteenth century. A July 25, 1849, decision of the senate provided the following benefits for those inorodtsy who became Christian: lifetime exemption from head taxes (podushnye), exemption from all other taxes for six years, and monetary rewards of 15 to 30 silver rubles per person, plus 30 silver rubles per family.[28]

Not only did these policies fail to increase the number of converts among the Tatars, but those who had earlier converted to Christianity also began to return to Islam in large numbers.[29] It could be argued that the mass return to Islam was partly the result of the revival and strengthening of the Muslim community around the muftiat created by Catherine II in 1782. Table 6 shows the situation that existed in the Kazan and Simbirsk gubernias between 1828 and 1829. These figures indicate that the majority of those novokreshchennye who had converted to Christianity during the eighteenth century had returned to Islam by the early nineteenth century. This trend intensified toward the middle of the nineteenth century. The May 19, 1848, report of the military governor of Kazan provided proof of the increasing return to Islam.

On May 21, 1849, Nicholas I responded to this situation by approving a state council resolution restricting the Orenburg muftiat's control over the appointment and activities of Muslim mullahs.[30] He also ordered the resettlement of Christian Tatars, both starokreshchennye and novokreshchennye, in Russian villages. In 1854, anti-Muslim, anti-Buddhist, and antischismatic (anti-raskolnicheskie) departments were organized by the Kazan Theological Academy, and in 1865, Professor E. A. Malov published an article stressing the need to maintain and reinforce the anti-Muslim department.[31] These measures, however, failed to reverse the missionary setback.

Against the background of this stalemate, N. I. Il'minskii (1822–1891), a

TABLE 6
CONVERTS TO CHRISTIANITY
AND THE RETURN TO ISLAM

	Total Converts to Christianity	Converts Who Returned to Islam
Kazan		
Starokreshchennye	19,016	3,251
Novokreshchennye	12,129	10,526
Simbirsk		
Novokreshchennye	2,667	2,532

SOURCE: Statistics of the Kazan consistory as given by E. A. Mozharovskii, *Izlozhenie khoda missionerskogo dela po prosveshcheniiu inorodstvev s 1552 po 1867. Chteniia v Imperatorskom Obschchestve Istorii i Drevnostei Rossiiskikh pri Moskovskom Universitete*, book 1, part 2 (Moscow, 1880), p. 151. They coincide with the figures given in *ITDM* (Moscow, 1937), pp. 336–37.

professor of Turkic languages at the Kazan Theological Academy and Kazan University, emerged as the promoter of a new, more subtle approach toward the inorodtsy. In a project presented to the academy in 1850, he pointed out that the main missionary weapons should be the school, the teacher, and the local language. This idea was not novel, having been promoted since the time of the *Novokreshchenskaia Kontora*. The difference between Il'minskii's policies and those of the eighteenth-century missionaries and government officials was not in kind but in degree. For Il'minskii, education through the local languages was not merely one of the policies to be pursued; it was the major policy. Il'minskii was also a sophisticated intellectual who realized that, to successfully attack Islam, one must know it, understand the sources of its strength, and recognize its vulnerability.[32]

Il'minskii's program was officially recognized on March 26, 1870, when the Ministry of Public Instruction approved the *Pravila o merakh k obrazovaniiu inorodtsev* (Rules concerning measures for the education of inorodtsy).[33] Il'minskii based his school system on these rules, which stressed the importance of native teachers and indigenous languages. Three types of schools, in particular, implemented his ideas: Russko-Tatarskie Shkoly (Russo-Tatar schools), Tsentral'naia Kreshcheno-Tatarskaia Shkola (the Central School for Baptized Tatars), and Kazanskaia Inorodcheskaia Uchitel'skaia Seminariia (Kazan Teachers' Seminary for inorodtsy).

The Russo-Tatar schools were those that included Russian language and arithmetic, as well as Muslim religion and Tatar language, in their curricula.[34]

The Central School for Baptized Tatars, founded in 1863 and existing until 1913, was set up to train teachers who would establish elementary schools in their own villages and thus bring under missionary control a much larger audience. Between 1863 and 1913, 4,454 boys and 1,885 girls studied at this school. Of these, 885 (635 men and 250 women) graduated as teachers: 163 became priests; 29, deacons; and 45, psalm readers. Also, a total of 565,139 copies of 77 different religious books were printed there.[35] The Kazan Teachers' Seminary for inorodtsy, which existed between 1872 and 1914, produced 231 teachers for inorodtsy schools between 1863 and 1881 alone.[36]

Il'minskii's system was criticized by both the Tatars and the Russians. Tatar criticism was based on fear of Russification; the Russians were apprehensive that Il'minskii's emphasis on native languages would generate nationalism and separatism among the inorodtsy. In defence, Il'minskii argued that, if native languages other than Tatar were neglected, the people would simply adopt the Tatar language and identity. He expressed fears of being confronted by a strong, united Tatar nation and openly stated that he would prefer to deal with a weak mass of inorodtsy. In this respect, his letter of June 27, 1891, to Pobedonostsev is remarkably candid:

> This is the dilemma: If from fear of separate nationalities, we do not allow the non-Russians to use their language in schools and churches, on a sufficient scale to ensure a solid, complete, convinced adoption of the Christian faith, then all non-Russians will be fused into a single race by language and by faith—the Tatar and Mohammedan. But if we allow the non-Russian languages, then, even if their individual nationalities are thus maintained, these will be diverse, small, ill-disposed to the Tatars, and united with the Russian people by the unity of their faith. Choose! But I believe that such diverse nationalities cannot have any solid existence, and in the end the very historical movement of life will cause them to fuse with the Russian people.[37]

To eliminate the possibility of the formation of a Tatar nation, and also to facilitate assimilation, the legal measures taken by the government were meant to support Il'minskii's policies. Tatar mektebs and medreses were required to hire teachers of Russian at their own expense. Furthermore, no approval was to be given for the construction of new mektebs and medreses unless their curricula included Russian. To promote the study of Russian, a series of new measures provided rewards for Tatars who had a good command of the language. They could be elected to zemstvo (local self-government) offices and could also perform religious functions without having attended the Muslim Theological Seminary.[38]

The Tatars, however, resented the idea of learning Russian in their own schools fully as much as they had rejected the idea of sending their children to Il'minskii's school.

Yet, despite the schools' ultimate goal of russification, and because his system emphasized bilingualism among the inorodtsy, Il'minskii indirectly rendered a great service to the Tatars. The heated discussions that took place among them concerning their acceptance or rejection of the idea and the futility or usefulness of the Russian language for their umma were a prelude to, and then a part of, the intellectual restlessness that characterized the Tatars toward the end of the nineteenth century.[39] These debates on the education of Muslim children became part of discussions of a more fundamental question regarding the place of Islam in a modern society and its compatibility with a rapidly changing way of life. Thus the gradual changes undergone by Tatar society, during the eighteenth and nineteenth centuries in particular, built, toward the end of the nineteenth century, a momentum for a reform movement that was a direct expression of the efforts the Volga Tatars undertook to adapt their entire life to the demands of an expanding, pluralistic, bourgeois society.

6 Reformism: A Re-evaluation of Religious Thought

Everywhere nations are awakening.

Här urïnda törle millät kuzgalïsha.

(S. Yahshigulov)

Tatar culture, both religious and secular, underwent significant change during the nineteenth century. A minority that had preserved its identity after living for centuries in a powerful Christian state, the Tatars had not blindly resisted assimilation, nor did they convert. Instead, they engaged in a continuous process of critically reassessing both their traditional values and their place in Russian society. In the process, a new sense of community developed, and Tatar society began to form its own secular character. During the course of this development, there existed two levels of dynamic tension stemming from Tatar connections—explicit or implicit—with two other main groups: the religiously identical, but historically dissimilar, Muslims of the Islamic umma and the religiously dissimilar, but historically adjacent, Russians.

The morphology of the Tatar reformist movement did not stem from a single source. One can recognize directly the Muslim fundamentalists of Islamic classicism as well as the nineteenth-century reformers who challenged them.[1] One can also distinguish both an indirect, but profound, influence of Russian philosophical and political thought and the influence of the Ottoman renewal brought about by the Tanzimat reforms.[2] The distinctive character of Tatar reformism, however, is a measure of the intensity and creativity with which the Tatars themselves approached these sources.

Tatar reformism had a broad scope. It began as early as the end of the eighteenth and beginning of the nineteenth centuries with a reassessment of their religious thinking, then turned toward cultural and educational reformism, and finally reached the realm of politics at the beginning of the twentieth century. Its earliest representatives were G. Utïz Imani (1754–1815), Abu-Nasr al-Kursavi (1776–1813), and I. Khal'fin (1778–1829).[3]

Abu-Nasr al-Kursavi (1726–1813) was the first to break the pattern of subservience and dependence the Volga Tatars had shown toward the Islamic scholastic centers of Central Asia.[4] His first contact with scholastic theology occurred during the years he spent in Bukhara and Samarkand. The combined effect of this direct contact with the conservative ulama and with the rich libraries of Central Asia led to Kursavi's rebellion against the established dogma and his commitment to a religious reform that would revitalize Islam through a return to its pristine purity. A serious scholar of the Qur'an and the Hadith (corpus of the sayings of the prophet Muhammad), Kursavi revealed himself as a strong adversary of the *kalamists*.[5] He resented the damage inflicted on Islamic dogma by the addition of the philosophical layer of interpretation for which he held the kalamists directly responsible.

Kursavi expounded these ideas in his work *Al-Irshad-al-Ibad* (Guidance for God's servants), which was never published. His main thesis warned, albeit indirectly, of the danger of remaining isolated from a changing world and stressed the importance of developing capabilities to adapt to new conditions of life. Kursavi emphasized the importance of making *ijtihad* (creative individual interpretations of the tenets of the faith) available to all Muslims, not just to those who had expertise in the intricacies of Islamic dogma. The insistence on participation of the entire umma in ijtihad, and the importance attached to it by Kursavi, seem to suggest that he felt the need to reinforce the meaning of Islam as a religion and as a way of life. The second idea developed by Kursavi was that of the need to give each scholar of Islam the right to provide his own interpretation of the Qur'an and the Hadith in searching for the true answer to any particular question. By advancing this belief, he denied the axiomatic value of *taqlid* (unquestioning acceptance of authority of the Islamic dogma and the adoption of precedents established by the ulama) and established the creative interpretation of the Qur'an and the Hadith as an important criterion for the vitality of the Islamic dogma.

These ideas outraged the conservative ulama of Central Asia and prompted a strong reaction on the part of Emir Haidar of Bukhara, himself an Islamic scholar. Kursavi had to flee Bukhara for his own safety and returned to his native village of Kursa in the upper Volga, where he began teaching at the local medrese. Although his innovative thinking soon made him popular among students, it aroused the suspicion and hatred of the other teachers and the Muslim clerics.[6] And because his was a single voice, too far ahead of its time, he was unable to gain a true following on any wide social basis.[7] Nevertheless, Kursavi's ideas, and the controversies they created, were the first signal of the restlessness that characterized the years to come.

It has often been argued that the special position of the Russian Muslims in the history of the intellectual, social, economic, and political development of the Muslim world is largely due to the influence of the Russian milieu. To the same extent, it would be valid to argue that the leading role the Tatars enjoyed among Russian Muslims during the nineteenth and twentieth centuries was partly because they shared in the climate of reforms that characterized the reign of Alexander II and were the beneficiaries of a new intellectual stimulus that emanated from the University of Kazan.

The first Tatar reformer to be indebted to the intellectual climate of Kazan as much as to that of Bukhara was Shihabeddin Merjani (1818–1889).[8] Merjani spent eleven years (1838–1849) in Central Asia studying at the medreses of Bukhara and investigating the manuscripts and rare materials of the Samarkand library. During the years he spent in Samarkand (1843–1845), Merjani's religious thinking shifted, and his critical approach to all established truth first revealed itself.

The Samarkand library prided itself in having among its holdings the famous Qufi Qur'an, which was believed to be one of only four copies of the Qur'an written by Othman, the son-in-law of the Prophet Muhammad. Merjani was interested in this Qur'an and studied its text and history while at Samarkand, coming to the conclusion that it had not, in fact, been written by Othman. He defended this thesis in a work entitled *Al-Fawaid-al-Muhimmatu* (Important goals).[9]

On his return to Bukhara, Merjani studied Kursavi's ideas and subscribed to them in a work called *Tanbih-i-Abna'-l-'Asr-bi-Tanzih-i-Anba'i Abu-Nasr* (Advice to the children of our time and a verification of Abu-l-Nasr's work). But Merjani had already drawn a beneficial lesson from Kursavi's boldness, and while in Bukhara, he never became too outspoken in his criticism of Central Asian scholasticism. Instead, he became deeply involved in the study of sciences and history and wrote his first historical essay on the history of the Uyghurs. It was not published until 1865, some fifteen years after his return to Kazan, where he had been appointed imam of the first mosque and teacher at the medrese attached to it.[10] Soon after its publication, his essay on the history of the Uyghurs came to the attention of the St. Petersburg Archaeological Society, which invited Merjani to join. Throughout his life, he remained an esteemed and active member of that society, taking part in its program and presenting papers on the history of the Tatars and of the Volga-Ural region.[11]

In 1886 and 1887, Merjani traveled to the Middle East. In the Ottoman capital, he was received with great honors by the Sheikh-ul-Islam and some of the most prominent ministers. He visited Ottoman institutions of learning and welfare and donated some of his books to the Hamidiye library. His travels also took him to Mecca and Cairo, but it is most likely that Merjani became acquainted with ideas of reform only in Cairo and Istanbul.[12]

Shortly after his return to Kazan in 1887, Merjani was appointed language teacher at the Russo-Tatar Teachers' School. His contact with the Russian teachers at this school, as well as with the professors at Kazan University, gave him a unique opportunity to compare the changes and movements toward reform in two different societies, Islamic and Russian. This exposure undoubtedly contributed to his critical assessment of the needs of the Volga Tatars.

Merjani wrote some 24 works on various issues. All were written in Arabic, with the exception of *Mustafad al-Akhbar fi-l-Ahwal Qazan wa Bulghar* (Select information on the situation of Kazan and Bulgar), which was written in the Volga dialect. This book represents the first attempt to present the Volga Tatars with their own history in their own language.[13]

The core of Merjani's reformist ideas is contained in his religious writing.[14] As a follower of Kursavi, Merjani advocated the need to bring ijtihad back to the umma to make it possible for everyone to use personal interpretation to find in the Qur'an the answers to religious questions.

For Merjani, this advocacy of the ijtihad was not just an intellectual exercise: He practiced what he preached, and there are sufficient instances to prove this point. One such instance was his approach to the practical question regarding the necessity or futility of the fifth daily prayer, *yatsy*. According to Islamic dogma, the fifth daily prayer must be performed after sunset, in the twilight. Because in Kazan and many other places in the distant regions of the northern hemisphere there is a sudden transition to night, many mullahs considered the fifth prayer to be unnecessary. Relying on ijtihad, Merjani warned against blindly observing dogmatic requirements and demonstrated the obligatory nature of this prayer.[15] Ijtihad was also the basis of Merjani's work on *fikh* (Islamic law), where he advocated the use of mathematical and astronomical principles instead of the principle of empirical observation for the delineation of Muslim months. Implementing this principle into practice when he was imam of Kazan, Merjani sent a note to the mullahs acknowledging that for that current year, 1873, the month of fasting (Ramadan) would begin (according to astronomical calculations) on a Wednesday. However, when weather conditions made it impossible to sight the new moon, mullahs accused Merjani of having acted against Shariat in establishing the beginning of Ramadan according to some calculations. They defied Merjani, and twelve of them sent a letter of complaint to the mufti on November 7/20, 1873. As a result, the mufti suspended Merjani's title of *imam* for six months.[16]

Merjani's approach to the educational system was also critical. The years he had spent in Central Asia had enabled him to scrutinize closely the medreses and identify their shortcomings. As a result, when he returned to Kazan in 1849, Merjani advocated that medreses be purged of books on conservative scholastic philosophy. He also urged that, together with the Qur'an and the Hadith, the history of Islam be taught in all medreses.

Merjani's activities at the University of Kazan and his direct contact with Russian and German professors reinforced his belief in the importance of science and the Russian language. At the university, he had the opportunity to study the beneficial effects of science on the life of Russian and Western European societies. It would be inaccurate, however, to believe that Merjani discovered the importance of science solely through his contact with Russian intellectual circles. Secularism must not be regarded as a purely Western importation into the Muslim world; it is to be found, to a certain extent, in medieval Islam. The ulama themselves contributed to the spread of secularism through their defense of worldliness against the influence of Sufi (mystic) orders.[17]

Merjani's thoughts on science and secularism and on the comparison of Islamic and non-Islamic cultures, as well as his reflections on the future of Islamic culture, were gathered in an impressive seven-volume work entitled *Wefayat al-Aslaf wa Tahiyat-al-Ahlaf* (The legacy of the ancestors and the response of their descendants). Written within the framework of biographies of famous figures of Islam, the book is an exposition of Merjani's ideas on Muslim culture. In the first volume, published in Kazan in 1883, Merjani deplored the state of Muslim education and science, especially in light of the remarkable achievements of medieval Islamic scholars in both areas. He viewed the stagnation in Muslim education and science as the direct result of the fact that for centuries scholasticism had stifled innovation and growth.[18]

Merjani emphasized the importance of science for the growth and advancement of a society, criticized his fellow Muslims for their lack of interest in modern science, and called on them to correct this shortcoming. At that time, the shortest bridge Tatars could cross to reach the world of modern science was that offered by Russian science. This bridge was open, however, only to those Tatars who were equipped with adequate knowledge of the Russian language. Consequently, while emphasizing the importance of becoming acquainted with modern science, Merjani also stressed the need for the Tatars to learn Russian. To those who equated learning Russian with russification, Merjani offered a subtle message: He never used a Russian idiom in Tatar, Russian endings for Tatar family names, or the Christian calendar. These examples were perhaps his indirect message to the Tatar umma, whom he wanted to reassure that becoming knowledgeable about science and the Russian language did not necessarily mean the loss of one's Islamic identity.[19]

The key to Merjani's reformist thinking was his belief that the main source of Islamic revival would spring from a return to the purity of pristine Islam. According to many reformers, including Merjani, the greatest damage to the purity of Islam had been inflicted by the philosophers. Hence, in his struggle for the reestablishment of the initial simplicity of Islam, Merjani aimed his writings at the kalamists. His most important work, written as an answer during his polemics with the kalamists, is *Al-Tarikat-al-Musla wa-l-Akidat Al-Husna* (The ideal path and the good beliefs).

Like Aristotle, the kalamists had circumscribed God to the philosophical category of necessity *(wajib)*, while assigning all remaining beings to the category of possibility *(imkan)*. They regarded God as infinite and eternal, whereas imkan was finite and changing. Because kalamists also attributed to God many qualities, such as knowledge, sight, speech, and hearing, they were faced with the dilemma of whether these qualities belonged to the category of necessity, as the nature of God Himself, or to the category of possibility.

Merjani criticized the kalamists and defended independent theology. Insisting that philosophy should not interfere with theology, he relied only on the Qur'an and the Sunna (traditions of the Islamic community consecrated by the Prophet's own example) for resolving the dilemma. According to Merjani, God, with all His qualities, had not been created but was eternal and infinite; He thus belonged to the category of necessity, and His qualities were inseparable from His nature.[20] Inherent in the answer formulated by Merjani was the question of the rationality of religion. This issue had preoccupied many scholars of Islam before him, the most famous of whom had been Abu-Hamid Al-Ghazali (d. A.D. 1111).[21] Following the intellectual tradition established by Al-Ghazali, Merjani employed a special set of criteria for dealing with such metaphysical issues as God and His qualities, while at the same time arguing in favor of reason and rationality for exploring descriptive sciences.

Although Merjani was a scholar who understood the ills of scholasticism and advocated changes, his advocacy of change was expressed mostly in theoretical writings. With his works, however, reformist thinking moved one considerable step ahead, due largely to the impact of Merjani's reevaluation of Islam as a religion and culture on the shaping of the political ideas of the Tatars.

Merjani's most famous disciples were Rizaeddin Fahreddin and Musa Jarulla Bigi, who through their provocative ideas revived religious thinking and polarized Tatar society into two groups: conservatives and liberals. The conservatives were committed to the preservation of the religious, social, and cultural status quo; the liberals were in favor of progress and secularism. This division was brought about by differences in opinion concerning religious matters, and as the differences between the two groups increased, the resulting tension became the main catalyst for renewal in the life of Tatars for several decades.

Rizaeddin Fahreddin (1858–1936) became acquainted with Merjani's reformist ideas while a student at the medrese and studied them in depth before formulating his own views on religion and on the future of Russian Muslims.[22] In 1891, Fahreddin was appointed a *kazi* (Muslim judge) and thus became a member of the Ecclesiastical Council and moved to Ufa. In Ufa, he had the opportunity to become acquainted with the problems of the Tatar community at a new level—that of the religious leadership, an opportunity that fell within the domain of his responsibilities. However, it was the archival work of the muftiat, which was not among his responsibilities, that appealed to him most. Consequently, he set about to organize the archives of the muftiat, a task that offered him the unique opportunity to collect materials for his future work, *Asar*, a series of biographies of famous Muslims from central Russia that began publication in 1900.

It has often been argued that Rizaeddin Fahreddin's thought developed under three equally important influences: Merjani; the newspaper *Terjuman*, published by the pan-Turkist Crimean intellectual Ismail Gasprali; and Jamal ad-Din al-Afghani, whom Fahreddin met in St. Petersburg. Evidence suggests that there was yet another influence: the Egyptian reformer Muhammad Abduh.[23] One proof of this influence is found in Fahreddin's own writing, wherein he analyzed Merjani's contribution to religious reform by comparing him with Al-Afghani and M. Abduh.[24] Moreover, Fahreddin's profound social orientation may stem from his dual experience as Islamic scholar and layman—as a journalist who in 1906 became coeditor of the Orenburg newspaper, *Vaqt*, and in 1908 began to publish a separate journal, *Shura*.[25]

Rizaeddin Fahreddin's social orientation emerges clearly in a book he wrote in 1911 to honor one of the wealthiest Tatar merchants, Ahmed Bay Huseinov, whose support of the reformist movement had gained him the respect of the community. In the introductory essay, Fahreddin made the following statement: "It is known that the cause of poverty and misery which exists in this world is wealth and the rich [*mal ve baylïq*]."[26] This statement may seem startling in a book about one of the wealthiest Tatars of the Volga-Ural area, but in fact, Fahreddin wrote those lines out of deep gratitude because Ahmed Bay had used his wealth to improve the education of the Tatars, and Fahreddin believed in education as the chief means of fighting poverty. The importance attached to education as a means of eradicating social ills was not novel; the Tatars, without realizing it, were perhaps as much indebted to the French Enlightenment as the Russians, who had imported its ideas to the Russian intellectual scene.

Fahreddin stressed the role of the press in disseminating information on the history of Islam and the Islamic world and emphasized the need to gather more information about the lives and deeds of those Tatars who had had an impact on the social life and progress of their communities. As a bad example, he mentioned the work of Ibn Khallikan (1211–1283), whose voluminous study of some 943 pages, entitled *Wafiat-al-'Ayan* (The demise of prominent people), leaves the reader with the impression that the most famous people of the Islamic world were the rulers.[27] In his criticism of Khallikan's work, Fahreddin revealed himself as a defender of the unity of the umma, whose future and prosperity, according to him, depended on the contribution of every one of its members. Thus, as he was to do elsewhere, he deplored the anonymity to which Ibn Khallikan had condemned all his contemporaries—those who through waqfs had contributed to the development of Muslim cultural and economic life. At the same time, Fahreddin viewed biographical studies of Tatar merchants, not as tributes to personal vanities, but as important records of the social and economic history of the Tatars and as valuable primary sources with considerable educational value.[28]

Rizaeddin Fahreddin wrote extensively. He was primarily concerned with theology and with the theoretical and practical aspects of religion, but he dedicated much of his energy toward such social issues as the education of women and the role of the family in Islam.[29] Of his religious and political writings, the most interesting include his multivolume work on Russian Muslims, *Asar*; a volume entitled *Meshhur Irler* (Famous men), which contains the biographies of medieval scholars; *Munasib Diniye* (On religion); *Islamlar haqinda hükümet tedbirleri* (Government measures regarding Muslims); and *Rusya Muslumanlariniñg ihtiyachlari ve anlar haqinda intiqad* (The needs of the Russian Muslims and a criticism regarding them).[30]

Fahreddin's religious philosophy can be summarized on the basis of these writings. Central to this philosophy is his sincere belief in the compatibility of Islam with science. Like Merjani, he valued the importance of science, Russian language, and schools. But in Fahreddin's case, rationalist thinking advanced even further, affecting the realm of theology itself and creating a skeptical attitude toward miracles, which he was ready to accept only when attributed to the prophets.

For Rizaeddin Fahreddin, only what was scientifically sound and ethically moral was acceptable, but he always extended tolerance and respect to other people's thoughts, regardless of their relationship to his own. He was also a man of outstanding intellectual curiosity, as is indicated by his choice of subjects for his six-part series on famous personalities of the Islamic world, which contains critical biographies of Ibn-Rushd (d. 1198), Al Ma'ari (d. 1118), Ibn al-Arabi (d. 1240), Ibn-Taymiya (d. 1328), Al-Ghazali (d. 1111), and Ahmed Midhat (d. 1913).[31]

What common denominator attracted Fahreddin equally to all these scholars? They all believed in the integrative capacity of Islam, and some, such as Ibn-Taymiya, claimed the right of absolute ijtihad and criticized taqlid. In addition, Ibn-Taymiya's restatement of Shariat (the totality of Islamic laws that govern all aspects of life) as an all-inclusive concept that integrates the legal and the spiritual into one religious whole must have reaffirmed Fahreddin's belief that a nondogmatic approach to Islam was a condition of Islam's future progress.[32] And Ibn-Rushd's belief in the radical dualism between body and mind, and Ibn al-Arabi's contribution to rationalism on the basis of its rational expression of the intuitive states of the mystics must have also appealed to Fahreddin.[33] Ottoman reformer Ahmed Midhat (1846–1913) probably interested Fahreddin not only as a reformer concerned with Muslim theology but most of all as a contemporary with whom he shared an interest in the development of the press and literature, in the political impact of religion, and in the critical relationship between religion and politics.[34]

Jamal ad-Din al-Afghani exercised a direct influence on Fahreddin by sensitizing him to the domain of politics. Al-Afghani's legacy as a reformer lay mainly in his political preachings. The cornerstone of his political and religious philosophy was the urgency of developing (or restoring) an ideological and political unity in the Islamic world as a defense against the encroachments of the West. Al-Afghani believed this unity could be achieved only if Islam proved able to adapt to the conditions of modern life. Moreover, he shared with other reformers the view that reason can serve the ends of religion and that a revised program of education can help update the thinking of Muslims. By restating the basis of the umma in terms of nationalism, Al-Afghani made an important contribution to the formulation of the pan-Islamic program.[35]

It seems that under these influences, Fahreddin became both more careful in listening to the needs of the Tatar community and more critical in establishing a rapport between these needs and the imperatives of the Russian society in which the Tatars lived. In 1906, he wrote an essay entitled *Rusya Mus-lumanlarïnïng ihtiyachlarï ve anlar haqïnda intiqad*, which was actually a critical response to the lists of grievances drafted by the ulamas of Qargalï and Oren-burg, grievances that had been published as a result of the more liberal attitudes toward inorodtsy that had characterized the period immediately following the Revolution of 1905.[36] Because Fahreddin recognized the ulama's intentions as laudable but considered the programs they suggested rather vague, he committed himself to commenting only on issues they raised related to Shariat and left out such issues as trading on Sundays, which he considered a purely political matter. Fahreddin's comments on two issues indicated that, despite his appreciation of the achievements of other cultures and his willingness to learn from them, he believed there were dangers involved in contacts with these cultures. For instance, he carefully weighed all arguments concerning point five of the suggested programs, which discussed the certificates of proficiency in Russian required for Muslim clerics. Although considering knowledge of Russian to be useful, Fahreddin pointed out that lack of a systematic program for its study compelled many Tatars to resort to private tutoring. Private tutors were available only in Russian villages, and Fahreddin stressed that visits to these villages exposed the Tatars to new and harmful habits, such as smoking and drinking, and led to a general deterioration of their morals. He favored having the Muslim Ecclesiastical Council control schools for Tatars, thus placing the entire responsibility for education upon the ulama and the community in general.[37]

Another major influence on Rizaeddin Fahreddin was exercised by the newspaper *Terjuman*, whose editor, Ismail Bey Gasprali, promoted and defended the idea of cultural as well as racial unity of all Turkic tribes. An offspring of the pan-Turkic ideology was Gasprali's concept of a common language for all Turkic peoples—a language called *Turki* and based on Ottoman—that might some day be spoken from the Volga to Kashgar. Ismail Bey's ideology was summed up in the formula *dilde, işte, fikirde birlik* (unity in language, action, and thought).[38]

Fahreddin did not adhere entirely to either the Ottoman or Ismail Bey's Turki. He used Turki to some extent but paid special attention to the peculiarities of the Volga dialect—without, however, becoming an exclusivist like Nasiri. Fahreddin did subscribe to Ismail Bey's concept of national identity, in which religion, and the social values deriving from it, played a crucial role.[39]

Ismail Bey's newspaper, *Terjuman*, discussed problems related to all aspects of the Russian Muslim's life: education, emancipation of women, political parties, and even reform of Muslim jurisprudence in Russia. An interesting idea was advanced in an article published in the summer of 1909, which suggested a sui generis codification of the Muslim legal practices in Russia based on the Ottoman model. *Terjuman* advised Russian Muslims to consult the Muslim legal journal, *Mijelle-i Ahkiam-i Shariye* (The journal of Shariat laws), published in the Ottoman capital, to educate themselves on the issue of codification of Muslim law.[40]

Fahreddin also became interested in the codification of Muslim legal practices in Russia and presented some of his ideas on Shariat, fikh, and a series of other issues connected with religious reform in a statement submitted to the ulama congress that met in Ufa between April 10 and 15, 1905.[41] On the second day of the congress, Fahreddin brought to the attention of the mufti, Muhammediar Sultanov, the need to present a written proposal for religious reform to the mullahs in order to provide a concrete basis for discussions. The mufti rejected the idea and replied to Fahreddin: "We should not submit anything in writing. It could be interpreted that we called this assembly in order to impose on it our views, and we shall be blamed. Therefore, do not write anything."[42] Despite this opposition, Fahreddin prepared a religious reform statement, which he intended, not for presentation at the congress but merely as a guide for the mufti. As the need for more organized and constructive discussions became evident, the mufti urged Fahreddin to present his project to the assembled ulama. With the modifications and improvements included during the discussions, the project was adopted as a resolution of the congress.

Several ideas proposed by Fahreddin illustrated a considerable evolution of the religious thinking and ideas of reform since the time of Kursavi and Merjani. The statement did not excel in boldness; Fahreddin justified its moderation by the need to make it feasible, which in turn depended on its conformity with the "rules of convenience vis-à-vis the Russian government."[43] He advocated reform of the religious administration, which would yield augmented power to the Ecclesiastical Council and place the mufti in a position subordinate to the council, as "an intermediary between the government and the people, an interpreter of the [needs of the] latter."[44] More interestingly, he called for reform of the fikh itself, arguing that, without a reform of Shariat, the administrative reform would not yield any results. Fahreddin believed that, to make reform work, the quality of the religious leadership must be changed to correspond to the needs of the people. Therefore, he advocated that the mufti should be elected, rather than nominated by the government, and that he should have equal competence in religious and secular sciences.[45]

To enable the Ecclesiastical Council to devote more time to solving the problems of the community, Fahreddin wanted to transfer to each medrese the responsibility for the examinations required for confirmation of mullahs. His main argument against leaving the council with jurisdiction over the mullah examinations reflected his commitment to the improvement of the quality, status, and prestige of medreses, which he eventually wanted placed on an equal footing with the Russian schools. Fahreddin complained: "The examination should be a function reserved to medreses, *muderrise*s [medrese teachers], and specialized ulama. Since in all civilized countries, examinations passed in schools serve a purpose, they should be the same in our medreses."[46]

Fahreddin considered it necessary that the educational process be supervised by the council, which perhaps could devise a centralized program for all medreses. But in the case of government control, he favored the Ministry of Education as the supervisory forum because he could not be reconciled to the political nature of the Ministry of Interior.

The idea of a merger of the religious administration of the Tatars with that of the Kazakhs of the steppes, which Fahreddin advanced in the same statement, is particularly interesting. It is difficult to point out any single reason that might have prompted such a proposal. The urge toward centralization could have meant that the muftiat was growing in strength and prestige; it could also have been a reflection of the pan-Turkist inclinations of the Muslims as well as a reflection of the special economic and social relationship the Tatars had enjoyed with the Kazakhs throughout the centuries and their willingness to maintain it.

The Russian government viewed the reforms as attempts to further increase the power of the Ecclesiastical Council, power that the Ministry of the Interior considered had already "exceeded that of any other institution or organization in Russia."[47] In 1910, the Ministry of the Interior organized a special conference, presided over by Count A. P. Ignatiev, the purpose of which was to devise measures that would counteract the Tatar-Muslim influence in the Volga area and decentralize the muftiat. This conference characterized the Ecclesiastical Council as an "artificially created Muslim center contributing to the tatarization of other inorodtsy tribes which profess Islam, but which do not belong to the Tatar tribe," and recommended that the council's power be reduced.[48] Some of the means by which the ministry meant to achieve this reduction were continuation of the practice that muftis be nominated by the government, the transfer of matters regarding inheritance to the jurisdiction of the civil authorities, and decentralization of the Orenburg muftiat, with the creation of smaller units based on regional-geographic, rather than ethnic, criteria.[49] The measures contemplated by the Special Conference of the Ministry of the Interior proved once more that "immobility did not represent a general feature of Islam in the same manner as the Inquisition and Catholic superstitions were not representative of the fundamental Christian belief."[50] The alarm sounded by the Ministry of the Interior proved that the earlier reformists were seen, not as accidental apparitions, but as people beginning an evolutionary chain of development.

Fahreddin was not alone in his commitment to the revival of the religious, cultural, and social life of the Russian Muslims in general and the Volga Tatars in particular. His best companion in this battle was his friend Musa Jarulla Bigi (1870–1949), who brought new dimensions to the development of the religious thinking of the Volga Tatars.

Bigi spent most of his youth studying at the medreses of Bukhara, Samarkand, Mecca, Medina, Cairo, Damascus, Istanbul, and India. When he returned to Russia in 1904, he had expertise in all aspects of Islamic theology, law, and philosophy. As a scholar particularly interested in *tafsir* (commentaries on, and interpretations of, the Qur'an) and fikh, he registered as an auditor at the Law Faculty of the St. Petersburg University to acquire the knowledge necessary to compare the Islamic and Western legal systems.[51]

Bigi's closer acquaintance with Russian society during his stay in St. Petersburg resulted in a politicization of his thought and a deeper appreciation of Islam as a political force.[52] But there was a great gap between stating an issue theoretically and becoming actively involved in politics. Whereas his good friend Abdurreshid Ibrahim, editor of the St. Petersburg *Ulfet*, was one of the most politically active defenders of pan-Islamism among Russian Muslims, including the Volga Tatars, Bigi dedicated most of his time to research and writing, and his only active involvement in politics was the contribution he made as secretary to the Muslim congresses held between 1905 and 1917.[53]

In 1909, Bigi had been extremely critical of mullahs when he discovered editorial changes in one of the copies of the Qur'an. These changes reflected the ignorance of those who had tampered with the original text, and he was determined to fight that ignorance. To that end, one of his first, and least controversial, works was a history of the Qur'an, *Tarihu'l Qur'an ve'l-Masahif* (A history of the Qur'an and the Qur'anic texts), in which he mainly dealt with the text of the Qur'an, protecting its integrity against harmful editing.

Bigi also advocated translation of the Qur'an into Tatar, which he felt would help make every individual's religious experience a more meaningful and conscientious act. He stressed that, in a civilized world, it was the duty of the community to translate the Qur'an into the languages of the people and that, where translations already existed, the most urgent task was to investigate their accuracy. He did not believe in blind adherence to religion, but in a conscious and active participation in it; and one of the means of encouraging this participation was to translate the religious books.[54]

In 1910, in Orenburg, Bigi published *Rahmet-i Ilahiye Burhanlari* (The storms of God's clemency), which is perhaps his most controversial essay. Not a voluminous work, it is a 97-page essay in which he challenged the official dogma that God's mercy and forgiveness were not extended to unbelievers, arguing that, on the contrary, God extended His forgiveness to everybody. Bigi had also expressed this opinion in 1908 in the pages of *Shura* and as a teacher of the Huseiniye medrese in Orenburg, but it was the publication of his opinions in book form that caused a storm of criticism to erupt. He was attacked by the conservative ulama, mainly through their publication *Din ve Magishat* (Religion and life), as much as he was criticized by the liberal mullahs or liberal reformist intellectuals (the jadids). The most vocal of the latter group of critics were Ismail Gasprali, in his article "Woe from Philosophy," and historian Hadi Atlasi, who wrote an article entitled "I Cannot Be Silent."[55] This controversy is a testimony to the fact that, although Tatar reformers were united in their opposition to the conservatives who denied change, they displayed divergent views regarding the nature and degree of change necessary to revitalize the Islamic umma. Insofar as their commitment to the advancement of Tatar society was concerned, however, a remark made by Herzen about the Slavophiles and Westernizers could be equally applied to the Tatar reformists, who also "reminded one of the ambivalent Janus, whose faces looked in opposite directions, and who yet had but one heart."[56] Rizaeddin Fahreddin was among the few defenders of Bigi, but he stated the issue from a different perspective and pointed to the historical precedents for the same interpretation.

In 1907, Bigi published *Sherhu'l-Luzumiyat* (Commentaries on Al-Luzumiyat), an equally controversial volume of commentaries, on *Al-Luzumiyat* (Obligation), the work of tenth-century Islamic poet and philosopher Al-Ma'ari (b. 973). Al-Ma'ari was a cynic and a highly skeptical thinker. Skeptical of all existing religions, Al-Ma'ari wrote, "Muslims, Christians, Jews, and Magians—all are following the path of error. In reality, humanity is divided into two: intelligent ones who doubt faith, and ignorant ones who are faithful.[57]

Bigi, whose adherence to some of Al-Ma'ari's skeptical ideas generated criticism, argued that none of the existing religions could be pleasing to God because they all contained moral, if not physical, oppression. An ideal religion, according to Bigi, must be totally lacking in oppressiveness. Bigi's comments were enthusiastically received by those who welcomed a critical approach to religion. A letter from an Orenburg reader to the paper *Musul'manin* read: "Our religion has not been subjected to this kind of criticism, especially on the part of the learned religious leaders. In my opinion, this [criticism] is a good sign. It is time we did something in this area. One should not oppress somebody who might have something fresh to say.... This [outspokenness] is what we need."[58]

In an essay entitled *Büyük mevzularda ufak fikirler* (Small thoughts on big issues), Bigi critiqued the works of Ziyauddin Kamali, an enlightened ulama and muderris at the Osmaniye and Aliye medreses. In this essay, one can see that Bigi valued the philosophical message of mysticism, was interested in Sufi orders, and attached a special meaning not only to the Muslim *tariqat* (mystic orders) but to Christian monasticism as well. He considered Kamali's approach to religion narrow because of Kamali's criticism of the tariqat. Bigi developed his concept of miracles in Islam in great detail, arguing that "they were not against the laws of Nature." This particular essay, written while Bigi was perhaps under the strongest Sufi influence, could be indicative of his disenchantment with political and social realities and a sign of his desire to withdraw from the realities of life.[59] It is conceivable that his interest in Sufism (Islamic mysticism) and the Muslim tariqat resulted not only from his inquisitive thinking and intellectual curiosity but also from a much closer acquaintance with the Sufi tariqa Naqshbandi of Kazan, which numbered some 10,000 members at the beginning of the twentieth century.[60]

For Volga Tatar reformers, nonconformism meant much more than the campaign being waged against scholasticism. It designated a whole spectrum of religious attitudes, including puritanism, mysticism, and even a renewed, more tolerant view of the Shiite sect. In fact, a re-evaluation of the Sunni/Shiite relationship had reached even the more conservative regions of Central Asia, and in 1907, the kazi of Ashkhabad, Haji Mir Ibrahim, recommended a union between the Shiite and Sunni Muslims in a *fatwa* (opinion on an issue of Muslim canonic law) delivered in Khiva.[61] It seems, however, that the still conservative Central Asia was not ready to consider this recommendation seriously, and the violent clashes between the two sects that took place in Bukhara during the winter of 1910 were a testimony to the enduring animosities. The Volga Tatars, however, remained consistently tolerant toward the Shiites and even collected money to send to the Emir of Bukhara for distribution among those who had suffered during the violence.[62]

The Volga Tatars did not extend the same toleration toward the puritanical, extremist religious sect of the Vaisites, known among the Russians as the *Vaisov Bozhii polk*. This lack of tolerance was based primarily on the fact that the social and political views of the Vaisites, who advocated an isolationist Utopia, conflicted with the Tatars' own determination to achieve progress and gain more rights within the existing state structure.

The Vaisites were a puritanical Muslim Sufi sect, founded in Kazan in 1862 by Bahaeddin Vaisi and directed against the authority of the Russian state and its institutions, which they refused to recognize.[63] They claimed to be the only true heirs of the ancient Bulgars, and always used the name Bulgar instead of Tatar. Theirs was, in fact, a different response to the economic and russifying pressures the Tatars confronted during the nineteenth century. Rather than emigrating or becoming reformists they took a passive stand.

Chiefly peasants and impoverished craftsmen, the Vaisites advocated a "return to the land of Bulgar instead of emigration to Turkey."[64] They argued that those who accepted the authority of the infidels were not Muslims anymore, and they called for strong opposition to civil registration. They also refused to pay taxes, perform military service, or attend mosques where prayer was led by mullahs who had conformed to the requirements of the Russian language examination.[65] They seceded from the Muftiat, organized their own autonomous Muslim leadership, and established a Chancellery of Muslim Old Believers.[66]

The conservatism of the Vaisites brought pressure upon them from two different directions: from the Russian government and from the majority of Tatars, who favored reform and development rather than a return to the distant past. In 1884, the Vaisite prayer house was closed, and the founder of the sect, Bahaeddin, was exiled to Siberia along with many of his disciples. Those who remained in Kazan were rounded up and brought to trial.[67]

The activity of the sect was revived in 1906 by Bahaeddin's son, Inan, as a result of the more tolerant laws regarding religion enacted after 1905. However, a denunciation of the sect soon came—from one of its own members, a Kazan meat merchant named Abdulla Kildishev.[68]

Despite this denunciation and the general contempt in which they were held, the Vaisites maintained a following until 1917, when they emerged on the national scene on the side of the Bolsheviks. The alliance between the atheistic Bolsheviks and the ultraconservative splinter Sufi sect could be regarded as unusual, although not surprising. What led to this strange rapprochement of Vaisites with Bolsheviks was not a common ideology; perhaps it was the social program of the Russian Social Democrats and the promises for self-determination that they made.[69]

One of the important social challenges Tatar reformers had to confront and provide an answer for was the position of women in Islam. This complex issue—which transcends the confines of family life and the laws of marriage, divorce, and inheritance as defined in the Shariat—first came to the attention of the Volga Tatars when use of the veil came under discussion. That this issue aroused discussion was not accidental, because the veil stood as the symbol of the traditional attitude toward women. Egyptian reformers had raised the issue of the legality of the veil for the first time in Cairo in 1899, and by doing so, had launched the campaign to abolish the veil from the lives of Muslim women.[70] The close contact of such Volga reformers as Bigi and Fahreddin with the Egyptian movement must have sharpened their sensitivities to this issue.[71] The Volga ulama was concerned with this problem, and in 1910, the imam of Ufa, Muhammed Sabir Hasan, emerged as the spokesman for those who believed that the veil had never been an obligation of the Shariat.[72]

The controversy regarding the veil was accompanied by discussions regarding the institution of marriage and the rights of women in it. Polygamy came under attack, not only in Tatar newspapers but also in articles written by Tatars in Russian newspapers. An article published in *Penzenskie vedomosti* in 1907, for instance, criticized the practice of polygamy because, according to its author, it had a detrimental effect on "the education of children as future citizens of their country."[73] It is interesting to note that the author of the article regarded the younger generation of Tatars not only as members of the Muslim umma but also as citizens of the Russian state. This statement, in itself, is a testimony to the fact that reformism was undergoing a metamorphosis and that cultural, social, and political issues would become much more important than settling controversies of a purely philosophical or theological nature.

The determination with which women defended their own rights on the national level in the years after 1905 was added proof of the fact that Tatar society had produced educated (or "liberated") women fully capable of grasping the dimensions of the issue of emancipation, of understanding its social and political implications, and of demanding consideration.[74] But the number of these women would have been much lower, or nil, had earlier reformers and enlightened religious leaders of the Tatar communities not fought the distorted interpretations of the Shariat by conservative mullahs.[75] By stressing the importance of education for girls as well as for boys, progressive mullahs had set in motion one of the valuable latent forces of Tatar society.[76] And it was within the framework of the Muslim religious organization that these forces received one of their major recognitions. In May 1917, at the All-Russian Muslim Congress in Moscow, Muhlise Bobi, a teacher and a native of the village of Izh-Bobi, became the first woman to be appointed kazi and a member of the Muslim Religious Board at Ufa.[77]

The appointment of a woman to the position of judge of the Muslim Religious Board epitomizes the scope of the changes that had taken place in the Tatars' outlook at the end of the nineteenth and the beginning of the twentieth centuries. These changes had been set in motion, to a great extent, by those

Tatar ulama who had addressed, with courage and creativity, the task of reassessing religious thinking. In doing so, they provided for the Tatars valuable guidelines and leadership in the general effort aimed at reassessing traditional Tatar culture and integrating into that culture new elements that would enable them to address the imperatives of a rapidly changing world.

7 Reformism at Work: The Emergence of a Religious-Secular Symbiosis

Do not think of yourself
Think of your country.

Uzeng turïnda uylama
Ileng turïnda uyla.

(T. Mingnullin)

The challenge of scholastic theology by the reform-minded ulama was the first step toward testing the strength of traditional Tatar culture in a modern secular world. The next step involved the forging of a viable symbiosis between tradition and secularism. The promotion of the Tatar literary language, the advancement of book printing in Arabic characters, the re-evaluation of the traditional approach to social problems, and the development of secular education emerged as crucial components of this process.

Merjani made a significant contribution to the shaping of Tatar national consciousness because, in his capacity as historian, he presented his people with their own history and was the first to use the name *Tatar* when writing about the Volga Muslims.

A contemporary of his, Kayyum Nasiri (1825–1902), was the first to raise the issue of preservation of the Tatar language and to defend the importance of language in shaping and maintaining one's identity. Nasiri was often called a "Tatar Lomonosov" or a "Tatar Encyclopedist," in recognition of his many contributions to the development of Tatar culture. Indeed, Nasiri advocated secular sciences, both as an important source of knowledge and as another alternative in man's struggle to understand the world. He wrote textbooks on a variety of secular subjects in an effort to spread science among the Tatars and was also interested in ethnography and anthropology. Most of all, however, Nasiri was a pioneer who urged building the Tatar literary language on the basis of the vernacular of the Volga region.

Born into a family of Tatar merchant mullahs from the village of Shirdan, near Sviazhsk, Nasiri's early education followed the pattern of many of his contemporaries and included the experience of the village mektep as well as the Kazan medrese. Unlike most of his contemporaries, however, Nasiri was not attracted by Central Asian medreses. He remained in Kazan, read intensively, became acquainted with Ottoman literature, and began to learn Russian secretly.[1]

Knowledge of Russian stimulated Nasiri's curiosity about the secular sciences and prompted his decision to register as an auditor at the University of Kazan. He read the works of the famous mathematician N. I. Lobachevski and the scientist and ethnographer K. F. Fuks and became deeply interested in the writings of K. D. Ushinskii and N. I. Pirogov. His association with the University of Kazan enabled him to become personally acquainted with such leading intellectuals of the time as the orientalist Radlov and the law professor N. P. Zagoskin.[2]

In 1850, Nasiri's knowledge of Russian gained him an appointment as teacher of the Tatar language at the Kazan Theological Seminary, and in 1873, with the intervention of Radlov, he received the same appointment at the newly opened Russo-Tatar Teachers' Seminary. He was also a private tutor of Russian for many a student of Tatar medreses, who received from him their first glimpse of European culture and gained access to secular sciences.[3]

Nasiri's may not have been an original mind; he may have been only a *perepischik* (in Validov's word), or translator, but his greatest merit rests in having translated literature and scientific knowledge into the language of the people.[4]

Nasiri's direct involvement in teaching, and his association with the University of Kazan, determined his intellectual interests and his publishing activity, which began in the 1860s. At that time, the Russian Muslims used three literary languages in their writing: Arabic, Persian, and Chagatay (medieval Turkish). Nasiri was the first Tatar intellectual to advocate development of a literary language based on the Tatar vernacular of the Volga region—a language free of Arabic, Persian, and Ottoman words and accessible to the people. He wrote grammars, dictionaries, and stylistic studies of the Tatar language, and translated Arabic and Ottoman literature into Tatar. Furthermore, in his anthology of Arabic folklore, which was published in 1884, he included a section on Tatar literary folklore.[5] Earlier, in 1880, he had published, in Russian, a study of

Tatar folk rituals and customs.[6] Recognition of Nasiri's contributions to the study of Tatar culture came in 1885, when he was elected a full member of the Kazan Archaeological Society and received the title of *uchenyi* (scholar).[7]

Nasiri's defense of the Tatar vernacular, and his struggle to establish it as the basis of the literary language of the Volga Tatars, did not remain unchallenged. His critics raised their voices, and they were found equally among the conservatives and the reformers. One of Nasiri's most vocal opponents on the issue of use of the Tatar vernacular was Ismail Bey Gasprali, who advocated a common Turkic language for all Russian Muslims.[8] Yet Tatarism had been raised as a linguistic issue by Nasiri, and it became an intrinsic part of the identity of the Volga Muslims. The move toward a Tatar literary language was also perhaps the key point in the transition from a purely Islamic identity to a still-Islamic, but also national, Tatar identity.

The Volga vernacular became the language of literature in the pages of the calendar Nasiri published between 1871 and 1897 as a sui generis substitute for the nonexistent periodical press.[9] After Nasiri's death in 1902, the tradition of his calendar was continued by a similar calendar, entitled *Zaman kalendari*, which was originally published by Sherafetdin Shehiddulin.

The *Zaman kalendari* appeared regularly until World War I. A comparative analysis of *Zaman kalendari* issues between 1903 and 1912, however, leads to the conclusion that, prior to 1905, it published more articles on current issues and that, with the development of the Tatar press, especially after 1906, it became more a collection of biographies and commemorative articles. For instance, in the 1903 issue, there were articles on the Muslim muftis of Russia and on the Muslim societies, as well as several articles dealing with the press in which the discussions of Russian and Muslim newspapers in Russian were aimed at emphasizing the urgent need for a periodical press in Tatar. Another article in the same issue not only explained the meaning of *usul-u jadid* (the new method of teaching) but defended it strongly.[10] The 1909 calendar, however, abounded in biographies and only the article written for the twenty-fifth anniversary of the Crimean newspaper, *Terjuman*, reminded the readers of the earlier calendars, which had echoed contemporary events.[11]

Despite its merits, Nasiri's calendar could not match the scope of *Terjuman*, the newspaper Ismail Bey Gasprali began to publish in 1883 in Bakhchisarai, because *Terjuman* alerted the Tatars to problems of undisputed urgency in their contemporary society.

Nasiri's contribution to the movement of reform and revival, which was vaguely called *izvestnoe dvizhenie* in an article published in 1892 in *Kazanskie vesti*, rests on both his establishment of the Tatar vernacular as the basis for the literary language and his advancement of secular sciences.[12] In recognition of his activity as a teacher and textbook writer, Nasiri was often called the first Tatar reformer-pedagogue.[13]

Nasiri's Tatarism was not unanimously accepted, although he had chosen this alternative as a result of careful observation and study of the needs of the Volga Tatars. One could perhaps argue that linguistic differentiation had advanced too far for people to aspire to a common literary language that could be understood by all Turkic peoples.[14] But it can also be argued to the same degree that, in the case of the Volga Tatars, an awareness of their heritage, which included such political entities as the Bulgar state and the Kazan khanate, made them defend the linguistic differentiation gained from the elevation of their vernacular to literary status.

The issue of Tatarism was not resolved during Nasiri's lifetime. It left its mark on every major development in the life of the Tatars during the first two decades of the twentieth century and was not stifled by the events of 1917.[15] The Tatar vernacular was promoted by the new generation of *jadid* (reformist) writers; its purity was defended in the press, as well as privately, by those who were concerned with the preservation of their national identity and the development of a national culture. An article published in the 1907 issue of *Vaqt* warned that "whoever neglects his mother tongue will perish."[16]

The concern with the Tatar language was primarily Nasiri's legacy, but it was also a result of the efforts of other Tatar intellectuals to promote the study of Tatar. Among these, Ibrahim Khal'fin (1778–1829) and two of Nasiri's contemporaries, Muhammed Gali Mahmudov (1824–1891) and Husein Feizkhanov (1821–1866), made outstanding contributions.

Ibrahim Khal'fin had been a teacher of the Tatar language at the Kazan gymnasium for twelve years when, on July 26, 1812, he was appointed a lecturer of Tatar at the Kazan University.[17] In 1819, he presented to the university council a paper entitled "Liubopytnoe soobrazhenie I. Khal'fina o prosveshchenii Tatar" in which he emphasized the need to teach the Tatars their own language and to acquaint them with secular sciences. He even proposed that Kazan University students be assigned as teachers of Tatar.[18] This never happened, but Khal'fin furthered his own efforts to provide adequate material for the study of Tatar. Between 1819 and 1820, he translated many textbooks into Tatar and also prepared a dictionary of the Tatar language. In 1820, the Russian officials awarded him a medal as a sign of recognition for his merits as a translator. In September 1823, Khal'fin was promoted to an assistant professorship for a translation regarding the rules of Muslim marriage practice, which he had prepared for the governor of the Orenburg guberniia.[19]

Gali Mahmudov began his career in 1842 as a teacher of calligraphy at the Kazan gymnasium. As a result of the direct intervention of mathematician N. I. Lobachevski, he received an appointment as instructor of Tatar at the faculty of oriental languages of the University of Kazan.[20] Mahmudov dedicated his entire life not only to the teaching of the Tatar language but also to the task of convincing the Tatars that knowledge of Russian would enable them to gain a better understanding of the society in which they lived. The task of teaching Russian or convincing the Tatars that knowledge of Russian should not be viewed as a sign of russification was difficult, and its fulfillment required a gradual and continuous effort in which Tatar educators and linguists were joined by writers. Its didacticism notwithstanding, Z. Bigiev's novella *Güzäl kïz Khädichä* (The beautiful girl, Khädichä) contributed to the education of the public because it depicted two Tatar youths who, despite their knowledge of Russian and enrollment in Russian schools, were successful in maintaining their Tatar identity.[21]

Husein Feizkhanov, another teacher of Tatar and a former student of Merjani, is commonly referred to as the first Western-style Kazan Tatar scholar. Feizkhanov perhaps owes this to the fact that he was the first Tatar to base his writings on history, archaeology, and language, using not only source materials available in Eastern languages but those in Russian as well.[22] Upon his appointment as a lecturer of Tatar and Arabic at St. Petersburg University, Feizkhanov began intensive studies of the Tatar language, which led to the publication of a grammar in 1862. One of his most important writings is undoubtedly an unpublished essay dealing with the reform of the medreses. The central idea of Feizkhanov's reform program was reorganization of the medreses to introduce into their programs secular subjects modeled on those of the Russian schools.[23] At the time of Feizkhanov's death in 1896, the reforms he advocated were still in the realm of unrealized dreams, but within just a decade, the new type of medreses and their supporters outnumbered the conservatives who defended the old scholastic system.

The essays, pamphlets, and books written by Tatar religious and cultural reformers and printed in Kazan at the end of the nineteenth and beginning of the twentieth centuries directly reflected the spectrum of intellectual changes undergone by Tatar society. Indirectly, book printing and book trade among the Tatars reveal another dimension of the cultural developments in which secular ideas began to play an increasingly important role.

Until the nineteenth century, all books—whether purely religious or adaptations for the use of the mektebs—were taken to the Volga area from Bukhara, Istanbul, or other centers of Islamic culture.[24] Only in 1801, as a result of the pressures of Muslim clerics who had become more vocal after the establishment of the Muftiat in 1782, did Paul I issue an ukaz regarding the establishment of Aziatskaia Tipografiia, a printing shop designed to fulfill the religious needs of Russian Muslims.[25]

Aziatskaia Tipografiia began its activity in 1802 and operated in the Kazan gymnasium for *raznochintsy* (founded May 10, 1759). Its sponsor was the Tatar merchant A. Burnashev. Within three years, Burnashev financed the printing of 11,000 textbooks and 19,000 religious books.[26] He then sold the press to another merchant, by the name of Apanaev.

When the University of Kazan was founded in 1804, it was also endowed with a press, which began its activity in 1809. Aziatskaia Tipografiia merged with the new press, the name *Aziatskaia* was dropped, and for almost a century, the university press enjoyed the monopoly of Tatar book printing. By mid-century the number of books in Arabic characters printed by the university press had reached 2 million annually.[27] The activity of the press became especially intensive at the times when the biblical society held its meetings in Kazan.[28] This increase in activity can be regarded as an effort by the Tatars to counteract the Russian missionary zeal by promoting even more Muslim religious books.

The university press had a particularly active business relationship with such publishers as U. Kadyrov and Sh. Khusainov. Despite the fact that business declined after 1905, when Tatar private book printing proliferated, the university engaged in an active effort aimed at reviving the Tatar "account." One measure designed to address the problem was a price reduction, which was undertaken because the university had been charging its Tatar customers a higher fee than it charged other customers for printing Russian books. This measure is particularly significant in view of the fact that at that time, burdened by a budgetary deficit, the university could hardly afford to lower its revenues.[29]

It has often been noted that the oldest Muslim-owned press in Russia was established in 1881, in Bakhchesarai, by the prominent Crimean intellectual Ismail Bey Gasprali. This contention was never challenged, perhaps partly due to the authority of Ismail Bey himself and, most of all, because his printing shop is associated with the activity of *Terjuman*, the first Muslim newspaper in European Russia.

There are, however, references indicating that, as early as 1843, a Volga Tatar, Rahimjan Saitoglu, organized the first Muslim printing shop in Kazan, where he printed mostly religious books, for which he charged much lower prices than the Kazan university press thus making his books accessible to the poor. Evidence further suggests that, in 1860, a second Tatar-owned printing shop opened in Kazan. It is difficult to ascertain which of these two shops endured until the 1880s. What is certain, however, is that one year prior to the opening of Ismail Bey's printing shop in Bakhchesarai, there were two Muslim printing shops in Russia, one in Kazan and the other in Tiflis.[30]

Despite references to these earlier printing enterprises, only the activity of the printing shop opened by Ilias Mirza Boraganskii in 1894 in St. Petersburg can be documented in some detail. By 1900, that shop had published 60 titles in various Eastern languages, for a total of 270,000 copies. After its reorganization as the Baiazitov-Boraganskii partnership in 1901 (when it was renamed Nur), the shop functioned without interruption until 1910. By then, it had published an additional 148,440 copies of 68 new titles.[31]

It is significant that, after 1894, and particularly after 1900, book printing among the Tatars grew as a result of the contributions of both Russian and Tatar-owned businesses. Among the Russian-owned printing shops of Kazan that specialized in printing Tatar books and catered to Tatar publishers, several should be noted: I. V. Ermolaeva, N. M. Chizhova, V. Eremeev, A. Shashabrin, B. L. Dombrovskii, M. Chirkova, I. V. Perov, and I. N. Kharitonov.

Of these, the I. N. Kharitonov enterprise gained the unequivocal respect of the Tatars for its outstanding contribution to their cultural growth.[32] The Kharitonov press was founded in 1896, but it was only in 1902 that it began to specialize in Tatar books. Between April 8, 1902, when the first Tatar book came off its presses, and 1917, the Kharitonov enterprise published 666 titles, totaling 3,300,126 copies.[33]

By 1900, printing shops owned and operated by Tatars had opened in Kazan, as well as in the major cities of the Middle Volga and Ural region. Their owners were either private individuals (usually merchants, sometimes peasants) or joint stock companies, such as Millät, Magarif, Umid, Karimov Bros., and Shäräf Bros. (Kazan); Karimov and Khuseinov and Co. (Orenburg); and G. Gumerov and Co. (Astrakhan). Printing developed so rapidly that Kazan alone boasted some twenty Tatar presses, which between 1900 and 1917 published 5,154 titles in 38,714,032 copies. Tatar books represented one-third to one-half of the total number of titles and three-fourths of the total number of copies published annually in the city of Kazan. Of all these enterprises, the largest publishing share belonged to the M. Karimov press, which, during this period, produced 32.98 percent of the total number of titles and 50.74 percent of the total number of copies of Tatar books printed in Kazan.[34]

Book printing developed so rapidly during the first decade of the twentieth century that lists and catalogs of books printed in the Arabic script in the Volga area were circulated at the St. Petersburg book exhibit of 1910. Each year, the number of printing shops increased as new businesses opened, and by 1910, those printing shops in Kazan alone had published 349 various titles, amounting to a total number of 3,115,871 copies.[35]

A common feature of all printing shops that opened after 1900 is that none of them, with the possible exception of Din ve Maghishet of Orenburg, printed exclusively religious books. The Karimov shop, founded in 1900 in Orenburg by Akhund Karimov, printed a considerable number of textbooks. The shop organized by the Shäräf brothers in Kazan in 1906 printed literature and some of the Kazan periodical press. The Gumerov shop, which opened in Astrakhan in 1907, did not print religious books at all, specializing solely in books on literature and science. The Millet shop, which opened in Kazan in October 1908, printed books in a variety of fields. During the first seven months of its existence alone, it produced some 202,600 copies of various titles.

The printing shops that opened in other cities were as active as those of Kazan, and the book mania that had swept across the Tatar communities of the

Volga-Ural region became a major source of concern for the government, which viewed it as a dangerous sign of growing pro-Islamic propaganda.

Of particular concern to the government was the impact of this book mania and the educational campaign on novokreshchennye, those Tatars who had converted to Christianity during the eighteenth century. In this regard, the activity of the Karimov printing shop is particularly telling. In 1907, because the owners wanted to educate the Tatar community about the impact of the recent political changes on their own lives, the shop published excerpts referring to Muslims from the October Manifesto of 1905 and from the statement of the Council of Ministers dated April 17, 1905. The company singled out the novokreshchennye for special attention. Among other declarations, the Manifesto proclaimed the religious freedom of all Russian subjects. At the end of the pamphlet excerpting the Manifesto, the Karimov shop attached several blank forms of petitions to the governor-general to grant freedom to return to Islam to those Tatars among the novokreshchennye who wished to do so. For the same novokreshchennye, Karimov also published, in 1906, books and pamphlets on Islam printed in Cyrillic characters; one such pamphlet is entitled *Islam dini*.[36] Equally alarming (if not even more so) in the government's view was the fact that books printed in Arabic characters in the Volga area did not stay within the confines of religion.[37] Numerous textbooks, calendars, books on science, and pamphlets on social and political issues were printed in each of the existing shops. Young writers were encouraged to print their works and at times received financial assistance from well-to-do and enlightened members of their communities. The will of Ahmed Bay, a wealthy merchant of Orenburg, for instance, provided that 500 rubles be allocated annually to assist writers in publishing their works, regardless of the nature of the items: religious or secular, original or translations. The only stipulation was that editorial changes could be made only with the knowledge and approval of the authors.[38] This stipulation, in itself, is significant and is indicative of the impact of reformist ideas that defended the right of individuals to formulate and express their own ideas on all areas of human life.

The government was equally concerned with the fact that Tatar pamphlets (which cost only between two and ten kopeks) and books (between ten kopeks and one ruble) were no longer the privilege of Tatar urban dwellers. Instead, they were becoming increasingly accessible to those who lived in rural areas. Tatar books in Arabic script were sold at all village fairs. Book business was particularly brisk at important fairs, such as those held at Irbit, Buinsk, Aktamysh, Simbirsk, Bakaly, Burkai, Amikai, Chakan, Buziak, Abdullino, and N. Novgorod.[39]

In 1907, having grown increasingly nervous about the impact of Tatar publishing activities on rural areas, the government banned the village book trade. The police vigorously enforced this new regulation, and on February 6,

1907, searched all Tatars selling books at the fair held in the village of Burai, in the Birsk uezd. Books that were found were confiscated or destroyed, and the peasants who had them were beaten; one was even killed.[40]

The village fair, which performed the same function as the city bookstore in spreading books and information among the Volga Tatars living in rural areas, was much more vulnerable to harassment than a bookstore, because it was a temporary, albeit periodical, institution that lacked organization. Yet despite this vulnerability, the village fair, and more particularly the itinerant book trader, had become so much a part of life and so ubiquitous in Tatar communities, that the book trader was immortalized in literature, in works published at the end of the nineteenth and the beginning of the twentieth centuries.[41]

Because opening bookstores in rural areas was profitable culturally but not economically, the Tatars chose to open libraries in many of the villages. Often, village libraries were sponsored by one of the Tatar benevolent societies in the area, and their activities were modeled on those of the already existing city libraries, of which Kazan offered an outstanding example.[42] A comparison of two library statutes—one for the city of Malmyzh, Viatka guberniia, and the second for the village Tiunteri, Malmyzh uezd, of the same guberniia—leads to the conclusion that all of the 29 articles of the two statutes were identical. Both libraries set as their goal "to make possible for our children not to forget to read and write, and even more, to improve [their reading]; also, to make possible for literate Muslims to obtain books, newspapers, and journals in the Tatar, Russian, and Arabic languages." Both libraries were administered by a board of trustees whose members were required to have a knowledge of Russian in addition to Tatar. The most important member of the administration was not the local imam but rather the secular figure of the librarian. Also, in the case of both libraries, article 16 of their regulations provided that "persons of both sexes, of all social classes and positions can use the library." Neither of the two libraries was class-oriented; instead, they were designed to serve the umma as a whole.[43]

The importance Tatars attached to the impact of education, books, and learning on those less fortunate members of their communities is illustrated by the efforts of the mullah of the third ward of Samara, Hadi Battalov, who took the initiative to collect Tatar books for a prison library. His goal was to contribute to the improvement of the educational level and moral character of those Tatars who were detained there.[44]

The outstanding feature of the Tatar book mania and book publishing at the beginning of the twentieth century is the growing interest that Tatars exhibited in secular knowledge. A comparison of eleven bookstore catalogs from Kazan for the years 1897 to 1911 illustrates this point. The Karimov bookstore of Kazan listed alphabetically in its 1897 catalog some 492 titles, only half of which were religious books. The remainder dealt with a variety of subjects, such as history, geography, zoology, medicine, literature, and lexicography. The section on literature contained short stories, travel accounts, plays, and poetry. The languages of these works were primarily Tatar and Kazakh, which suggests the continuation of the close cultural ties between the Kazakhs of the steppes and the Tatars.[45] The 1899 catalog for the Sharif bookstore provides a similar picture, with a slight increase in the number of works published in Turkic dialects.[46]

The Karimov catalog for 1903 lists some 786 titles, almost double the number of titles published in 1897. The format was still the same, and the most noticeable change in content was the addition of a section on philosophy (which, incidentally, featured a translation of Schopenhauer). There was also a new section on mathematics, which might suggest a growing interest in science on the part of the Tatars. The languages of the listed publications were the same—Arabic, Persian, Tatar, and Kazakh—with the difference that the short stories in Kazakh were more numerous than those in Tatar.[47]

The 1906 Sabah catalog resembled the Karimov catalog; it featured books on mathematics and, in addition, listed the memoirs of K. Nasiri.[48]

The 1907 Karimov catalog featured slightly more books on science, including books on building and construction, and at the same time contained more books printed outside Kazan—in St. Petersburg, Istanbul, Egypt, and India. It also featured more translations, not only from Arabic, Persian, and Ottoman but also from Russian. The translations from Russian were those of the genealogy of the imperial family, a book on the education of young children, and a book on preventive medicine.[49]

The Idrisov and Galiev catalog for 1907–1908, issued for the bookstores of Kazan and Ufa, reflected a change in presentation and format, as well as in content. This catalog was much better organized, listing books by both author and subject and also providing brief reviews of the listed items. This format could suggest that the audience to which the bookstore appealed had become more sophisticated and that the number of printed literary works had increased considerably, thus requiring a more rigorous organization. The catalog still featured a considerable number of books on religion, but the textbooks and books on secular subjects outnumbered them. As far as textbooks were concerned, there was a special section that listed books recommended by the teachers' meeting of 1907.

The increasing Tatar concern with the new type of schools and education is indirectly revealed by a new item listed in the 1907–1908 Idrisov and Galiev catalog. This listing was some sort of grade-report book, and the publisher recommended that parents buy two copies for each of their children, so they could receive a report on their children's behavior and progress in school.[50]

Two other 1907 catalogs, Iqbal (Kazan) and *Ahmed-al-Ishaqi* (Orenburg), were similar in the increased number of maps and geographic atlases and biographies of famous people they featured. In addition, the Iqbal catalog listed, in pamphlet form, the report of the Kazan zemstvo meeting, which could mean that an increasing number of Tatars were interested in following the activity of the Russian administrative and political institutions.[51] A similar interest in current events and domestic life is evident in a 1909 Orsk catalog, which featured many pamphlets and journalistic accounts of the Russo-Japanese War and the activity of the Duma.[52]

Compared with those of Kazan, the Orenburg and Ufa bookstore catalogs for 1910 and 1911 were much better organized, and books were listed according to their publishers. This format could be indicative of the overall increase in the volume of printed material but could also suggest the emergence of competition and, as a result, the need to organize bookstore holdings much more judiciously to make them easily accessible to the public.[53]

As a whole, the development of printing and the book trade among the Volga Tatars reflected their growing interest in the advancement of learning and revealed the emergence of a new approach to science and secularism, the study of which the Tatars had come to view as complementary means for achieving a better understanding of the dimensions of their own culture.

In addition to the increase in book printing and the rise in book trade, the changes that occurred in the attitude of the Tatars toward traditional correctives to social ills also testify to the fact that the ideas of the reform-minded ulama had come to bear fruit in a very short period of time.

Individual acts of charity usually performed under the obligation of *zakat* (the alms tax) were not only a social corrective whose legitimacy the Volga Tatars accepted but also the traditional response to their overall material and spiritual needs until the end of the nineteenth century. Wealthy merchants and industrialists of the Volga-Ural area usually cared for the orphans, provided food and shelter for the poor, and aided in the building of new mosques and the upkeep of old ones. Temirbulat Akchurin, for instance, donated the land on which the Muslim community of Samara began the construction of a new mosque in 1895.[54] In 1844, the wealthy merchant family of Iunusov had organized the first orphanage for Muslim children (Musul'manskii Iunusovskii detskii priiut) in Kazan; it was still open in 1909, one of only two orphanages (the other one was in Ufa) for a population of 20 million Muslims living in Russia.[55]

Under the impact of the reform-minded ulama, communities as a whole began to re-evaluate their traditional approach to social ills and to corrective charity. Abdullah Bobi, a teacher of Arabic and religion at the Izh-Bobi medrese, addressed the issue of zakat in a six-part commentary on the Qur'an, published in 1904 under the title *Haqiqat* (The truth). Among other issues, he provided a new interpretation of zakat.[56]

Although according to *Sura* (Chapter) II-215 of the Qur'an, and according to the Hadith, only parents, relatives, the poor, travelers, beggars, and slaves could be recipients of zakat, Bobi argued that it was permissible to give zakat not only for the personal use of individuals but also for the use of benevolent societies or for building mosques as well, thus challenging one of the main tenets of the traditional fikh.[57] He also stressed that it was preferable to collect zakat for the benefit of the poor through benevolent societies that could provide organized and coherent assistance.

Bobi stopped short of accounting for the causes of poverty. Viewing zakat, not as a temporary answer to the needs of the poor but rather an institutionalized means of fighting and eradicating poverty, he nevertheless made the transition from transcendence to imminence, rationalizing poverty as an ill amenable to social policies. Furthermore, he criticized the hypocritical approach toward zakat on the part of some rich Muslims who had devised means of avoiding the fulfillment of its requirements. In the case of assets valued at 100,000 rubles, the zakat (which represented $\frac{1}{40}$ of the total value of assets) would be 2,500 rubles. Often rich Muslims would pay the required amount of zakat, then have part of the donation rebated, thus converting payment of zakat into a symbolic act. In his *Haqiqat*, Bobi stressed not only the need to reevaluate the implementation of zakat but also the need to explore new means of addressing a variety of social problems.[58]

To be sure, zakat was not replaced or disregarded. The Volga Tatars supplemented it and used it within the secular context of the benevolent societies. Although the goals and concerns of various Tatar benevolent societies varied greatly, all of them were functioning beyond the confines of the original sphere of zakat.

It is difficult to establish with certainty the date when the first benevolent society, Jemgiyet-i Hayriye, was organized in the Volga-Ural region. It is known, however, that by 1901 there were benevolent societies not only in Kazan but also in Astrakhan, Troitsk, and Ufa.[59] A survey prepared by the department of religious cults of the Russian Ministry of the Interior indicated that, as of January 1, 1912, there existed in Russia some 87 authorized Muslim societies. Although the survey did not provide a regional breakdown of the total figure, it did indicate that 48 of these societies were benevolent; 34, educational; and only 5, religious.[60]

An investigation of the Tatar societies at the beginning of the twentieth century is inherently handicapped by the contradiction between their names and the nature of their activities. The contradiction is twofold: Often the activities of benevolent societies surpassed the concerns of purely charitable organizations, and societies that listed themselves as religious or educational always extended charitable help of one kind or another. With the exception of a very few societies, such as the Society Against Polygamy or the Society for the Assistance of New Muslims, which were organized to deal with only one issue, all of the Tatar societies were eclectic.[61] Activities of societies such as those of the Tatar ulama, for example, transcended problems of religion and included active involvement in educational policies to such an extent that they actually functioned as ad hoc boards of education.[62]

In 1910, Kazan was a city of 182,653 people, of which 30,486 were Tatars and 149,060 were Russians. It had 60 churches and 15 mosques.[63] It also had an active benevolent society. According to a report published in *Kazan mukhbiri* (Kazan reporter) on February 14/27, 1907, the financial report of the Kazan Benevolent Society for 1906 indicated that, after having distributed 4,135.6 rubles for various causes, the society was left with 25,000 rubles in bank deposits and 689.4 rubles in its treasury.[64] This money was used to aid the needy and to encourage education. The society opened a school for poor children and also founded a school where Tatar children could learn the craft of printing. In 1905, the same society had provided care for some 1,301 students who were in ill health.[65]

Despite its general laudable record, the charitable activity of the Kazan region seems hardly to have been immune to criticism or to shortcomings. The Kazan correspondent of the Paris newspaper *Musul'manin*, Iusuf Almamedov, complained about the selfishness and apathy of some Kazan Muslims who failed to extend their help to those less fortunate in the villages.[66] It is difficult to assess accurately the success or failure of the Kazan Benevolent Society based on this single voice of criticism; the criticism is, however, indicative of the fact that most of these societies had a rather parochial attitude, being usually concerned with local issues, even though with a variety of them.

At the end of the first decade of the twentieth century, the Tatars of Orenburg were well acquainted with the activities and achievements of the local benevolent and cultural society. In 1910, Orenburg was a city with a population of 91,240. There are no data available concerning the national composition of that population, but the ratio of churches and mosques could at least serve as a point of reference. In 1910, there were fifteen churches and seven mosques in Orenburg.[67] Yet, in 1911, the Muslims represented 23 percent of the entire population of the Orenburg guberniia.[68]

The Orenburg Tatars' petition to organize a benevolent society had been ignored by the Russian government early in 1905, but later that year, permission was granted, and a Society for the Defense of the Material and Moral Interests of the Muslims, with some 30 contributing members, was organized.[69] Besides direct material assistance to the needy, the society was charged with advancement of education among Tatars. By 1910, it had opened five elementary schools (two for boys and three for girls) and one vocational school.[70]

The Tatar concern with secular education, especially with vocational education, could be indicative of their willingness to take part in all areas of life within the Russian state. Traditionally, the Volga Tatars had been either merchants or peasants. There were among them a small number of craftsmen, almost all of whom were exclusively involved in producing eastern footwear, clothing, or jewelry. Emphasis on vocational schools that would provide training in industrial crafts could, therefore, be interpreted as an open commitment by the Volga Tatars to play an active role in the economic life of the Russian state, which at the time was engaged in rapid industrial growth.

Some members of the Orenburg Muslim Society also took part in the activities of the Orenburg section of the archaeological society. This participation may have prompted the abortive effort to organize a Tatar National Museum in 1906.[71]

The Muslim societies, although an outgrowth of reformist ideas, were also adopted by the conservatives and became the ground on which both groups tested their plans for betterment of life in the community. Tatars generally gained from this competition, but there were instances, such as that involving the city of Astrakhan, when rivalry between overzealous societies also harmed the community.

In 1910, there were two societies in Astrakhan: Shura-i-Islam (Islamic council) and Jamgiia-Islamiia (Islamic society). They had similar goals, both being concerned with charitable activities and with sponsoring the foundation of new schools, libraries, and reading rooms. But they also competed fiercely in achieving these goals. Shura-i-Islam missed no opportunity in a prolonged effort to demonstrate its superiority over the more conservative Jamgiia-Islamiia.[72]

Shura-i-Islam had been organized in 1906 and was credited with opening several schools during that year. In March, the Dar-ul-Ädäb (House of education), a school with a staff of four teachers and a student body of 144, had begun its operations. Numune-i-Terakki (An example of progress), a girls' school with two teachers, was opened on April 23, 1906. These openings were followed in May by the start of a preparatory school and later by a secondary school.[73] In 1907, the society earmarked 20,000 rubles for the foundation of a medrese that, according to *Yulduz*, was to provide complete (that is, including secular) education and whose teachers came from Bukhara and Istanbul.[74] The school, however, aroused the suspicion of the Russian officials, and in 1910, it was briefly closed on the grounds that the Turkish background of its teachers made their loyalty questionable. The apprehensions of the Russian authorities regarding the school may have been augmented by the fact that Shura-i-Islam had openly fostered a certain cultural philo-Ottomanism. In August 1909, for instance, it had organized a feast honoring three young students from Astrakhan on their way to Istanbul where they intended to further their education.[75] As a result of protests by members of the community and a personal petition by the president of the Shura-i-Islam, the school was reopened.[76]

Shura-i-Islam sponsored a variety of activities, but most of its energies and resources contributed to the development of its medrese, which had been conceived as a model national school and which also became the testing ground in the unfolding contest between Shura-i-Islam and Jamgiia-Islamiia.

Instead of improving the quality of education, the efforts of Shura-i-Islam to prove its superiority over Jamgiia-Islamiia deprived the children of Astrakhan of a solid education. In its zeal to attract students from schools sponsored by the rival society, the Shura-i-Islam medrese lowered admission standards at a time when the medrese curriculum had become similar to a university program designed for a highly qualified student body. At the same time, the medrese lifted time limitations for new registration, which led to a higher enrollment but detracted from the coherence and congruity of the programs.[77]

Shura-i-Islam and Jamgiia-Islamiia were the best known, most active societies of Astrakhan, but they were not the only ones. In fact, Muslim societies were so active in the city of Astrakhan, and in the entire area surrounding it, that when a new society was organized at Khanskaia-Stavka, the Russian press reacted strongly.[78] A Russian newspaper correspondent warned against the awakening of the Muslims and viewed the existing Muslim societies as unifying forces within a larger, nationalist, pan-Turkic movement.

To view the Muslim Tatar societies of the Volga area as local chapters of some centralized pan-Turkic movement would perhaps credit them with more organization than they actually enjoyed; it would also lead to an exaggeration of their merits. It is true, however, that one of their main contributions rests in the fact that, by promoting science and supporting secular education, they helped shape a religious-secular symbiosis, a new type of identity. In this regard, the agenda for a 1911 meeting held by the Samara Muslim Society is particularly relevant. At the meeting, which was a part of the routine activities of the society at the time, the society heard two lectures: One, on the lives of the imams, was delivered by Fatih Murtazin; the second, "Inventions and Discoveries," on science, was delivered by a young student, Hasan Mamichev, and drew heavily on examples from the Islamic world.[79] There is a symbolism to the choice of lecture topics: a sign of reformist-conservative coexistence, a willingness to shape a symbiotic religious and secular identity.

All Muslim societies attached an overwhelming importance to education in general, and to secular education in particular, as a means of self-improvement and national progress. Some societies, such as the *Society for Cultural, Economic, and Charitable Activities* organized by the Tatars of Perm, attached particular importance to the value of vocational education.[80] The need for vocational schools became even more urgent as the community sought to improve the economic status of unskilled Tatar laborers and poor peasants. By 1910, the Perm society had a vocational school that trained carpenters and also provided useful information on rotation of crops and use of fertilizers. In the same year, the society opened a carpenters' vocational school and a craft shop for twenty students in the village of Koian. In this project, the society was joined by the local zemstvo, which in 1908 had provided the building for the school and had also earmarked 210 rubles annually for its needs. In 1910, the society applied for an increase in zemstvo subsidies (to 290 rubles per year) and also made plans to rent an experimental plot on which to plant clover as a way of convincing Tatar peasants that planting "grass" could be profitable.[81] On September 15, 1911, the vocational school opened a new class for teaching crafts, and that same autumn, its students participated in the Omsk Exhibition, where they earned a silver medal.[82]

Between 1905 and 1910, the number of societies organized by the Volga Tatars increased continually. After 1910, stricter government controls made authorization for founding new societies more difficult to obtain. In some cases, organizers were obliged to drop the word *Muslim* from the name of their group in order to obtain approval.[83] This change in government policy seems to have been a direct result of the warnings issued by the Missionary Congress of 1910, warnings that also moved the Ministry of the Interior to request information from the Orthodox religious authorities not only on conversions to Islam but also on the extent to which the Muslim societies played a role in these conversions.[84]

Although a society to assist new Muslims did exist, it is difficult to view that society as the cause of any significant number of conversions to Islam during the early years of the twentieth century. In fact, these conversions occurred in the heady climate of religious and political freedoms following the Revolution of 1905, and the society was born more from a need to cope with these new converts than from any desire to trigger the conversion process.

Evidence of some Tatar proselytizing is contained in an Okhrana document that indicates that such activities were carried out mainly outside the Volga-Ural area, especially in the Baltic region. Tuhfatulla Mamaliev, an active Okhrana agent, claimed in one of his reports that, toward the end of the first decade of the twentieth century, the mullahs and bays (rich merchants and landowners) of Kazan had organized a missionary committee, the most vocal members of which had been Sulaiman Aitov, Sadïq Galikaiev, and Ahmädjan Saidashev. The activities of the committee seem to have been concentrated primarily on educa- tion of the youth: It provided the means for Chuvash children and for the children of novokhreshchennye Christian Tatars to attend Muslim medreses.[85]

The committee, however, was principally interested in the Lithuanian Tatars, who had been assimilated by the Poles and the Russians to such an extent that only their religion had been preserved. These Tatars were Muslim, but they could neither speak nor write in any of the Tatar dialects; culturally, they were alien to their own heritage. The task of the Kazan Tatar Missionary Committee was to try to add an awareness of national feeling, heritage, and continuity to the Lithuanian Tatars' Islamic identity. The committee chose to achieve this aim in two ways: by bringing Lithuanian Tatar children to Kazan and enrolling them in local medreses where they could learn the language and culture of their ancestors, and by sending teachers from the Volga area to the Baltic region. The background of these teachers is indicative of the attention given to the program; for example, Husein Abuzerov, who was sent to Poland, was a former student of Alimjan Barudi and a graduate of the Russo-Tatar Teachers' School.[86]

Although neither the successes nor failures of the activities of the Tatar Missionary Committee can be ascertained on the basis of the available information, it is quite clear that Kazan Tatars remained interested in the fate of the Lithuanian Tatars up to the end of World War I. They organized a Committee for the Help of Lithuanian Muslims to assist those refugees who had sought temporary shelter in the Kazan area, launched an appeal to all Muslims for help, and sponsored a benefit play, the proceeds of which were to be used in aiding the refugees.[87]

The activities of the Tatar Missionary Committee could be viewed as an offspring of the benevolent societies, which continued to have an eclectic character in the entire Volga-Ural area until their dissolution after the revolutions of 1917. A comparison of three statutes belonging to benevolent societies from Khanskaia Stavka (Astrakhan), Temir (Uralsk), and Imankul (Orenburg) indicates that the very broad and identical goals these societies set forth for themselves led ultimately to their eclectic character. Each society aimed to contribute to the material and moral progress of the Muslims in all aspects of life. To this end, these societies ascribed to themselves the task of providing food, clothing, medical assistance, and shelter to the poor, sick, and old.[88] Problems of adult and child education, vocational schools, libraries, and scholarships for institutions of higher learning were also made the object of concern for all benevolent societies, which invariably emphasized the fact that their membership was open to all Muslims regardless of nationality, sex, or social status.[89] What is interesting is that, in the case of the benevolent society of Temir, in addition to tea houses and soup kitchens, the poor were to receive assistance through workhouses, modeled probably on the pattern of the Russian work-help (*trudovaia pomoshch*), that provided employment for the poor through shops organized especially for this purpose.[90]

Although benevolent societies were the main type of organization designed to assist the Volga Tatars in fulfilling their material as well as spiritual needs, two other types of societies that were formed concerned themselves only with economic issues; these were the cooperatives and the credit associations.

Benevolent societies had a long tradition with the Tatars, but cooperatives were initially organized during the first decade of the twentieth century. A novel institution (even among the Russians) when many Tatar communities in the Volga-Ural region began to adopt them, after 1910 cooperatives were organized in an increasing number of Tatar communities.[91] Aimed at providing cheaper goods for the community, while at the same time helping the participating members market their own products, cooperatives became increasingly popular in the communities beyond the Urals, which were inhabited by both Tatars and Bashkirs and had lower economic status. One can note that village cooperatives were organized as a result of the combined efforts of village teachers, mullahs, doctors, and the medical staffs of the zemstvo hospitals and that there was a concerted effort to exclude the religious leaders of the community from the administration of the cooperatives.[92]

Credit associations also became increasingly widespread among the Tatars at the beginning of the twentieth century.[93] These associations owed their existence mainly to local initiative and were intended to provide assistance to rural communities through short-term credits that enabled peasants to modernize their agricultural inventories and acquire goods at the retail market price. Taking advantage of this form of assistance, many Tatar peasants replaced their plows with more efficient McCormick agricultural machines.[94]

The success of the credit associations resulted in their growing popularity among the Volga-Ural Tatars. Through their credit association, the villagers from Qïzan (Astrakhan guberniia), for instance, purchased all the machinery necessary for a tomato-canning factory.[95] And the Tatar press advocated joining credit associations to buy electric generators that would improve the productivity of antiquated village windmills.[96]

At times, the organization of small credit companies was the result of a need to cope with an emergency. In 1905, for instance, the Tatar village of Malchin, near Tiumen, was completely destroyed by fire. Nigmetullah Karamshakov, one of the wealthy merchants of the area and an ardent supporter of the reformist movement, founded a credit company to assist in reconstructing the village according to more modern standards. The company was based on long-term credit that Karamshakov had opened at the Samara Credit Bank. By 1906, the village had been entirely rebuilt, and by 1910, the peasants had paid off their debts.[97]

At the end of the nineteenth century, and especially at the beginning of the twentieth, benevolent societies, cooperatives, and credit associations were fulfilling many of the cultural, social, and economic needs of the Volga-Ural Tatars, thereby becoming a fundamental part of the life of their communities. The support the entire Tatar umma gave to benevolent societies reflected its readiness to use organizations modeled on Russian institutions as a means of supplementing the traditional Islamic response to social ills and needs. The popularity of credit associations and cooperatives represented acceptance of the need to extend to economic life the quest for change and improvement voiced by the first reformers. Tatar societies, as a secular response to the socioeconomic needs of the umma, represented yet another proof that the reformist movement had gained a large audience among the Volga-Ural Muslims. Along with acceptance of the integrative value of knowing Russian and the emphasis on a secular educational system that would reinforce the commitment of the Tatars to their religion and tradition, Tatar societies stood as a new, strengthening element in the emerging religious-secular symbiosis.

8 Education

> When we shall acquire the first fruits of your science in our own
> schools, when we shall learn about our motherland Russia and
> about its laws from our Tatar books, be convinced that we will
> have the desire and the means to fill your gymnasia and univer-
> sities so that we may work together with you for the benefit of
> science and life.
>
> . . . kogda my v svoem mektebe priobretem pervonachal'nye
> plody vashei nauki i znanii, kogda my iz Tatarskikh knig
> uznaem nashu rodinu Rossiiu i ee poriadki, bud'te uvereny, u
> nas iaviatsia zhelaniia, i sredstva napolnit' vashi gimnazii i
> universitety, chtoby trudit'sia riadom s vami na poprishche
> zhizni i nauki.
>
> (I. Gasprali, *Russkoe musul'manstvo* [Russian Muslims].)

The viability of a symbiosis between tradition and secularism underwent the
crucial test in the field of education. The Volga Tatars had always attached great
importance to education, even though until the end of the nineteenth century,
being educated generally meant nothing more than possessing the ability to
read and write, which was essential to the fulfillment of religious obligations.
Despite the limited scope of each person's reading and writing ability, literacy
was widespread among Tatars. In fact, K. Fuks, a leading professor at Kazan
University, was sufficiently impressed to have noted in 1844: "A Tatar who does

not know how to read and write is looked down upon by his people, and as a citizen he does not enjoy the respect of others."[1]

The Volga Tatars maintained the Islamic pattern of organizing schools into the twentieth century. Their children learned the fundamentals of literacy in mektebs, or primary schools, where they were taught by a mullah whose combined duties included those of elementary school teacher as well as those of mosque custodian and community leader.[2] Those Tatars who wanted to further their education and achieve a level of knowledge beyond the ability to decipher only the text of the Qur'an attended the medreses, which were higher schools. There, under the guidance of the *muderris* (teacher), students engaged in an intensive study of the Arabic language as a preparatory step toward the study of the Islamic disciplines. Of these Islamic disciplines, tafsir (commentaries on, and interpretations of, the Qur'an), Hadith, *fikh*, *usul-u-fikh* (jurisprudence), *kalam* (Muslim dialectics), *mantïq* (logic), and the history of Islam were the most important. Arithmetic, natural sciences, and geography were also part of the medrese curriculum, but only as supporting subjects whose importance was recognized only insofar as they facilitated the understanding of the Islamic disciplines.[3]

Until the last decade of the nineteenth century, all but a very few Tatar confessional schools, mektebs and medreses alike, carried on their educational tasks in humble one-room buildings adjacent to the mosques.[4] Children entered mektebs at the age of seven or eight, and the average term of study was four years. As for the medreses, there was no general rule or age limit. In Bukharan medreses, where the term of study was nearly twenty years, there were students who had reached the fourth decade of their lives. The length of study was ten years in Crimean medreses; in the Volga area, it fluctuated between a minimum of eight and a maximum of fifteen years. Neither mektebs nor medreses had standard curricula. Examinations as means of testing knowledge were not a part of school life; the judgment of the teacher, alone, verified one's progress and knowledge.[5]

The schools, which lacked standard furniture so students sat on the floor and recited combinations of syllables to learn the Arabic alphabet, might have looked and sounded like "living pictures" of medieval schools to the occasional Russian or Western visitor. The picture might have seemed odd or antiquated to the outsider, but until the final decades of the nineteenth century, the Tatars showed little or no discontent with their schools and expressed no desire to alter the old pattern. They also remained oblivious to other educational opportunities, such as Russian missionary schools, government-sponsored schools, and Russian gymnasia and universities, that were within their reach during the nineteenth century.

The missionary schools, which had been designed for Christians and therefore remained outside the interests of Muslim Tatars, had failed to attract even Christian Tatars because the teaching was conducted in Russian. In 1867, the organization of the missionary brotherhood of Gurii led to a revival in school activity, and by 1870, there were 62 brotherhood schools in the Volga area.[6] In addition to the numerical growth of missionary schools, there was also an effort aimed at reforming them. N. I. Il'minskii was mainly responsible for designing the new school system (since named after him), which was meant to provide a Christian education in the native languages of the Volga area.[7]

Il'minskii's system was introduced on March 26, 1870, under the provisions of the "rules concerning measures for the education of inorodtsy inhabiting Russia."[8] Besides encouraging schools for Christian inorodtsy (such as Kreshcheno-Tatarskaia Shkola), the rules of 1870 recommended the organization of schools for Muslim Tatars. These were the so-called Russko-Tatarskie Shkoly, where students acquired a general education in Russian in addition to studying both Tatar and Russian as required subjects. At these schools, Tatars were allowed to hire, at their own expense, a teacher of Muslim religion.

This concession contributed little to the popularity of Russo-Tatar schools, and Tatars remained reluctant to send their children there. This is not surprising in view of the major goals of the Russo-Tatar schools, as stated in their statutes: "The Russification of Muslim-Tatars can be achieved only by disseminating the Russian language and education."[9] Adding to the apprehensiveness of the Tatars toward these schools, where instruction was carried out in Russian and Tatar was relegated to the status of just another subject, were the punitive actions taken against those students who were caught speaking Tatar at school.[10]

The rules of 1870 also required that Muslim mektebs and medreses open classes of Russian at their own expense. A report presented to the meeting of the council of the Ministry of Public Instruction on February 2, 1870, emphasized the key role of the Russian language in achieving a rapprochement (*sblizhenie*) between the Russians and the Tatars that would lead ultimately to the assimilation (*sliianie*) of the latter.[11] This emphasis was one of the main reasons the Volga-Ural Muslims resisted attending the Russo-Tatar schools, and their refusal postponed the possibility that the Volga-Ural Muslims would encounter secular education through government-sponsored schools.

For those Tatars who wanted to further their education beyond the primary level, the only alternative to medreses, besides missionary-sponsored teachers' seminaries, were the Russian gymnasia and universities. The first two gymnasia opened in Kazan on January 21, and May 10, 1759, as a result of the senate ukaz of July 21, 1758. By 1808, 13 of the 54 gymnasia that existed in the entire Russian empire were located in the Kazan school district, but very few Tatars chose to enroll, even when some of them included Tatar in their curricula. In fact, on August 24, 1838, the inspector of the Kazan school district presented the minister of education with a report concerning the attitude of the Muslims toward the Kazan and Astrakhan gymnasia, in which he observed that, although the introduction of Eastern languages (Tatar and Persian) into the curriculum had been aimed at attracting Muslim students, very few had responded positively to the improvement.[12]

As still another means of promoting attendance at the gymnasia, all Muslims of the Volga area, the Crimea, and the Caucasus were invited to enroll their children in these schools. The invitation stressed awareness of the Muslims' respect for knowledge and their contributions to world culture while also emphasizing that the basic rule of the gymnasia included high standards of morality and observance of Muslim religious requirements.[13] This appeal was apparently successful in securing higher enrollments at the Astrakhan gymnasium. On June 6, 1843, the Ministry of Education approved the hiring of two additional teachers—of Tatar and Persian—for that school.[14]

On June 17, 1872, the Ministry of Education provided that Muslim religion be introduced into the gymnasia curricula, thus giving official support to the efforts to attract Muslim students. But the decision also specified that Muslim religion could only be taught in the Russian language and that the Muslim religion teachers must be paid by the Muslim communities. These provisions, plus the fact that teachers of Muslim religion were treated as pariahs in the school (they could only attend faculty meetings when the administration deemed their presence necessary, and they had no voting rights at such meetings) in addition to the financial burden placed on those communities, probably contributed to the Tatars' continuing reluctance to attend and led them to question the government's sincerity about opening the doors of gymnasia to Muslims. The charge of tokenism overshadowed any positive aspects of this government decision.[15] Apparently, between 1801 and 1917, only 20 to 30 Tatar young people obtained the gymnasium diploma.[16]

Tatar attendance at Russian gymnasia and universities could have contributed to the growth of secular education and to a rapprochement with the Russians, but for more than three centuries, the only links between the Tatars and Russian society in the area of education had been the pressures of the Russian missionaries, and the government control and police surveillance of the mektebs and medreses. And government educational policies at the end of the nineteenth century contributed little or nothing to dissipating the Tatar fear that Russian schools were merely vehicles for russification. As a result, the Tatars were forced to critically assess the alternatives available to them in the area of education.[17]

The Tatars may have claimed that "our awakening does not come from outside, for it is a natural feeling, born and fostered in the interior of our society," but the education reform movement, which embraced all Russian Muslims, developed under a double influence.[18] It received a strong impetus both from the climate of political, social, and cultural transformations that existed in Russian society after the 1860s, and from the influence of the movement of Islamic revival that swept through the entire Muslim world toward the end of the nineteenth century.

During the course of the nineteenth century, Tatar intellectuals became increasingly aware that mektebs and medreses were not keeping pace with changing times.[19] The choice the Tatars faced, however, was a difficult one: To perpetuate the tradition of the mektebs and medreses unaltered meant to remain completely cut off from the realities of the Russian state, whereas to opt for Russian schools—which were secular, but aloof to the national cultural diversity of their students—meant to render themselves vulnerable to assimilation. The Tatars rejected the Russian schools but not the need for a secular and more sophisticated education.

The missing link was a secular Tatar school. Yet the mektebs and medreses were too intimately bound up with the Islamic identity of the Tatar umma to make room for totally new institutions.[20] The unique place they occupied in the life of the Muslim communities prompted the effort aimed at reforming the old schools to enable them to address the educational needs of a modern society.

The Muslims of the Crimea and the Volga-Ural region took the initiative and provided the leadership for the movement within Russia. The Crimean Tatar Ismail Bey Gasprali, an educator and journalist whose lifelong credo rested in the belief that education represented the remedy to the ills and backwardness of the Muslim world, offered a new method of instruction aimed at reforming the mektebs and medreses in Russia. In his own school, founded in 1884, Ismail Bey replaced the old syllabic method of teaching the Arabic alphabet with a phonetic one, *usul-u-savtiye*, and used a primer (*Huja-i-sibyan* [Children's teacher]) based on the phonetic principle.[21]

Ismail Bey outlined several basic principles for his phonetic method. First, the students were to learn the sound and the sign for each individual letter, instead of memorizing their combinations. Second, they were to practice the alphabet in drills that combined various letters in actual words of their native tongue instead of using the arbitrary combinations of the old system. Third, the teaching of the alphabet was to be accompanied by drills in writing.[22] Gradually, Ismail Bey developed usul-u-savtiye into an articulate, multifaceted program for a new system of education that challenged the content of education itself and aimed at ridding the Russian mektebs and medreses of medieval scholasticism and traditionalism. Usul-u-jadid (literally, "the new method") soon lent its name to the general movement of reform and intellectual renewal among Russian Muslims, a movement that became widely known as jadidism.[23]

In the Volga area, as everywhere else in Russia, change occurred gradually. Each innovation in the school system, or in the way of life of the Tatars, raised controversies that polarized the entire umma into two hostile camps. The history of the transformations undergone by the mektebs and medreses to provide the requirements of a modern education is, in fact, a history of the clashes between the jadidists (proponents of the new method) and the qadimists (defenders of the old). By the end of the first decade of the twentieth century, the jadidists were the victors in their campaign against the qadimists. Even Faizkhan Davudov, editor of the conservative Orenburg journal *Din ve Magïshat*, represented jadidism as a positive movement in a July 1910 interview for the Samara journal, *Iqtisad*. He also admitted that *Din ve Magïshat* had begun disregarding the anti-jadid letters of the conservatives.[24]

The changes that had already been adopted by many mektebs and medreses by the end of the 1890s were incorporated into an official proposal for school reform only in 1906, when the Third Muslim Congress, which met in N. Novgorod, drafted a 33-point resolution regarding Muslim schools. Because most of the points summarized the changes that had already taken place, or were in the process of being implemented in mektebs and medreses, the intent of the document was to sanction and generalize the experience of jadid schools while also legalizing them, as much for the Muslim umma as for the Russian government.

The resolution spelled out the role of the native tongue as the language of education in all jadid schools and also made Russian a compulsory subject in schools beyond the elementary level.[25] Point 23 of the resolution provided that all medreses include secular sciences in their programs. Point 26 demanded that medrese graduates be granted rights and privileges equal to those of graduates of Russian secondary schools; its implementation would have made it possible for the medreses to replace gymnasia as a springboard for higher education.[26]

The 1906 resolution on education contributed further to the secularization of the Tatar mektebs and medreses by addressing the issue of the separation of the religious and academic duties of the mullah. Point 27 stated that "the title of medrese teacher should be separated from that of imam," thus sanctioning the separation of the two functions that had already begun at the end of the nineteenth century.[27] In 1898, Gani Bay, a wealthy Orenburg merchant and an ardent supporter of jadidism, had written to his friends from the village of Ilek and advised them to hire a teacher for their school because the mullah, who had religious obligations in addition to academic ones, could not devote sufficient time to his students.[28]

The Russian government was equally concerned about the direction the education of its inorodtsy was taking, especially after the failure of the Il'minskii system. In 1905, the Ministry of Public Education organized a commission of educators, headed by N. Miropiev, to elaborate an educational program that would halt the Tatarization of inorodtsy. With regard to the mektebs and medreses, the commission pointed out that it would be desirable to place purely

religious schools under efficient control, while at the same time avoiding interference with their internal organization. The commission submitted to the
Duma an eleven-point list of measures meant to create a new educational
program.[29] When the Duma adopted the decision to introduce compulsory
elementary public education in Russia, the Tatar press, fearing russification,
urged the Muslim deputies to take a stand against public schools and state
school systems. Instead, the Muslims proposed that the government train
teachers for their schools, pay the salaries of the existing *muallims* (mekteb
teachers), and guarantee that the native languages remain the language of
instruction in all Muslim schools.[30]

At the local level, the zemstvos took a direct interest in the education of the
inorodtsy; but in 1908, the Muslims in general, and Tatars in particular,
debated the character of the schools the zemstvos planned to organize for them.

The discussion continued until the eve of the Moscow zemstvo conference
on education in 1911. The issues on the agenda of the preliminary meetings
were school programs, textbooks, teacher training, and the language of education. The Tatar press urged all committees to debate and prepare comprehensive programs and submit them to the zemstvo meetings through their representatives.[31] A meeting that took place in Kazan on January 10 and 11, 1911,
brought together the zemstvo administration and the representatives of the
Muslim community. They debated whether Russo-Tatar schools were desirable
for the Tatars and whether it was necessary to organize a special network of
Russo-Tatar schools, instead of opening such schools gradually, as the need
developed.

The Tatars who attended the meeting recommended that the organization
of Russo-Tatar schools be a gradual process. They saw each Russo-Tatar school
as a two-part institution that, in fact, perpetuated the differences between the
two types of educators and traditions instead of blurring them. The Russo-Tatar
school day was as follows: In the morning, a muallim (not a mullah) was in
charge of religion and native language classes, for which twelve hours were set
aside weekly; in the afternoon, classes were set aside for subjects of general
education and Russian.

Although because of the controversies that surrounded the Russo-Tatar
school proposal, few communities opened such schools, communities did
become increasingly interested in finding the best avenues for improving the
education of their children.[32] At the end of 1910, the Tatars of Ufa held a
meeting to discuss the question of schools. Some 500 people attended and
elected a nine-member permanent committee to develop a detailed program
around three crucial points: education in the native language, teaching of
Russian as a second language, and the need for Muslim representation on
school boards.[33]

A year later, when Ufa Tatars gathered to celebrate the twenty-fifth jubilee of mufti M. Sultanov, they again discussed the future of Muslim education. At this time, they specifically addressed the decision of the Ufa zemstvo to introduce compulsory public elementary education. This Ufa meeting of the Tatars concluded that all zemstvo schools for Muslims should conduct teaching in their native languages and that school programs should contain no fewer than three hours of religion and six hours of Tatar weekly. Teachers to be trained for these schools were to be Tatars, and there was also the suggestion that the zemstvo sponsor a Tatar teachers' school.

With regard to textbooks, those present at the meeting stressed the general abundance of Tatar textbooks and suggested that, for disciplines that were poorly covered, the zemstvo could appoint a committee to supervise the compilation of texts.[34]

Indeed, there was a remarkable increase in the number of Tatar textbooks published between the 1890s and the eve of World War I. In the 1890s, Ismail Bey Gasprali, A. Osmanov, and Menulla Sabirjan's textbooks were among the handful available.[35] By the beginning of the second decade of the twentieth century, however, the number of textbooks had increased so greatly that one bookstore in the city of Orsk (Orenburg guberniia) listed seventeen titles in its 1911 catalog, and Tatar newspapers often published reviews of textbooks.[36] What was remarkable about the Tatar textbooks was the fact that none of the prominent Tatar intellectuals considered writing them a trivial task. They wrote textbooks instead of devoting their entire time to theological, philosophical, or literary writings of a more theoretical nature. Thus, Musa Bigi wrote a textbook, *Kavaid-i-fikhiye* (The principles of law); Rizaeddin Fahreddin wrote a reader (*Ehliyal*) for first and second graders; the young poet Majid Gafuri published a volume of poetry for girls' schools; and Z. Kamali wrote, in a clear and simple language, a 330-page textbook on dogmatic philosophy, *Felsefe-i-itikadiye* (The dogma of philosophy), in which he developed the thesis of the compatibility of science and religion.[37]

In addition to their own texts, whenever the Russian government authorized it, the Volga Muslims used books from Istanbul.[38] Although the Tatars had some inadequate and poor textbooks, their effort to mobilize the best intellectual forces of their community to produce better textbooks indicated an overall concern with the quality of jadid education. Still, better—and even excellent—textbooks could not improve the quality of education for all Tatar children of Russia as long as such books were not adopted by all schools, and as long as medreses where scholasticism dominated existed side by side with modern medreses that could rival the best gymnasia. What was needed was a uniform implementation of jadid principles in all Tatar schools.

The resolutions of the Third Muslim Congress of 1906 had responded to this need and had charged the local congresses on education with the responsibility of advancing and discussing proposals for a centralized mekteb and medrese school program. Such congresses took place in many cities and villages between 1906 and 1914, but they failed to produce a program that would answer the needs of all Muslim communities in Russia.[39] In the absence of a centralized school program, the initiative rested with individual communities, and the balance between religious and secular subjects in each school program directly reflected the degree to which the teachers, the sponsors of that school, and the community as a whole adhered to jadid ideas.

A review of the program for jadid medreses suggests that, on the average, the number of weekly hours devoted to secular sciences at the intermediate and superior class levels surpassed those for religious subjects. At the intermediate level, a student attended 30 hours of classes in secular subjects and only 3 hours of religious education each week. During the last three years of the medrese, the ratio was 17 to 5. The secular education consisted of language and literature classes for Tatar, Arabic, and Russian; history, philosophy of history, and history of Islam; psychology; logic; methodics; arithmetic, algebra, geometry, and trigonometry; geography; natural sciences; physics and chemistry; agriculture; bookkeeping; calligraphy; and hygiene. French and German were optional. For religious study, the students concentrated on the Qur'an, systematic theology, Islamic law, fundamentals of law, rules of morals, laws concerning inheritance, commentaries on the Qur'an, the Hadith, and the fundamentals of Hadith.[40]

The change in the medrese program represented a remarkable improvement toward providing a coherent general education, and many Russian educators considered medreses to be equal to the European secondary schools. The requirements for entrance examinations to each of the sections of the medreses similarly reflected the growing concern for the quality of education.[41]

It is striking that, in almost all medrese programs, the number of hours devoted to the study of Russian surpassed the number of hours designated for the study of the native language or Arabic, or of the two combined. Medrese students studied Russian from six to twelve hours weekly, whereas they spent only three to four hours weekly on the study of Tatar or Arabic. The intensive Russian-language program was perhaps still another indication of the efforts of the jadids to end the isolation of the Tatar umma and to prepare the community for becoming actively involved in the cultural, economic, and political life of the empire.

The dramatic change in the attitude of the Tatar communities toward learning Russian, as well as the growing tide of secularism in mektebs and medreses, did not trigger a positive reaction on the part of the Russian government. Prompted by fears that the integrative forces of secular education might raise the expectation of the Tatars and unduly politicize their thinking, the government prohibited the teaching of secular subjects in medreses. The contention was that, as long as the language of education was Tatar, these schools were officially confessional schools where there was no room for science. School inspectors visited the medreses to see that restrictions regarding the teaching of science were being observed, and these representatives of the school district became known among Tatars as *fen kuvuji* (science hunters). To cope with this surveillance, schools kept two class schedules: one for the use of the students (which contained the real daily sequence of classes) and another (from which secular subjects were excluded) that replaced the real schedule as soon as a school inspector entered the school.[42]

In 1910, the department for inorodtsy of the Ministry of the Interior appointed counselor M. Platonnikov and two other employees to a committee, the purpose of which was to investigate whether the content of medrese teaching exceeded the confines of religion. When the teachers and directors of the Galiye medrese of Ufa had to answer a 34-point questionnaire related to the investigation, they stressed the fact that the program of education in their medrese did not have an antigovernment nature and defended the teaching of secular subjects, adding that learning these subjects was necessary because the knowledge facilitated the study of religion.[43]

Despite government pressures, the number of jadid schools increased steadily. In 1912, 90 percent of the 1,088 Tatar schools functioning in the Kazan guberniia were jadid. The city of Kazan, alone, had ten medreses; four of them with a student body of 200 or more: Kasimiye had 200; Tainbiye, 250; Muhammediye, 400; and Apanaev, 800.[44]

The most secularized Kazan medrese was perhaps Muhammediye, which continued the traditions of the smaller medrese opened by the enlightened ulama, Alimjan Barudi, in 1881. The new Muhammediye, which Barudi built with the financial assistance of his merchant father, opened its doors in 1901 and functioned without interruption until 1917.[45] Entrance examination requirements for Muhammediye consisted of Tatar language and literature, Russian, arithmetic, geography, history of Islam, and knowledge of the Qur'an.[46] Its program contained twelve secular and four religious subjects.[47] It had many able teachers; among them, Yusuf Akchura, who had a law degree from the Sorbonne and who taught literature between 1904 and 1905.[48] Yet the secularism of Muhammediye did not fully satisfy the needs of its students, who considered its secular training superficial and criticized Barudi for keeping alive "the spirit of Bukhara" because Barudi believed that the ultimate truth still rested in religion and viewed secular sciences only as the path toward achieving it.[49]

In 1904, the students of Muhammediye founded the society El-Islah (the reform), which was responsible for the militancy of the Tatar shakirds (medrese students) during the following years. Theirs was an unrest of rising expectations, and paradoxically, it might have been the first dramatic proof that secularism had not only arrived in Tatar schools but also begun to transcend the realm of education. For the Islahist shakirds listed among their grievances not only demands for an increased emphasis on secular subjects but also the need to develop cultural jadidism into a struggle for political rights. In February 1906, there were clashes between students and officials of the medrese; 4 shakirds were expelled and 82 others left the medrese as a gesture of protest. The militancy of the students and the solidarity they displayed was a political act, but one of modest proportions. Despite this rebellion, and although El-Islah was the reservoir from which many or most of the intellectuals who represented the left wing of Tatar politics came, its concern with politics was mostly rhetorical.

The concrete actions of El-Islah remained confined to the domain of medrese reform, as in the case of the meeting held between May 1 and 15, 1906, to which shakirds from the medreses of Orenburg, Troitsk, Samara, Chistay, Biklen, and Bobi were invited. El-Islah proposed that each town or village combine all its intermediate and higher-level medreses into one large institution of learning. They also wanted to discontinue the tradition of naming medreses after their founders or sponsors, and they wanted to make Russian and Arabic compulsory for all programs. The participants demanded improvements in living conditions and life-style that would enable Tatar students to enjoy standards comparable to those enjoyed by Russian students. To establish a forum for further expression of their grievances, the students wanted permission to publish a newspaper and requested that medreses be administered by a joint student-faculty committee. They also demanded the right to strike when the administration failed to answer their grievances.[50]

Between 1905 and 1914, medrese unrest spread from Kazan to the entire Volga-Ural region. The shakirds supported the strikes for reform in one medrese by organizing solidarity strikes throughout the region. The militancy of the students increased after the Revolution of 1905, and there were strikes at Apanaev and Akhundov medreses in Kazan, at Huseiniye in Orenburg, and at Galiye in Ufa.

In 1905, 50 students from Galiye and 85 from Huseiniye medreses were expelled for participation in strikes that aimed at securing a reform in the school program. In 1907 and 1908, the causes of unrest at the Galiye medrese of Ufa were the delay in the arrival of the science teacher, the insufficiently intensive program in Russian, and the poor living conditions.

Almost every year, Galiye hired new science teachers: U. Starkov, a graduate of the Istanbul Pedagogical Institute was hired in 1907; a year later, two other Istanbul graduates, A. Shinasi and Ahmed Nuri, were hired, as well as a Muhammediye and Beyrut graduate named Z. Sadretdinov; in 1911, A. Fahri and A. Vali, graduates of the Istanbul faculty of mathematics and physics joined the Galiye teachers.[51] Despite this rapid buildup of science faculty, both the students and their supporters on the outside were frustrated that their medrese was not moving fast enough toward becoming a modern institution of learning.

In 1912, the emphasis on religious subjects was still heavier than the students might have desired, but Galiye's program also included mathematics, geography, geology, mineralogy, and pedagogy, along with the traditional Islamic disciplines. An overnight change of the medrese into a purely secular school was impossible, simply because, if it were to remain a Tatar school, Galiye had to correspond, at least to some extent, to the profile of a confessional school as defined by the Russian government.

Other important Ufa medreses were Hasaniye and Osmaniye. Hasaniye was founded by the Duma deputy M. Hasanov; Osmaniye was founded by the jadid intellectual H. Osmanov, who was also active in writing textbooks for new schools. The expenses of Osmaniye were covered partly by the benevolent society, partly by private donations, and partly from tuition. Its teachers were former graduates of the medrese, as well as graduates from Russian schools. The ratio of secular and religious subjects was similar to that of Galiye or Muhammediye, but the pace of the secularization of the medrese curriculum was not as intense as the 400 students of Osmaniye would have desired, and strikes became a measure of their discontent.[52]

There were several large medreses in Troitsk: Rahmankulov, Rasuliye, Valiev, and Muhammediye. Of these, Muhammediye, founded and sponsored by the industrialist Iaushev, was the best. It contained three sections: *iptidaye* (elementary), *sahavi* (intermediate), and *galiye* (superior). The introductory paragraph of the program of Muhammediye for the 1912–1913 school year stressed that one of the goals of that medrese was the promotion of the Tatar language to develop and enrich the students' ability to think in Tatar. The teaching of Russian received equal attention because it was the language of the Russian state.[53]

In the elementary section of the medrese, a four-year term, the shakirds studied the Tatar language, orthography, orthoephy, calligraphy, arithmetic, natural science, history of Islam, the Qur'an, drawing, crafts, and physical education. In the intermediate section, also a four-year term, the curriculum consisted of Tatar grammar and composition, Russian grammar, orthography and conversation, arithmetic, geometry, natural history, geography, history (Islamic, Tatar, and Russian), anatomy, commerce, drawing, methodics, the Hadith, and gymnastics.

The duration of studies was five years in the superior section. But after the first two years, the students were divided into two classes: those who studied to become imams and those who wanted to become teachers or pursue other careers. As a result, the list of subjects for this section of Muhammediye read: Tatar composition; literary analysis and criticism; Russian etymology, syntax, composition, and literature; Arabic language, rhetoric and literature; algebra; geometry; trigonometry; physics; zoology; mineralogy; astronomy and chemistry; logic; psychology; pedagogy; political economy; general history; Russian law; rules of ethics; gymnastics; religion; Qur'an; Hadith; Muslim law and jurisprudence; commentaries on the Qur'an; history of religion; philosophy of religion; comparative religion; and history of Arabia.

Muhammediye's program was much more comprehensive than those of the Ufa or Kazan medreses; in fact, the breadth of its curriculum rivaled those of Russian gymnasia or the technical schools. There might have been several reasons for this. Unlike Ufa, Troitsk was not handicapped by the status of being the religious center of the Volga-Ural Muslims, and as a result, the Tatars of Troitsk perhaps felt freer to carry the secularization of their schools beyond the level of maintaining a parity between secular and religious subjects. Troitsk also enjoyed an economic advantage over Kazan, which had lost its momentum when it had been bypassed by the Siberian railroad. Troitsk's economic boom perhaps made its community more receptive to change and therefore supportive of innovations, even in the traditional school system. Last, but not least, the Iaushevs, who sponsored the Muhammediye, were among the handful of Tatar millionaires; thus they could afford to keep up with the increasing costs of a comprehensive secular education. Even so, beginning with the academic year 1912–13, the Muhammediya shakirds paid a tuition of fifteen rubles annually, which was deemed necessary "in order to improve the quality of education."[54] The quality of education at Muhammediye was, and remains today, a matter of pride for the Tatars of Troitsk.[55]

Orenburg had its own modern Huseiniye medrese. The educational goal of Huseiniye was outlined by its founder, Ahmed Bay Huseinov, who believed that:

> Our nation's children should acquire the knowledge of the Muslim [i.e., Tatar] and Russian languages to such an extent that, when they join the mainstream of life, they will be competent in any work. For instance, they will be able to become administrators, teachers, accountants, and clerks. For those youths who desire to engage in scientific pursuits, entrance to Russian schools will become easier. This medrese-i-Huseiniye must also provide sufficient training for those who want to pursue a higher education in Islamic studies, to enable them to become "two-eyed"—i.e., open-minded scholars of Islam or teachers of religion.[56]

Huseiniye opened in 1906. The new medrese, which had cost 100,000 rubles to build, was a three-story stone structure equipped with central heating and containing a library, reading rooms, cafeterias, dormitories, and modern classrooms. Its curriculum reflected the equal emphasis on science and religion that suggests the commitment of the administration to respect Ahmed Bay's will and provide an education that would be equally valuable for those who wanted to pursue secular and religious careers.[57]

Bobi was a village medrese in the Sarapul uezd, Viatka guberniia, and it was the best jadid medrese in Russia.[58] When the government closed the school in 1912 as a result of the intrigues of qadimist mullahs, it wrote the final chapter to a tradition of almost 200 years in education, even if the tradition as a modern medrese was a recent one. The jadid medrese of Bobi owed its fame to the efforts of Abdullah, Ubeydullah, and Muhlise Bobi. At the end of the nineteenth century, Abdullah and Ubeydullah Bobi had returned to Russia from their studies abroad. At the encouragement of their father, they had spent several years in Turkey and Egypt, where in addition to traditional Islamic sciences, they had acquired knowledge in science and pedagogy. On their return to their native village, the Bobi brothers embarked on the task of modernizing both the form and content of teaching at the medrese. A. Bobi travelled annually to the N. Novgorod and Menzelinsk fairs to explain to his fellow Tatars the new type of education at his medrese, to discuss his goals with them, and to secure financial assistance from the merchants assembled there. The study of secular sciences at Bobi surpassed, in both breadth and intensity, that at any other Russian medrese. In addition to the secular subjects that appeared in the programs of other jadid medreses, Bobi also offered French, the only jadid medrese to do so.[59]

A telling comment on the quality of education at Bobi was perhaps given by one of its former students, J. Validov, who reminisced: "In the small, but rich, village of Izh-Bobi, situated on an island between the two branches of the river, stood large modern buildings, which through their appearance reminded one of a zemstvo hospital. The aspirations of the young people, not only from the various guberniias of central Russia but from the distant Siberia and Turkestan, were directed toward this little village, then still far away from any water or rail routes.[60]

After 1905, according to G. Mansurov and to the reports of the Okhrana agent H. Kaibyshev, the teachers of Bobi focused their attention on social and political problems. To develop an ability to deliver public speeches, the students prepared weekly reports and made oral presentations on current issues.[61] This addition to the medrese program could be viewed as an effort to acquaint Tatar students with the changes that were taking place in Russia after 1905 and to prepare them to understand the impact of these changes on their own lives. The combination of secular orientation and perceptiveness concerning current issues made Bobi a target for police surveillance, and its dramatic departure from the tradition of purely religious medreses angered the conservative members of the Tatar umma. Paradoxically, the campaign against the jadid medrese brought together the Russian authorities and the qadimist mullahs, who had traditionally been hostile toward each other but who cooperated to bring about the demise of Bobi.

On January 29, 1911, the staff of Bobi learned from Stepan Krivonogov, a peasant living in a neighboring village, that the Russian police planned to raid the medrese.[62] During the night of January 30, 1911, some 160 mounted police, accompanied by high-ranking police officers, surrounded the school and began to search it. The police seized the school archives, which contained information on current and former students and their places of employment. Later, some of those students were put under police surveillance and then imprisoned. The school was closed, and ten of its teachers were arrested and accused of pan-Islamic propaganda. Among those arrested were Abdullah and Ubeydullah Bobi, K. Kumavi, A. Samatov, and A. Selimov. Instrumental in preparing the raid and the accusations against the Bobi teachers were qadimist mullahs, such as Ishmuhammed Dinmuhammedov, Husein Abubakirov, and Shahmurad Gadilov. There were also accusations made by such teachers as Sh. Apakov, M. Yunusov, and F. Davudov, who had become Okhrana informers— perhaps because they could not fit into the modern school that Bobi medrese had become.

Sixteen months after the raid, the trial of the teachers began. The Kazan police department appointed M. Katanov, professor of oriental languages at the Kazan Theological Academy, as official translator for the trial and, to secure a maximum of accuracy in translation, even acquired a dictionary of Arabic political terms from Algeria. The main defense lawyer was V. A. Maklakov, a Duma deputy from Moscow guberniia and a member of the Constitutional Democrat party. (Muslim deputies in the Duma adhered to the policies of that party.) Maklakov, who took the case free of charge, was joined by the Kazan lawyer A. G. Bat, by Egorov from Sarapul, and by I. Ahtamov from Ufa.

The main witness for the prosecution was the qadimist mullah Ishmuhammed Dinmuhammedov, who in his deposition, labeled the Bobi brothers and their school as antigovernmental and, on the basis of the narrow interpretation of those verses from the Qur'an dealing with obedience, argued that whoever raises against the Qur'an and Shariat raises against the government.[63] Dinmuhammedov considered the teachings at Bobi anti-Qur'anic and, consequently, antigovernmental. What he could not grasp, and what the prosecution ignored, was the fact that the Qur'anic verse referred to the support of Islam as a political force as it emerged as a trifaceted system: religion, way of life, and system of government.

On the day of the trial, the streets of Sarapul were filled with Russians and Muslims who had come from distant places to follow its development. The entire city was in a state of emergency because prodefendant feelings were so strong among Russians and Muslims that the police had to offer special protection to Dinmuhammedov. Despite the able defense of Maklakov, who pointed out that the teachers were merely partisans of reforms and not pan-Islamists, the defendants were convicted on three grounds: operation of a medrese that propagated pan-Turkic and pan-Islamic ideas, making anti-government statements, and mishandling the portrait of the tsar.[64]

The trial revealed that the dividing line between prosecution and defense cut across national groups; it was a showdown between progressive and conservative forces. The first advocated change, the second defended the status quo, both religious and political. The Bobi teachers had been equally victims of the ignorance of qadimist mullahs and of the anti-Muslim policies of the Stolypin government, as promulgated in the December 1910 measures of the *Osoboe soveshchanie po vyrabotke mer protivodeistviia Tatarsko-Musul'manskomu vliianiiu v Povolzhskom krae*.[65] The Bobi medrese never reopened, although the support its cause had received from the majority of Tatars was a measure of the success of the jadid schools.

A similar qadimist reaction to the new schools had failed in 1907, when the Stolypin reaction was in its opening stages. At that time, the Tatar community of Tomsk had opened a jadid *rushdiye* (preparatory) school for which they hired teachers from Kazan, Cairo, and Istanbul. This enraged the local imam, who denounced the school to the local authorities as a nest of subversive and pan-Islamic ideas. His efforts were futile, however; the school continued its activities, and soon another jadid school was added to the first, although the imam continued to warn in mosque against the evil effects of the new medreses.[66]

In addition to economic and curriculum problems and the constant clashes with qadimist conservatives and government officials, jadid schools wrestled with another major problem: shortage of adequately trained teachers. In 1897 and 1898, merchants who favored jadid reforms provided an ad hoc solution to this problem by sponsoring summer courses for mekteb teachers and, in many cases, finding employment for them.[67] These summer courses, organized at Bobi between 1908 and 1910, became so famous that, during the summer months, it was difficult to find housing in Izh-Bobi or its environs. The class notes of those who attended the summer courses became basic texts for jadid teachers. They were saved and forwarded to those who could not attend the courses.[68]

Summer courses alone could hardly solve the teacher shortage, and Tatars explored other alternatives as well. In 1908, the Muslims of Orenburg petitioned the Ministry of Education for an annual subsidy of 2,000 rubles to sponsor a two-year pedagogical course. Their request was denied.[69] Then the Muslim press took the initiative in campaigning for the establishment of a Tatar teacher's school (Dar-ul-muallimin).[70] The need for such a school was further emphasized by the fact that medrese graduates preferred to take positions as teachers rather than taking the examinations for the post of imam. Traditionally, the medrese graduate was expected to perform as both teacher and imam, but the growing trend to separate the duties of the imam and those of the teacher made it necessary to consider establishment of schools that would train teachers.[71]

An integral part of the jadid effort aimed at improving the education of the Tatars was the campaign to establish jadid schools for girls. Until the end of the nineteenth century, the only form of education available for Muslim girls throughout Russia was the quasi-private tutoring they received from the *abïstay* (the wife of the mullah), who taught basic reading skills and knowledge of rituals and prayers.

The jadid thinkers had stressed the need to begin the emancipation of Muslim women by educating them. As jadid schools won a growing number of supporters and their number increased, the gap between the education of boys and that of the girls became even greater, and the need for girls' schools became more urgent. The first step toward changing the old attitudes regarding education of women was to win recognition of their right to learn to write as well as read. Abïstays were the first to undergo training to become teachers for girls' schools.[72]

In the summer of 1898, the number of women who received teacher's training at the courses sponsored by Gani Bay Huseinov had reached 60, and some 500 more had announced their plans to attend the September courses.[73] A generation of young jadid women teachers was gradually replacing the abïstays.

As early as 1904, Lebibe Huseinova, who herself had been educated by Magrui abïstay, the wife of A. Barudi, had opened a jadid school for girls in Kazan. By 1906, there were some 40 students in her school, and what was most remarkable was the fact that some of them were women 30 or 40 years of age. Between 1906 and 1913, the student body grew from 40 to 170, and the program of the school was almost entirely secularized to include, among other subjects, Tatar and Russian languages, geography, biology, music, and crafts.[74] Because the teachers feared government repression, this secularization took place secretly. As the number of women teachers grew, they became instrumental in mobilizing entire communities to open schools for girls. A. Osmanov opened a school for girls in Ufa; Yusuf Akchura financed the building of a similar school at Khauly (Simbirsk guberniia). In 1906, the Tatar women of Ufa founded a society for the promotion of education of women.[75] In 1907, the society opened three schools for girls, each of which provided elementary as well as secondary education.

In 1908, Baghbestan Khalaf opened a school in Orenburg where girls learned geography and arithmetic in addition to writing and religion.[76] Student response to this new school prompted Baghbestan Khalaf to launch a campaign in 1910 to open a reading hall for girls. She made an appeal for book donations through the Muslim press.[77]

The first Tatar girls' school to have a comprehensive secular curriculum was the one in the village of Izh-Bobi. By 1910, it had become an eight-year school that taught senior students methodology and pedagogy, thus contributing to the emergence of the first generation of women teachers with formal training.[78] In 1912, in the aftermath of the Bobi affair, the Russian authorities closed down Muhlise Bobi's school, and she received and accepted an invitation to teach at the Suyumbike girls' school in Troitsk. By 1913, Suyumbike had become the best girls' school in Russia. Its success has been attributed to the financial support of the Troitsk merchants, to the strength of the jadid forces in Troitsk, and to the fact that it had attracted the best teachers from Bobi after the closing of the jadid schools there.[79] The Suyumbike school became the nucleus from which the campaign for girls' schools spread to the entire area around Troitsk.[80]

In 1913, the Tatars considered joining the celebrations of the tricentennial of the Romanov dynasty by opening the first girls' gymnasium. Between January and March of that year, the Tatar press discussed the issue. F. A. Aitova, who was already leading an elementary girls' school, became the main force behind the effort aimed at opening the gymnasium. Aitova endured three years of frustrating clashes with the aloofness of the Russian authorities. Only after the intervention of the Muslim Duma deputies was the first gymnasium for girls opened on October 29, 1916.[81] This event marked a new phase in the process aimed at secularizing the Tatar schools and building up a comprehensive system of education in the national language.

Another phase in the process of secularization was marked by the growing interest Tatars exhibited at the beginning of the twentieth century in Russian vocational schools and vocational training. The Tatars approached such schools differently from the way they approached Russian secondary schools: They advertised Russian vocational schools and encouraged their children to attend them.[82]

There was a special emphasis on the need for commercial schools because only 153 of the 53,000 students enrolled in the 290 commercial schools of Russia in 1909 were Muslim.[83] Tatar newspapers always considered the graduation of Tatar youths from technical or commercial schools to be newsworthy; thus in 1908, *Iqtisad* reported the graduation of S. Agishev, R. Akchurin, A. Bulatov, I. Utamishev from the Siberian Commercial School.[84] In 1911, the same journal noted that almost half of the 27 students of the commercial school sponsored by the Society of Orenburg Clerks were Tatar.[85] The popularity of commercial schools among Tatars is not surprising because trade was a traditional occupation for them.

Leading members of the Tatar communities also encouraged vocational training.[86] In an article written in 1911, imam Nejip Shikiev welcomed the initiative of those Tatar youths who entered Russian schools but deplored the fact that so many of them favored the theoretical gymnasia. Shikiev urged the young generation of Tatars to take a more practical attitude toward life and undergo vocational training.[87] The Tatar press published similar articles discussing the importance of acquiring practical skills for improving one's economic situation; often these articles both pointed to the relationship that seemed to exist between delinquency and the lack of skills and encouraged vocational training.[88]

By the end of the first decade of the twentieth century, the Tatars had come to accept the need for vocational schools; and the isolated attempts at providing vocational training for Tatar children, although unsatisfactory, marked a transition to the development of a school that, by definition, was secular and represented a departure from the tradition of mektebs and medreses.

The number of medrese and gymnasium graduates was growing steadily at the end of the first decade of the twentieth century, but those pursuing academic or professional careers were still a small minority. Until 1905, St. Petersburg and Kazan were the main university centers where Tatar youths went to earn their degrees.[89] Outside Russia, the Middle East attracted them by its excellence in Islamic studies. After 1905, Cairo, Medina, Beirut, and Istanbul still enjoyed popularity, but Western European universities began to emerge as increasingly popular centers of learning for Tatars. Simultaneously, a diversification of the career interests of Tatar students occurred: The medical field—which had always been popular—still attracted many youths, but it was joined by such fields as law, international studies, and engineering.[90]

The sex distribution among university students also changed; women began to attend the Sorbonne or the University of Geneva, although their numbers were still very small.[91] All of these changes suggest that the reform of Tatar schools, which had begun modestly with the introduction of the phonetic system, had ultimately led to a profound re-evaluation of the attitude toward education as a whole.

In some twenty years of catalyzing tension between jadidist and qadimist forces, Tatar schools entered the twentieth century. They retained an Islamic character because the moral foundations of education remained religious. Yet from this basis, mektebs and medreses developed as national schools that became increasingly secular. The national character of the jadid schools rested in the emphasis on national language and culture that accompanied the special attention given to the secular sciences in the curriculum.

One of the beneficial effects of this dichotomy between jadidist and qadimist was that it ended the passivity of the medrese students. The active interest many youths took in educational policies was perhaps one of the early tests regarding the Tatar schools' adequacy in preparing the entire umma to question and challenge the nature as well as the scope of the changes the Tatar society was experiencing. This growing inquisitiveness on the part of the Tatar community was particularly important after 1905, when Tatars had to re-evaluate their relationship with the Russian state in political terms.

Finally, but not least in importance, the success enjoyed by jadid schools in the Volga-Ural area led the Tatars to become the teachers and the sponsors of similar schools throughout a territory that extended from the Kazakh steppes to China.[92] The Tatar teacher became the companion of the Tatar merchant in travels to the East.[93] The merchant returned, while the teacher stayed in the East. The teacher's gifts, less tangible than the goods of the Orenburg or Kazan merchants, were more durable because jadid schools were a living presence in the Far East long after the merchants had abandoned the trade routes that linked Kazan with Harbin or Peking.[94]

9 Tatar Jadids in Politics

> "The time will come!"—they said
> And waited with hope.
> But when the time came, how many of them,
> How many of them, were already gone.
>
> "Shundïy vakït kiler!"—diep,
> Ometlänep kötkännär.
> Vakït jitkäch, ällä kemnär,
> Ällä kemnär kitkännär.
>
> (A. Minhajeva)

The early Tatar reformers approached Islam not only as a religion but also as a culture that united the spiritual and temporal on a religious foundation. In so doing, they also stressed the need for a solution to the tension between Islam and its sociopolitical milieu. The ulama, however, were not capable of carrying on the task of reform to its ultimate fruition—political organization. To the degree that original political thought and political activities developed among Tatars between 1905 and 1917, such thought and activities were primarily the work of lay Muslims who had had a liberal education. Even for those enlightened ulama, such as Musa Bigi and Rizaeddin Fahreddin, who demonstrated originality and boldness in approaching the issue of religious reform, the realm of politics remained of marginal interest. They participated in the political activities of the liberal jadids but did not contribute original ideas or programs. The more conservative ulama chose to join the political arena either by subscribing to the policies of the Russian conservative parties or by reassessing their allegiance to the ideals of an Islamic umma whose constituency transcended the borders of the Russian empire.

The Volga Tatars welcomed, with great hope, Tsar Nicholas II's Manifesto of October 17, 1905, because the pronouncement seemed to promise the people of Russia rights and liberties that would endow their status as citizens of the Russian empire with meaning. The November 10, 1905, issue of the Tatar newspaper *Kazan muhbiri* noted that "greatest in its importance, the law of October 17 will change radically the structure of our state."[1] This optimistic tone was based on the promises contained in the Manifesto: freedom of speech, of the press, of assembly, and of organization; a commitment to the inviolability of the individual; and even the proposed formation of the State Duma as a legislative organ.

The Volga Tatars received these promises with hope because, by 1905, jadidism had matured enough to prompt at least some of them to contemplate the issue of political organization.[2] Their political ambitions found expression in the activities of the four Muslim congresses called after 1905, in the organization of a Muslim party, in adherence to Russian parties, and in involvement in national politics through participation in the State Duma. After 1905, involvement in politics projected some Tatars into Russian socialist circles while encouraging others to put in motion a political mechanism aimed at fulfilling their nationalist aspirations. It would be inaccurate, however, to regard the events of 1905 as a Tatar political deus ex machina. For even if modest, their interest in politics had emerged at the end of the nineteenth century.

The first Tatar literary-political circle was organized in 1895 by a few Tatar youths. Tuhfatullah Mamaliev, a former graduate of the Kazan Teachers' School and a Socialist Revolutionary between 1905 and 1906, commented on Tatar student circles in an essay, entitled *Pan Turkizmniñg tuuvï* (The birth of pan-Turkism), that he prepared for the Okhrana.[3] Mamaliev stated that, between 1895 and 1900, a few students of the teachers' school who had strong nationalist inclinations, but showed no receptivity to socialist ideas, had organized a circle aimed at investigating the best course for the new Tatar literature to take. Some of its members were to become leaders of Tatar political life: Sadri and Hadi Maksudov as Liberals; Ayaz Ishaki, Aliagsar Kemal, and Fuad Tuktarov, Socialist Revolutionaries; Husain Yamashev, Bolshevik; and Ümer Teregulov, Menshevik. After studying the Turkish, Persian, and Russian literatures, they chose the pan-Turkist ideals of the Crimean newspaper *Terjuman* and the civic traditions of Russian literature as models for a new Tatar literature.[4] The group published its own newspaper, *Tarakki* (Progress), in mimeographed form, but there is no evidence that the students had any concrete political goals or were connected with either of the two illegal Russian parties.

In 1901, according to A. Ishaki, who belonged to the circle, the members organized a party named Shakirdlik (Student life) while continuing to publish *Tarakki*. Ishaki argued that, in 1904, Shakirdlik took the character of a purely political party and changed its name to Hürriyet (Freedom), publishing a paper under the same name. He further claimed that upon the dissolution of Hürriyet in 1905, the younger generation formed the Tangchï party, and the remainder of the membership formed the Ittifak.[5]

The initiative to transform the student circle into a party in 1901 may have been taken under the influence of the radicalism that was growing among the students of Kazan University, although there is no indication that any of the members of Shakirdlik were taking part directly in the radical activities organized by the Russian students.

In the fall of 1905, however, the situation changed. On October 11, the students of the Tatar Teachers' School began to participate in the meetings organized by the students of the Russian gymnasia, of the pedagogic and technical institutes, and of the art school. In response, the administration closed the teachers' school between early November 1905, and January 1, 1906.[6] In the fall of 1905, former students of the teachers' school organized the socialist party, Brek (Union), which existed until the fall of 1906 and which, throughout its existence, published a paper first called *Azat* (Liberty) and then *Azat Halk* (The free people). The party's program was built around the issues of "freedom for the people, land to the peasants," reflecting the influence of the Social Democrats and Socialist Revolutionaries.[7]

Modest in scope at the time of its organization, Shakirdlik made a contribution to Tatar politics as a result of the role its former members played in the Socialist Revolutionary and Social Democratic parties. In 1906, A. Ishaki and F. Tuktarov, former members of Shakirdlik and two of the founders of Brek, together with Sh. Muhammedyarov and A. Davletshin, organized a Tatar Socialist Revolutionary party, Tangchï, whose organ was the newspaper *Tang Yulduzï* (The morning star).[8] At about the same time, Husain Yamashev, one of Ishaki and Tuktarov's companions from Shakirdlik, chose to join the Russian Social Democratic party of Kazan and emerged as one of its active members and propagandists among the Tatars.[9] Despite his sustained propaganda, Yamashev had little success in attracting more than a handful of Tatars into the party, and they left Kazan and scattered throughout the Volga region when the police destroyed the Kazan organization of the party in 1905.[10]

Yamashev, accompanied by a few of his friends, left for Orenburg, where in 1907, they organized a legal Social Democratic group, called Uralchïlar (The Uralists), which opened its membership to Bolsheviks and Mensheviks alike. The group published its newspaper, *Ural*, which enjoyed a brief life of only 31 issues between January 4 and April 27, 1907.[11]

Throughout its short existence, *Ural* was critical of the liberal and revolutionary-nationalist Muslim parties, emphasizing the need for class, rather than national, consciousness. In its third issue (January 12, 1907), it published an article entitled "Ittifak-al-Muslimin" (The Muslim union), which declared: "The Tatar bourgeoisie is trying to prove that there are no exploiting classes among Muslims—landowners, capitalists—and that Muslims represent a homogeneous entity. This is pure demagogy. Despite their common religion, not all Muslims can join the same party, the so-called Muslim Union, because their economic interests are not identical by any means."[12]

Uralchïlar was dispersed by the police in April 1907, and with the death of Yamashev in 1912, the task of spreading Marxism among the Tatars and organizing them along class lines seemed even less attainable.

The Tatar bourgeoisie may have been at fault in denying the existence of class differentiation among Muslims. Equally unperceptive, however, were the editors of *Ural*; to require their fellow Muslims to disregard or belittle an identity responsible for their survival as a people in order to join a brotherhood of the exploited was a colossal tactical error.

The best evidence of the price Tatar Social Democrats had to pay for their political naïveté is the fact that, between 1905 and 1907, the liberal nationalist groups emerged almost unchallenged on the Russian political scene as the spokesmen for the Tatars, and at the time of the February Revolution, the membership of the Kazan Bolshevik organization was almost exclusively Russian.[13]

Those Tatars for whom ethnic and religious concerns took precedence over class issues chose to use the Muslim congresses as a means of identifying the priorities of the umma and articulating plans for action. Credit for taking the initiative to organize the first Muslim congresses goes to Abdurrashid Ibrahimov, a Siberian Tatar and former member of the Muslim Ecclesiastical Council.[14] After almost nine years of self-imposed exile in Europe, the Middle East, and the Far East, Abdurrashid Bey had returned to Russia in 1904, having been deported by the Ottoman Sultan Abdulhamid, who was becoming increasingly weary of political émigrés, regardless of their race and religion.[15]

On his arrival in Odessa on August 12, 1904, Abdurrashid Bey was promptly arrested by the Russian authorities, only to be released on August 21 because of the protests of Muslims throughout Russia. He then traveled to Moscow, where he established contacts with Russian politicians for the purpose of discussing a course of action for improving the situation of the Muslims. To this end, he met on September 20, 1904, with M. A. Stakhovich, who was the head of the zemstvo liberal movement. They agreed that Muslims should participate in the general movement for reforms, and Stakhovich gave Ibrahimov a copy of the zemstvo report regarding the types of reforms that were necessary.[16] It is conceivable that, during that meeting, Ibrahimov raised the issue of the types of autonomous administration most suitable for different groups of Muslims, a topic in which he had had a long-standing interest and one on which he later published two essays in which he summarized his ideas.[17]

After his meeting with Stakhovich, Abdurrashid Bey continued his tour of the political circles in the Russian capital. He secured an audience with Prince D. P. Sviatopolk Mirsky, the minister of interior, and brought the grievances of the Muslims to his attention. Although sympathetic to Abdurrashid Bey's concerns, Prince Mirsky could make no promises, but he did suggest that Muslims present an official list of grievances for the government to consider.

Abdurrashid Bey's enthusiasm when he left St. Petersburg for the Volga-Ural region indicates that he must have interpreted Prince Mirsky's suggestion as a commitment to give prompt consideration to the demands of the Muslims. His journey took him to Kazan, Chistay (Chistopol), Bobi, Perm, Troitsk, Kyzylyar (Petropavlovsk), and Ufa. In each community, he pointed out to the Tatars that, to be able to give coherence to the grievances they submitted to the government, they must organize.

In Ufa, his call fell on receptive ears. M. Tevkelev, justice of the peace and zemstvo deputy for Belebeev and Ufa; H. Sytrlanov, justice of the peace and president of the Belebeev zemstvo council between 1887 and 1891; and journalist B. Ahtamov, son of lawyer A. Ahtamov, were convinced that: "Certainly there will be one day in Russia a general revolution. In view of this [event], the Tatars must not remain inactive."[18]

In Kazan as well, Abdurrashid Bey's call received an enthusiastic response. On January 29, 1905, some 200 Tatars attended a meeting to draft a petition to the tsar. The petition contained demands for reforming the religious organization of the Muslims in a way that would secure the election of the mufti and of Ecclesiastical Council by the Muslims themselves. The petition also stressed the need to emancipate Muslim schools from the supervision of Russian school inspectors and to allow Muslim communities to freely open libraries, reading rooms, and vocational and general educational schools, as well as to publish their own newspapers. In addition, the Volga Tatars demanded that their representatives participate in the drafting of the proposals for laws regarding religious and cultural affairs in the Russian empire.

One of the important grievances articulated in the Volga Tatars' petition took the form of a request for the abolishment of laws that limited the right of the Tatars to enter the Russian civil service and to join certain professions, such as law and book publishing. The same petition contained requests for lifting all restrictions on Tatar trade, real estate ownership, and settlement beyond the Urals. This last set of requests was in response to those policies of the Russian government designed to halt, or at least curtail, the influence of the Tatars on other Russian Muslims, policies that had prohibited Tatars from settling in regions inhabited by the Kirghiz, from owning landed estates in Turkestan or the steppe regions, and from engaging in book trade.

On March 9 and 17, 1905, the Muslims of Chistay and Buinsk, respectively, elected the delegates who were to present their petitions to the president of the Council of Ministers, Count Witte, and to the minister of the interior, Bulygin.[19]

Throughout the spring months of 1905, delegations of Volga Muslims traveled, one after another, to St. Petersburg, where they accomplished nothing beyond personally presenting their petitions either to Minister of the Interior Bulygin or to Count Witte. The lack of coordination among the efforts of various communities suggests that their enthusiasm could not overcome their lack of experience in politics. Instead of cooperating, the various groups of Volga Tatars almost competed with each other for the attention of the government.

Between April 10 and 15, 1905, the ulama held a congress (kurultai) of its own in Ufa. Its aim, too, was to draft a petition to the government. During the congress, the ulama discussed numerous petitions that individuals or entire villages had sent for consideration. The medrese students of Ufa presented the congress with a 28-point memorandum dealing mainly with the reform of schools along jadid lines and calling for Muslim schools to be placed only under the supervision of the Ufa Muftiat. The reform proposal drafted by the ulama congress restricted itself to the confines of religious, educational, and administrative grievances and contained no suggestions for political organization.[20]

In the spring of 1905, the Kazan community was perhaps the only one that concerned itself with establishing contacts between the Muslims of the Volga area and those of the Crimea, the Caucasus, and Turkestan in an effort to prepare for common political action. In early spring, Kazan Tatars held a meeting at the residence of journalist Yusuf Akchura, where they discussed the plan for a Muslim congress to be held in Kazan.[21] That meeting was followed by another one at the residence of Ahmed Bay Huseinov and still another gathering hosted by the merchant A. Saydashev. The task of drafting the list of grievances to be presented to the government fell upon Sayid Giray Alkin, a lawyer and a graduate of the Law Faculty of the University of Kazan. Yusuf Akchura and Abdurrashid Bey wrote to the Muslims of the Crimea, the Caucasus, Kazakhstan, and Turkestan, inviting them to a congress of all Russian Muslims.[22]

On April 8, 1905, when the delegates of various Muslim communities arrived in St. Petersburg to present their petitions to the government, they gathered first at the residence of Abdurrashid Bey to discuss future action. The focal point of their deliberations was the issue of centralization: the organization of a joint religious center for Sunni and Shiite Muslims and the creation of a political committee for all Russian Muslims. They also decided to hold an All-Russian congress in N. Novgorod to consider the problem of political organization.

The preparatory meetings for the first All-Russian Muslim Congress took place on May 20, 1905, in Chistay. Like all previous, and many future, meetings of the Tatars, these sessions were held under the disguise of a social function to avoid harassment by the Russian authorities: The ulama Zakir Hazret invited prominent Muslims from throughout Russia to attend the wedding ceremony for his daughter.

Once in Chistay, however, the representatives of the Muslim communities planned the congress. Guests joined their hosts at the mosque for prayer. After the prayer, they engaged in deliberations regarding the best course of action. On the grounds that the government could not deny them the right to found an organization whose aim was only cultural, Abdurrashid Bey insisted that Muslims unite under the auspices of an association for the propagation of education and culture.

In the evening of May 20, 1905, the guests gathered at the house of Mustafa Vahab, where the meeting was dominated by students who opposed the mild project of Abdurrashid Bey, insisting that Russian Muslims had no need for cultural associations and arguing that what Muslims needed was political organization.[23]

The date of the first All-Russian Muslim Congress was set for August 15, 1905, at N. Novgorod, to coincide with the annual fair that always attracted Muslims from all over the empire. By August 13, many delegates were already present in the city and were attending informal meetings. During one such meeting, the lawyer A. Ahtamov accepted the task of securing an authorization for the congress. On August 14, he was received by the governor, who denied the authorization on the grounds that the entire city was under curfew.

The news disappointed the majority of the delegates and angered the students into declaring, "If they don't give us the authorization, we must organize demonstrations with red flags."[24] This radicalism on the part of the Tatar students was a result of their exposure to the Russian student movement, to the strikes and demonstrations that had troubled Kazan during that year, and to the propaganda materials distributed by the Kazan committee of the Russian Social Democratic Party.[25]

The flamboyant student proposal was met with indifference by others present at the meeting, who, choosing to avoid a direct confrontation with the government, searched for loopholes in the laws regarding the right of assembly. Finally, Abdurrashid Bey pointed out that, because there was no law prohibiting assembly on water, a riverboat trip on the Oka would be the best, and politically safest, location for the first All-Russian Congress of the Muslims. Consequently, he rented the boat *Gustav Struve* for a "congress trip."

All delegates, with the exception of the students, were told to assemble at the pier on August 15, 1905, at 9:00 A.M., instead of 10:00, which was the officially announced departure time. This manner of attempt to bar the students from participation at the congress indicates that the organizers must have regarded the radicalism of the students as disruptive, if not outright dangerous. The delegates agreed, however, that if the students arrived they should be taken on board.

The *Gustav Struve* left the pier some ten minutes earlier than the official departure time because the commander spotted some Okhrana agents at the docks, but latecomers caught up with the ship in a motorboat. Among these latecomers there were some twenty students, led by socialists A. Ishaki, F. Tuktarov, and A. Davletshin. They were all taken aboard, but only after having been reminded, "This is not an assembly of Social-Democrats but an assembly of alliance; arrogant and far-fetched points of view shall not be tolerated; it is necessary to submit to conventions."[26]

The students apparently complied with this request because the documents of the first congress contain no evidence of their views, dissenting opinions (if any), or contributions. Most likely, they honored the request that reduced them to silence because, numerically, they represented a minority of less than 20 percent of the total number of 108 delegates assembled aboard the *Gustav Struve*.[27]

The First All-Russian Congress of Muslims, presided over by Crimean journalist I. Gasprali, Baku lawyer and journalist A. Topchibashi, and Volga journalist Y. Akchura, and dominated numerically and ideologically by the Volga Tatars, was a congress of the landowners, the traditional ulama, and the industrial and merchant bourgeoisie, as well as of the jadid intelligentsia. The main goal of this congress was to forge a political union of all Russian Muslims, but when it was over, although the participants had recorded the importance of organizing the Muslims into a political force, they had stopped short of creating a party by merely announcing the formation of a union (Ittifak) of all Russian Muslims, regardless of their social class. They had arrived only at the theoretical approval of a union, and there had been little, if any, discussion of political action.

The five-point document of the First All-Russian Muslim Congress spelled out the following goals:

Unification of Russian Muslims for the purpose of carrying out political, economic, and social reforms

Establishment of a democratic regime in which elected representatives of the people belonging to all nationalities would share in the legislative and executive power

Legal equality of Muslims and Russians

Freedom to develop Muslim schools, press, book publishing, and cultural life as a whole

Periodic reconvocation of the congress.[28]

The First All-Russian Muslim Congress recorded one significant accomplishment: The participants accepted the idea of a religious union, or rather of reconciliation between the Shiite Muslims of the Caucasus and the Sunni from the Volga and the Crimea. The leaders of the Volga and the Caucasus Muslims sealed the reconciliation with banquets in honor of each other, and the people in the streets welcomed, although with surprise, the fact that Sunni and Shiite Muslims were greeting each other. Perhaps one of the best summaries of the meaning of this reconciliation for the average Muslim was provided by a merchant from the Caucasus who noted: "I have been trading at N. Novgorod for many years; Tatars never bought from us; this year my sales to them amounted to six thousand rubles." A peasant, however, remarked, not without irony: "My friends, this alliance is indeed a good thing; we should have arrived at it a long time ago. There is one thing, however, which I don't understand. Are we the ones who converted to the religion of the Shiites, or did they adopt ours? Whatever the situation, it is all right now."[29]

The comments of this Tatar peasant could be interpreted as still another proof of the fact that, compared with the Shiite Muslims of the Caucasus and Central Asia, the Sunni Volga Tatars placed much less weight on sectarian differences within Islam. This religious tolerance might have been an indirect result of the fall of Kazan; after 1552, the Tatars were probably too concerned with the dimensions of the Muslim-Christian confrontation to seriously consider dissent within Islam.

The task of organizing the Second All-Russian Congress of Muslims fell on the Kazan group of Ittifak. In the months after the August session in N. Novgorod, representatives of the Volga, Crimea, and the Caucasus Muslims drafted proposals for the statute and program of Ittifak to be submitted to the second congress for discussion.

During the same months, however, political events that took place in Russia added new concerns to the agenda of their meetings. After the promulgation of the October Manifesto, the issue of elections to the State Duma was of particular interest to members of Ittifak, who welcomed the prospects of political representation but were ill-prepared to take advantage of the opportunities a constitutional system could offer.

In the fall of 1905, Ittifak was an alliance, not yet an official political party, and Muslim liberals still believed that adherence to one of the existing Russian parties was the best answer to the problem of participation in elections for the State Duma. The choice of which Russian party this would be proved to be a contested issue, for among the Muslims, there was no unanimous approval of any of the existing parties. The Kazan group favored the Kadets (Constitutional Democrats), a choice in which they were joined by the Orenburg group, and, because Kazan Tatars were better organized than any other group of Ittifak, they were able to acquaint the Tatar public with the Kadet party by launching a sustained press campaign. The newspaper *Kazan muhbiri* published not only translations of the Kadet program but also commentaries on the party.

The Muslim religious leaders favored the more conservative Russian parties. To facilitate a final decision about which party to follow, the members of Ittifak decided to invite a few prominent Kadet leaders and some representatives of the conservative parties to their December 9, 1905, meeting, which took place in St. Petersburg at the Muslim benevolent society. The meeting was chaired by the famous linguist, Professor Baudouin de Courtenais, and was attended by P. Miliukov, I. Rodichev, and P. B. Struve, all very important members of the Kadet party.[30] It was a meeting of promises and courtship, at the conclusion of which, in a gesture of goodwill, the Kadet leaders proposed the election of Yusuf Akchura to membership in the Central Administrative Committee of the Kadet party.[31]

The Kadet leaders' decision to elect Akchura to their Central Administrative Committee may have been prompted by the fact that, in addition to his Sorbonne education, Akchura was perhaps the most ardent supporter of collaboration with the Russian liberal parties during the winter of 1905–1906. What the Kadets were oblivious to, however, was the fact that this same Yusuf Akchura had authored a political essay that developed the theory of Turkism or pan-Turkism.[32] The Kadets' ignorance of Akchura's political philosophy is not only of theoretical interest; it has practical implications in that Akchura's adoption of the Kadet program, rather than being an ultimate gesture of Westernization, was an attempt to gain access to political participation and to integrate the specific demands of the Volga Tatars into the programs the Russians themselves were advancing at the time. The rapprochement between the Kadets and Akchura could have become an alliance if the commitment of the Kadets had been genuine and not a cover for tactical maneuvering. In any case, despite the rationale behind it, the election of Akchura sealed a de facto commitment of Ittifak to the political game of the Kadet party. To formalize the commitment, however, the issue of the Kadet-Muslim alliance had to be submitted to the Second All-Russian Congress of Muslims.

The Second All-Russian Congress of Muslims took place in St. Petersburg between January 13 and 23, 1906. The program and the statutes of Ittifak were discussed, and the creation of a party called Union of Russian Muslims (Rusya Musulmanlariniñ Ittïfakï) was made official. Cooperation with the Kadets in the elections to the First Duma was also approved, although one of the leading figures of Ittifak, Ismail Bey Gasprali, opposed such a move and suggested a boycott of the elections.[33] His major opponent in this was Yusuf Akchura.

Akchura returned from the Kadet convention with a firm conviction that the Constitutional Party best suited the interests of the Muslims. As a gesture of goodwill, the Kadets had agreed to adjust some of the articles in their party's program to make it more acceptable to the Muslims. For instance, the Muslims had requested that revisions of the Russian civil or penal codes take into account the Muslim canonic and common laws, that full autonomy be granted to the Ecclesiastical Council, and that use of the national language be permitted in schools.[34]

Ittifak's 23-point statute proposed a territorial organization of Russian Muslims that would reflect the imperatives of political action. This new organization would be in addition to, not in lieu of, the existing territorial divisions that were the basis for the religious administrative structure. Each of the proposed sixteen regions was to be represented at the annual congress by an assembly elected at regional congresses. Baku was chosen as the seat of the Central Assembly, but regional centers were to host the annual congresses by rotation.[35]

All regional committees, with the exception of the Kazan Committee for the Upper Volga, remained projects on paper.[36] Factors that may have hindered the emergence of the other regional committees include the paucity of material and human resources and the reluctance of the Muslim communities to commit themselves to political action in a year marked by political violence in most of Russia and by racial violence in the Caucasus.

Whether political action at the regional level was hindered by apathy, ignorance, or fear, the failure of other Muslim groups to develop political action allowed the Kazan Tatars to gain the upper hand in Muslim politics and dominate the political life of the Muslims of Russia until 1917. The prominence of the Kazan group, which monopolized the affairs of the second congress, generated dissatisfaction, and even alienation, because many Muslims began perceiving Ittifak as a party of the Kazan Tatars. One delegate complained: "We are not being informed of anything; everything is being done in secret; under the circumstances I cannot understand how one could speak of an alliance . . . The Muslims of Baku elected us as their delegates; how could we adopt unknown programs in such grave circumstances, brothers?"[37]

Frustrated by the behavior of the Kazan Tatars, the alienated delegates from the Caucasus returned home to maintain a conspiracy of silence about the deliberations of the congress because they deemed it useless to popularize a political event that had been monopolized by a single group. This perception of the events of the congress, one shared by many of the participants, led to a political apathy that, ironically, contributed to greater strengthening of the Kazan committee, which emerged as the only active regional chapter of Ittifak.

The Kazan committee's active involvement in the issues of Ittifak had a catalytic effect on the Tatar communities of the Volga-Ural area. They organized town and village meetings at which to discuss issues raised at the second congress and to assess the impact of the political changes occurring in their lives. One of these meetings, held in February 1906, brought together some 2,000 ulama from the entire Orenburg region. Also in February 1906, 700 members of the Ufa Tatar community met to discuss the organization of an eight-member commission of lawyers to study land reforms. At that same meeting, they also discussed the opening of vocational schools and proposed a series of measures aimed at maintaining high moral standards among Muslims.

Other groups also met that spring. In March 1906, the villagers from Burai met to discuss the equality of Muslims and Russians before the law. They demanded that Muslim muftis be nominated to the Duma, just as the six Christian Orthodox religious leaders were. They also raised the issues of the proportional representation of the Muslims in the zemstvos, of state subsidies for Muslim schools, and of equal rights for Muslim teachers. That same spring, the Tatars of Kuznitsky organized an association that demanded affiliation with the Kazan chapter of Ittifak. Finally, on July 20, 1906, the Orenburg community met to name its delegates to the Third All-Russian Muslim Congress.[38]

The Third All-Russian Muslim Congress was held in N. Novgorod, between August 16 and 20, 1906. It was the first congress whose assembly was authorized by the government. Although Abdurrashid Bey deserves credit for securing that approval, his achievement was overshadowed by criticism from the majority of the delegates, who considered it unethical for him to criticize pan-Islamism in his memorandum to the authorities, even if he had done so as a concession aimed at securing government sanction for the congress. The works of the congress began only after Abdurrashid Bey's public apology, delivered in a lengthy speech that was in fact less a mea culpa than a reiteration of the need for Muslim unity within the framework of a single political party in order to resist missionary attacks and to safeguard the religious and cultural traditions of the Islamic umma of Russia.[39]

The 800 delegates present at the first session of the third congress elected the presidium as well as the membership of the three commissions designated to study the issues of political organization, education, and reform of the religious administration. This congress was even more overwhelmingly dominated than the second by the Volga Tatars, who represented at least 80 percent of the membership in each commission. Ten of the fourteen presidium members were from the Volga-Ural region, and even though the presidium chairman was the Azeri journalist A. Topchibashi, the secretary was Yusuf Akchura.[40]

When the delegates assembled for the second session on August 17, the debates registered the first major differences of opinion regarding the scope and goals of Ittifak. One line of thought was represented by the patriarch of jadidism, Ismail Bey Gasprali, who suggested that the discussion of political programs be postponed until the fourth congress and expressed his belief that perseverance would be more successful than flamboyance in securing rights for Muslims. He reminded the participating delegates that approval for the congress had been granted on the condition that only religious and cultural issues be addressed, which would make it illegal to introduce political issues into the agenda.[41]

The second line of thought was represented by young Volga Tatar intellectuals, such as historian Hadi Atlasi and Socialist Revolutionaries A. Ishaki and F. Tuktarov. Opposing Gasprali's apolitical stand, they welcomed the political aspirations of Ittifak but found its program too moderate to be satisfactory.[42] Hadi Atlasi considered that, in a century marked by wars of liberation, putting trust in political debate for gaining rights and freedom was not only unrealistic but also outright irresponsible to future generations. He believed that action and direct participation were needed.[43] Following a similar line, F. Tuktarov and A. Ishaki spoke from a class position, although at first glance, Tuktarov's emphasis on the antagonism between the views of the young and the old generations might have given the impression that he saw the disagreement as a fathers-and-sons conflict. A. Ishaki was much more outspoken in his criticism of the shortcomings of Ittifak: He stressed that, even though they shared the same faith, no single political party could accommodate all Muslims because Muslims belong to different social classes. He also pointed out that a union of all Muslims, an Ittifak, would be possible only if it were confined to educational and religious issues and as long as it excluded the idea of one political program for all.

A third line of thought found expression in the opinions of Volga Tatars S. Alkin, S. Sytrlanov, and Y. Akchura, who represented the voice of the liberal majority. They answered the criticism of the Left by emphasizing the need for a program and a political party for all to give national exposure to the problems of the Muslims. Yusuf Akchura replied as follows to the objections of Socialist Revolutionaries Tuktarov and Ishaki: "There should be unions based on principles of nationality and ethnic origin; despite economic differences, it is always possible to unite and organize the most powerful party on principles of nationalism and religion."[44]

If the discussions on politics were divisive, the deliberations on educational reforms that took place on August 18 and 19 unfolded in an atmosphere of agreement. No substantive objections were registered to the 33-point report prepared by the commission, which was headed by A. Apanaev.[45]

During the second half of the August 19 session, the commission on religious reform, presided over by A. Barudi, presented its thirteen-point report, which advocated election of muftis to the Duma and emphasized the need to press for government guarantees that muftis would enjoy rights equal to those of the Orthodox clergy of the same rank.[46]

On August 19 and 20, the third commission presented the report on Ittifak's political program. Despite opposition from Socialist Revolutionaries, such as A. Ishaki and F. Tuktarov, the congress adopted a 72-point program influenced so heavily by the Kadets that Ittifak could even claim to be a chapter of the Kadet party.[47] The Tatar Social Democrats, who had grouped around the newspaper *Ural*, called Ittifak "Tatar Kadetism in *chalma* (national dress) and *tiubeteika* (national head dress)."[48] Despite such criticism, the majority of the delegates were resolved to give Ittifak formal organization as a Muslim popular party. To accomplish this end, they outlined the framework of the political bureaucracy necessary for establishment of a party, and the congress elected, by secret ballot, a central committee comprised of fifteen members, eleven of whom turned out to be Volga Tatars.[49]

Even though formally elevated to the status of a party and endowed with its own bureaucracy, Ittifak could hardly develop an effective political machine. It suffered from a double handicap: The close association with the Kadets made it impossible to pursue an independent course of political action at the national level, and its very raison d'être, unity, ruled out any receptiveness to the demands of the dissenters. The Kadet connection was undeniably clear when the Muslims sent their deputies to the first Russian Duma (parliament), which was convened in April 1906.

The brevity of the life of the First Duma (April–July 1906) made it impossible for the first generation of Muslim deputies to develop a collective identity and a coherent course of action as a Muslim bloc. Instead, all 25 deputies, of whom 12 were from the Volga-Ural region, chose to register their adherence to the Kadet party as individual choices rather than a corporate choice.[50] The activities of the Volga Tatar deputies in the First Duma were confined to the speeches delivered by Akhtiamov, Matinov, and Syrtlanov, who were neither bold nor original in reiterating some of the religious and cultural concerns voiced by jadid reformers.[51] (See the Appendix for the names of Volga Tatar and Bashkir deputies to the First through Fourth Dumas.)

When Nicholas II dissolved the First Duma on July 7, 1906, a group of mainly Trudoviki deputies assembled in Vyborg to register their protest and to sign a manifesto that called on all Russian citizens to refuse to pay taxes or to report for military service. Six Muslims signed the Vyborg manifesto, three of them—S. Alkin, S. Janturin, A. Akhtiamov—were from the Volga-Ural region. This action prevented them from running for election to the Second Duma and led to their harassment by the Russian authorities.[52]

The Second Duma met from February 20 through June 1, 1907. Its composition was much more radical than that of the first because the socialist parties had abandoned their boycott tactics and joined the elections. The Kadets were able to seat only 99 deputies; the Trudoviki, 98; Socialist Revolutionaries, 37; Social Democrats, 66; national minorities, 94; Octobrists, 12; moderate conservatives, 23; extremists, 10; independents, 52; and splinter groups, 7.[53] The Russian Muslims gained 35 seats in the Second Duma; of these, 15 belonged to Volga Tatars.[54]

The sessions of the Second Duma took place shortly after the Second

Muslim Congress, which had formalized the plan for an all-Russian Muslim union, although Ittifak had not yet been registered as a party. Under the impact of this reasserted commitment to Muslim union, Ali Mardan Topchibashi set forth to organize the Muslim deputies into a separate faction within the Duma. His attempt was partly successful: 29 deputies responded to his call; the remaining 6, who almost all belonged to the socialist revolutionary Tangchï group, formed a separate bloc called Musulman Hizmet Taifesi (Muslim Labor Party) and joined the Russian Trudoviki, whose agrarian policies they found most representative of their interests.[55] These 6 dissenters—H. Atlasi, A. Nejmetdinov, A. Massagutov, K. Khasanov, A. Badamshin, and Z. Zeinalov— soon became known as Dumachïlar because they published a newspaper entitled *Duma*.[56] Within the group, Zeinalov (an industrial worker) was the only member who was from the Caucasus. The remainder were all from the Volga-Ural region. Their adherence to the Trudoviki agrarian program does not necessarily indicate that they were all peasants. Hadi Atlasi was a teacher and a writer.[57] K. Khasanov, the spokesman of the group, was also a teacher. A. Badamshin and H. Massagutov were merchants. Only A. Nejmetdinov was a peasant, and he owned 37.8 acres of land and was also a mullah.[58]

As a group, the Dumachïlar were not representative of the poor landless peasantry, and, despite the fact that they advocated free distribution of land to the peasants, they never gained a large audience among the Muslims.[59] When the Second Duma was dissolved on June 2, 1907, the members of the Muslim Trudoviki group joined either the Socialist Revolutionaries or the Social Democrats.

Those Volga Tatars who remained loyal members of the Muslim faction of the Duma adhered closely to the political philosophy and program of the Kadets. The land issue was central to the deliberations of the Second Duma, deliberations that were dominated by the Russian Constitutional Democrats, whose agrarian program favored land sale to the peasants at market value rather than an established general price. Despite their adherence to the Kadet program, most members of the Muslim faction paid special attention to the problems of land tenure in the borderlands. S. Syrtlanov and M. Khasanov pointed out in their speeches that, in Bashkiria and in the steppes, the resettlement policies of the government were in direct conflict with the economic interests of the local population (which was mainly Muslim).[60]

When the Second Duma concluded its term on June 2, 1907, neither the Muslim faction nor the Dumachïlar, nor for that matter, the Russian parties whose philosophies they adhered to, could pride themselves on major accomplishments. Once more, the life of the Duma had been too short to make possible the emergence of coherent economic or political programs.

The new electoral law of June 3, 1907, reflected the Russian government's efforts to efface the liberal and national minority groups from the political scene and establish the supremacy of the conservatives. The number of Kadet deputies elected to the Third Duma under the terms of this new law dropped to 53; they were opposed by 288 right-wing conservatives. The Trudoviki and the Social Democrats could send only 14 and 19 deputies, respectively, and large areas on the eastern borderlands were deprived of the right to participate in elections.[61] The number of Muslim deputies dropped to 10; of these, 7 were Volga Tatars belonging to the Muslim faction.

The social background of the Volga group was the same as that of Ittifak: jadid intelligentsia, bourgeoisie, and landowners.[62] The social background of the entire Duma can be discerned from the observations of the British correspondent for the London *Times*, which need no additional comment: "The deputies struck me as being not only better-dressed, but generally more cultured than their predecessors. An entire absence of peasants straight from the plough, and a large contingent of priests were equally noticeable. For the first time the Left benches were empty and the Right benches were crowded."[63]

The strong representation of the Orthodox clergy in the Third Duma led to a revival of missionary designs toward the inorodtsy. The educational policies of the government came under the influence of Bishop Nicholas of Warszaw, who in one of his speeches to the session of the Duma, argued that the task of the government was "to russify all non-Russians and to convert to Orthodoxy all non-Orthodox elements."[64] In response, the Volga Tatar deputies once again concentrated their efforts on issues of education and religious rights.[65]

The Third Duma addressed the issue of elementary school reforms. The Muslims defended the right to provide their children with an elementary education in the national language. In this request, they were opposed by the Russian nationalists, represented by deputy Alekseev who argued that the Russian language should be given more attention in the Muslim elementary school curriculum.[66]

Perhaps the most vocal defender of the Muslim viewpoint in the Third Duma was the deputy from Kazan, S. Maksudov. He challenged the state budget, which allocated to Muslims only 54 thousand out of a total of 2.5 billion rubles and defended the religious rights of Muslims and their right to a national education, pointing out that Muslims did not reject Russian culture in principle; they just kept away from it because its messengers had been either the priest or the *uriadnik* (village policeman). As a representative of the liberal jadid intelligentsia who favored a rapprochement with the Russian people and Russian culture, however, Maksudov made a distinction between the Russian government and the Russian people. In one of his speeches, he noted: "We, and the Russian people, we understand each other; we have never confused the Russian people with the Russian government. Speaking against the government, we know perfectly well that it represents a handful of individuals who do not have anything in common with the Russian people and who most of the time misjudge their interests.[67]

The Muslims were a weak minority in the Third Duma. Their allies, the Kadets—whose support they relied on—were also weak. The only hope for the liberals seemed to be to unite in a coalition and, as Maksudov suggested, to advance a purely political platform void of all economic concerns.[68] Such a coalition never materialized, and Muslims grew increasingly dissatisfied with the results of the Duma. One of the deputies, M. Haidarov, blamed the poor performance of the Muslim faction on the paucity of human resources. He noted that the Muslim faction was under-represented and understaffed; it was not able to challenge some of the resolutions because it lacked the manpower to prepare the adequate background information. Hence, the Muslim deputies in the Third Duma were strangers working for other commissions.[69]

The Muslim faction of the Fourth Duma (November 15, 1912, to February 16, 1917) was comprised of only six deputies. Five of them were Volga-Ural Muslims.[70] Sadri Maksudov, who had been one of the most active Muslim deputies in the Third Duma, was not re-elected, but as a Kadet, he spoke on behalf of the Russian Muslims at the Central Committee meetings of the Kadet party. The negligible size of the Muslim faction and the irregular sessions (interrupted by long intermissions) of the Fourth Duma, were perhaps among the causes of its failure to achieve any concrete results toward meeting the grievances of the Russian Muslims.

Some of the jadid leaders, including previous Duma deputies, such as Topchibashi, however, believed that what the Muslim faction in the Fourth Duma needed was an infusion of new ideas from the communities. Consequently, in February 1914, some jadid leaders held a meeting in St. Petersburg, to draft a list of issues to serve as a guideline for the Duma deputies. The list reiterated the requests for improvement of education and religious autonomy; it also raised the issue of bank credits for Muslims.[71]

The energizing, revitalizing effect the ideas stemming from the meetings of jadid leaders had on the Muslim faction of the Fourth Duma contributed to increased involvement of the Muslim deputies in the deliberations of that body. The lobbying of the Muslim deputies was responsible for the fact that the Fourth Duma approved the proposal that provided state subsidies for teaching Muslim religion in Tatar schools, a proposal that had met strong opposition in the senate. Monseigneur Nicholas, the archbishop of Warzsaw, for example, argued that granting state subsidies for the teaching of Muslim religion would mean "placing Islam on the same level with the Christian religion."[72]

This rather minor gain in the area of education did not render the Muslim faction immune to criticism. Tatar newspapers carried articles that suggested solutions to their apparent lack of political power: these ranged from replacement of the existing deputies with more energetic ones, to proposals for new coalitions within the Duma.[73]

One such proposal came from Fuad Tuktarov, who in 1906, had opposed Ittifak's Kadet connection, but who in 1914, suggested: "It is necessary to hide (even if only for the moment) behind the more powerful. And the more powerful can be neither the Rightists, nor the Oktobrists, but only the Progressists."[74] What Tuktarov in fact implied was that the success of the Tatars in the Duma would depend on their alliance with a political party that was even more conservative than the Kadets, whom he had bitterly criticized in 1906.

The Muslim faction reacted to the wave of grass-roots criticism and worked hard at improving its image. Between 1910 and 1916, in an effort to reach the people and inform them about the political life in St. Petersburg, it published its own newspaper, *Millet*.[75] The publication did little to alleviate Muslim communities' dissatisfaction with the Duma, however, and the jadid intellectuals reached out for the last resource: the convocation of the Fourth All-Russian Muslim Congress.

As compared with its earlier counterparts, the fourth congress, which took place in St. Petersburg between June 15 and 25, 1914, was a modest gathering, both in size and scope. Some 40 delegates, 6 of whom were Duma deputies, attended and discussed primarily matters concerning education and religious reforms.[76] Despite the attempt of the fourth congress to boost the life of the Muslim faction, the existence of such a faction was eventless and self-effacing until 1917.

The fate of the Muslim faction in the Duma was perhaps the best indicator of the destiny of the political aspirations of the Volga Tatars as a whole. The jadid intellectuals, who in 1905 and 1906 had undertaken the task of bringing the Tatar umma into the stream of Russian politics, had been insufficiently prepared to accomplish this task. Their timidity in approaching politics was indicative of a conflict between an intellectual orientation toward the West and a strong, emotional attachment to Islam—if not as a faith, at least as a cultural heritage.

The Volga Tatars were also handicapped by problems of political leadership. Y. Akchura had a strong emotional commitment to the political future of the Russian Muslims, but having lived most of his life abroad, knew little about the details of Russian political life and societal development. His achievements in Russian politics registered a gap between ideal and performance, namely because much too often he gave literal interpretations to the promises of the Russian liberals.

The conservative backlash, which began in Russia in 1907 as a reaction to the liberal euphoria of the period 1905 to 1907, struck a major blow to the political leadership of the Tatars as many intellectuals (Y. Akchura included) emigrated to Turkey, Europe, or the Middle East.[77] Poor in human resources and handicapped by an almost exclusive commitment to education and religion—the only concerns shared by the entire umma—the Tatars did not succeed in developing an independent political life. Ittifak never became a party. The best recognition it achieved was as a political faction, much too small to justify the ambitions the jadids had outlined in 1905 and 1906 or to satisfy the needs of the Tatar umma.

THE VOLGA
TATARS
AND THE
SOVIET STATE

PART THREE

10 The Revolution: From Cultural Autonomy to the Tatar ASSR

People who have holidays—are rich people:
Their name is carried by the festive winds of holidays.
Their flags always waving.

Bayrame bar khalïk—bay khalïk:
Gasïrlarnïng bayram jillärenda
Jiri Kala
Bayraklarï bara chaykalïp.

(Kharras Ayupov, *Bayramnar* [Holidays].)

The February Revolution, which entered on the chariot of insurmountable problems faced by a war-exhausted Russia, created a general euphoria that became filled with meaning when the traditional tensions between the Russians and the ethnic minorities of the empire were pushed into oblivion, or at least relegated to the background for the time being.

That the Muslims were no exception, and the Tatars welcomed the fall of the monarchy with anticipation and renewed hopes, was reflected in an editorial published in *Shura*: "The peoples of Russia were helpless and defenseless slaves to this very day. Now they are free, they are in a position to decide their own affairs according to their own wishes... The main principles of the new government—freedom, equality, and justice—will now be implemented voluntarily, as dictated by the conscience of everybody and not because of police fear. And this is in accordance with the teachings of Islam as well."[1]

One of the by-products of this euphoria was the centripetal force of Muslim unity, which brought together liberals and socialists alike. Between February and May 1917, to paraphrase Herzen, the Russian Muslims reminded one of the ambivalent Janus whose two faces looked in opposite directions and who had but one heart. The heart of the Muslims was committed to their nationalist aims, even if, when articulating their programs, some remained indebted to Russian liberalism, while others still embraced Russian socialism. Euphoria was translated into action as the Muslims responded to the promises of the February Revolution with a flurry of organizational activity.

To coordinate their political actions immediately after the fall of the monarchy, the Muslims organized a Muslim Central Executive Committee (ISKOMUS) with regional chapters throughout eastern Russia. This committee was the result of cooperation between the progressive clergy, the liberal-minded bourgeoisie, and the moderate members of the parties of the Left. This diversity is perhaps best illustrated by the political affiliations of the most prominent members of the Kazan Muslim Committee, which was organized on March 7, 1917: A. Apanaev (a mullah), S. Maksudov and S. Alkin (liberals), and F. Tuktarov (a Socialist Revolutionary). The Kazan committee became the voice of the Tatar nationalist forces, a voice that was echoed by similar committees in other cities of the Middle Volga and the Urals as much as it was supported by dynamic press organs, such as *Koyash* (The sun) and *Yulduz* (The star) in Kazan, *Tormüsh* (Life) in Ufa, and *Vaqt* (Time) in Orenburg.[2]

The March 7 meeting of the Kazan Muslim Committee, presided over by the lawyer Tanachev, adopted a program that, in its eclecticism, reflected the political affiliations of its members while also epitomizing the Muslim drive for unity. In addition to demands of general nature—for an end to the war, for convocation of the Constituent Assembly, and for equality of rights between Muslims and Russians, to name a few—the program contained demands for the organization of Muslim military units and adhered to the programs of the Russian Social Democratic Labor Party (RSDLP) and the Socialist Revolutionaries on issues of labor and land.[3]

The emergence of the Kazan Socialist Committee on April 7, 1917, only a month after the organization of the Muslim committee, could suggest that the Tatars represented the exception to the rule of Muslim unity. There are valid reasons, however, not to exclude them from the front of Muslim unity, for they illustrated best the dynamics of unity in diversity. Dominated by people who belonged to all shades of the Left, the Kazan Socialist Committee did not affiliate itself organically with the Bolshevik party, but maintained ties with the Tatar nationalist organizations even as it adhered to the policies of the Bolsheviks on the issues of war, land distribution, and transfer of power to the Soviets.

The Kazan Socialist Committee, which was the heir to the Workers' Committee organized in early March by the Left Socialist Revolutionary Sh. Akhtamov, embraced an ideology that, despite its socialist label, was a mélange of Marxism and pan-Islamism. Its president was the charismatic Muslim revolutionary Mullanur Vakhitov; the position of vice president was entrusted to a woman, E. Mukhitdinova; and its secretary was I. Kuliev. In June 1917, M. Sultangaliev joined the presidium. As in the case of the Muslim committee, the Kazan Socialist Committee relied on its own press organs for reaching the Tatar masses, a task fulfilled by the newspapers *Avaz* (The echo) and *Qzil Bairaq* (The red banner).

Despite the Kazan Socialist Committee's lack of political homogeneity, the Bolshevik party supported it because, as an organization that brought together Bolsheviks, Mensheviks, and Socialist Revolutionaries, the committee's eclecticism was outweighed by the benefits derived from gaining access to a channel of communication with the Tatar masses.[4]

The decision of the Bolshevik party to support the Kazan Socialist Committee should not be viewed as an aberration. It illustrates once more the tactical flexibility of the Bolsheviks, who disregarded ideological incongruities and chose to gamble on the opportunity to use the Kazan Socialist Committee as a training camp for genuine Marxism. What they failed to see, however, was that, even for the most ardent self-acknowledged socialists and communists of the committee, commitment to Marxism was only secondary to allegiance to nationalist goals.

The manner in which the Muslims perceived class and ethnic and religious solidarity is illustrated by the statement of their Central Provisional Bureau when the call for an All-Russian Muslim Congress was launched in the spring of 1917:

> Our slogan is "Muslim citizens, organize!" We Muslims belong overwhelmingly to that middle segment of the society which is democratic [*sic*]. We have a pitiful number of the representatives of capital and those of the big landowners. Class differences among Muslims are still weak. This is our plus and our minus. Class differences lead to intense political activity—and this is a plus; but they also weaken the general unity of the nation—and this is a minus. Let us weaken the minus and strengthen the plus.[5]

Once launched, the call for the All-Russian Muslim Congress was the moving force behind the guberniia congresses of Muslims held in Ufa (April 14 through 17) and Kazan (April 23 through 29). In addition to these congresses (which addressed issues of general concern, such as national self-determination, cultural autonomy, and education), Kazan hosted, at the end of April, the First Congress of Muslim Women from the Volga region, Siberia, Turkestan, Caucasus, Crimea, and Lithuania, as well as the Congress of Muslims from the Armed Forces.[6]

On May 1, 1917, the First All-Russian Congress of Muslims brought to

Moscow some 900 delegates covering a broad political spectrum from the conservative Right to the revolutionary Left. Only the handful of Muslims who had formally adhered to the Bolshevik party chose to ignore this political event, which unfolded under the banner of unity and religious and ethnic solidarity in the best of jadid traditions.[7]

The detailed work on specific issues was entrusted to nine commissions that addressed the issues of state organization, local administration, elections to the Constituent Assembly, education, religion, armed forces, land, labor, and women. The delegates supported the development of a school system along jadid lines and favored the creation of exclusively Muslim national military units and the establishment of an Islamic Religioius Board (Mahkämä-i-Shargiia) at Ufa, a board that would be independent of the Russian authorities.

On May 11, during its session devoted to the issue of religious administration, the congress fulfilled another dream of the Muslims: Putting an end to the tsarist practice of nominating the members of the religious administration of the Muslims, it elected the members of the newly established religious board. The congress elected the new mufti (G. Barudi) and the six kazis (judges)—one of whom, Muhlise Bobi, was a woman.[8]

The spirit of unity at the congress went unchallenged, even by the resolutions on the issues of land and labor and despite the radicalism of the platforms borrowed from the Social Democrats and Socialist Revolutionaries. Demands for an eight-hour working day and for abolition of private landed property were, to some extent, stripped of their radicalism when they were presented within the context of a program that made demands for construction of mosques and of schools for Muslim workers at their places of employment and that also argued in favor of giving Muslim workers the option of celebrating their religious holidays if they wished.[9]

It was on the issues of state organization and the role of women in the new society that social conservatism and inertia, as well as the imperatives of diversity in national experiences, strained the unity of the Muslims. And in both cases, the Tatars rode against the general tide.

Of the 30 delegates (22 men and 8 women) who addressed the women's issue, the majority of those who supported equality of the sexes in politics and spoke against polygamy and the veil were Volga Tatars. The arguments of G. Barudi and M. Bigi and of women delegates, such as E. Mukhitdinova, I. Tuktarova, and F. Kulakhmetova, although clearly articulating the importance of equality of the sexes, were incapable of drawing unanimous support, and the resolutions on this issue were contested by 226 delegates, who signed a letter of protest.[10]

As for the issue of state-building, the majority of the Volga Tatars supported an extraterritorial cultural autonomy within the confines of a centralized, but democratic, Russian republic. However, they ran into staunch opposition from the federalists (Azeris, Crimeans, and Central Asians) who were in favor of territorial autonomy within a federal republic. The federalists won by 446 votes to 271, and among them was a handful of Volga Tatars who did not share the centralist view of their conationals. A. Suleimani, F. Tuktarov, and F. Karimi saw the danger of denationalization and russification as a natural outcome of extraterritorial cultural autonomy. This concern was articulated very clearly by Karimi: "Should there be no federation, then people from regions with a high density of population will be resettled to areas that are sparsely populated . . . Turkestan will be flooded with Russians. Turkestan will look like Tambov guberniia and this, no doubt, is not in Turkestan's favor."[11]

The cultural autonomy platform was implicitly pan-Turkic because, without the forbidding walls of statehood among them, the various Turkic peoples of Russia could borrow from each other more freely and eventually bring about a form of political symbiosis. The defeat of the cultural autonomy platform dealt the most serious blow to Muslim unity.

In an effort to salvage this unity, the congress established the Milli Shura (Central Muslim council), which was conceived as an organization aimed at building bridges and coordinating the political actions of all Muslims. There were some Muslim leaders, such as the Volga Tatar A. Ishaki, who went so far as to view Milli Shura as a Muslim counterpart to the Provisional Government. He argued that, as a central agency, Milli Shura's decisions should be binding on all Muslims until the convocation of the Constituent Assembly. His opinion was not generally shared, and one of the most articulated challenges came from a fellow Volga Tatar, G. Ibragimov, who warned: "No, this is not an organ with decision-making powers. This is merely an organ that can implement decisions."[12] Thus, the Milli Shura and ISKOMUS set forth to coordinate the political actions of the Muslims.[13]

The delegates at the congress accepted the usefulness of periodically convening all-Russian congresses of Muslims and even suggested locations for the next three: Kazan, Tashkent, and Baku. Consequently, the Second All-Russian Congress of Muslims was held in Kazan between July 21 and August 2, 1917.

The Second All-Russian Congress was an almost exclusively Volga Tatar political event because the Central Asians and the Azeris, who did not share the Volga Tatars' views on extraterritorial autonomy, chose not to join. Furthermore, those few delegates from Crimea, Bashkiria, and North Caucasus who attended the second congress had, in fact, been assimilated politically by the Volga Tatars. Although the limited attendance was tangible proof of the rift in general Muslim unity, the second congress ironically emerged as an example of Tatar unity—as the proof of the leveling effect of Tatar nationalism that had rendered meaningless, at least for the time being, the ideological differences between various shades of socialists, on one hand, and between socialists and liberals, on the other.

The Second All-Russian Congress was a much more mature, structured political event for at least two reasons: It was void of the national festival euphoria of the first congress, and it unfolded in a much more sober, businesslike, organized fashion, benefiting greatly from the careful preliminary work the Volga Tatars had done in preparation for it.[14]

The delegates addressed the same issues that had been discussed in Moscow, focusing especially on the substance and implications of extraterritorial autonomy. The new issue that drew unanimous attention was the importance of preparing Muslims adequately for elections for the Constituent Assembly. The Volga Tatars won the day on the issue of autonomy when the extraterritorial cultural autonomy of the Muslims of inner Russia and Siberia was proclaimed at the July 22, 1917, joint session of the Second All-Russian Congress of the Muslims and at the congresses on Muslim religious and military issues that were being held simultaneously in Kazan.[15]

The Muslim Military Congress was convened at the initiative of the Harbi Shura (provisional Muslim military council), which had emerged in April 1917 under the leadership of I. Alkin. The congress confirmed the authority of Harbi Shura and decided to proceed with the organization of Muslim military units because "the standing army had to be reorganized on the national principle."[16] On July 22, however, the military congress relegated specifically military issues to the background and shared in the purpose and meaning of the joint session, which proclaimed the extraterritorial cultural autonomy of the Muslims of inner Russia and Siberia. Any additional symbolism notwithstanding, the green and red banners that were raised when autonomy was solemnly proclaimed were first of all symbols of Tatar unity born of the belief and hope that Islam, nationalism, and socialism were the ingredients of a viable political symbiosis. Thus July 22 became the official national holiday of the Muslims of inner Russia and Siberia.

The joyful occasion, however, did not affect the political realism and pragmatism of the delegates. They were aware that, to convene a Muslim deliberative body, a Millet Mejlisi (national assembly) of their own, there was much preparatory work to be done. With this purpose in mind, they organized a Milli Idare (national board), which, from its headquarters in Ufa, was to coordinate implementation of extraterritorial cultural autonomy while also doing the preparatory work for convening the Millet Mejlisi.[17]

The only bystanders to the flurry of organizational activity that brought together the socialists and liberals during the spring and summer of 1917 were the few Tatars who had joined the Kazan Bolshevik party organization. The Bolshevik leadership, who fully appreciated the political implications of Tatar unity and nationalism, set forth to weaken it, and Tatar Bolsheviks, such as K. Iakubov, A. Mukhitdinova, Kh. Gainullin, Ia. Chanyshev, and V. Shafigullin, directed their efforts toward encouraging defections from among socialists and liberals alike.[18]

During the spring and summer of 1917, this minority seemed to be engaged in an exercise in futility, but its fortunes changed when the October Revolution pushed the Bolsheviks into the limelight of history. The events between February and October 1917 revealed the strength of the nationalist forces among Muslims, and in the true tradition of Bolshevik tactical flexibility, the Soviet of People's Commissars adopted the proposal for the Appeal to the Muslim Workers of Russia and the East, on November 20, 1917. The fact that the appeal was personally signed by Lenin and Stalin illustrates the importance the new government placed on reaching the Muslim masses. The message of the appeal was direct, linking the promise for a bright future for the Muslims with the future of the revolution: "Build your national life freely and without hindrance. You have the right to it. Know that your rights and the rights of all the peoples of Russia are being protected by the full force of the Revolution and its organs, the Soviets of Workers, Soldiers, and Peasant Deputies."[19]

The appeal was followed by a series of goodwill gestures. The Suyumbike Tower of Kazan was transferred to the trusteeship of the Kazan Socialist Committee, and the holy relic of Islam—the Qur'an of Othman—was taken from the Petrograd National Library and placed in the care of the Muslims of Petrograd. For a short period of time, the Bolsheviks even tolerated the crescent moon that the Tatars placed on the Suyumbike Tower after taking down the double-headed eagle.

These acts, however, were only a prelude to substantive political moves aimed at attracting the Muslims to the cause of the Revolution. That these were shrewd tactical maneuvers on the part of the Bolshevik leadership is suggested by the fact that, referring to the issue of the Suyumbike Tower, Stalin commented: "If the transfer of the tower and the mosque will bring even the smallest contribution to the cause of the Revolution, Lenin will regard it as a matter of utmost importance."[20]

At least two imperatives called for prompt action on the part of the Bolshevik government:

> In all Muslim areas, the Muslims had been spectators in the October events. The Revolution had been a "Russian affair," as epitomized by the composition of the various revolutionary organizations.[21]

> Muslim nationalist organizations, such as Mulli Shura, Milli Idare, Harbi Shura, and Millet Mejlisi, continued to function in the Middle Volga until the spring of 1918. They were participants in a de facto *dvoevlastie* (dual power) in which parallel Soviet and Muslim administrative bodies competed for the control of the Muslim populations.

The National Assembly of the Muslims of Inner Russia and Siberia convened in Ufa between November 20, 1917, and January 11, 1918. In the interval since the Second All-Russian Congress of Muslims held in Kazan in July and August of 1917, the Volga Tatars' view on the issue of autonomy had changed substantially. The more than one hundred delegates attending the meeting of the National Assembly in November were almost equally divided between the supporters of extraterritorial cultural autonomy (Turkchïlar) and those who favored territorial national autonomy (Tufrakchïlar). Under the new political conditions that had emerged after the Bolshevik revolutions of 1917, the assembly opted for territorial autonomy. On November 19, 1917, it proclaimed an autonomous Idel-Ural state. The founding principles of the state required that the Tatars and the Bashkirs represent the majority of the population within the boundaries of a territory that had to be contiguous while also possessing economic and cultural unity.[22]

The assembly met in closed session to hear a presentation by S. Mamliev, a member of the Petrograd Executive Committee of Milli Shura, who reported to the deputies that Stalin had approached the Milli Shura with a project for the organization of a Central Commissariat for Muslim affairs (Muskom) and invited Tsalikov to become its first commissar on the condition that Milli Shura merge with Muskom.[23] The deputies turned down the invitation, but its significance should not be ignored, for it reflected the urgency with which the Bolsheviks approached a tactical alliance with the Tatar nationalists, even if it was a precarious and temporary one.

The decision of the assembly did not lessen the perseverance of the Bolshevik leadership, whose search for allies continued until Mullanur Vakhitov, chairman of the Kazan Socialist Committee, accepted the chairmanship of Muskom, which was created by the January 17, 1918, decree of the Council of People's Commissars as an agency of the People's Commissariat of Nationalities (Narkomnats).[24] Vakhitov was joined by G. Ibragimov and Sh. Manatov, who became Muskom's first vice-chairmen.[25] Their decision to take positions of leadership in a body not sanctioned by the National Assembly created the most serious rift in Tatar unity.

In March 1918, Muslim commissariats were organized in the provinces. They had their own press organs—Esh (Labor) in Kazan and Mamadïsh Tavïshï (The voice of Mamadysh) in Mamadysh—both of which followed the tradition of Chulpan (published by the Petrograd-Moscow Muskom) and embarked on the urgent task of contributing to the political education of the Tatar masses.

The creation of the Central Muslim Commissariat was the first tangible proof that the government was determined not to tolerate any longer the peculiar dual power and parallel Muslim infrastructure that had emerged since the spring of 1917. Unable to dismantle the Muslim agencies, the government could only hope (at least for the time being) to weaken them by setting up rival organizations, such as the Central Muskom. The events of early 1918, however, forced the government's hand and provided a pretext for dissolution of all Muslim nationalist bodies.

The Second Muslim Military Congress began its proceedings in Kazan on January 21, 1918. Its main task was to address the issue of the autonomous Idel-Ural state. The majority of the 150 delegates present at the congress were Tatars and Bashkirs who supported the decision of the National Assembly to create the Idel-Ural state, but they were confronted with opposition from the Tatar Bolsheviks and their sympathizers. When, on February 17, navy captain Tokumbetov, one of the members of the Harbi Shura, warned the Bolsheviks that "you cannot teach us how to implement self-determination, this is our business," the Bolsheviks responded by staging a walkout.[26]

The open rift in Muslim unity was fully exploited by the Kazan Soviet. On February 26, it sponsored the organization of a Revolutionary High Command led by Ia. Sheikman but staffed by the Tatars K. Iakubov and S. Galiev, the main task of which was to prepare a counteroffensive against the Harbi Shura and the Muslim Military Congress. To ensure success and paralyze their opponents, the Soviets decreed martial law in Kazan on that same day. Two days later, they arrested the entire leadership of Harbi Shura, including Tokumbetov, Muzaffarov, and the Alkin brothers, all of whom the Soviets agreed to free on the condition that they recognize Soviet power in the Kazan guberniia, renounce their plans for an Idel-Ural state, dismantle all national organizations, and place the Muslim national units under the control of the guberniia Muskom. They refused and escaped to the Tatar suburb of the city of Kazan located across the Bulak River. There, they reiterated their commitment to the Idel-Ural state and proclaimed a national government, which the Soviets pejoratively labeled the Trans-Bulak Republic.

The flight of the nationalists from Kazan marked the beginning of the end of their aspirations for a large Turkic state in the Middle Volga. Their stronghold across the Bulak was stormed on March 28, and within a few days, Kazan was completely under the control of the Soviets and the Red Army. Hopes for resurrecting the dream of an Idel-Ural state dimmed after a March 26, 1918, decree of Narkomnats abolished Harbi Shura. By mid-April, Milli Shura and Millet Mejlisi had fallen victims to the same harsh measures.[27]

Freed of the hindering presence of the rival Muslim national organizations, the Bolshevik government turned to Muskom as the Muslims' only representative body and enlisted its aid in rallying the support of the Muslim masses for the new regime.

The spring of 1918, which saw the beginning of the Civil War, was a critical time for the Bolshevik regime, and developing military preparedness and building up the army took precedence over other concerns. It is within this context that the emergence of the Central Muslim Military Collegium acquires significance and additional meaning as a much needed tactical move and not a response to the needs of the Muslims.

The Central Muskom had a military section led by In. I. Ibragimov, a member of the Executive Committee of Muslim soldiers on the Northern front. The main task of the section was to assist local Muskoms "in organizing battalions of the Worker-Peasant Red Army."[28] On April 28, 1918, the military section was reorganized as a military collegium under the name of Central Muslim Military Collegium (CMMC) and staffed by four Tatars and two Russians: M. M. Vakhitov, In. I. Ibragimov, M. G. Aliev, I. Abdrashitov, A. K. Malikov, and M. G. Konov.

The fortunes of the Civil War in the Middle Volga affected the organization of the collegium. The White occupation of Kazan between August 7 and September 10, 1918, delayed organization of the CMMC and caused its leadership a serious loss when M. Vakhitov was shot by the White occupying forces on August 19. As soon as the Red Army recaptured the city on September 10, 1919, all Soviet and Soviet-sponsored Muslim organizations were resurrected.

The CMMC resumed its activity on September 12. Under its new president, Mirsaid Sultangaliev, a draft for the statute of the CMMC was developed promptly and was adopted at the November 2, 1918, meeting. As stated in the statute, the main goal of the collegium was "to assist the People's Commissariat of War [Narkomvoen] in organizing loyal Muslim units of the Red Army throughout the republic, to assume leadership in the political education of the Muslim soldiers of the Red Army, and to disseminate the ideas of Communism among them."[29]

The goals of the CMMC determined its structure. The Bolshevik leadership placed special importance on its political section, whose primary domain was agitation and propaganda. The main vehicle for propaganda work was the newspaper *Qzl Armiia*, published in Tatar, an added testimony to the prominent role of the Volga Tatars among Russian Muslims.

Order no. 276 issued on November 20, 1918, by the Revolutionary War Council (Revvoensovet) confirmed creation of the CMMC as an agency of Narkomvoen. The proposal for the statute, however, was yet to be approved. In fact, the struggle for the collegium itself was closely intertwined with the efforts of its leadership to secure Narkomvoen and Narkomnats' approval for the statute proposal.

Narkomnats had discussed the proposal first at their January 16, 1918, meeting. At a second meeting, held on January 27, they decided to abolish the CMMC on the grounds that it would duplicate the work of the existing Soviet and Muslim organizations.

Sultangaliev, who was president of the CMMC and a member of the Collegium of Narkomnats, had been absent from those crucial meetings. On learning of the decision to abolish, he approached Stalin personally to secure his support for the collegium.

The struggle for the collegium continued, and an amended proposal for the statute was finally approved on July 12, 1919. This decision could be interpreted as a tactical retreat within the context of the Civil War crisis that confronted the Soviet regime during the spring and summer of 1919, a crisis that made it imperative for the party and the government to win over the loyalty of the Muslims. Such a hypothesis is supported by the fact that as soon as the danger of the Civil War had ended, the Revolutionary Military Council issued its order no. 2005 of October 1, 1920, and dismantled the CMMC.[30]

The precarious existence of the collegium was governed from its inception by a peculiar quid pro quo for which the Muslim perception of the nature and purpose of national units, and of the collegium as a whole, was responsible. The Muslims genuinely believed in a symbiosis among Communism, Islam, and nationalism and viewed their national units and the collegium as the catalysts of this symbiosis. Initially swept up by revolutionary zeal, they were oblivious to the fact that Moscow regarded the collegium and the national units as only temporary and convenient instruments for overcoming the language barrier and mobilizing the Muslim soldier. Neither the party nor the government leadership ever intended to allow the collegium to escape their control, and neither considered the needs and specific problems of the Muslims to be a priority.

Despite the brevity of its existence, the most important contribution of the CMMC was in the area of literacy—both basic and political literacy. It is certainly here that hidden factors revealed themselves with full force: Because no other texts were available, Tatar primers were used for all Muslim soldiers, and it was the Tatar theater that was mobilized to carry the political message of the new regime to the Muslim soldier. This Tatar dimension of the education of the Muslim soldier testified once more to the cultural resourcefulness of the Volga Tatars, and revealed their potential for assuming the leadership of a Turkic commonwealth in Russia.

Education and propaganda emerged as the most important goals of the CMMC, because as early as the summer of 1918 it was deprived of decision-making powers in the military domain.

In August 1918, in an effort to control the pan-Turkic nationalism of the soldiers, all Muslim units (50,000 soldiers commanded by native officers) were placed under the general command of the Russian Army. The Volga Tatars and the Bashkirs provided the soldiers for most of these units. For instance, the First Tatar-Bashkir Infantry Battalion of the Worker-Peasant Red Army, which had been formed on April 1, 1918, proved its loyalty to the new regime when it participated in the battle to recapture Kazan from the Czechs and the Whites in September of 1918.

In the fall of 1918, the First Tatar-Bashkir Battalion and the First Muslim

Communist Battalion were merged under the command of Tatar Kh. Z. Gabidullin, who also doubled as the political commissar of what became the First Soviet Muslim Reserve Infantry Regiment of Kazan. Similar battalions and regiments were organized at Astrakhan, Saratov, Samara, Belebeev, Menzelinsk, Bugul'me, Elabuga, Chistopol, and other places in the Tatar-Bashkir country, which provided not only the core but also the bulk of the Muslim units of the Red Army. By October 1919, two Tatar rifle brigades had been organized as part of the ongoing effort to increase the number of Muslim units in the Red Army.

Once more, the Tatars were singled out for special attention, and an appeal published in *Qzil Armiia* (The red army) on April 6, 1919, read: "Freedom-loving Tatar youth, rally under the red banner!"[31]

Apparently Muslims fought bravely and distinguished themselves as good soldiers.[32] On November 9, 1918, the Highest Military Inspection of the Red Army concluded: "Muslim regiments are an example of discipline and fortitude."[33]

The fortitude and loyalty of the Muslim units was so crucial in the summer of 1919 that the government did not shy away from enlisting the symbolism of the crescent moon to its aid. In July 1919, the Red Army High Command approved a special badge that only soldiers of the Muslim units were to wear on the sleeves of their uniforms: a crescent moon and a star embroidered in gold colored thread on the green background of the rhomb in which they were enclosed.

These measures, however, were merely temporary concessions, and in the fall of 1920, they came to an end. By that time, having emerged as the victor in the Civil War confrontation, the Bolshevik government felt more secure and became less willing to accommodate the needs of the various segments of the population that had rallied to its support. By 1920, the return of the Qur'an of Othman and the Suyumbike Tower, and the crescent moon embroidered on the sleeve of the Muslim soldier were gestures that belonged to a past saturated with symbolic behavior. The realities of 1920 were void of similar symbolism, and these realities had a sobering effect on the Volga Tatars, who awakened to the truth of shattered national aspirations as revealed by the fate of the Tatar-Bashkir republic.

On March 23, 1918, just as the menacing clouds of Civil War were gathering over the young Soviet state, *Pravda* carried in its pages the Narkomnats decree proclaiming the "territory of Southern Ural and Middle Volga the Tatar-Bashkir Soviet Republic of the Russian Soviet Federation." The signatures of I. V. Stalin, M. Vakhitov, Sh. Manatov, and G. Ibragimov gave weight to the decree.[34]

Although not sanctioned by the Bolshevik party organization, the decree was welcomed by the majority of the participants in the Moscow Conference of the representatives of the Soviets and Muskoms of Kazan, Ufa, Orenburg, Perm, and Ekaterinburg, which was held on May 10 through 16, 1918, and by the representatives of the Chuvash and Mordvinian peoples. Only the representatives of the Kazan, Ufa, and Ural Soviets, echoing the opposition of the Bolshevik party, opposed the idea of a Tatar-Bashkir republic on the grounds that it would represent a concession to nationalism; all other delegates supported it. Moreover, there was even a request from the representatives of the Chuvash and Mordvinian peoples that their territories be included in the projected republic.[35]

These initial discussions, and the plans for a Turkic republic in the Middle Volga, were rendered meaningless by the outbreak of the Civil War in May 1918, when the Tatar-Bashkir country found itself in the heart of the confrontation between the Soviet regime and the White counterrevolution. Plans for a Tatar-Bashkir republic were shelved for at least a year, but discussions were resumed in 1919 at the initiative of M. Sultangaliev, chairman of the Central Muskom and a member of the Collegium of Narkomnats. He submitted the project for a Tatar-Bashkir republic to the Second All-Russian Congress of the Communist organizations of the Peoples of the East, which met in Moscow between November 22 and December 3, 1919. There the delegates renewed their support for the formation of a Tatar-Bashkir republic, but at the December 13 meeting of the Politbureau of the Central Committee of the Russian Communist (Bolshevik) Party, which was presided over by Lenin, it was decided to halt all efforts to create a Tatar-Bashkir republic.

This decision did not remain unchallenged. The Central Bureau of the Communist organizations of the Peoples of the East met on December 16, 1919, and adopted a resolution to submit the issue of creation of a Tatar-Bashkir republic to the plenary meeting of the Central Committee for its review. In the same spirit, one of the prominent Tatar Communists, M. Burundukov, made his position clear at the joint meeting of the Kazan guberniia party organization and Muskom. He emphatically stated his refusal to bow to the December 13, 1918, decision of the Politbureau.[36]

Burundukov, Sultangaliev, and all those who shared hopes for a Middle Volga state of the Tatars and the Bashkirs, however, were engaged in a futile effort. The die was cast against a large Turkic state on the Middle Volga when the Bashkir Autonomous Soviet Socialist Republic (BASSR) was established on March 23, 1919. The decree announcing formation of the Bashkir republic was the key to erecting administrative, and even cultural, barriers between the Tatars and the Bashkirs, whose cultures and historical paths had always been closely intertwined. The Idel-Ural or the Tatar-Bashkir state had been divided up before it ever came into existence because its existence would have become a danger too real to be overlooked by the Soviet government, which was already weary of the nationalism of its Muslim minorities. A Tatar-Bashkir republic with the capital at Kazan would have further enhanced the role of that city as the political and cultural center of the Muslims of Russia. To prevent Turkic unity and the emergence of a dynamic republic in the Middle Volga, the Soviet government chose to sponsor the formation of smaller republics; by doing so, it also fostered isolation and even nourished old jealousies and rivalries, thus facilitating its control over the peoples of the area.

The idea of creation of a Tatar autonomous republic followed soon after the birth of the Bashkir ASSR. The first step toward making such a republic a reality was taken at the January 26, 1920, meeting of the Politbureau, when it was decided to proceed with the organization of a Tatar republic as an autonomous entity of the Russian republic. The proposed resolution regarding the territory and borders of the Tatar Autonomous Soviet Socialist Republic (TASSR) was submitted to Lenin on March 22, 1920, when in a last effort to reverse the clock of history, Sultangaliev tried to resurrect the issue of the Tatar-Bashkir republic, only to encounter Lenin's unbending opposition to the project.

Throughout the spring of 1920, party organizations at all levels discussed the tasks deriving from the decision to organize an autonomous Tatar republic. Those discussions culminated with the joint meeting of the Central Executive Committees of the Party and of the Soviet of People's Commissars, which on May 27, 1920, issued the decree declaring the formation of the Tatar ASSR.[37] (See maps 4 and 5.)

The territory designated for the republic covered an area of 68,000 square kilometers and was much smaller than the 220,000 square kilometers that would have made up the Idel-Ural state. Only 1,459,000 of the 4,200,000 Tatars living in the Middle Volga area were included in the new republic. Despite the fact that, in 1920, the Tatars represented 51 percent of the population of the republic, as compared with the 39.2 percent that was Russian, the Tatars could hardly rejoice. The borders of the republic, as they stood in 1920, excluded such areas as the Belebeev, Birsk, and Ufa uezds, where Tatars represented the majority of the population.[38] Moreover, the arbitrary drawing of the borders of the Tatar and Bashkir ASSRs not only left 75 percent of the Tatar population outside the boundaries of the Tatar republic but also was at the root of a paradox whereby the Tatars represented the ethnic majority in the Bashkir ASSR. Consequently, the creation of the Tatar ASSR, instead of alleviating some of the national tensions, led to growing dissatisfaction on the part of nationalists and Communists alike, who became disillusioned with the *divide et impera* policies of the new regime.

These disappointments seriously tested the loyalties of the jadid intellectuals, who had only recently joined the new regime and adopted its ideology. The outcome of their soul-searching was an even stronger commitment to the national path, the development of the national culture nourished by the belief that Communism and nationalism were compatible.

MAP 4.   USSR: POLITICAL AND ADMINISTRATIVE DIVISIONS

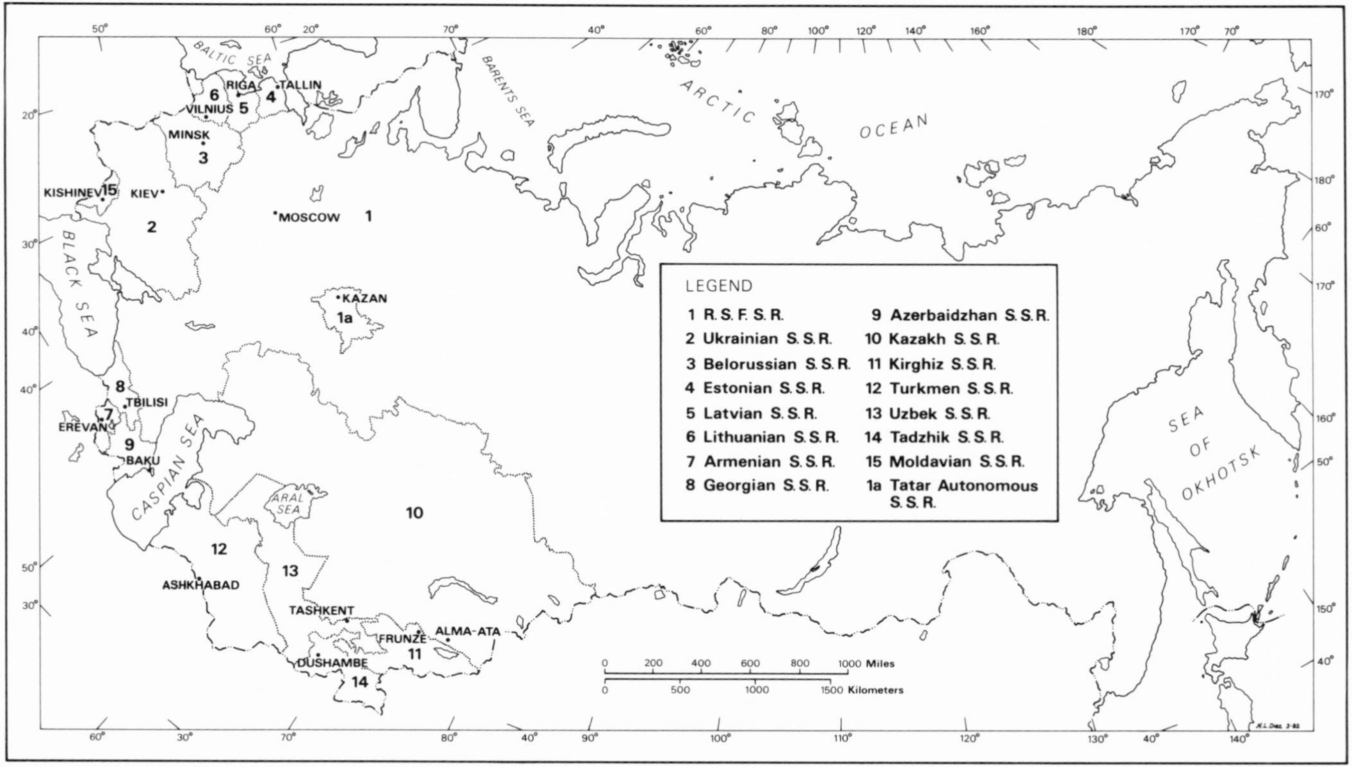

LEGEND

1 R.S.F.S.R.	9 Azerbaidzhan S.S.R.
2 Ukrainian S.S.R.	10 Kazakh S.S.R.
3 Belorussian S.S.R.	11 Kirghiz S.S.R.
4 Estonian S.S.R.	12 Turkmen S.S.R.
5 Latvian S.S.R.	13 Uzbek S.S.R.
6 Lithuanian S.S.R.	14 Tadzhik S.S.R.
7 Armenian S.S.R.	15 Moldavian S.S.R.
8 Georgian S.S.R.	1a Tatar Autonomous S.S.R.

ARCTIC OCEAN

SEA OF OKHOTSK

BARENTS SEA

BALTIC SEA

BLACK SEA

CASPIAN SEA

ARAL SEA

MOSCOW
KAZAN
1a
1
TALLIN
RIGA
VILNIUS
MINSK
KIEV
KISHINEV
15
5
4
6
3
2
TBILISI
EREVAN
7
8
BAKU
9
ASHKHABAD
12
13
TASHKENT
FRUNZE
ALMA-ATA
11
DUSHAMBE
14
10

0   200   400   600   800   1000 Miles
0   500   1000   1500 Kilometers

MAP 5. THE TATAR AUTONOMOUS REPUBLIC: MAIN URBAN CENTERS

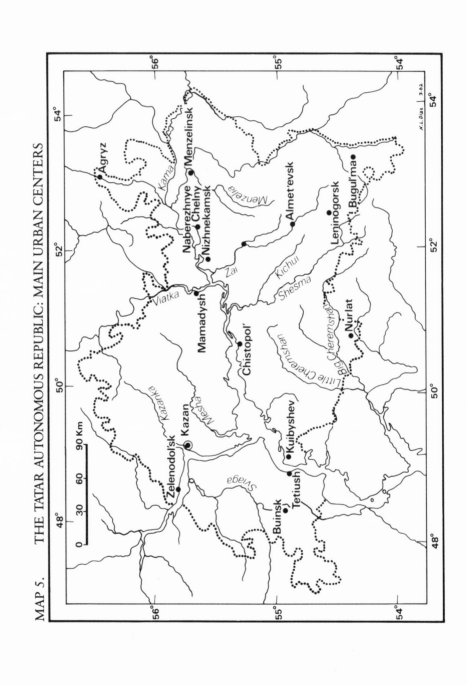

The decade that opened with the formation of the Tatar ASSR was dominated by the political waves made by those who attempted to join Communism and nationalism. In the early 1920s, national communism blossomed in Tatarstan because its seeds had been planted in the fertile soil of jadid reformism, which had thrived on the double catalysts of secularism and nationalism.

11 National Communism and the Tatar ASSR Before World War II

The winged horse charges and the earth shakes
He is a free soul—Dreams and Hopes!

Kanatlï at chaba jir buylatïp—
Azat jan ul-Khiyal häm Ömet!

(Zöl'fät, *Sak bul!*) [Be careful!].)

The Volga Tatars were among the first Muslims to be subjected to communist rule. As such, their conflicts and cooperation with the Soviet authorities established precedents for other Muslim groups and determined the evolution of future attitudes on all sides. The strength of nationalism and its ability to overwhelm and efface the political differences among the Volga Tatars surfaced many times after February 1917 and was to leave an indelible mark on their political life in the decades to come.

The Soviet declarations of the establishment of the Bashkir Autonomous Republic on March 23, 1919, and of the Tatar Autonomous Republic on May 27, 1920, washed away the political and administrative foundations of what could have become the Idel-Ural state of the Tatars and the Bashkirs.[1] Yet this political reality, despite the brutality of its consequences, or because of them, was partly responsible for the endurance of the dream of a Tatar state. Paradoxically, the dream was nursed by Tatar Communists whose jadid nationalism had been responsible for their own emergence as national Communists who addressed themselves to the complex issues of the relationships between communism and Islam, communism and colonial nations, and communism and peasant societies.

The most articulate spokesman and original thinker of Tatar national communism was Mirsaid Sultangaliev. A jadid teacher by training, and a sincere Communist by way of a rather late conversion to Marxism in November 1917, Sultangaliev had become the most influential Muslim Communist in the hierarchy of the Bolshevik party by 1920. No matter how sincere his conversion, however, it had not occurred at the expense of his belief in the ideals and national aspirations of his people, and on this issue Sultangaliev stated his position clearly: "It is not to sell my nation, to 'drink its blood' that I am marching with the Bolsheviks. No!...No!"[2]

As a leading figure in the Narkomnats, the president of the Muslim Military Collegium, chairman of the Central Muskom, editor of *Zhizn' Natsional'nostei*, and a professor at the University of the Peoples of the East, Sultangaliev reached a wide audience. It was through these various channels that he articulated his own original interpretations of the relationship between communism and Islam, of the dynamics of the revolutionary process, and most importantly, of the relationship between social and national revolution in the economically backward countries of the East, which as a rule, had experienced colonial oppression. Sultangaliev argued that, in an overwhelmingly peasant and semicolonial Muslim society, the goal of national revolution represented a higher priority than the goal of social revolution. This position was, indeed, a departure from Marxist orthodoxy, but the statement is hardly surprising. Sultangaliev was a jadid who was rationalizing the experience of the Islamic umma of Russia when he argued: "The Muslim peoples are proletarian peoples. There is a great difference between the economic situation of the English and French proletariat and the proletariat of Morocco and Afghanistan. It should be stressed that national movements in Muslim countries have the characteristics of a socialist revolution. The national aspirations of the Muslims of Russia have the same characteristics."[3]

A companion of Sultangaliev, Veli Iskhakov, justified the urgency of the national revolution by arguing that, objectively, "Tatars are more revolutionary than Russians because they have been more heavily oppressed by Tsarism than the Russians."[4]

Galimjan Ibragimov—a member of the Russian Communist Party (Bolshevik) [RCP(b)] since 1918, a leading writer and journalist, and the chairman of the academic center of the People's Commissariat (Narkom) between 1919 and 1929—was not a follower of Sultangaliev.[5] They shared, however, the same jadid background, which nurtured their nationalism and shaped their thinking and perception of culture and politics. As a result, the radical nationalist Ibragimov, who at times even criticized Sultangaliev, echoed Sultangaliev's concerns for national unity. Ibragimov's speech at the Ninth Tatar Regional

Party Conference implicitly justified the prevalence of national solidarity over class solidarity among the Tatars: "Our republic differs from the Tambov [and] Moscow guberniias not only in its population and way of life but also by virtue of the fact that here, the local population experience the Tsarist [i.e., Russian] yoke."[6]

Russian conquest and rule had been equally devastating for the Tatar rich and poor. Centuries of discriminatory policies had had a leveling effect, blurring class differences and providing the umma with at least one issue on which it stood firmly united: the defense of Islam. Hence, for Sultangaliev and his fellow national Communists, all Muslims—and for that matter all Tatars—were a proletarian nation by virtue of the colonial oppression they had experienced. As such, they constituted an exception to the orthodox Marxist concept of class struggle, even if their societies featured some identifiable class distinctions.

In 1918, Sultangaliev argued that, because Tatars and all other Eastern peoples had neither a proletariat nor antagonistic classes, they should embark on the road of moderate socialism.[7] Sultangaliev envisaged intellectuals of bourgeois background and the progressive jadid clergy marching on this road together with the peasants and the not-too-numerous workers in a common effort to accomplish the crucial task of national liberation and progress. The idea of a united national front as the key to the success of the struggle for national liberation, which emerged in the program of the Tatar national Communists, was in fact the secular replica of the religious concept of the umma. The only concession the national Communists made to the Marxist concept of class struggle was their willingness to exclude the feudal overlords and the upper bourgeoisie from the community of the downtrodden believers.

The commitment of the Tatar national Communists to the unity of the umma, and their defense of the uniqueness of class relations in their society, can only be compared with the fascination Kireevskii and his fellow Slavophiles had with the concept of *sobornost'*, the wholeness of the Russian nation. It was this belief in Tatar uniqueness that prompted Sultangaliev to call for the replacement of the hegemony of the Russian people over other nations with the dictatorship of these same nations over the Russians.[8] Projected to the world scene, this call translated into a mandate for the domination of colonial oppressors by their former colonies.

How did Tatar national Communists plan to implement this part of their program? First of all, by uniting the Muslim masses into an autonomous communist movement of their own.[9] "To be tied to Moscow in every way is to ignore greatly the interests of the local people," argued G. Maksudov, one of Sultangaliev's companions.[10]

Aware of this danger of total alliance with Moscow, the Tatar national Communists embarked on the effort to organize a Muslim Communist Party as early as 1918. The Conference of the Muslim Toilers of Russia, which was held in Moscow in March 1918, adopted the decision to organize a party of Muslim Socialist-Communists that would be open to "all revolutionaries who adhered to its program."[11] The leadership of the new party—M. Vakhitov, M. Sultangaliev, and B. Mansurov—urged the Muslims to commit themselves to a purely Muslim Communist Party and refrain from joining the Russian Communist Party (Bolshevik).

In June 1918, at the First Conference of Muslim Communists, held in Kazan, the Party of Muslim Socialist-Communists was transformed into the Russian Party of Muslim Communists (Bolsheviks). It was conceived as an entity separate from the RCP(b) because it was to be open to Muslims only, was to have equal status with the RCP(b), and was to enjoy organizational independence to the extent of electing its own Central Committee—a major sign of emancipation from the tutelage of the Central Committee of the Russian Communist Party.[12]

This move toward party autonomy, although not applauded by the RCP(b), was tolerated for purely tactical purposes under the stress of the Civil War. As soon as the fortunes of the Bolsheviks changed and they regained the upper hand in the Civil War, especially after recapturing Kazan in September 1918, Moscow moved to reassert its control over the Muslim Communists. Stalin used the First Congress of Muslim Communists, which met in Moscow in November 1918, to halt the centrifugal forces that had set the course for the emergence of a parallel and rival party organization of the Russian Muslims. The Congress of Muslim Communists was forced to bring the Russian Party of Muslim Communists under the control of the RCP(b). Consequently, the Russian Party of Muslim Communists underwent a substantial metamorphosis, re-emerging in the process as the Central Bureau of Muslim Organizations of the RCP(b), whose central committee became the Central Muskom, presided over the Sultangaliev.

The process of centralization had not yet been completed, however. The Eighth Congress of the RCP(b), held in Moscow between March 18 and 23, 1919, signaled the nature of changes yet to come. The congress resolved that "all decisions of the RCP(b) and of its guiding organs are compulsory for all party organs, regardless of their national composition."[13] And indeed, in the spring of 1919, the Central Bureau of Muslim Organizations of the RCP(b) was stripped of its sociocultural meaning and was instead endowed with a geographic attribute. It became the Central Bureau of the Communist Organizations of the Peoples of the East. For Moscow, this new name had a double advantage: It was politically safe and it was neutral from the sociocultural standpoint. Similarly, the Central Muskom became the Tatar-Bashkir Commissariat.

The events of early spring 1919 left no doubt that the RCP(b) and its chief expert on nationality problems, Stalin, had reversed the tide of organizational independence that the Tatar national Communists had set in motion in 1918. Despite this major setback, however, the Communists of Tatarstan were not yet resigned to the demise of the Russian Party of Muslim Communists, and they made a bid for autonomy for their party organization at the local level. In October 1919, Tatar Communists organized the Muslim Bureau of the Kazan Guberniia Committee (Gubkom) of the RCP(b) as the nucleus of a future party organization that would be independent of the Gubkom of the RCP(b). The president of the bureau was I. Kazakov, an ardent follower of Sultangaliev. Its members included G. Enbaev, I. Firdevs, and the top leadership of the Muslim Military Collegium: M. Sultangaliev (president), Sh. Usmanov (his deputy), and M. Burundukov (military adviser). Encouraged by the promises for autonomy contained in the proclamation of the TASSR on May 27, 1920, the First Regional Conference of Tatar Communists, held in Kazan on July 26, 1920, adopted the decision to rename the Muslim Bureau of Gubkom the "Tatar Regional Bureau of Communist Organizations."

The August 6, 1920, resolution of the RCP(b), however, emphasized that the Regional Committee (Obkom) of the RCP(b) was, in fact, the highest party organ of the republic and alone had the power to appoint and replace party cadra. The fact that only three of the twelve Communists who served on the Obkom Bureau were Tatars is indicative of Moscow's commitment to tighten its controls over the party organization of Tatarstan. Even those three—Izmailov, Said-Galiev, and Kasymov—were orthodox Bolsheviks who belonged to the small pro-Russian left wing of Tatar communism and whose membership in the Obkom Bureau strengthened Moscow's grip over Tatarstan's party life (at least for the time being), while at the same time paying lip service to the notion of national equality and representation.[14]

The same August 6 resolution indicated that Sultangaliev's duties and assignments in various party and cultural organizations required his presence in Moscow. That the issue of Sultangaliev's place of residence should become the concern of a party resolution reveals how much the Central Committee of the RCP(b) sought to weaken the Tatar Communists and their independent stand by removing their most prominent leader from Kazan.

In 1920, Moscow also launched a concerted effort aimed at gradually stripping Kazan of its role as the political center of the Russian Muslims. During that year, despite the opposition of the Military Collegium, the Muslim military courses were transferred from Kazan to Moscow, and the Muslim Military Collegium itself was relocated in Moscow, despite the fact that the Tatar Regional Bureau of Communist Organizations had opposed such a move.

In August 1920, when the First Tatar Obkom conference of the RCP(b) met in Kazan, the Tatar bureau moved to enhance its autonomy. By doing so, it not only sealed its own demise but also triggered a series of measures aimed at checking the influence of the national Communists even further. In the aftermath of the conference, Shamil Usmanov, the vice president of the Military Collegium, was accused of national agitation among the soldiers and transferred to Central Asia, a move that set the pattern for a practice soon to become widespread in Moscow's dealings with the unorthodox Tatar Communists.[15]

Such actions, taken at the level of local party organizations, indicated that a campaign to isolate the national Communists was under way, but it was the Congress of the Peoples of the East, held in Baku, in September 1920 that provided perhaps the first clear warning that the fundamental principles on which the national Communists had sought to give the East a special role in the revolutionary process were not acceptable to the Bolshevik leadership. The congress, rejecting Sultangaliev's thesis that the Eastern peoples were proletarian nations par excellence, pointed to the revolutionary potential of the Western proletariat and stressed the fact that the East could be saved only through the victory of the Western proletariat.[16] This thesis, articulated from the podium of the congress, provided some of the ideological justifications for the campaigns against national communist "heresies," such as those of Sultangaliev. As a result, during the 1920s, party life was dominated by the war against nationalist deviation, and in the Tatar country, nationalist deviation occupied a place of importance on the agenda of the republican conferences held after 1920.

The efforts of the Tatar Communists to build a party organization of their own independent of Moscow were paralleled by similar actions undertaken by the Komsomol (communist youth organization). The need for a National Bureau of Communist Youth was articulated for the first time at the August 16, 1920, Conference of the Komsomol of Tatarstan. This conference preceded by one month the first All-Russian Conference of the Young Communists of the East, which was chaired by Sultangaliev and which resulted in the foundation of an autonomous Central Committee of the Komsomol Organizations of the East. By a majority of 50 to 36, the Conference of the Komsomol of Tatarstan adopted a resolution to organize Eastern Komsomol sections in the republics of the East. The most important impact of the conference, though it was not spelled out in the resolution, was the emergence of various national youth organizations—called unions—under such names as the Union of Tatar Readers (Ufa and Kazan) and the Union of Tatar Youth (Simferopol, Crimea).

No doubt, Sultangaliev, who was elected an honorary member of the Tatar Komsomol, influenced the thinking of the leadership of the youth organizations. The Komsomol conferences held in 1922 and 1923 reiterated the main theses of Sultangaliev's program regarding the absence of a Tatar proletariat and the need for a united national front, but discussions of these issues were not confined to conferences. They were continued in the pages of *Tatarstan Khabärläre* (Tatarstan news), in articles signed by Sultangaliev's disciples, H. Mukhtarov, F. Burnash, and Sh. Usmanov, and in the pages of *Qzïl Yashler*

(Red Youth) and *Qzil Shark Yashlere* (Red Youth of the East), which were in nationalist hands until 1923 and to which Sultangaliev himself often contributed.[17]

Between 1920 and 1923, despite the centralizing web that was growing from Moscow, Sultangaliev and his followers still had a firm grip on the political and cultural life of the Tatar republic. They dominated the Central Committee of the Communist Party of Tatarstan, and they represented the right-wing majority in the party organization as a whole. Similarly, they still monopolized the key posts of the state bureaucracy: K. Mukhtarov was chairman of the Central Executive Committee of Tatarstan; V. Iskhakov, deputy chairman of Gosplan (the state planning committee); and M. Burundukov, people's commissar for national education, in which capacity he played a major role in ensuring that the jadid intelligentsia would take its rightful place in shaping the cultural life of Soviet Tatarstan.[18]

The stubbornness with which the Tatar national Communists fought for the autonomy of their party organization reflected both their belief that only a national party organization could be receptive to problems specific to the Tatar milieu and their conviction that there could be a Muslim road to communism. Recognizing the all-encompassing quality of Islam as a religion that is, above all, a way of life, the national Communists were careful to integrate in their program both the teachings of Islam and those of the secular western ideology to which they had adhered, even pointing out the compatibility of some of the basic fundamental precepts of Marxism and Islam.

Sultangaliev not only urged a very careful approach toward Muslims but also warned his fellow Communists not to confuse antireligious struggle with antireligious propaganda. It would be unwise, he argued, to attack Islam openly because it represented the religion of an oppressed people, suffering—or having suffered, as was the case in Russia—from the economic and political encroachment of Western European imperialism. Not religion, not Islam, but economic and political backwardness was the main weakness of the Muslims. The chains of political and economic backwardness could be broken, not by antireligious propaganda, but by political socialization, by drawing the Muslims into the leadership of the political, economic, administrative, and cultural institutions.[19]

Sultangaliev also pointed out that what accounted for the strong commitment of Muslims to Islam were some of its intrinsic positive characteristics, such as collectivism; egalitarianism; emphasis on education (the thirst for knowledge from cradle to grave advocated in the prophetic tradition); industriousness; negation of private property for agricultural lands, water, and forests; and existence of a progressive tax system in the form of the obligatory almsgiving. In addition, he stressed the desirability of a type of antireligious propaganda that would convince the Muslim believer that "Communists are not struggling against religion but merely using their right to be atheists." Sultangaliev's critics claimed that he was waging a propaganda war for jadidism (i.e., secularism), not atheism, and criticized what they called his "vegetarian Communism, which did not have anything in common with the ideology of Marx, Engels, Lenin."[20]

Sultangaliev was committed to secularism, and as a high-ranking official in the party bureaucracy, he was committed to the separation of church and state. The difference between him and his Russian comrades was that he linked the success of the movements of national liberation with the ability of their leaders to understand the role that religion played in the lives of people engaged in such a struggle. He argued that "no antireligious propaganda will succeed as long as the Eastern people remain exploited."[21] And in 1920, as he was still trying to break the barrier of aloofness and convince the Bolshevik leadership about the special place of Islam in the Tatar umma, Sultangaliev took the initiative to replace the double-headed eagle on the Suyumbike Tower with the crescent moon. His was a symbolic act, indeed, but one that could not be relegated to the domain of empty symbolism because it epitomized visually Sultangaliev's belief in the primacy of Islam in the life of the Tatars and his conviction that Islam and communism were compatible.

He warned his Russian colleagues in the party bureaucracy to use extreme caution in dealing with Islam, given the special role it played in the life of Russian Muslims.[22] His words of caution, however, fell on not-too-receptive-ears. Instead of using Sultangaliev's inside knowledge of Russian Islam to find ways in which Islamic values would be compatible with those of communism, the party leadership in Moscow chose to pursue a policy that ignored the basic promises of the January 23, 1918, decree of the Council of People's Commissars "On the Separation of Church and State, School and Church," which stated: "Every citizen may profess any religious belief, or profess no religious belief at all. All restrictions of rights, involved by professing no religious belief at all, are canceled and void."[23]

Even during the early implementation of the Degree of Separation of Church and State, even when the antireligious zeal of government agencies was toned down by the realities of the Civil War, mosques were closed and some were profaned, and often mullahs who were labeled as counterrevolutionaries were shot. What distressed the Tatars was the fact that, at least initially, many of those in charge of antireligious propaganda were Russians who had a missionary background.

This situation led to a rather unflattering comparison between Tsarist and Bolshevik policies vis à vis Islam. Aware of this connection, but still rejecting Sultangaliev's approach, Lenin wholeheartedly supported the proposal submitted to the Central Committee of the party in 1921 by Russian comrade G. V.

Chicherin, who stressed that, for tactical reasons, there was an urgent need for especially careful antireligious propaganda among Muslims.[24]

The recognition of this need for a special approach to Islam was responsible for the modus vivendi that emerged between Russian Islam and the Soviet state between 1921 and 1928. It was this climate of coexistence in 1922 that allowed Tatar national Communists to take the initiative and create a Shariat Commission that, working under the jurisdiction of the Commissariat of Justice, would undertake the formidable task of coordinating and making compatible Qur'anic and Soviet law. The same circumstances encouraged Sultangaliev in 1923 to begin organizing festivities to mark the first Islamic millenium in the Tatar country. Sultangaliev's boldness seems to have stretched the limits of the modus vivendi too far: In 1923 he was arrested on charges of nationalist deviation, and preparations for the Islamic millenial festivities were canceled. Just by launching the preparations, Sultangaliev had once more made his case for the role that Islam played in shaping the identity of the Tatars.[25]

The Bolshevik leadership refused to accept the validity of the Tatar nationalist Communists' thesis on the relationship between Islam and communism for Soviet Russia and rejected the idea of a Muslim road to communism. Having done so, the party and government leadership had to win Muslim allegiance to the new regime by proving in some fashion that the revolution's promises to eliminate the existing inequities between Russians and non-Russians were not empty phrases.

To achieve this goal, the government chose, until the mid-1920s, not to interfere to any great extent with the approach of the Tatar party and government officials to the implementation of the policy of *korenizatsiia* (indigenization) in their republic. This policy, which went into effect in 1920 in Soviet Russia, was designed to promote the formation and growth of national cadra and thus to eliminate some of the tensions between Russians and non-Russians that stemmed from the frustrated national aspirations of the latter.

On Tatar soil, korenizatsiia became the policy of Tatarization— Tatarization of the party and government apparatus, the intellectual cadra, and the language—and had the support of all Tatars, no matter what their affiliation. In fact, the aspect of korenizatsiia that became the cause célèbre for many intellectuals was the Tatarization of the language, which was understood to mean its purification—the restoration of its integrity and wholeness after eradication of the damaging effects of the centuries-old russification policies.

The congresses of the Tatar-Bashkir teachers and intellectuals held in Kazan and Moscow in 1924 and the Congress on Terminology held in Kazan that same year could be singled out as major efforts in the campaign to halt Russification and implement Tatarization. To this end, when the participants at the Congress on Terminology discussed the principles that would be adopted for the development of the Tatar language, the main emphasis was on the need for the Tatars to abstain from borrowing from any other language whenever their own language contained enough resources for enriching its own vocabulary. The congress further recommended that the Tatar language be weeded of Arabic and Russian words. Whenever the language lacked a word or a term, the terminology most widely used in Western languages should become the repository from which the missing term would be selected, and then adapted to the pattern and rules of the Tatar language.[26]

The most outspoken and ardent supporter of the Tatarization of the language was G. Ibragimov, for whom the endurance of the Arabic alphabet—a strong reminder of the Islamic heritage of the Tatars—was a prerequisite for the cultural continuity and linguistic vitality of the Tatars. An orthodox Communist, and not a political Sultangalievist, Ibragimov became the staunchest opponent of the Latin alphabet (Yanalif), the adoption of which was discussed at the First Turcological Congress held in Baku between February 26 and March 5, 1926.

From the podium of the congress, Ibragimov defended the validity of the Arabic alphabet for the Tatar people. His principal argument was that Tatarstan had an old and significant culture based on the Arabic script. Furthermore, for fifty years, the Tatars had been using a modified Arabic script that best met the needs of their language. Conceding that the old Arabic script was not perfect, he argued that there were only two ways to replace it: either reform or revolution. The Tatars, he pointed out, preferred reform to revolution.[27]

G. Ibragimov lost. The congress passed a resolution adopting the Latin alphabet the Azeri delegation had introduced.[28] The decree issued by the Presidium of the Central Committee of Sovnarkom on August 7, 1929, gave the resolution the force of law. The significance of the decree was manyfold. Overnight it produced an instant crop of millions of illiterate Muslims who found that a wall had been erected between them and their pre-Soviet cultural heritage. Another major impact was the elimination of a vital channel of communication with the Islamic umma outside the Soviet Union and, as a result, the further isolation of the Muslims of the Soviet Union.[29]

A loser in the Yanalif battle, Ibragimov perceived the adoption of the Latin alphabet as a means of facilitating the russification of the Tatar language, and he was determined to defend the cultural heritage and cultural integrity of his nation. Ibragimov's essay, *Which Way Will Tatar Culture Go?*, published in 1927 in Tatar in the Arabic script and never translated into Russian or published in either of the alphabets (Latin and Cyrillic) that were imposed upon the Tatars, was designed as a warning.[30] It posed two alternatives for the future of the Tatar culture: russification or survival. In the introductory paragraph, Ibragimov stated that Communists, such as S. Atnagulov, who regarded the Tatar culture with distrust, had become partisans of russification.[31] Ibragimov saw the emphasis on internationalism in the proletarian revolution as an effort to wipe out national cultures and create a single, generally acceptable and viable international culture. Ibragimov was eager to determine what would be the place of the Tatar culture in such an international entity, should the revolution create one, and whether the Tatar culture, as a part of an international proletarian culture, would grow closer to its national past and to the needs of its people, using its own language, or whether it would be absorbed by other cultures. Should this absorption happen, who would assimilate the Tatar culture? The Russian, Chuvash, German, or French culture? Or would it perhaps be assimilated by a new, international culture, yet to be born?

It is obvious that Ibragimov was not really worried about the Tatar culture being assimilated by the Chuvash or French cultures and that his target was the growing tide of russification. He posed the question in still another way: Should not the Tatar people voluntarily deny their national culture and replace it with the higher, Russian culture? His answer was that the Russian culture was indeed rich, and in the years after the October Revolution it had acquired more strength, having been enriched by proletarian elements. This superior culture, nonetheless, was not close to the Tatars. According to Ibragimov, the road to be followed by the Tatars was a cultural development resting on the foundations of their national heritage and using their own language.

Ibragimov considered the national language to be the primary ingredient of a national culture and saw the future of Tatar culture as dependent on the future of the Tatar language. Noting the difficult conditions under which the Tatar language had defended itself and grown in tsarist Russia, he pointed out that, only with the October Revolution, had Tatar become an official state language. But, Ibragimov stressed, russification efforts had not disappeared; on the contrary, they were perpetuated in the new socialist society.

For Ibragimov, the key word and solution was *Tatarization*. To resist russification, a defense of the linguistic status quo would not be sufficient. The tatarization of the language had to be intensified, and Ibragimov saw clear signs that Tatars had embarked on the road to do so. He documented this point by providing a chart containing the percentage of Tatar words in books published between 1919 and 1920, as compared with those in books published between 1924 and 1927. Although not dramatic, the figures for the latter period indicated an increase in the percentage of Tatar words, a sign of the growing awareness of the danger of russification and an attempt to shield the Tatar language from it.

On the basis of other charts, Ibragimov also elaborated on the efforts aimed at the tatarization of the national institutions. Here, the crucial issue was the link between the national cadra and the development and improvement of education. He argued that Tatar should be the language of instruction at all levels of the educational process. The fact that the studies of Tatar language and literature had been introduced in the curricula of the Kazan Pedagogical Institute and the Tatar Communist University gave Ibragimov hope that in the near future Tatar would take its rightful place in the curriculum of the 125-year-old Kazan University. Despite the existing difficulties, Ibragimov asserted that, in the years between 1920 and 1927, Tatar culture had demonstrated its viability and vitality, which prompted him to conclude that "the Tatar language and literature are not disappearing, they will not be russified, they will grow on their own Tatar foundations, enriched by their proletarian essence."[32]

In the first years of korenizatsiia, when Tatar national Communists still held important positions in the party and government apparatus, the Tatar party organization supported the efforts of the intellectuals to promote the Tatar language. The ninth conference of the Tatar party organization, held in Kazan in 1924, criticized the chauvinism that had characterized the attitude of some Russian Communists toward the Tatar language. Addressing the delegates from the podium of the conference, Gil'fanov and Bashkirov deplored the fact that, in Tatarstan, political literature was still being produced in Russian. They argued that library and school buildings alone were not sufficient to accomplish the enlightenment of the Tatars. Lack of books and materials in Tatar hindered Tatar political education more than the paucity of buildings. Discrimination against the Tatar language was so blatant as to prompt even a Russian Communist, Turshchin, to call for a more careful, balanced attitude, vis-à-vis the Tatar language. He argued that, at a Tatar party conference, such as this one he was attending, it was an anomaly to hear the major report delivered in Russian. Equally unsatisfactory, in his opinion, was the attitude of the Russians who were studying at the Communist University but who refused to learn Tatar, whereas Tatars were studying Russian in increasing numbers.[33]

The campaign for the defense of the Tatar language was an unplanned result of the korenizatsiia effort as intended by Moscow because, when it had been launched, korenizatsiia had amounted to assigning to non-Russians the percentage of administrative posts that would be proportionate to their share in the total population of a republic. On the Tatar soil, this aspect of korenizatsiia had been translated into efforts aimed at the Tatarization of the government and party apparatus and technical and intellectual cadra. Tatar leaders demonstrated a genuine commitment to make good on the promises of korenizatsiia, especially between 1920 and 1923, when national Communists, Sultangaliev's companions, still had control over the party and government apparatus of the republic.

The purges of national Communists that began with Sultangaliev's first arrest in 1923 did not end Tatar korenizatsiia efforts abruptly. In fact, testimonies of national Communists who were purged suggest that Tatarization efforts continued at least until 1929, one year after the official phasing out of korenizatsiia. One such testimony belongs to R. Sabirov, a companion of Sultangaliev and the president of the Tatar Central Executive Committee between 1922 and 1923. He admitted that, until as late as 1929, Tatar leaders made a special effort to reserve as many positions as possible for their *millet* (nation).

An original approach to tatarization came from another of Sultangaliev's companions, I. Kazakov, who as president of the election commission for one of the districts of Kazan disregarded the disenfranchised status of some 2,000 Tatars and allowed them to vote in the 1929 elections because he wanted to enable the Tatars to have as strong a voice as possible in deciding the fortunes of their republic. His official explanation of the decision pointed to his belief that franchise, or lack of it, was irrelevant because "after the revolution the bourgeoisie disappeared from Kazan."[34]

Korenizatsiia benefited from the fact that in the years between 1921 and 1928 a modus vivendi was forged between communism and Islam; and between communism and nationalism. This was a fragile and precarious modus vivendi, indeed, because, even as it was beginning to take shape, Sultangaliev—the most outspoken of the Tatar national Communists—was purged at the Twelfth Party Congress held in April 1923, and one month later was arrested for a short period. He was expelled from the Communist Party at the Fourth Conference of the Central Committee of the Russian Communist Party held in 1924 in Moscow and was condemned for nationalist deviations in the resolutions of the same conference. The party cadra of the autonomous and national republics and regions had been expressly summoned to Moscow to attend this conference, probably in order that they might better understand the consequences of persevering on the nationalist road.

If the party leadership in Moscow intended to use the conference to intimidate other national Communists and isolate Sultangaliev, they were unsuccessful. Until 1928, Sultangaliev wielded influence through his companions who occupied positions of responsibility in the party and government apparatus and who, in fact, organized petition campaigns to protest his ouster and defend his program ("The petition of the 39") as well as to oppose the adoption of Yanalif ("The declaration of the 82").[35]

During the period between his first arrest in 1923 and his final arrest and banishment in 1928, Sultangaliev gave impetus to the nationalist drive—organizing, leading underground nationalist societies, and continuing to add new theses to his program.[36] One such thesis advanced the concept of creation of the republic of Turan, an independent and ethnically homogenous state that would include the Middle Volga, Azerbaidzhan, Dagestan, North Caucasus, and Turkestan and would bring about the administrative unity of all the Turkic peoples of Russia.[37] The extent to which such an idea received support among various Turkic groups is difficult to assess, for we lack documentary evidence. It can be assumed, however, that the issue gained the attention of the underground political circles that had sprung up in both the Middle Volga and Central Asia.[38]

It is possible that even underground literary circles, such as Dzhidigan (organized in 1927 in Kazan), may have addressed the issue of the impact of administrative unity on the cultural unity of the Turks of the Soviet Union.

The boldness exhibited by the Tatar Communists in defending their national culture proved to be counterproductive, however, and it brought about the ultimate demise of national communism as a political force in Tatarstan. In 1927, at a time when Ibragimov's essay underlined the urgency of finding out "Which Way Will Tatar Culture Go?", a high-ranking delegation of Tatar commissars of the people traveled to Moscow to call to the attention of the Central Committee of the RCP(b) the harmful effects the chauvinism and imperialist policies of the Russian Communists were having on the national interests of their republic. It was this action that opened the lid on Pandora's box. Accusations of nationalist deviations triggered Sultangaliev's second arrest, justified the final purge of the Tatar national Communists, and launched the frontal attack on Islam as a religion.[39] Nobody was spared. This final purge eliminated the Tatar nation's most talented and dedicated leaders and intellectuals of the years preceding the outbreak of World War II.

Although the Party Control Commission had expelled the Sultangalievists from membership in the Communist Party in 1928, their destinies were sealed only in 1929.[40] The Tatar Obkom held its Third Plenum in November 1929, and on the basis of the decisions of the Sixteenth All-Russian Party Conference and of the Fourteenth Party Conference of Tatarstan, the Third Plenum adopted a resolution condemning once more the Sultangalievists and even claiming an initial victory over this national deviation.[41] After their explusion from the party, K. Mukhtarov, chairman of the Central Executive Committee [CEC] of Tatarstan; K. Mansurov, head of the propaganda section of the CEC; R. Sabirov, first secretary of the Tatar Obkom; M. Burundukov, people's commissar of education; V. Iskhakov, vice president of the Tatar Gosplan; and M. Budaili, first secretary of the Tatar Komsomol were arrested and convicted for sins that included "plotting against the dictatorship of the proletariat" and maintaining ties with émigré circles.[42]

The purge of the top leadership was soon followed by a general purge of the party organization of Tatarstan. In 1930 alone, 2,056 Tatar Communists, representing 13.4 percent of the total membership, were expelled from the party; 2,273 received the death penalty for their nationalist deviation, and 329 were fired from the posts they had occupied.[43]

Equally important targets were the cultural, educational, and scientific institutions of Tatarstan. The first to feel the brunt of the cultural purge, the Society of Tatarology was dismantled in 1929. This was followed by similar action against the Oriental Institute of Kazan in the spring of 1930, the demise of Dzhidigan in the fall of the same year, and virulent attacks on the Union of

Tatar Proletarian writers and Tatgosizdat (the Tatar State Publishing House) in the spring of 1932.[44]

The purge of the top establishment in the world of culture, science, and education was only the beginning of the overall purge of the cultural institutions and cadra, a purge that touched writers and humble village teachers alike simply because Tatar Communists had dared express openly a firm commitment to the national values, culture, and aspirations of their people.

By the end of 1932, Sultangalievism had ceased to exist, not only as an organized political movement but also as a coherent cultural movement. Yet the cultural dimensions of Sultangalievism, more elusive to the control of the party, endured; although not once in the 1930s was the sin of Sultangalievism resurrected to punish any deviation from ideological orthodoxy. Political national communism was dead, but the hopes and dreams of the national Communists regarding the future of their culture were vindicated to a great extent by the resilience exhibited by the Tatar culture in the decades following World War II.

12 Cultural Resilience and National Identity in the Post– World War II Period

Motherland, Tukay, and mother are one.

Vatan da-ber, Tukay da-ber, äni da-ber.

  (K. Mostafin)

You do not have the right to forget, do you understand?

Sezneng onïtïrga khakïgïz yuk, anglïysïzmï?

  (A. Eniki, *Aytelmagan vasiyät* [Unspoken testament].)

The four decades following the end of World War II represent a period in the history of the Volga Tatars that is characterized by an increasing sense of their ethos of distinctness and by an even greater commitment to the cultivation and promotion of that ethos, reflected in their efforts to identify to what extent the Soviet sociopolitical milieu affected the ingredients of Tatar ethnicity and to re-evaluate the attributes of their national culture and identity. This re-evaluation has been largely the result of the Volga Tatars' response to their historical past, a response based on recognition of the value of having historical roots, of being endowed with a measure of antiquity.

    Long before the formation of the TASSR in 1920, the Volga Tatars forged a collective consciousness in which the twin ingredients of a sense of antiquity rooted in their common history traceable at least to the Bulgar state and a sense of belonging to the Islamic umma figured prominently.

    In trying to understand the cultural resilience of the Volga Tatars and the nature of their national consciousness and identity in the postwar period, one must give due importance to the role played by the Soviet regime. After October 1917, Tatars were forbidden to nurture any political aspirations that could conflict with the ideology and politics of the Bolshevik state, despite the promises of freedom of choice contained in its official declarations. The trauma of this reality was matched only by its unique irony: A people who had been deprived of political freedom since 1552 were again to be confined to the same status after having been allowed to nurture hopes for an Idel-Ural state in 1917 and after riding on the Bolshevik promises for a Tatar-Bashkir republic until 1919.

The demise of the plans for a Tatar-Bashkir republic and the emergence in 1919 and 1920 of separate Bashkir and Tatar republics are at the root of what can be considered at the least a demographic oddity. According to the data furnished by the 1979 census, Tatars represent 47.6 percent of the population of the TASSR and 24.5 percent of the total population of BASSR, where they outnumber the Bashkirs, whose share of the population amounts to only 24.3 percent.[1]

Despite the administrative fragmentation, Volga Tatars exhibit an intense and pervasive consciousness of national history, of self-image as a nation, which has been forged in a centuries-old struggle for survival and translated into their resistance to assimilation and a remarkable cultural resilience. In this respect, Tatar attitudes toward the mainstays of ethnicity—historical roots, language, literature, religion, customs, and traditions—are keys to understanding the nature and scope of their cultural resilience in the post–World War II period and assessing their relationship vis-à-vis the concepts and realities of Soviet culture and Soviet man.

If the twin prerequisites of socialist content and national form have to some extent lifted the veil of elusiveness still floating around the concept of Soviet culture today, the concept of Soviet man—*homo sovieticus*—is still as vague an entity today as it was in the immediate postrevolutionary years when the term *Soviet man* was first coined by Bolshevik leaders to describe him. Homo sovieticus is an abstraction, a concept that, rather than suggesting a concrete national profile, suggests adherence to an ideology, and to the set of values and behavior that derive from it. Divorced from a national milieu, from national roots, the culture of Homo sovieticus would be as hybrid and sterile as the Communist Esperanto G. Ibragimov criticized while attacking Kautsky's vision of a socialist society in which all national languages would disappear and a language common to all nations would be born.[2]

The emergence of new and intense forms of ethnicity and nationalism among the nationalities of the Soviet Union during the post–World War II period has been traced by some scholars to the general breakdown of the attempt to create a Homo sovieticus.[3] Yet perhaps what we are witnessing is not so much the breakdown of the attempt to create a Soviet man as it is an effort to re-evaluate and redefine the concept from the perspective of the nationalities that make up the ethnic mosaic of the Soviet Union.

At various times, and with varying degrees of enthusiasm, hope, and emphasis, the official Soviet ideology has endowed the processes of *sblizhenie* (drawing together) and *sliianie* (merger) with an almost magical power to accomplish the birth of the Soviet man. The state machine has implemented a broad range of policies aimed at furthering, encouraging, and even speeding up sblizhenie and sliianie, in order ultimately to create the genuine Soviet man.

Soviet sociologists have devoted a great deal of attention to the study of sblizhenie and the socioeconomic, cultural factors that facilitate it. V. Iu. Arutiunian and L. M. Drobizheva have argued that the urban setting provides optimum conditions for ethnic consolidation because the urban environment, by its very nature, fosters social and cultural uniformity and discourages ethnic isolation.[4]

Tatars share with the Russians, Armenians, Estonians, and Latvians the distinction of belonging to the group of nationalities with the highest level of urbanization (between 50 and 69 percent) in the Soviet Union. Their linguistic behavior validates Arutunian's thesis to some extent, although one should approach the available data with caution. The number of Volga-Ural Tatars who declared the language of their nationality as their native tongue has decreased from 89.3 percent in 1959 to 85.9 percent in 1970. Although not a significant drop, the change deserves attention, for it might indicate that the peoples of the Soviet Union are "drawing together."[5]

On the basis of the existing incomplete data, however, it is difficult to assess which direction sblizhenie is taking in the Volga-Ural area. The level of urbanization is highest for those Tatars who live outside their republic, which would render them, at least theoretically, even more vulnerable to ethnic consolidation and assimilation. In the case of Siberian Tatars, however, statistics for the years 1969 through 1971 suggest that urbanization and remoteness from the traditional centers of Tatar culture have affected their linguistic behavior little (if at all), since 85.2 percent of Siberian Tatars declared Tatar their native language, a figure that almost matches the overall linguistic behavior of the Tatars.[6]

Soviet scholars have emphasized the positive role of bilingualism as a major step toward ethnic integration, and educational policies have been geared toward making bilingualism a reality for all ethnic groups living in the USSR. The number of hours allocated for the study of Tatar language and literature, as compared with those for the study of Russian language and literature, in the school curriculum approved by the Ministry of Education of TASSR for the academic year 1981/82 proves this point. If, in grades one to three, Tatar children benefit from a more intensive study of their language and literature, in grades four to six the emphasis shifts in favor of Russian, only to shift back to Tatar in grades seven and eight and then to even out during the last two years of high school.[7]

The intensive Russian-language training that Tatars receive at the level of secondary education is probably largely responsible for both the growing bilingualism of Tatar children and their ability to enter institutions of higher education in increasing numbers.[8] Still, Tatar youths are underrepresented in institutions of higher education because of the discriminatory impact of the Russian language examination, which is a requirement for entrance to any such institution. As a result, it is not surprising that, during the academic year 1969/70, only one-third of the 61,000 students who attended the eleven institutions of higher education in TASSR were Tatars, despite the fact that Tatars represented 49.1 percent of the total population of their republic.[9]

The issue of the linguistic behavior of the Tatars is of major importance to Tatar educators, scholars, and writers. They support the road of bilingualism on which the Tatars seem to have embarked but are neither complacent nor jubilant with regard to the status of the Tatar language in their republic. On the contrary, an ever-increasing demand for quality in education and a growing concern with the role the national language plays in shaping national culture permeates the thinking and the efforts of Tatar intellectuals. They have assigned a particularly important role to literature, which they see as the standard bearer of the national language, as one of the main vehicles for promoting and enriching it, and as a mirror of a people's historical experiences. Tatar scholars have stressed the importance of the links between language, literature, and history in defining, maintaining, and promoting one's national culture and identity.

Khatip Mingnegulov, for instance, brought a discussion of literature textbooks for eighth graders to the pages of the prestigious literary, sociopolitical journal, *Kazan Utlari* (The fires of Kazan). He pointed out that the history of Tatar literature should be studied within the context of the history of the nation, stressing that students who attended Russian-language schools were already enjoying such an approach because those schools included Russian history classes in their curricula. Mingnegulov took issue with M. Gainullin and M. Mahdiev, who in the pages of their textbook contended that, although the emergence of Tatar prose can be traced to the twelfth century, no texts have survived. In correcting their lapse of memory, he renewed his call for accuracy and quality.[10]

The importance Tatars attach to the endurance and growth of their national language is also epitomized by Sh. Galiev's stanza addressed to children, published in the section for children's literature of *Kazan Utlari*. It is entitled *Tugan tel* (Native tongue) and reads:

Tugan tel—ing tatlï tel,

Tugan tel—ing tämle tel,

Tämle dip, teleng yotma,

Tugan telne onïtma!

The native tongue is sweet, indeed.

The native tongue is dear, indeed.

Don't swallow it because it's sweet

And don't forget this tongue so sweet.[11]

Tatar writers of the postwar period have echoed G. Ibragimov's concerns in emphasizing the role of the language in preserving a nation's heritage. S. Khakim, speaking in June 1958 at the Fourth Congress of the Writers of Tatarstan, pointed out that "national color, national peculiarities are not embellishments. They reflect the richness of a people's language, which has developed over the centuries."[12] More recently, the overall emphasis Tatar scholars have put on their national language as the backbone of the national heritage has been reflected in studies aimed at investigating its richness and evolution. In 1976, N. Fattakh published a three-part etymological study entitled *Erak gasïrlar avazï* (The voice of bygone centuries) in the pages of *Kazan Utlarï*.[13] Undertaking such a project, M. Fattakh's main goal was, in his own words, "to share [his] thoughts on the history and ethnography of the Turkic peoples."[14] In some of the discussions of etymology, he advances a theory of the Turkic origins of Russian words, such as *tvorog* and *tovar*, which he traces to *tuar agï* and *tuar*, respectively. In doing so, Fattakh not only acquaints his readers with the richness of their language but also aims indirectly at increasing their pride in it and warns against borrowing indiscriminately from Russian.

Islam has played a crucial role in shaping the national-cultural identity of the Tatars. Today, the Volga Tatars' ethnosocial and cultural behavior bears, to a great extent, the imprint of the Islamic heritage; and their adherence to religion-based values and social conduct, rather than strict observance of the ceremonial duties, is the measure of their commitment to a cultural heritage forged by a centuries-old history.

Soviet sociologists have pointed out that an outstanding feature of the consciousness of Soviet Muslims results from the juxtaposition of their national and Islamic identity. Hence, Muslims perceive religious rituals and holidays as elements of their national culture, and certain sociocultural attitudes initially motivated by religion have become components of their secular ethnic profile. The attitude of the Volga Tatars toward mixed marriages and observance of religious rituals and holidays is a case in point.

Because endogamy among Muslims is largely a result of religious restrictions, it would follow that the attitude of secular Muslims, or atheists, toward mixed marriages would be overwhelmingly positive. Yet a survey conducted among the Tatar population of the Gorky village revealed that even among those 243 Tatars who had declared that they were atheists, some 17 percent considered mixed marriages undesirable, while 48 percent of the 267 believers were of the same opinion.[15] Interestingly enough, however, the percentage of those who looked favorably upon mixed marriages was not much higher in Kazan and Almet'evsk (52 and 68 percent, respectively). In urban areas, the negative attitude toward mixed marriages is apparently triggered by a Tatar belief that, in an environment that by its very nature has a leveling effect on national cultures, marriage within one's own ethnic group enhances the chances of hindering assimilation. Such behavior relegates to the realm of fantasy, or at least to social anomaly, the model union depicted in S. Shakurov's drama *Tugan tufrak* (Native land). The marriage between the Tatar agronomist and the Ukrainian girl—his comrade-in-arms from the years of World War II— is celebrated according to Russian customs and presented rather programmatically as the model for future social engineering and behavior. Whatever Shakurov's intentions, the test of time and present trends among the Tatars seem to have reduced his ideal couple to a mere hybrid model.

Equally telling is the choice Tatars make in the areas of social contacts and personal friendships. Although the majority of the Tatars approve of an ethnically integrated work environment, and most favor social contacts with other nationalities, 47 percent still prefer to choose their friends from among Tatars.[16]

Social segregation along ethnic lines seems, at least partly, to result from the endurance of a set of sociocultural values and attitudes that have guided the behavior of the Russian and Tatar communities vis-à-vis each other for centuries. The racial and cultural slanders and the discrimination to which the Tatars grew accustomed prior to 1917 have lingered on with varying degrees of aggressiveness, ranging from the more or less benign cartoon ridiculing the Tatar who has drafted a resolution in poor Russian to the graffiti that read "Beat the Jews!" "Down with the Tatars!" "We'll get rid of the ugly Tatar faces!" on the wall of the Kazan Municipal Soviet.[17]

If attitudes toward mixed marriages and social contacts outside their ethnic group can be traced to the role Islam has played in shaping the way of life of the Tatars, observance of religious rituals and ceremonial duties provide even stronger proof of their commitment to Islam, not so much as a system of theology, but as an all-encompassing way of life. In this allegiance, mullahs and average believers alike have exhibited equal degrees of creativity in addressing the issue. The official declarations of the mufti of Ufa, the kazis, and the imams, however, show less of their creativity than do the fatwas they deliver by way of answering the questions submitted by the believers during the Friday congregational prayers. In 1968, N. Mufliukhanov, the mullah of the Chistopol mosque, was asked whether he could see a conflict between the belief in the existence of God and an acceptance of the discoveries of science. He answered: "As one cannot see Reason, one cannot hold it, or prove that it exists, [so] one cannot see the Almighty Allah; and the proof of the fact that He exists shall never be found."[18]

The mullahs' declarations regarding the role of women in an Islamic society are still another solid proof that Soviet Islam is modernizing and creatively using the forces of revival unchained by jadidism. Today, most mullahs do not concentrate their efforts on promoting the education or political socialization of women. Success in this area has been achieved, and credit belongs to the Soviet government.[19] Mullahs are mainly concerned with religious socialization, which would enable women to participate and share in all areas of the religious life of their community, and to this end, they have opened the doors of mosques to women and have encouraged women to break with the old tradition of praying at home. Praying together as a congregation, Tatar men and women would add a new meaning to the concept of community, for manifest acts of common worship cement communal bonds and stimulate the individual's sense of belonging. During Friday congregational prayers, mullahs emphasize the role of the mosque not only as a place for prayer but also as a place where people meet in friendship, equality, and happiness to further their moral improvement.[20]

Furthermore, mullahs creatively approach the rules regarding salah, the obligation of daily prayers, to make it possible for more and more Muslims to fulfill this duty. In many mosques, prayers are scheduled in such a way as to avoid conflict with the work schedule.

Muslim clergy have a similarly flexible attitude toward some of the ceremonial duties of Islam. Throughout the month of Ramadan, each day of fasting ends with a festive dinner, *iftar*, which begins at sunset. When his parishioners asked K. Iarullin, the imam of the Kazan mosque, whether it would be proper to invite atheists as well as people of other religious persuasions to iftar, his answer was positive, provided that atheists did "not hinder Muslims in their observance of iftar and prayer."[21] This ecumenical approach could be indicative of efforts to modernize Islam; it could also indicate a desire on the part of the clergy to allow even acknowledged atheists from among the Tatars and Bashkirs to share in some of the traditional rituals of their families. Soviet criticisms of party organizations that "even tolerate the observance of religious practices by Communists" suggest that such an assumption may be valid.[22]

Circumcision and observance of other religious rituals connected with the life cycle of birth, marriage, and burial and the observance of dietary restrictions are other expressions of faith still practiced by a considerable number of Tatars, although failure to observe any of these rites does not necessarily exclude a person from the community of believers. When asked about the obligatory nature of circumcision, the mufti of Ufa replied in one of his fatwas of 1963 that it was not compulsory. Moreover, when questioned whether it would be acceptable to marry a man who had not undergone the ritual of circumcision but who claimed to be a Muslim, the same mufti replied that such a marriage would be allowed "since lack of circumcision does not indicate that a man is not a believer."[23]

Equally important in revealing the crucial role Islam has played in shaping the national identity of the Tatars is the resurgence of interest in Islam among the Tatar intelligentsia, who have found avenues to examine the Islamic roots of Tatar culture within the framework of the officially sanctioned ideology and cultural policies.

This interest should be read, not as a step on the path to becoming practicing Muslims who conform strictly to the five pillars of Islam, but rather as the fulfillment of what these Tatar intellectuals see as a moral duty to reacquaint the people with their culture and traditions and, ultimately, with one of the main shapers of their identity.

Along these lines, the publication in Kazan in 1981 of a second enlarged edition of the *Reference Dictionary of Islam* stands as a landmark. A number of factors validate this contention. First, this work is officially sanctioned and is published in Tatar for a domestic audience. The demand for the book must have been overwhelming because the 27,000 copies of this second edition by far exceed the 5,500 copies of the 1978 edition. Second, the review of the dictionary carried in the October 1981 issue of the journal of the Tatar Oblast Party Committee, *Tatarstan Kommunisty* (The Communist of Tatarstan), was written by K. Faseev, who is a leading scholar and staff member of the Institute of Language, Literature, and History of the Kazan Branch of the USSR Academy of Sciences and the former head of the Propaganda and Agitation Department of the Tatar Oblast Party Committee. Faseev described the book as a valuable aid in learning about Islam, even as he emphasized that the book could serve as a tool for eradicating the residues of religious superstition.[24] Third, the dictionary was compiled by a prominent group of scholars led by Ia. G. Abdullin, who in his discussion of religious thought emphasized clearly the link between the Tatar enlightenment and religious reformism.

In his review of the book, Faseev deplored the brevity of the atheistic propaganda in the pages of the dictionary. This shortcoming, however, is more than compensated for by the intensification of the anti-Islamic propaganda in the pages of the journal *Tatar Kommunisty* and in the newspapers of the Tatar republic. A case in point is the article entitled "An Important Aspect of Ideological Work" written by A. Kalaganov, the head of a group of lecturers attached to the Tatar Oblast Committee of the Communist Party of the Soviet Union (CPSU) and published in the first issue of *Tatarstan Kommunisty* for

1983. Kalaganov delineates 352 schools of Marxism-Leninism in the Tatar ASSR, with 6,115 students engaged in the study of religion and atheism. He points out that, in 1982 alone, approximately 60 people's universities of atheism were organized in cultural and trade union clubs at which 9,000 lectures on atheistic themes were delivered to various audiences throughout the republic.[25]

The impressive atheistic propaganda activity, however, has apparently failed to yield the expected results because Kalaganov proceeds to list areas, such as the Aksubaevo, Vysokaia Gora, and Verkhnii Uslon *raions*, where religious practices are still tolerated by party organizations. Moreover, he singles out the cadra of atheistic propaganda in the Oktiabr'skii Raion for criticism for having taken no action against a signature collection campaign aimed at supporting a petition to open a mosque. The same atheistic propaganda cadra are also criticized for having been complacent about Muslim preachers who are active in rural areas. These remarks regarding Muslim preachers and not mullahs may be interpreted as an indirect reference to the stepped-up activities of Sufi preachers and leaders (ishans, imams).

This surmise about increased Sufi religious activity is reinforced by information contained in one of the latest substantial studies of Islam in Tatarstan authored by Z. A. Ishmukhametov and published in 1979 in Kazan.[26] In this book, dedicated to the study of the social role and evolution of Islam in Tatarstan, Ishmukhametov has devoted an entire chapter to the discussion of Sufism and Muridism, and his reference therein to the attention paid in the atheistic literature of the 1920s and 1930s to the social role of "ishanism" both indicates that Sufi beliefs and practices had not died with the advent of the Bolshevik regime and represents an implied criticism of the absence of anti-Sufi literature in the 1970s.[27]

In his analysis of the nature of Sufism, Ishmukhametov underlines its emphasis on asceticism. He notes that in the past the Sufis laid out the path (*tariqah*) that would lead to a mystic knowledge of God (*ma'rifah*) and that traditionally Sufism has had an appeal because it has provided a personal and emotional approach that fulfills the needs of those who are reacting against the abstract and impersonal teachings of the orthodox. Today, this appeal could be a reaction to the sterility and impersonal nature of a secular doctrine imposed from above, as much as it could be a reaction to the elitism and corruption of a society that claims to be egalitarian.

For the Sufi, the path of ascension to divine union (*tawhid*) with God passes through stages commonly known as states or stations. The last stage is that of *fana*, or passing away in God, which is the ultimate desire of a successful mystic because at this point one ceases to be aware of one's physical identity although one continues to exist as an individual. The practice of *dhikr*—uttering the name of God in order to concentrate the mind on God—plays an important role in achieving fana. With time, however, the Sufi dhikr has begun to embrace clear liturgical tendencies marked by the recitation of chants and litanies. It is this form of dhikr that Ishmukhametov mentions while discussing Sufi ceremonies and practices in general, and he points out that dhikr is still performed in many Tatar mosques as part of the prayer.

The resilience of Sufism in Tatar lands comes as no surprise; Ishmukhametov himself traces its roots to the earliest period of Tatar history, the Bulgar khanate, mentioning the names of Iusuf Cholba and Sahib Keremet Sheikh Khazar Baba, two of the more than one hundred known sheikhs and preachers who were active during Khan Iadigar's rule. By the nineteenth and twentieth centuries, Sufism had spread from perm to Astrakhan, from Troitsk and Orenburg to Omsk and Irkutsk. There were even dynasties of Sufi leaders (ishans), such as those of Z. Rasulev and B. Vaisov, and brotherhoods, such as the one led by Ishan Gabdelsattar. These groups numbered from 5,000 to 6,000 members.[28]

The ideological motivations of Ishmukhametov's inquiry notwithstanding, his study belongs to the growing number of scholarly and literary works that focus on the Tatar past. One of the tangible measures of the cultural resilience of the Volga Tatars is their engagement in the effort to reclaim their past. The study of the Tatar past and cultural heritage has attracted, with equal enthusiasm, historians, archeologists, ethnographers, linguists, and literary critics. The precariousness of the alternating Soviet thaws and freezes has not substantially affected the ascending line in scholarship, literature, and art. *Miras* (national heritage) and *mirasism* (pride in the national heritage), long relegated to the position of taboos after the campaign against nationalist deviation of the 1920s, have been gradually restored to their rightful place in the pantheon of values of the Tatar people and have almost become catchwords. Respect for heritage is openly advocated in the pages of the prestigious journal *Kazan Utlari*.[29]

The avalanche of reference works published since the 1960s leaves no doubt that Tatar intelligentsia is intent on retrieving the national heritage of its people and is making this task a multidisciplinary endeavor. In addition to the *Reference Dictionary of Islam*, the first volume of the bilingual bibliography of the Tatar historiography of the Soviet period—the history of Soviet Tatar literature that acknowledges the writers rehabilitated after 1956—has been published, as has the three-volume encyclopedic dictionary of the Tatar language. All these publications illustrate this trend.[30]

In addition, the papers presented at the First and Second Volga-Ural Archeological and Ethnographic Conferences, held in 1976 and 1977, reflected an ever-increasing interest on the part of the scholars from various disciplines in the culture of their people. P. G. Mukhamedova, for instance, reported on the progress on the ethnographic atlas of the Tatar people; F. L. Fattakhova, P. G. Mukhamedova, and Iu. G. Mukhametshin devoted their papers to the study of dwellings of Tatars; F. Sh. Safina and D. K. Valeeva discussed Tatar textiles and the decorative arts of the Bulgars; and E. A. Khalikova investigated the penetration of Islam into the Volga area on the basis of materials collected from 600 tombs.[31]

A direct reflection of the government's uneasiness with the Tatars' and other Turkic peoples' increasing awareness of the common bonds they share through their religion and culture can be found in S. I. Vainshtein's paper, presented at the 1977 All-Union Turkological Conference. Vainshtein summarized the achievements of Soviet ethnographers, only to point out that there was no Turkic culture common to all peoples speaking Turkic languages.[32]

One of the most striking features of Tatar scholarship today is the preoccupation of scholars with the more distant past of their people; this is evidenced by a wealth of studies (from essays to monographs) on early Bulgars, the emergence of Kazan, and the history of Kazan during the period of the khanate. There is visible effort in the pages of *Kazan Utlari* to acquaint the readers with accounts of Arab travelers, such as Ibn-Fadlan (tenth century) and Abu-Hamid-el-Garnati (twelfth century), whose impressions provide a valuable source of information on the life and society of the Bulgar state. It is perhaps neither accident nor chance that the editors of *Kazan Utlari* chose to publish the exact excerpts from Garnati's travel account that contained information on the adoption of Islam by the Bulgars.[33] A. Kh. Khalikov, a prominent Tatar archeologist and historian, has devoted a new work to the study of the Volga-Kama region in the eighth to sixth centuries B.C. F. Kh. Valeev and D. Valieva have concentrated on investigation of the ancient and medieval art of the Middle-Volga region.

The areas of inquiry seem benign enough, at first glance, and void of any messages with political undertones. The criticism M. Gosmanov advances with regard to Valeev's book, however, may suggest another possibility. Gosmanov argues that Valeev conducts his analysis in such a manner as to seem to provide an answer to the question "Who were our ancestors?" Furthermore, Gosmanov warns against claiming the Bulgars or the Kypchaks as direct ancestors of the Kazan Tatars for, he points out, the Kazan Tatars, as is the case of many other peoples, have emerged as a result of a complex process of ethnogenesis that has involved many ethnic groups.[34]

The new trends in Tatar historiography are probably represented best by the revisionist approach to two major topics: the interpretation of the Russian-Tatar relationship and the assessment of jadidism.[35]

In addition to breaking the frontiers of the immediate past that had held them captive, those Tatar historians who increasingly have paid attention to the Bulgar and Kazan khanates, to the eighteenth century, have also been audacious enough to challenge some of the old axioms. S. Kh. Alishev's analysis of the Kazan khanate—its socioeconomic and political problems as well as its relationship with Muscovy—annihilates the postulates of the 1950s as represented by Gimadi.[36] A. Karimullin's studies of the history of Tatar book publishing and Kh. Khasanov's study of the emergence of the Tatar bourgeois nation contribute to a much more sophisticated understanding of the evolution of the Tatar society and culture.[37]

Tatar scholarship has also been enriched by Ia. Abdullin's boldly new interpretation of jadidism, its roots, and its legacy. In keeping with the tradition of Soviet scholarship, however, Abdullin calls jadidism the Tatar enlightenment.[38] The economic determinism responsible for Abdullin's characterization of jadidism as a class-oriented intellectual phenomenon produced by a capitalist society does not diminish the value of his interpretation of the intellectual roots and socioeconomic milieu of jadidism and its relationship to Islam. Abdullin argues that, because Shariat governs not only the individual life of the believer but also Muslim society as a whole, any atheistic propaganda in the radical form inaugurated by the French Revolution is self-defeating for the Muslims. Consequently, he interprets the success of Tatar jadidism as the result of the careful approach of the reformers, who did not criticize religion in general but rather embarked on a criticism of Muslim theology as a system of philosophy. Furthermore, he believes that what gave Tatar enlightenment dynamism and a distinct profile were its intellectual roots deeply planted in the progressive traditions and spiritual heritage of the people.

Abdullin also addresses the issue of the relationship between the Tatar and Western European enlightenments, on the one hand, and the Tatar and Russian enlightenment on the other. Interestingly enough, he not only gives credit to the intellectual heritage of the Muslim East (Al-Farabi, Ibn-Sina, and Ibn-Rushd) for the growth and coming of age of Tatar sociopolitical thought but also argues that this same Eastern philosophical system became the channel through which Tatars became acquainted with the foundations of Western culture—ancient Greek philosophy and culture. As for the Russian culture, he relegates it to the role of a transmission belt that brought to the Tatars the riches of modern European culture, including its achievements in science and philosophy.

The latest contribution to the history of jadidism comes from M. Usmanov in the form of a documentary story about the life of Khusain Faizkhanov (1828–1866) entitled *Zavetnaia mechta Khusaina Faizkhanova*. While reiterating some of the theses on jadidism formulated in the 1960s, Usmanov also calls attention to the specific problems of the Tatar milieu. His discussion of Merjani points out that attempts to exclude him from the circle of jadids were based on the fact that many considered the very concept of a mullah-jadid a contradiction. This approach resulted from the inclination of some scholars to apply mechanically to the Tatar milieu concepts viable for the Russian society, in which as a rule, an enlightener was a lay person, a secular figure.[39]

Jadidism was also a topic for consideration during the 1977 celebration of the founding of Kazan 800 years before. That festive occasion augmented the general interest in the history of the khanate, triggered controversies, and offered a forum for discussing the greatness of Kazan as the economic, political, and cultural center of an Islamic state. Along with contributions from contemporary scholars, such as A. Alishev and Khalikov, *Kazan Utlarï* marked the celebration of Kazan's eight-century-long history by honoring Tatar intellectuals of the jadid generation who had contributed to the study of early Tatar history. Thus, in evaluating Merjani's heritage, Ia. Abdullin and A. Khairullin stressed his contribution as a historian, pointing to the value of Merjani's study on Bulgar and Kazan: *Mustafad al-Akhbar fi-l-Ahwal Qazan wa Bulgar.* Even the contribution of a less known jadid—Fazyl Tukyi's *History of the Turks*—received attention in the overall effort to unearth and bring to light and life the roots of Tatar history.[40]

Tatar scholars seem to have chosen to respond to government policies that encourage sblizhenie and ultimately aim at sliianie, not by promoting secession, but by arguing that there can be unity in diversity. The message seems to be that the Tatars of today can better understand themselves by learning to understand their past and can remain themselves by maintaining an awareness of their past in its undiluted complexity.

Tatar intellectuals and writers have also exhibited a growing interest in assessing the part that the continuity of historical experiences and traditions of a people play in shaping their culture and national consciousness. "Contemporary Tatar culture and literature did not come out of nowhere," points out M. Gainullin in his analysis of the poetry of Därdämänd; "it emerged from the literature and culture of bygone ages which matured meeting new challenges."[41] The thesis of cultural continuity as a prerequisite to vitality is also present in the thought of G. Bashir, who values the many customs and traditions that have emerged over the course of centuries and can greatly benefit the Tatars today if they can be carried on successfully. Rafael Mustafin notes with hope the encouraging trends in poetry: Even dedicated avantgardists, such as R. Faizullin, R. Mingalimov, R. Kharisov, M. Agliamov, and Zöl'fät, could not ignore the creative potential inherent in the traditional national culture and are bringing to their poetry the wealth and beauty of folk imagery and rhythms.

R. Mustafin's definition of national traditions is so broad as to include material culture as expressed in monuments of architecture, crafts, and agricultural patterns; spiritual culture in the form of folk literature, literature, and the arts; ethical values; a common spiritual profile; and "all that is handed down from generation to generation together with mother's milk." Such a definition enables Mustafin to contrast the spiritual and moral profiles of the simple, solid peasant woman, Gil'mänisa, the heroine of F. Khusni's story with the same name, who has raised seven children against the "superficiality of marriages and hastiness of divorces among some people."[42] Taking into account the low birth rate of the highly urbanized Tatars and projecting that rate against the background of the high birth rates of the Central Asians for whom families with six and seven children are the norm, Gil'mänisa's example seems to be used as an argument for a Tatar return to the healthier patterns of the traditional Muslim family.

Tatar literature today has to a great extent overcome the handicaps of the immediate postwar period, when uncompromising ideological orthodoxy forced it to wear a "dress uniform" for too long. In the 1940s and 1950s, too many poets strove "to speak not for themselves, but in the name of millions; they walked on their toes with their chests out and raised their voices to look better, taller, and more important."[43] The fresh winds that have been testing the wings of Tatar literature since the 1960s have brought to the shores of Idel and Kama not only the names of R. Faizullin, R. Gäray, R. Mingalimov, R. Kharisov, F. Shafigullin, M. Agliamov, and Zöl'fät but also new talent and boldness. Zöl'fät's poetry is perhaps the best measure of this boldness.

In his poem entitled *Tukay dogasï* (A Tukay prayer), Zöl'fät ponders the role of the artists and the role of the Tukays of every generation. Artists alone, it seems, can intercede with the future on behalf of their people and pray for a magic fountain of strength that will render the people equally immune to the devastation of water and fire:

> Yalvaralar alar kilächäkkä
> "Tilsim duäse bir khalkïma:
> Suga töshkäch—suda batmasachï
> Yanmasächi—kergech yalkïnga!"

> They beg the future:
> "Give my people a magic prayer
> [So that] they will not drown if they fall into the water
> [So that] they will not burn if they are caught in fire."

What is hidden behind Zöl'fät's metaphor is not an unqualified optimism in the bright communist future but an uncertainty that is tamed only by the hope that the artist can have an impact on the future of his people.

Zöl'fät's poem *Jeza* (The punishment) carries the subtitle "From the Journal of N Who Is on Board the Time Machine as Participant in the Expedition to the XXI Century Organized in the Year of the Swine." As the expedition is about to begin, the "Child of Dreams" participating in it is urged to say a prayer or cross himself. Zöl'fät's choice of word for "prayer" is worth noting: It is *Bismillah*, the Muslim recitation "In the name of God," and as such, it places the prayer in as concrete a cultural setting as the meaning of the act of crossing oneself.[44] The message of the poem is twofold. First, there is the implication that in the twenty-first century prayer will not have lost its meaning. Second is the suggestion that the Year of the Swine—a cultural taboo for Muslims—does not exactly hold the promise for a bright twenty-first century. Hence, the need for prayer.

Zöl'fät may excel in the boldness of his metaphors and literary techniques, but his concerns are not unique. In the biographical novel *Ayle Tonnar* (Nights with moonlight), dedicated to the revolutionary Kh. Yamashev, A. Rasikh reiterates the importance of the unshakable bonds that must exist between the artist, the artist's nation, and the people whose ideals the artist must serve. N. Fattakh's novel *Itil suu aga turïr* (And thus flows the Volga), which brings to life the Bulgar period of Tatar history, was considered by Tatar critics, not an exercise in escapism, but "a search for answers to contemporary issues."[45] This comment indicates a discernment of specific attributes that have been forged in the course of history and an appreciation of the role they play in giving a distinct character to the ethnic consciousness of the Tatars and in determining their responses to the challenges of the society in which they live.

G. Bashir's 1967 novel *Tugan yagïm-yashel bishek* (My home is a green cradle) is a tribute to the beauty and endurance of Tatar national traditions and folk culture. Bashir's detailed descriptions of old Tatar customs were not appreciated by some official reviewers, who labeled the novel as an ethnographic novel and accused Bashir of mirasism. The adjective *ethnographic*, within the context of the criticism, represents a rather negative assessment of Bashir's efforts to reveal to his readers the richness of their traditions and culture. The initial negative assessment, which some reviewers gave Bashir's novel, was rendered meaningless by the numerous reviews and analyses that praised its contribution to the rediscovery of national traditions and culture. It is likely that these positive assessments more accurately represented the opinion of the majority of the intelligentsia and the population in general.[46]

One of the remarkable characteristics of the postwar Tatar cultural upsurge is the commitment of the native intelligentsia to the promotion of Tatar national culture and to the vital role that culture plays as a catalyst—as the conscience of the nation in encouraging the growth of a corporate sense and cultivating an ethos of distinctness. The roots of this cultural upsurge are historical; its thrust is essentially, but not exclusively, cultural; and its threshold of fulfillment implies claims of ancestral territory with ethnic homogeneity and cultural cohesiveness.

The first signs of an emerging militancy that is rooted in cultural as well as political concerns have come from Tatar *samizdat*, a development of the late 1970s. Until 1977, only the Crimean Tatars used samizdat as an alternative channel of communication to challenge the government monopoly on information and media. The three Volga Tatar samizdat documents that have reached the West were compiled in April 1977. One of the authors chose the pseudonym Kukshar, while two others chose to remain anonymous, indicating only the collective authorship of a group of Tatars for one document and twenty-six Tatars and Bashkirs for the other.

TABLE 7
ETHNIC COMPOSITION
OF THE POPULATION OF TATAR ASSR
BETWEEN 1926 AND 1970

Census Year	Total Population (thousands)	Tatars (%)	Russians (%)	Others (%)
1926	2,594	44.9	43.1	12.0
1939	2,915	48.8	42.9	8.3
1959	2,850	47.2	43.9	8.9
1970	3,131	49.1	42.4	8.5

SOURCE: V. I. Kozlov, *Natsional'nosti SSSR. Etnodemograficheskii obzor* (Moscow, 1975), p. 108.

The seeds of politicization that seem to have been sown into the soil of the Tatar cultural upsurge are easily identifiable in one of the documents in particular. Its authors seem to be aware, even if vaguely, of the existence of Sultangaliev and of his plans for a state that would have united the Turkic peoples of the Volga area. The platform from which the authors of this document spoke was clearly pan-Turkic as they called upon their countrymen: "Our task is clear: We have to fight, not fearing for our lives; we have to find, to raise those 'populists' who will have to carry the national consciousness to the people without fearing the consequences of whether their grandchildren and great-grandchildren will be Tatars or Bashkirs, Uzbeks or Kazakhs, etc., because Turks they will all have to be. Our task is to endure."[47] The same authors also expressed the hope that "the Turks [of the republic of Turkey] would not forget that they are our closest brothers."[48] The pan-Turkic solution these authors chose stemmed from their frustration with the Soviet government's discriminatory policies toward the languages and cultures of the Tatars and Bashkirs. The authors deplored the suppression of religious life and demanded that Russian-language examinations be dropped from the requirements for admission to institutes of higher education.

The issues of language and religion play a central role in the other two documents. The authors of these documents reacted against discriminatory programming by the Tatar and Bashkir television and radio stations: The audience was forced to listen to programs in Russian most of the day, including during prime time, thus reducing to tokenism the few hours of native-language programs scheduled and rendering them almost useless from the viewpoint of the promotion of national cultures.

The ubiquitousness of the issue of national language in all three documents provides further evidence on the relationship between language behavior and

TABLE 8
ETHNIC COMPOSITION
OF THE POPULATION OF BASHKIR ASSR
BETWEEN 1926 AND 1970

Census Year	Total Population (thousands)	Bashkirs (%)	Russians (%)	Others (%)
1926	2,695	23.7	39.8	36.5; of these, 17.1 Tatars
1939	3,159	21.2	40.6	38.2; of these, 24.6 Tatars
1959	3,340	22.1	42.4	35.5; of these, 23.0 Tatars
1970	3,818	23.4	40.5	36.1; of these, 24.7 Tatars

SOURCE: V. I. Kozlov, *Natsional'nosti SSSR. Etnodemograficheskii obzor* (Moscow, 1975), p. 109.

national consciousness and points to the complexity of the relationship between language ability, language preference, and language use, which is adequately illustrated by the fact that a 1967 survey indicated that even those 19.2 percent of the urban Tatars who claimed Russian as a native language used only Tatar at home, whereas only 27 percent of those rural Tatars who claimed to have a better command of Russian than Tatar used only Tatar at work and 55 percent used only Tatar at home.[49] (See tables 7, 8, and 9 for ethnic composition and linguistic data in general.)

The authors of the samizdat documents were equally vocal on the issue of official attitudes toward mixed marriages. They deplored the fact that the state encouraged mixed marriages between Russians and Tatars or Bashkirs by bestowing upon such couples favors that ranged from promotions to trips abroad.

An even angrier reaction was triggered by the disrespect with which Soviet officials treated cradles of Tatar culture, such as the former medrese Galiye, which had housed a Tatar school in the years after 1917 only to be converted in the 1970s into an asylum for retarded children.[50]

Mosques did not fare any better with the officials, and the author of the third document pointed to the fact that although Kazan had tens of well-maintained churches, its only standing mosque was in a deplorable state of disrepair. It was probably in response to these realities, and in hope of dissipating public dissatisfaction, that in April 1980, the government of TASSR adopted a decision that focused "On the situation and measures regarding the

TABLE 9

TATARS AND BASHKIRS LINGUISTIC DATA:
1959 AND 1970

ETHNIC GROUP	TOTAL POPULATION (THOUSANDS)		THOSE WHO DECLARED AS MOTHER TONGUE THE LANGUAGE OF THEIR NATIONALITY (IN % OF THE TOTAL POPULATION)		THOSE WHO IN 1970 WERE FLUENT IN OTHER LANGUAGES OF THE SOVIET UNION (IN % OF THE TOTAL POPULATION)	
	1959	1970	1959	1970	Russian	Other
Tatars	4,968	5,931	92.1	89.2	65.2	5.3
Bashkirs	989	1,240	61.9	66.2	53.3	2.6

SOURCE: *Naselenie SSSR (Chislennost', sostav i dvizhenie naseleniia). 1973. Statisticheskii Sbornik* (Moscow, 1975), p. 37.

continuing improvement of the protection, restoration, and use of the monuments of history and culture in TASSR."[51]

The authors of these samizdat documents exhibited an overt militancy that is understandably absent from the general picture of Tatar cultural and political life. Their centuries-old coexistence with the Russian state—whether in its Tsarist or Soviet form—seems to have taught the Tatars that the key to their survival is not only a strong commitment to their culture and traditions but also caution in pursuing this goal. As a result, the majority of the Tatars seem to have chosen to respond to the government policies that encourage sblizhenie and ultimately aim at sliianie, not by promoting militancy and secession, but by arguing that there could be unity in diversity. Tatar scholars come to the defense of this diversity by reminding the Tatar people of the continuity of their history and by pointing to the strong bonds that link them with bygone generations. Their message seems to be that Tatars today can better understand themselves by learning to understand their past and can remain themselves by maintaining an awareness of their past.

There is a poetic equivalent to this message rendered in the form of a Testament (a Tatar folk genre) a father leaves for his son during World War II. It reads:

> My son!
>
> Far away countries, far away lands, far away people—may you see all there is to see in this world, but—not what I have seen!
>
> The taste of honey, the taste of sweets, the taste of fruits, the taste of milk—may you taste them all in this world, but not what I have tasted!

My son!
Search for riches in forests and mountains, search for oil, search for metal and coal; search for pearls in the depths of waters, search for golden fish, . . . search for new moons, search for new suns—there are no secrets and mysteries in this world—search for them all, but first of all, do not forget our graves![52]

The realities of Tatar culture in the postwar period represent living proof of the fact that Tatars today have not forgotten the graves of their ancestors and that the unbroken link between their past and their present is the key to their survival as a people and to the vitality of their cultural resilience.

Conclusion

*Nations live only by the memories which bygone centuries left
in their souls and by their interaction with other peoples.*

*Narody zhivut lish' moguchimi vpechatleniami kotorye ostav-
liaiut v ikh dushe proteskishie veka, da obshcheniem s drugimi
narodami.*

(P. Ia. Chaadev, *Filosoficheskie pis'ma*
[Philosophical letters].)

The Volga Tatars became the earliest Muslim subjects of Muscovy after the
conquest of Kazan in 1552. The coercive administrative and socioeconomic
policies the Russian state adopted vis-à-vis the Muslim inorodtsy of the Volga-
Ural area between the sixteenth and twentieth centuries failed to bring about
wholesale russification. The overwhelming majority of Volga-Ural Muslims
rejected assimilation and engaged in a defense of their Islamic identity and
heritage.

Against the background of this precarious modus vivendi with the Russian
government, the Volga Tatars became the first Muslims of the Russian empire to
engage in a process of re-evaluation and reform that their traditional Islamic
values brought under scrutiny. Their contacts with Russian society, as well as
with Islamic centers throughout the world, gave further impetus to the movement of revival.

Their religious thinkers and the teachers provided the intellectual leadership for the Tatar reformist movement, while the bourgeoisie displayed a deep

sense of obligation toward the Tatar umma by becoming its financial supporter. What these several groups had in common was their remarkable continuity in Tatar history. The dynamism of the bourgeoisie was also a result of the capacity it displayed throughout the centuries to adapt itself to changing economic and social conditions. The bourgeoisie shared in the pride of all Tatars as heirs to those Turkic tribes that had enjoyed an early statehood in the khanates of Bulgar and Kazan.

Thinkers and teachers like A. Kursavi, Sh. Merjani, R. Fahreddin, and M. Bigi emphasized the urgency of ridding Russian Islam of scholasticism to revive its capacity to fulfill the changing needs of the umma. All Tatar reformers regarded secularism as an alternative view of man and society, coexisting with and not excluding a religious perception of the world. They stressed the importance of science, secular education, and emancipation of women for the advancement of the Tatar umma, while also pointing out the importance of learning Russian to be able to come out of isolation and achieve a cultural rapprochement with the Russian society.

The criticism to which the religious reformers subjected traditional Islam created a climate that was adequate for the first expressions of Tatar national identity in addition to, and not in lieu of, the Islamic identity. K. Nasiri's efforts at promoting a literary language based on the Tatar vernacular and M. Bigi's and Z. Kamali's projects for translating the Qur'an into Tatar were representative of this trend.

Jadidism owes at least its etymological beginnings to the search for a new method (usul-u-jadid) of teaching the Arabic alphabet. The introduction of the phonetic system, however, was only the first of a series of innovations that gave an increasingly secular and national character to Tatar mektebs and medreses. A common denominator for all Tatar reformers was the importance they attached to education. They valued the role of jadid mektebs and medreses in maintaining and reinforcing the religious and national identity of the Tatar children and viewed secular education as a major contribution of these schools to the revival of the Tatar umma.

The controversy that developed around the jadid schools polarized Tatar communities into two hostile camps that confronted each other on all levels of societal life. Jadidism, moreover, transcended the realm of education and came to symbolize the general effort of the Tatars to renew and improve all aspects of their life.

The thirst for secular knowledge, the rapid growth of book publishing and book trade at the beginning of the twentieth century, and the organization of secular societies in response to the cultural, social, and economic needs of the umma were still other dimensions of Tatar jadidism.

National identity and statehood were central issues in Y. Akchura's political essay, which laid the foundations of pan-Turkism. Ismail Bey Gasprali's design for a language to be understood by all Turkic peoples from the Volga to Kashgar was the linguistic counterpart of Akchura's political pan-Turkism. Yet by choosing to develop and promote their own dialect instead of adopting an all-Turkic language, the Volga Tatars exhibited boldness and confidence in their ability to assume the cultural and political leadership of Russian Muslims. At the beginning of the twentieth century, they realistically approached the issue of their relationship to the Russian state by deciding for cultural autonomy within the framework of the Russian state as an alternative to a pan-Turkic state.

Cultural autonomy, however, may have been the only realistic choice the Volga Tatars could make in politics. Not until the beginning of the twentieth century, had cultural jadidism matured enough to consider a political dimension to the life of the Volga Tatars. The events of 1905 only speeded up their entry into the political scene of the Russian state.

Although a dominant force at all Muslim congresses, the Volga Tatars proved incapable of organizing independent Muslim political parties because the traditions of their umma had fallen short of providing them with an apprenticeship in politics. Although committed to Muslim unity, the Volga Tatars may have hindered that unity by antagonizing other Muslim peoples of Russia by their monopoly of political activities. Political jadidism failed because it developed within the framework of a conflict between the moral commitment of the Tatar jadids to Islamic unity and the intellectual attraction they demonstrated to Western political ideas. The political experience of the Tatar umma was much too brief to provide the necessary time for a synthesis of the two sets of values into original political ideas at the level of Tatar communities; as a result, political jadidism remained elitist. It copied rather than created, and it never equaled the strength of religious and cultural reformism that had begun at the level of both village and city communities and had grown with the participation and support of the entire umma.

The legacy of cultural and religious reformism was the viable synthesis between secular and Islamic values that came to characterize the life of the Volga Tatars at all levels. The presence of jadid schools and Tatar teachers in the Kazakh steppes, Central Asia, and even China was proof of the fact that the legacy of Tatar jadidism transcended the boundaries of the Volga-Ural region.

The success of the Bolshevik revolutions of 1917 renewed the life of the left wing of political jadidism. Paradoxically, however, the emphasis on class consciousness that had been the left wing's dissenting point was no longer its most important concern. Tatar Communists, such as M. Sultangaliev and G. Ibragimov, became increasingly concerned with the future of their people, first as Tatars and only then as Communists. They accepted the value of the national consciousness, which had been one of the main achievements of cultural reformism, and in a defensive reaction to the centralizing tide spreading to the borderlands of the Soviet state from Moscow, they resurrected Akchura's idea of a state of all Turks in the form of the Republic of Turan advocated by Sultangaliev. They lost.

The demise of political jadidism in its national communist metamorphosis, however, added strength to cultural jadidism in the 1920s. And it was the legacy of cultural jadidism that prompted the Tatar Bolshevik G. Ibragimov to inquire in 1927, not what the future of the Tatar proletariat would be, but to ask: "Which Way Will Tatar Culture Go?"

The very deep sense of history and the remarkable security with which the Volga Tatars perceived their national identity were largely responsible for their cultural resilience in the postwar period. This resilience continues today. The creative approach of the Volga Tatars to Islam—true to the legacy of jadidism, their scholarship, literature, and their sociolinguistic behavior—seems to have answered rather clearly G. Ibragimov's rhetorical question. If anything, accomplishments and trends in these areas suggest the deep commitment of the Volga Tatars to their culture and national heritage. Their choice of biculturalism emerges not only as a means of survival but also as a means of reasserting a genuine cultural vitality. In addition, the isolated, but rather articulated, voices of Tatar samizdat reflect a level of intellectual sophistication and political awareness that make it possible to expect that political dynamism might become the extension of Tatar cultural vitality in the future.

APPENDIX

Volga Tatar and Bashkir Deputies to the First, Second, Third, and Fourth Dumas

FIRST DUMA

Total Muslim Deputies: 25
Volga Tatars and Bashkirs: 12

Akhtiamov, Abussugud abd-el-Kholikovich
Deputy from Ufa guberniia. Tatar. Born 1843. Constitutional Democrat (hereafter, KD). In 1871 graduated from the law school of the University of Kazan. Between 1871 and 1881, held special assignments for the governor of Ufa and was also a court investigator. Member of the zemstvo guberniia council and honorary justice of the peace. Between 1895 and 1901, secretary of the Muslim Ecclesiastical Council.

Alkin, Said-Girei Shagiakhmetovich
Deputy from Kazan guberniia. Tatar. Born 1867. KD. Graduated from the law school of the University of Kazan. Wealthy real estate owner, editor of the Tatar newspaper *Kazan Muhbiri.*

Badamshin, Gafir Serazetdinovich
Deputy from Kazan guberniia. Tatar. Born 1865. KD. Received traditional Muslim education. Peasant merchant.

Dzhanturin, Salim-Girei Seid-Khanovich
Deputy from Ufa guberniia. Tatar. Born 1864. KD. In 1889, graduated from the Mathematics and Physics Faculty of Moscow University. Between 1891 and 1894, justice of the peace for the Belebeev district; between 1894 and 1902, land captain for the same district; between 1903 and 1906, permanent member of the Ufa guberniia

zemstvo council. He also served three consecutive three-year terms as member of the district zemstvo.

Khuramshin, Yamaletdin Khuramshin

Bashkir. Born 1977. KD. Graduated from the Karamovo village medrese. Took the mullah examination at the Belebeev municipal public school. Mullah in the village of Karamovo.

Khusainov, Shamsutdin Khusaianovich

Deputy from Viatka guberniia. Tatar. No information on date of birth. KD. Peasant. Elementary education. Mullah.

Maksutov, Sahipzada Davletshin

Deputy from Ufa guberniia. Tatar. Born 1874. KD. Graduated from the medrese in Kazan; also attended the four-year Russo-Tatar school. In 1902, elected member of the district zemstvo and trustee of the zemstvo elementary school. Wealthy landowner and merchant.

Matinov, Shagisharif-Medet-Galievich

Deputy from Orenburg guberniia. Bashkir. Born 1856. KD. Received his education at the Muslim medrese in Kazan.

Mindubaev, Gaizakdaz Mindubaevich

Deputy from Kazan guberniia. Tatar. No information on date of birth. KD. Peasant.

Rameev, Muhamed-Zakir Muhamed Sadykovich

Deputy from Orenburg guberniia. Tatar. Born 1860. KD. Educated by private tutors; also attended Muslim schools and completed his education abroad. Owner of gold mines in the Urals. Representative of the goldmine owners to the Orenburg Fiscal Board. Publisher of the newspaper *Vaqt*.

Syrtlanov, Shakhaidar Shakhaidarovich

Deputy from Ufa guberniia. Bashkir. Born 1847. KD. Graduated from the Orenburg Cadet Corps. Upon graduation, served nine years in Turkestan. In 1874, retired from the army and returned to his estate in Belebeev. Member of the district and guberniia zemstvo. In 1876, elected honorary justice of the peace for the Belebeev district; in 1878, elected member of the guberniia zemstvo council. Between 1887 and 1891, president of the guberniia zemstvo council.

Tevkelev, Kutlu-Muhamed Batyrgireevich

Deputy from Ufa guberniia. Tatar. Born 1850. KD. Received his education in the Page Corps. Guard officer between 1870 and 1885. In 1881, elected member of the Belebeev district zemstvo and Ufa guberniia zemstvo; also, honorary justice of the peace for the Belebeev uezd. In 1886, elected marshal of the nobility for the same district; in 1891, elected member of the city Duma.

SOURCES:

M. M. Boiovich, *Chleny gosudarstvennoi dumy (Portrety i biografii). Pervyi sozyv. 1906–1911. Sessiia 27 IV–9 VIII 1906* (Moscow, 1906), pp. 109–10, 113, 116, 212, 214, 364, and 368–73.

Chleny pervoi gosudarstvennoi Dumy s portretami (Moscow, 1906), pp. 20, 28, 43, and 65–66.

Gosudarstvennaia Duma. Ukazatel' k stenograficheskim otchetam. 1906 god. Sessiia pervaia. Zasedaniia 1–38 (27 IV–4 VIII 1906) (St. Petersburg, 1907), pp. 25, 28, 50, 79, 82, 84, 104, 120, and 127–28.

V. A. Maksimov, ed., *Sbornik rechei deputatov gosudarstvennoi dumy I i II sozyva. Kniga pervaia.* (St. Petersburg, 1908), p. 284.

N. Pruzhanskii, ed., *Pervaia Rossiiskaia gosudarstvennaia duma* (St. Petersburg, 1906), pp. 46–47, 53, 57–58, 61–62, 64, 67–68, 129, 133, 139, and 146–47.

SECOND DUMA

Total Muslim Deputies: 35
Tatars and Bashkirs: 16

Atlasov, G. M.
Deputy from Samara guberniia. Tatar. Born 1876. Member of the Trudoviki faction. Mullah.

Badamshin, Gafir Serazetdinovich
Deputy from Kazan guberniia. Tatar. Born 1865. Member of the Trudoviki faction. Also member of First Duma.

Biglov, M. A. M.
Deputy from Ufa guberniia. Tatar? Born 1871. Member of the Muslim faction. Graduated from the Page Corps. Landowner.

Khasanov, K. G.
Deputy from Ufa guberniia. Tatar. Born 1878. Member of the Trudoviki faction. Teacher.

Khasanov, M. S.
Deputy from Ufa guberniia. Tatar? Date of birth not listed. Member of the Muslim faction.

Kumvakov, Sh. A.
Deputy from Ufa guberniia. Tatar? Born 1849. Member of the Muslim faction. Secondary education. Graduated from the Kadet Corps.

Maksudov, Sadrutdin Nizamutdinovich

Deputy from Kazan guberniia. Tatar. Born 1879. Member of the Muslim Faction. Landowner, lawyer. Graduated from the Law Faculty of the Sorbonne University, Paris.

Maksiutov, S. D.

Deputy from Kazan guberniia. Tatar? Born 1859. Member of the Muslim faction. Medrese graduate. Mullah, landowner.

Massagutov, H. V. S.

Deputy from Viatka guberniia. Tatar. Born 1862. Member of the Trudoviki faction. Medrese graduate. Merchant.

Musin, Gumer

Deputy from Kazan guberniia. Tatar. Born 1854. Member of the Muslim faction. Mullah, landowner.

Nidzhemetdinov, Abdulla Aimatdinov

Deputy from Simbirsk guberniia. Tatar. Born 1869. Member of the Trudoviki faction. Graduated from Buinsk medrese; continued his studies in Bukhara and India. Mullah, landowner, and merchant.

Seifutdinov, Shahbal Sahautdinovich

Deputy from Orenburg guberniia. Bashkir. Born 1846. Member of the Muslim faction. Landowner.

Syrtlanov, Shakhaidar Shakhaidarovich

Deputy from Ufa guberniia. Bashkir. Born 1847. Member of the Muslim faction. Also deputy to the First Duma.

Tevkelev, Kutlu-Muhamed Batyrgireevich

Deputy from Ufa guberniia. Tatar. Born 1850. Muslim faction. Also deputy to the First Duma.

Tukaev, Muhammed-Shakir Muhamed Kharisovich

Deputy from Ufa guberniia. Bashkir. Born 1862. Member of the Muslim faction. Graduated from the medrese; also completed two years at the Orenburg Tatar Teachers' School. Landowner.

Usmanov, Hairullah Abdrahmanovich

Deputy from Orenburg guberniia. Tatar? Born 1866. Member of the Muslim faction. Graduated from medrese. Mullah.

SOURCES:
Chleny 2-oi godsudarstvennoi dumy. Biografii. Sravnitel'naia kharakteristika chlenov 1-oi i 2-oi dumy. Alfavitnyi ukazatel' (St. Petersburg, 1907), pp. 16, 29–30, 59, 75, 94, and 109–10.

Godsudarstvennaia Duma. Ukazatel' k stenograficheskim otchetam. Vtoroi sozyv. 1907 god. Zasedaniia 1–53. (20 fevralia–2 iiunia 1907) (St. Petersburg, 1907), pp. 4, 7, 9, 19–20, 24, 28, and 80.

THIRD DUMA

Total Muslim Deputies: 10
Tatars and Bashkirs: 7

Baiburin, Zigangir Nurgalievich
Deputy from Orenburg guberniia. Bashkir. Born 1852. Member of the Muslim faction. Completed four years of study at the medical school of Kazan University. Secretary of the Orenburg Muslim Benevolent Society.

Enikeev, Gaisa Khamidulovich
Deputy from Kazan guberniia. Tatar. Born 1864. Member of the Muslim faction. Secondary education. Teacher at the school for inorodtsy, employee of the State Bank, and director of a cloth factory. Also manager of the educational and charitable institution founded with capital from A. G. Khusainov.

Maksudov, Sadrutdin Nizamutdinovich
Deputy from Kazan guberniia. Tatar. Born 1879. Member of the Muslim faction. Also member of the Second Duma.

Mahmudov, Sharafutdin Zemelitdinovich
Deputy from Ufa guberniia. Bashkir. Born 1853. Member of the Muslim faction. Graduated from the Ufa Tatar Teachers' School. Teacher of Russian at the medrese.

Syrtlanov, Ali-Oskar Shakhaidarovich
Deputy from Ufa guberniia. Bashkir. Born 1865. Member of the Muslim faction. Son of First and Second Duma deputy Sh. Sh. Syrtlanov. Higher education. Reserve captain, assigned to the military court.

Tevkelev, Kutlu-Muhamed Batyrgireevich
Deputy from Ufa guberniia. Tatar. Born 1850. Muslim faction. Also deputy to the First and Second Dumas.

Tukaev, Muhamed-Shakir Muhamed Kharisovich

Deputy from Ufa guberniia. Bashkir. Born 1862. Member of the Muslim faction. Also deputy to the Second Duma.

SOURCES:

Gosudarstvennaia Duma. Ukazatel' k stenograficheskim otchetam. Chasti I–III. Tretii sozyv. Sessiia I. 1907–8 (St. Petersburg, 1908) pp. 63, 128, 187, 193, 262, 264, and 275.

FOURTH DUMA

Total Muslim Deputies: 7
Tatars and Bashkirs: 5

Akhtiamov, Ibniamin Abussugutovich

Deputy from Ufa guberniia. Tatar. Born 1877. Secretary of the Muslim faction. Son of lawyer and First Duma deputy, A. Akhtiamov, brother of Social Democrat I. Akhtiamov. Entered the Faculty of Physics and Mathematics of St. Petersburg University in 1878. In 1901, arrested and exiled to Ufa. In 1905, resumed his studies, and in 1910, graduated from St. Petersburg University with a degree in law. Lawyer for the Kazan district court.

Baiteriakov, Gabdullatif Khabibullich

Deputy from Ufa guberniia. Tatar. Born 1873. Member of the Muslim faction. Elementary education. Peasant from the village of Tashlykul, Ufa guberniia. *Volost'* elder and member of the district zemstvo council (1904–1907); from 1908 to 1913, in charge of military service obligations and also accountant for the volost' board.

Enikeev, Gaisa Khamidulovich

Deputy from Orenburg guberniia. Tatar. Born 1857. Member of the Muslim faction. Also deputy to the Third Duma.

Minnigaleev, Mingazetdin

Deputy from Samara guberniia. Tatar. Born 1857. Member of the Muslim faction. Traditional Muslim education. Peasant merchant in the village of Kakri-Elgi, Samara guberniia. Member of the zemstvo district council and president of the volost' court.

Tevkelev, Kutlu-Muhamed Batyrgireevich

Deputy from Ufa guberniia. Tatar. Born 1850. President of the Muslim faction. Also deputy to the First, Second, and Third Dumas.

SOURCES:

Gosudarstvennaia Duma. Ukazatel' k stenograficheskim otchetam. Chasti I–III. Chetver-tyi sozyv. Sessiia I. 1912–13. (St. Petersburg, 1913), pp. 22, 66, 103–4, 149, and 198.

N. N. Olshanskii, ed., *Chetvertaia Gosudarstvennaia Duma. Portrety i biografii.* (St. Petersburg, 1913), pp. 17, 19, 66, 124, and 193.

Glossary

Abïstay—wife of a mullah

Ädäbiyat—science of proper upbringing; in literature, it relates to belles lettres

Baskak—tax official of the Golden Horde who was also a military representative of the central government

Bays—wealthy Tatar merchants and landowners

Caravanserai—inn on a commercial route traveled by caravans

Daruga—civil officials of the Golden Horde who were in charge of the collection of taxes

Duma—State council, a parliamentary institution introduced in Russia in 1906; also a city council introduced in Russia after 1870

El-Islah—"The reform," a militant society of Tatar medrese students

Fatwa—opinion on an issue of Muslim canonic law

Fen kuvuji—science hunters, term used for certain Russian school inspectors

Fikh—Islamic jurisprudence

Galiye—superior level of the medrese

Golden Horde—the portion of Ginghis Khan's empire that included the Russian principalities, the Middle Volga, and the steppes west of the Volga

Gosplan—state planning commission

Guberniia—a province in the Russian empire

Gubkom—party guberniia committee

Hadith—corpus of sayings of the Prophet Muhammad

Harbi Shura—provisional military council under the control of Muslim Nationalists; tolerated by the Bolshevik government until April 1918

Ichki—insiders; most likely military stationed inside the fortress of Kazan proper

Iftar—festive dinner ending each day's fast during Ramadan

Ijma—principle in Islamic jurisprudence; legislating by consensus of those in the community who know Islamic dogma

Ijtihad—creative interpretation of the Islamic dogma

Ilytvar—title of nobility, probably meaning "ruler" among the Bulgars

Imam—head of the community and leader of the congregational prayer among the Sunnis

Iptidaye—elementary section of the medrese

Ishan—Sufi leader

ISKOMUS—Muslim central executive committee organized after the February Revolution

Islam—"submission," i.e., total submission to God

Ittifak-al Muslimin—The Union of Muslims, Muslim Liberal Party, which emerged in Russia after 1906

Jadid—proponent of the new method, reformer

Jadidism—movement of reform and intellectual renewal

Kalam—science of Islamic dialectics

Kalan—land tax in the Kazan khanate

Karachi—overseer, royal council in the Kazan khanate

Kazi—Muslim judge

Khan—head of state in a khanate

Komsomol—Communist Youth Organization

Korenizatsiia—indigenization

Kurultai—council, gathering of all leaders for legislative or other decision-making purposes; initially, a meeting of the clan leaders in the khanates

Mahkämä-i-Shargiia—the Islamic Religious Board

Mantiq—logic

Medrese—Muslim school of higher learning

Mekteb—Muslim primary school

Minbar—pulpit in a mosque

Miras—national heritage

Mirasism—pride in the national heritage

Mïrza (Murza)—hereditary Tatar noble

Muallim—Mekteb teacher

Muderris—teacher at the medrese

Mufti—head of the Muslim Ecclesiastical Council

Mullah—a member of the Muslim religious hierarchy, usually combining the duties of leader of the congregation and teacher

Muskom—central commissariat for Muslim affairs

Naqshbandi—Sufi brotherhood founded by Baha ed-din Naqshbandi in the fourteenth century

Narkomnats—People's Commissariat of Nationalities

Narkomvoen—People's Commissariat of War

Novokreshchennye—Tatars who converted to Christianity during the eighteenth century

Obkom—regional party committee

Pistsovye knigi—population registers and tax records

Podushnye—soul taxes

Qadimist—defender of the old method

Qufi—style of Arab calligraphy characterized by angular letters

Ramadan—the month of fasting

Raznochintsy—people of various ranks

Revvoensovet—revolutionary war council

Rushdiye—Muslim preparatory school

Saban—heavy plow used by the Bulgars

Sabantui—festival of the plow, now celebrated in May and June by the Volga Tatars

Samizdat—underground publications

Shakirds—medrese students

Shariat—the totality of Islamic laws that govern all aspects of life

Shiite—a follower of the fourth Caliph, Ali

Soiurghal—service people in the Middle Volga during the Golden Horde period

Sufism—Islamic mysticism

Sunna—body of traditions of the Islamic community consecrated by the Prophet's own example

Sunni—orthodox Muslim who adheres to the Sunna

Tafsir—commentaries on, and interpretations of, the Qur'an

Tamgachï—tax collector from among the Bulgars during the Golden Horde period

Taqlid—uncritical acceptance of the authority of the Islamic dogma and the adoption of precedents established by the ulama

Tariqat—Muslim mystic orders; path followed by the Sufis to achieve gnosis

Tarkhan—privileged nobility of the Kazan khanate; enjoyed hereditary land tenure

Thuluth—style of Arab calligraphy that evolved from the Qufi; it is less angular, more slender

Tufrakchïlar—those who favored territorial national autonomy

Turkchïlar—supporters of extraterritorial cultural autonomy

Tütün sanï—household tax

Ulama—Islamic scholars

Ulans—probably Tatar commanders of cavalry units who at times performed diplomatic services

Ulozhenie—Russian law code

Ulu Karachi—main overseer

Ulus—lands

Umma—community of believers

Usul-u fikh—jurisprudence

Usul-u savtiye—phonetic system

Waqf—pious foundation

Yanalif—Latin alphabet adopted for the Muslims of the Soviet Union between 1926 and 1937

Yarlyk—a charter, a patent of authority from the khan

Yasachnye—tributary peasants

Yatsy—fifth Muslim daily prayer

Yer khablasï—tax imposed on the sale of land

Yltyvar—ruler of the Bulgar state

Zakat—alms-tax, one of the principal obligations of Islam; offered on the day ending the month of fasting

ABBREVIATIONS

ChPGD	*Chleny pervoi gosudarstvennoi Dumy s portretami*
CMMC	*Central Muslim Military Collegium*
CMRS	*Cahiers du monde russe et soviétique*
ITASSR	*Istoriia Tatarskoi avtonomnoi sovetskoi sotsialisticheskoi respubliki*
ITDM	*Istoriia Tatarii v dokumentakh i materialakh*
KU	*Kazan Utларï*
PSRL	*Polnoe sobranie russkikh letopisei*
PSZRI	*Polnoe sobranie zakonov rossiiskoi imperii*
RLRB	*Radio Liberty Research Bulletin*
RMM	*Revue du monde musulman*
RN	*Revoliutsiia i natsional'nosti*
SA	*Sovetskaia arkheologiia*
SE	*Sovetskaia etnografiia*
SR	*Slavic Review*
SRMNP	*Sbornik rasporiazhenii po Ministerstvu Narodnogo Prosveshcheniia*
SV	*Sovetskoe vostokovedenie*
ZMNP	*Zhurnal Ministerstva Narodnogo Prosveshcheniia*

Notes

INTRODUCTION

1. *Naselenie SSSR. Po dannym vsesoiuznoi perepisi naseleniia 1979 goda* (Moscow, 1980); Ann Sheehy, "Data from the Census of 1979 on the Tatars and the Bashkirs," *RLRB*, July 15, 1980, pp. 2–4; Shirin Akiner, *Islamic Peoples of the Soviet Union* (London, Boston, Melbourne, and Henley, 1983), pp. 55–105.

2. E. Allworth, ed., *Soviet Nationality Problems* (New York, 1971); A. Bennigsen and Chantal Lemercier-Quelquejay, *Islam in the Soviet Union* (New York, 1967), *La presse et le mouvement national chez les musulmans de Russie avant 1920* (Paris, 1964), *Les mouvements nationaux chez les musulmans de Russie. Le "sultangalievisme" au Tatarstan* (Paris, 1960), and *Les musulmans oubliés. L'Islam en Union Soviétique* (Paris, 1981); A. Bennigsen and S. E. Wimbush, *Muslim National Communism in the Soviet Union: A Revolutionary Strategy for the Colonial World* (Chicago, 1979); H. Carrère d'Encausse, *L'empire éclaté: La révolte des nations en URSS* (Paris, 1978). T. Rakowska-Harmstone, *Russia and Nationalism in Central Asia. The Case of Tadzhikistan* (Baltimore and London, 1970); Michael Rywkin, *Moscow's Muslim Challenge. Soviet Central Asia* (New York, 1982); S. A. Zenkovsky, *Pan-Turkism and Islam in Russia* (Cambridge, Mass., 1960).

3. A. W. Fisher, *The Crimean Tatars* (Stanford, 1978).

4. A. Kh. Khalikov, *Proiskhozhdenie Tatar Povolzh'ia i Priural'ia* (Kazan, 1978); R. G. Fakhrutdinov, *Arkheologicheskie pamiatniki Volzhsko-Kamskoi Bulgarii i ee territorii* (Kazan, 1975); G. V. Iusupov, *Vvedenie v bulgaro-tatarskuiu epigrafiku* (Moscow and Leningrad, 1960); S. Kh. Alishev, "Prisoedinenie narodov Srednego Povolzh'ia k Russkomu gosudarstvu," in *Tatariia v proshlom i nastoiashchem. Sbornik statei* (Kazan, 1975), pp. 172–86; and *Tatary Srednego Povolzh'ia v Pugachevskom vosstanii* (Kazan, 1973); A. G. Karimullin, *U istokov Tatarskoi knigi* (Kazan, 1971) and *Tatarskaia kniga*

nachala XX veka (Kazan, 1974); Ia. G. Abdullin, *Tatarskaia prosvetitel'skaia mysl'* (Kazan, 1976); Kh. Kh. Khasanov, *Formirovanie Tatarskoi burzhuaznoi natsii* (Kazan, 1977).

5. The use of the terms *ethnogenesis* and *ethnonym* is not limited to Soviet scholarship. The most recent illustration of their use in Western scholarship is in Andreas Kappeler, *Russlands Erste Nationalitäten: Das Zarenreich und die Völker der Mittleren Wolga vom 16 bis 19 Jahrhundert* (Vienna, 1982), pp. 18–20 and 84–87.

CHAPTER 1

1. A. Kh. Khalikov adds to these two groups yet a third one, the Kriashens—the Christian Tatars. Linguistic and ethnogenetic criteria place them very close to the Kazan Tatars, thus rendering superfluous a category based solely on the religious criterion. A. Kh. Khalikov, *Proiskhozhdenie Tatar Povolzh'ia i Priural'ia* (Kazan, 1978), pp. 13–15.

2. As quoted by Ahmet Temir from an 1885–1900 edition of Sh. Merjani's *Mustafad al-Akhbar fi-l-Ahwal Qazan wa Bulgar*, in Ahmet Temir, "Tatar sözünün menşei hakkında," *Kazan* 3 (1971): 43.

3. Giuzel' Amalrik, *Vospominaniia o moem detstve* (Amsterdam, 1976), pp. 103 and 107.

4. See R. H. Mathews, *A Chinese-English Dictionary Compiled for the China Inland Mission* (Shanghai and Cambridge, 1969), p. 853. For a discussion of the name *Tatar*, see also A. Vambery, "The Awakening of the Tatars," *The Nineteenth Century* 54 (February 1905): 217.

5. V. Thomsen, *Inscriptions de l'Orkhon* (Helsingfors, 1896), pp. 140–41; Carl Brockelmann, *History of the Islamic Peoples* (London, 1979), pp. 163–64; W. Barthold, "Tatar," in *Enzyklopedie des Islam*, vol. 4 (Leiden and Leipzig, 1934), pp. 759–61. On Bartol'd's interest in the history and culture of the Volga Tatars, see Mokhammät Mähdiev, "Rus orientalistlariining eshchänlege häm tatar vakïtlï matbugatï," *KU* 3 (1980): 173–74.

6. Brockelmann, *History of the Islamic Peoples*, p. 29; for a detailed account of the Mongol Tatars, see *Men-da bei lu (Polnoe opisanie mongolo-tatar)* (Moscow, 1975).

7. Khalikov, *Proiskhozhdenie Tatar*, p. 59; R. G. Kuzeev, *Proiskhozhdenie Bashkirskogo naroda. Etnicheskii sostav. Istoriia rasseleniia* (Moscow, 1974), pp. 170–74. In his analysis of the terms *Tiurk*, *Tiurkskii* (Turkic), A. N. Kononov draws a sharp line between the ethnic and political concepts behind the term and concludes that *Tiurk* stands for a political concept. It is a "collective name designating a union of warring tribes." A. N. Kononov, "Opyt analiza termina 'tiurk,'" *SE* 1 (1949): 40–47.

8. *ITASSR*, vol. 1 (Kazan, 1955), p. 73.

9. Khalikov quotes from Plano Carpini's travel notes in *Proiskhozhdenie Tatar*, pp. 82–83; on Carpini's travels, also see N. P. Shastina, *Puteshestvie na Vostok Plano Karpini i Gil'oma Rubruka* (Moscow, 1957); Gil'om Rubruk is Guillaume de Rubriquis

(Willem van Ruysbroeck), the envoy of Louis II of France to Mangu Khan; Ebulgazi Bahadir Han, *Histoire des Mongols et des Tatares* (St. Petersburg, 1871–1874; St. Leonards, 1970).

10. A. Kh. Khalikov, "Kazanskoe khanstvo," in *ITASSR* (Kazan, 1973), p. 29. On adoption of the name *Tatar* by the peoples of the Golden Horde, see A. P. Smirnov, "K voprosu o proiskhozhdenii Tatar Povolzh'ia," *SE* 3 (1946): 43.

11. For reference to this dictionary, see Muhtar Tevfikoğlu, "Ali Emir Efendi," *Türk Kültürü* 8 (1970): 244–52; Rifat Bilge Kilisli, "Divanu Lugat it-Turk ve Emiri Efendi," *Türk Kültürü* 8 (1970): 253–70; M. Şakir Ulkutasir, *Kaşgarlı Mahmut* (Istanbul, 1946); Kh. Kh. Khasanov, *Makhmud Kashghariy. (Khaeti vä geografik merasi)* (Tashkent, 1963); S. M. Mutallibov, ed., *Mahmud Kashghariy: Törkiy süzler devani (Devanu lughat it-Turk)* (Tashkent, 1960).

12. Ahmet Temir, "Tatar sozünün menşei hakkında," *Kazan* 3 (1971): 44 and "Türk-moğol imparatorluğu devrinde askeri teşkilat," *Kazan* 7–8 (1972): 7–24; also see Akdes Nimet Kurat, "Malazgirt zaferi sıralarında Idil boyu ve Karadeniz'in kuzeyindeki Türk kavimleri," *Kazan* 7–8 (1972): 2.

13. Khalikov, *Proiskhozhdenie Tatar*, pp. 108–9.

14. A concise discussion of the main theses advanced by Russian/Soviet scholars until 1976 has been provided by A. Kappeler, "L'Ethnogenèse des peuples de la Moyenne-Volga (Tatars Tchouvaches, Mordves, Maris, Oudmourtes) dans les recherches soviétiques," *CMRS* 2–3 (April–September 1976): 311–34.

15. S. M. Solov'ev, *Istoriia Rossii s drevneishikh vremen*, 15 vols. (Moscow, 1959–1965); G. I. Peretiatkovich, *Povolzh'e v XV i XVI vekakh (Ocherki iz istorii kraia i ego kolonizatsii)* (Moscow, 1877); N. I. Ashmarin, *Bolgary i Chuvashi* (Kazan, 1902); A. Zeki Velidi-Togan, *Türk ve Tatar tarihi* (Kazan, 1912); Abdullah Battal-Taymas, *Kazan Türkleri: Türk tarihinin hazin yaprakları* (Ankara, 1966).

16. A. Kh. Khalikov, "K voprosu o nachale tiurkizatsii naseleniia Povolzh'ia i Pruiral'ia," *SE* 1 (1972): 100–110; P. V. Golubovskii, *Pechenegi, polovtsy i tiurki do nashestviia tatar* (Kiev, 1884).

17. Of the prerevolutionary scholars, I. Berezin's contribution should be noted: I. Berezin, "Bulgary na Volge. S risunkami Bulgarskikh drevnostei i nadpisei," in *Uchenye zapiski Imperatorskogo Kazanskogo Universiteta*, vol. 3 (Kazan, 1853). Among Soviet scholars, the most active and prolific on this issue is A. Kh. Khalikov; in addition to the works already cited, his following works are particularly relevant: *Tatar khalkïnïng kilep chïgïshï* (Kazan, 1974); "Istoki formirovaniia turkoiazychnykh narodov Srednego Povolzh'ia i Priural'ia," in *Voprosy etnogeneza tiurkoiazychnykh narodov Srednego Povolzh'ia i Priural'ia* (Kazan, 1971), pp. 1–18; and "Kazan tatarlarïnïng kilep chiguïna karata," *Sotsialistik Tatarstan* 155 (July 3, 1966): 4.

18. Noted by A. Kappeler, *Russlands Erste Nationalitäten: Das Zarenreich und die Völker der Mittleren Wolga vom 16 bis 19 Jahrhundert* (Vienna, 1982), p. 320.

19. Firsov's book is still widely used: N. N. Firsov, *Proshloe Tatarii* (Kazan, 1926).

20. G. Gubaidullin, *Tatarlarnïng kilep chiguvï häm Altïn Urda* (Kazan, 1924), *Tatar Tarihi* (Kazan, 1923), *Burungu Bulgarlar* (Kazan, 1927), and "Iz proshlogo Tatar," in

Materialy po izucheniiu Tatarstana, vol. 2 (Kazan, 1925), pp. 71–111; S. Alishev, "Gaziz Gubaidullin kak istorik," in *Issledovaniia po istoriografii Tatarii* (Kazan, 1978), pp. 46–54.

21. V. F. Smolin, *K voprosu o proiskhozhdenii Kamsko-Volzhskikh Bolgar. Razbor drevneishikh teorii* (Kazan, 1921); A. Rakhim, *Materialy dlia bibliografii po tatarovedeniiu (1918–1930)* (Kazan, 1930); Sh. F. Mokhammed'iarov, *Osnovnye etapy proiskhozhdeniia i etnicheskoi istorii tatarskoi narodnosti* (Moscow, 1968).

22. The papers delivered at the June 1946 session of the Academy of Science were published in *SE* 3 (Fall 1946). See A. P. Smirnov, "K voprosu o proiskhozhdenii Kazanskikh Tatar po dannym etnografii," pp. 75–86; T. A. Trofimova, "Etnogenez Tatar Srednego Povolzh'ia v svete dannykh antropologii," pp. 51–74; L. Z. Zaliai, "K voprosu o proiskhozhdenii Tatar Povolzh'ia (po materialam iazyka)," pp. 87–91. The following works should also be noted: A. P. Smirnov, *Volzhskie Bolgary* (Moscow, 1951) and *Nekotorye voprosy srednevekovoi istorii Povolzh'ia* (Kazan, 1957); N. I. Vorob'ev, *Kazanskie Tatary. Etnograficheskoe issledovanie material'noi kul'tury do-oktiabr'skogo perioda* (Kazan, 1953); T. A. Trofimova, *Etnogenez Tatar Povolzh'ia v svete dannykh antropologii* (Moscow and Leningrad, 1949); and K. A. Smirnov, *Velikie Bolgary* (Moscow, 1960).

23. F. Kh. Valeev, *Drevnee i srednevekovoe iskusstvo Srednego Povolzh'ia* (Ioshkar-Ola, 1975); Ia. G. Abdullin, "Rukhi asïlïbïz," *KU* 6 (1980): 150–56. Khalikov's works have been cited in previous notes.

24. Mirkassyïm Gosmanov, "Tarikhlïk fänneng zaruri taläbe," *KU* 4 (1976): 178–83; and "Yanga säkhifälär achïla," *KU* 10 (1980): 150–58. On the role the Kypchaks played in the ethnogenesis of the Bashkirs, see Kuzeev, *Proiskhozhdenie Bashkirskogo naroda*.

25. M. Z. Zäkiev, *Tatar khalïk teleneng barlïkka kilue* (Kazan, 1977); V. Khakov, "Katlaulï mäs'älälärne khal itu yulïnda," *KU* 11 (1978): 169–74.

CHAPTER 2

1. A. Kh. Khalikov, *Proiskhozhdenie Tatar Povolzh'ia i Pruiral'ia* (Kazan, 1978), p. 52. For an account of the very early history of the Bulgar lands also see his *Volgo-Kam'e v nachale epokhi rannego zheleza. VIII–VI v.v. do n.e.* (Moscow, 1977) and *Arkheologiia i etnografiia Tatarstana* (Kazan, 1976) and, with V. F. Genning, *Rannie Bolgary na Volge: Bol'she Tarkhanskii mogil'nik* (Moscow, 1964). For other accounts of the history of the Bulgar state, see A. P. Smirnov, *Volzhskie Bolgary* (Moscow, 1951) and "Nekotorye spornye voprosy istorii Volzhskikh Bolgar," in *Istoriko-arkheologicheskii sbornik k 60-letiiu A. V. Artsikhovskogo* (Moscow, 1962), pp. 160–74; and A. Zabiri, *Kïskacha tarih-i Bolghar* (Kazan, 1907).

2. A. P. Kovalevskii, ed., *Kniga Akhmeda Ibn-Fadlana i ego puteshestvie na Volgu v 921–922g. Stat'i, perevody i komentarii* (Kharkov, 1956), p. 131. There is an earlier edition of Ibn-Fadlan's work: I. Iu. Krachkovskii, ed., *Puteshestvie Ibn-Fadlana na Volgu* (Moscow and Leningrad, 1939); Kovalevskii also produced a monograph based

on Ibn-Fadlan's travelogue: *Chuvashi i bulgary po dannym Akhmeda Ibn-Fadlana* (Cheboksary, 1954). On the issue of historical topography, see A. Iu. Iakubovskii, "K voprosu ob istoricheskoi topografii Itilia i Bolgar v IX i X vekakh," *SA* 10 (1948): 255–70.

3. A. Kh. Khalikov, *Proiskhozhdenie Tatar*, pp. 56–57 and 63.

4. M. V. Fekhner, *Velikie Bulgary. Kazan'. Sviazhsk* (Moscow, 1978), p. 8; B. D. Grekov, "Volzhskie Bolgary v IX–X vekakh," in *Istoricheskie zapiski*, vol. 14 (Moscow, 1945), pp. 3–37; B. D. Grekov and N. F. Kalinin, "Bulgarskoe gosudarstvo do mongol'skogo zavoevaniia," in *Materialy po istorii Tatarii* (Kazan, 1948), pp. 97–184.

5. Kovalevskii, *Kniga Akhmeda Ibn-Fadlana*, pp. 13 and 160.

6. Ibid., p. 138.

7. Dinä Välieva, "Bolgar sängate säkhifälärennän," *KU* 1 (1977): 139; for Ibn Rusta's account, see D. A. Khvol'son, ed., *Isvestiia o Khozarakh, Burtashakh, Bolgarakh, Mad'iarakh, Slavianakh i Russakh Abu-Ali Akhmeda Ben Omar Ibn-Dasta, neizvestnogo dosele arabskogo pisatelia nachala X veka, po rukopisi Britanskogo Muzeia v pervyi raz izdal, perevel i ob'iasnil D. A. Khvol'son* (St. Petersburg, 1869).

8. *ITASSR* (Kazan, 1973), p. 18.

9. Fekhner, *Velikie Bulgary*, p. 9; Kovalevskii, *Kniga Akhmeda Ibn-Fadlana*, p. 140.

10. Kovalevskii, *Kniga Akhmeda Ibn-Fadlana*, p. 140.

11. Ibid.

12. Ibid.

13. Khalikov, *Proiskhozhdenie Tatar*, pp. 66–67.

14. *ITASSR* (1973), p. 19.

15. Kovalevskii, *Kniga Akhmeda Ibn-Fadlana*, pp. 131 and 136.

16. Ibid., pp. 140–41.

17. Fekhner, *Velikie Bulgary*, p. 9.

18. Änäs Khälid, "Äbu Khämid el-Garnatyiniñ Bolgarga säyakhäte. Säyakhätche häm aniñ äsärläre, *KU* 6 (1976): 153. Garnati's first trip took place in 1135 and 1136, when he spent a year among the Bulgars; in 1150, he stopped briefly in Bulgar on his way to the lands on the Danube. For an analysis of his trip, as well as a Tatar translation of an excerpt from Garnati's travel notes, see the Änäs Khälid article mentioned above, pp. 148–58. For other editions of Garnati's travelogue, see O. G. Bolshakov and A. L. Mongait, eds., *Puteshestvie Abu Khamida al-Garnati v Vostochnuiu i Tsentral'nuiu Evropu (1131–1153)* (Moscow, 1971); G. Ferrand, ed., *Le Tukfat al-albāb de Abū, Hamid al-Andalusī al-Garnatī édité d'après les Mss. 2167, 2168, 2170 de la bibliothèque nationale et le Ms. d'Alger* (Paris, 1925).

19. Khalikov, *Proiskhozhdenie Tatar*, p. 69.

20. A. Battal, "Kazan Türkleri," in *Türk ili* (Istanbul, 1928), p. 616; N. Asim, *Türk tarihi* (Istanbul, 1898), pp. 157–200. The date of N. Asim's book is given according to the Muslim lunar calendar. Its equivalent in the Christian (Gregorian) calendar would be 1898. For synchronic charts of the Muslim and Christian years, see Faik Reşit Unat, *Hicri tarihleri miladi tarihe çevirme kılavuzu* (Ankara, 1959), p. 88.

21. *ITASSR* (1973), p. 16.

22. Khalikov, *Proiskhozhdenie Tatar*, p. 79.

23. Välieva, "Bolgar sängate säkhifälärennän," p. 140.

24. *ITASSR* (1973), p. 16.

25. Samples of household objects and tools used by the Bulgars are contained in the collection of more than a hundred iron objects that were discovered in 1971 in the Kuibyshev region of the Tatar republic; see Khalikov, *Proiskhozhdenie Tatar*, p. 80. On architectural and epigraphic evidence concerning Bulgar history, also see I. Berezin, "Bulgar na Volge. S risunkami Bulgarskikh drevnostei i nadpisei," in *Uchenye zapiski Imperatorskogo Kazanskogo Universiteta*, vol. 3 (Kazan, 1852), pp. 74–160, and I. Kazakov, *Pamiatniki Bolgarskogo vremeni v vostochnykh raionakh Tatarii* (Moscow, 1978).

26. A. Kh. Khalikov, *ITASSR* (1973), p. 17. The architecture and the beautiful baths of the city of Bulgar impressed other travelers, such as Ibn Haukil (tenth century), Shehabeddin-abu-Abdullah Yakut-et-Himavi (1184–1229), Ismail abu-l-Fida (1273–1331), Zekeriya-ibn-Muhammad-el-Kazvini (d. 1283), and ibn Batuta (1304–1377). The ruins that stand today on the site of Bulgar reveal vestiges of stone-paved streets, water pipes, and stone buildings of the ninth and tenth centuries. See "Büyük Bulgar şehri ve onun tarihi hakkında," *Kazan* 7–8 (1972): 4–5. For the history of Bulgar, see also K. F. Fuks, *Kratkaia istoriia goroda Kazani* (Kazan, 1817). Born in Germany, Karl Fuks (1776–1846), attended the Nassau Academy and Marburg University, from which he graduated in 1798 with a degree in medical sciences. In 1805, he traveled to Russia, where he had been appointed a professor of botany and natural sciences at the newly opened Kazan University. Fuks, who never returned to Germany, died in Kazan at the age of 70. He had married a Russian woman, the poetess A. A. Apekhtina, and throughout their lives they took a deep interest in both the academic life of the university and the ethnography and economic and social life of the region. Students of Tatar culture are especially indebted to Fuks for his studies of Tatar ethnographic history. For more biographic data on Fuks, see M. V. Kazanskii, *Putevoditel' po Kazani* (Kazan, 1899), pp. 207–8.

27. Khalikov, *Proiskhozhdenie Tatar*, p. 78; *ITASSR* (1973), p. 18.

28. N. N. Firsov, "Nekotorye cherty iz istorii torgovo-promyshlennoi zhizni Povolzh'ia (s drevneishikh vremen do osmotra etogo kraia imperatritsei Ekaterinoi II-oi)," in *Izvestiia Obshchestva Arkheologii, Istorii i Etnografii pri Imperatorskom Kazanskom Universitete*, vol. 14 (Kazan, 1897), part 1, p. 481; P. Savel'ev, "O torgovle Volzhskikh Bulgar," in *ZMNP* (St. Petersburg, 1846), p. 32.

29. Fekhner, *Velikie Bulgary*, p. 10.

30. *ITASSR* (1973), p. 17; Khalikov, *Proiskhozhdenie Tatar*, p. 69; Fekhner, *Velikie Bulgary*, p. 10.

31. For an excellent account of the written culture of the Bulgars, see Gamir Dauletshin, "Bolgar yazma kul'turasy," *KU* 3 (1980): 176–80; also see Kh. R. Kurbatov, *Tatar alfavity häm orfografiyäse tarikhï* (Kazan, 1960); and G. V. Iusupov, *Vvedenie v bulgaro-tatarskuiu epigrafiku* (Moscow and Leningrad, 1960).

32. Ahmet Temir, "Kuzey Türk ebediyatı," in *Turk Dünyası El Kitabı*, vol. 1 (Ankara, 1976), pp. 505–6.

33. Nurmokhammat Khisamov, "Ädäbiyatka tarikhi karash," *KU* 1 (1981): 184; Mirkassyim Gosmanov, "Yanga säkhifälär achïla," *KU* 10 (1980): 155–58. Also see Khisamov's monograph *"Kyssa-i Yusuf" Kul' Ali. Analiz istoricheskogo siuzheta i avtorskogo tvorchestva* (Moscow, 1979).

34. S. M. Solov'ev, *Istoriia Rossii s drevneishikh vremen*, vol. 5–6 (Moscow, 1959–1965), p. 476.

CHAPTER 3

1. B. Spuler, ed., *The Muslim World. The Mongol Period*, part 3 (Leiden, 1960), p. 7, and *History of the Mongols Based on Eastern and Western Accounts of the Thirteenth and Fourteenth Centuries* (Berkeley and Los Angeles, 1972), p. 52; *ITASSR* (Kazan, 1973), p. 23; A. N. Kurat, "Altın Ordu devleti," in *Türk Dünyası El Kitabı*, vol. 2 (Ankara, 1976), p. 929.

2. R. G. Fakhrutdinov, *Arkheologicheskie pamiatniki Volzhsko-Kamskoi Bulgarii i ee territorii* (Kazan, 1975), p. 50; F. V. Ballod, *Privolzhskie Pompei* (Moscow and St. Petersburg, 1923).

3. Spuler, *Muslim World*, pp. 12–14.

4. A. N. Kurat, "Altın Ordu kaganlığı," in *IV–XVIII yüzyıllarında Karadenizin kuzeyindeki Türk kavimleri ve devletleri* (Ankara, 1972), pp. 119–52.

5. A. G. Mukhamadiev, "Bulgaro-Tatarskaia monetnaia sistema serediny 13v," in *Issledovaniia po istoriografii Tatarii* (Kazan, 1978), pp. 126–31.

6. Those who settled among the Bashkirs are considered the ancestors of the Teptiars. For a discussion of their ethnogenesis, see G. N. Akhmarov, "Teptiari i ikh proiskhozhdenie," *Izvestiia obshchestva arkheologii, istorii i etnografii pri Kazanskom universitete* 28 (1908): 340–64; R. G. Kuzeev, *Istoricheskaia etnografiia Bashkirskogo naroda* (Ufa, 1978); and A. Kh. Khalikov, "Obshchie protsessy v etnogeneze Bashkir i Tatar Povolzh'ia i Priural'ia," in *Arkheologiia i etnografiia Bashkirii*, vol. 4 (Ufa, 1971), pp. 30–37.

7. In Khalikov's definition of *anthropological purity*, interaction with various local Finnic and Turkic tribes is acceptable although any Mongol contribution to the ethnic processes of the area is ruled out. A. Kh. Khalikov, *Proiskhozhdenie Tatar Povolzhia i Priural'ia* (Kazan, 1978), pp. 98–99. A similar position is held by Kalinin, who argues that the Bulgar settlers mixed with the local population and set in motion the ethnogenetic process that was to result in the emergence of the Kazan Tatars and to which the Mongols made no contribution. N. F. Kalinin, *Kazan. Istoricheskii ocherk* (Kazan, 1952), p. 23.

8. *ITASSR* (1973), p. 28.

9. Kazan, or Iski-Kazan (old Kazan), emerged around 1238 to 1240. However,

because present-day Kazan is located at a distance of 45 km. from Iski-Kazan, this date is not valid as the date of its foundation. M. V. Fekhner, *Velikie Bulgary. Kazan'. Sviazhsk* (Moscow, 1978), p. 11.

10. V. G. Tizengauzen [Tiesenhausen], ed., *Sbornik materialov otnosiashchikhsia k istorii Zolotoi Ordy*, vol. 2 (Moscow and Leningrad, 1941), pp. 34–36.

11. *ITASSR* (1973), p. 23. On the vassal status of the Bulgar emirs, see G. V. Iusupov, *Vvedenie v bulgaro–tatarskuiu epigrafiku* (Moscow and Leningrad, 1960), pp. 102–3, and G. V. Vernadsky, *Zolotaia Orda. Egipet i Vizantiia v ikh vzaimo-otnosheniiakh v tsarstvovanie Mikhaila Paleologa* (Prague, 1927).

12. The khans had their winter residences in Gulistan, a suburb of Saray. During the summer, they moved to the country, setting up their tents on the open plains to the north. It was probably this practice that was responsible for the entrenchment of the belief that the capital of the Golden Horde was a tent city. Kurat, "Altin Ordu devleti," p. 930.

13. G. A. Fedorov-Davydov, *Obshchestvennyi stroi Zolotoi Ordy* (Moscow, 1973), pp. 25–32.

14. A. Battal, *Tatar tahiri. Qazan Türkleri. Tarihi ve siyasi görüshler* (Istanbul, 1925), pp. 20–27; I. Berezin, "Ocherk vnutrennego ustroistva Ulusa Dzhuchieva," in *Trudy Otdeleniia Imperatorskogo Russkogo Arkheologicheskogo Obshchestva*, part 8 (St. Petersburg, 1864), pp. 387–494.

15. For a discussion of political and administrative practices of the early Turkic state formations in order to identify their influence on the Mongols, see L. N. Gumilev, "Udel'no-lestvichnaia sistema u tiurok v VI–VII vekakh. K voprosu o rannikh for-makh gosudarstvennosti," *SE* 3 (1959): 11–16. For a discussion of the impact of Mongol rule on the nomadic peoples, see G. A. Fedorov-Davydov, *Kochevniki Vostochnoi Evropy pod vlast'iu zoloto-ordynskikh khanov. Arkheologicheskie pamiatniki* (Moscow, 1966).

16. *ITASSR* (1973), p. 25.

17. Spuler, *The Muslim World*, p. 48; Davydov, *Obshchestvennyi stroi*, pp. 25–32. According to Bartol'd, darugas were military governors; see V. V. Bartol'd, *Raboty po istorii i filologii tiurkskikh i mongol'skikh narodov. Sochineniia*, vol. 5 (Moscow, 1963–1968), p. 529.

18. R. G. Fakhrutdinov, "Posledstviia Mongol'skogo zavoevaniia v Volzhskoi Bul-garii," in *Issledovaniia po istorii Tatarii* (Kazan, 1978), p. 122.

19. *ITASSR* (1973), p. 24; I. P. Petrushevskii, "K istorii soiurgala," *SV* 6 (1949): 227–47.

20. Kurat, "Altın Ordu Kaganlığı," p. 931. For a discussion of the term and concept of *tarkhan*, see V. V. Bartol'd, *Sochineniia*, pp. 182, 284, and 599.

21. The elaborate burial monument erected in 1307 for a jeweler named Shakhidulla, and later discovered in the cemetery of Bulgar, suggests that some craftsmen had joined the notables of their communities. See *ITASSR* (1973), pp. 25–26.

22. Fakhrutdinov, *Arkheologicheskie pamiatniki*, p. 123. Based on the size of the

mosques, Berezin estimated the size of the population of Bulgar to have been around 50,000. See I. Berezin, "Bulgar na Volge. S risunkami Bulgarskikh drevnostei i nadpisei," in *Uchenye zapiski Imperatorskogo Kazanskogo Universiteta* (Kazan, 1852), part 3, pp. 74–126; Mukhamadiev, "Bulgaro-Tatarskaia monetnaia sistema," pp. 133–39.

23. Khalikov, *Proiskhozhdenie Tatar*, pp. 101–4. For a detailed analysis of the disintegration of the Golden Horde, see B. D. Grekov and A. Iu. Iakubovskii, *Zolotaia Orda i ee padenie* (Moscow and Leningrad, 1950).

CHAPTER 4

1. Despite the fact that most scholars accept 1177 as the year of its birth, the date of the founding of the city-fortress of Kazan is also a subject of debate. For a discussion of the old and new hypotheses, see A. Kh. Khalikov, "Kazan kaychan häm kaydan bashlagan kitken," *KU* 8 (1976): 137–44; and *Ukazatel' dlia puteshestviia ego Imperatorskago Vysochestva Nikolaia Maksimilianovicha kniazia Romanovskogo, gertsoga Leikhtenbergskago na Ural'skii khrebet. 1866.*, vol. 2 (St. Petersburg, 1866), Manuscript, University of Wisconsin Manuscript Collection, MS 115, p. 436.

2. Evidence provided by Moiseeva's sixteenth-century Russian chronicle *Kazanskaia istoriia* and by such historians as M. G. Safargaliev and A. Temir supports the earlier-date theory, whereas V. Veliaminov-Zernov, N. F. Kalinin, A. Khalikov, B. Nolde, and others view 1445 as the date of the founding of the Kazan khanate. See G. N. Moiseeva, ed., *Kazanskaia istoriia* (Moscow and Leningrad, 1954), pp. 52–54; M. G. Safargaliev, *Raspad Zolotoi Ordy. Uchenye zapiski Mordovskogo Gosudarstvennogo Universiteta. Vypusk XI* (Saransk, 1960), pp. 244–56; Ahmet Temir, "Kazan Hanlığı," in *Türk Dünyası El Kitabı*, vol. 2 (Ankara, 1976), p. 933; V. Veliaminov-Zernov, *Izsledovanie o Kasimovskikh tsariakh i tsarevichakh*, vol. 1 (St. Petersburg, 1863), pp. 3–13; N. F. Kalinin, *Kazan. Istoricheskii ocherk* (Kazan, 1952), p. 27; A. Kh. Khalikov, "Kazanskoe khanstvo," in *ITASSR* (Kazan, 1973), p. 28; and B. Nolde, *La formation de l'empire russe. Etudes, notes et documents*, vol. 1 (Paris, 1952), p. 2. Pelenski offers the most original approach to this question, proposing that the formation of the Kazan khanate be regarded as an evolutionary process that began in 1437 and was completed in 1445. See J. Pelenski, *Russia and Kazan; Conquest and Imperial Ideology (1438–1560s)* (The Hague, 1974), p. 23. On documentary evidence and discussion of the emergence of the khanate of Kazan, see also A. N. Kurat's *Kazan Hanlığını kuran Uluğ Muhammed Han yarlığı* (Istanbul, 1937), *Topkapı Sarayı müzesi arşivindeki Altın Ordu, Kırım ve Türkistan hanlıklarına ait yarlık ve bitikler* (Istanbul and Ankara, 1940), and "Kazan Hanlığı," *Ankara Üniversitesi Dil ve Tarih-Coğrafya Fakültesi Dergisi* 12 (1954): 227–46.

3. Veliaminov-Zernov, *Izsledovanie o Kasimovskikh tsariakh i tsarevichakh*, p. iv. On the history and culture of the khanate of Kasimov, see R. R. Arat, "Kasım Hanlığı," in *Islam Ansiklopedisi*, vol. 7 (Istanbul, 1955), pp. 380–86; V. A. Gordlevskii, *Elementy kul'tury u Kasimovskikh Tatar. Trudy Obshchestva Issledovaniia Riazanskogo*

kraia. (Riazan, 1927); E. D. Polivanov, *Foneticheskie osobennosti Kasimovskogo dialekta* (Moscow, 1923); and N. I. Shishkin, *Istoriia goroda Kasimova s drevneishikh vremen* (Riazan, 1891).

4. Of the sixteen khans who ruled in Kasimov, two came from the dynasty ruling in Kazan, three from Crimea, seven from Saray, and one belonged to the Kazakh and three to the Siberian line. Siberian khan Kuchum's line was the only one that laid claim to Kasimov, but it did so very late, toward the end of the khanate. Ahmet Temir, "Kasım Hanlığı," p. 941.

5. On the history of the Kazan khanate, see Ioan Glazatyi, *Skazanie o tsarstve Kazanskom* (Moscow, 1959); M. N. Tikhomirov, *Rossiia v XVI stoletii* (Moscow, 1962); M. Khudiakov, *Ocherki po istorii Kazanskogo khanstva* (Kazan, 1923); G. Z. Kuntsevich, *Istoriia o Kazanskom khanstve ili Kazanskii letopisets* (St. Petersburg, 1905); K. F. Fuks, *Kratkaia istoriia goroda Kazani* (Kazan, 1817); M. Pinegin, *Kazan' v eia proshlom i nastoiashchem* (Kazan, 1890); S. P. Singalevich, *Staraia i novaia Kazan'* (Kazan, 1927); A. Ahmerov, *Kazan tarihi* (Kazan, 1909); and H. Atlasi, *Qazan Hanligi* (Kazan, 1913; 1920). On H. Atlasi's contribution as a historian, see A. N. Kurat, "Kazan Türklerinin tanınmış tarihçi ve milliyetçilerinden Hadi Atlas (1875–1940)," *Kazan* 16 (1975): 4–5. The contribution made by Fazil Tuikin, a jadid poet, writer, and historian, to the study of the history of the Kazan khanate has been noted in a recent article by El'mira Sharifullina, "Ilebez-kaderle jerebez," *KU* 6 (1977): 163–69.

6. Pelenski, *Conquest and Imperial Ideology*, pp. 50–51.

7. K. V. Bazilevich, *Vneshniaia politika Russkogo tsentralizovannogo gosudarstva* (Moscow, 1952), pp. 35–37 and 60–62; S. O. Shmidt, "Vostochnaia politika Rossii nakanune 'Kazanskogo vziatiia,'" in *Mezhdunarodnye otnosheniia, politika, diplomatiia. (Sbornik statei k 80-letiiu akademika I. M. Maiskogo)* (Moscow, 1964), pp. 538–59; A. A. Zimin, *Rossiia na poroge novogo vremeni* (Moscow, 1972), pp. 68–69.

8. The clashes over the control of the Viatka-Perm region are among the first of this nature. See *PSRL*, vol. 26 (St. Petersburg, Moscow, and Leningrad, 1959), p. 217; and K. N. Serbina, ed., *Ustiuzhskii Letopisnyi svod* (Moscow and Leningrad, 1950), pp. 84–85.

9. *PSRL*, vol. 12 (1965), p. 118.

10. *PSRL*, vol. 18 (1913), p. 217.

11. In 1963, R. Stepanov found Ibrahim Khan's yarlyk in the Central state archives (Tsentral'nyi gosudarstvennyi arkhiv drevnikh aktov) in Moscow. Its text, with a translation into modern Tatar, was published by M. Gosmanov, Sh. Mokhammad'yarov, and R. Stepanov, "Yanga yarlïk," *KU* 8 (1965): 146–50.

12. *PSRL*, vol. 18 (1913), pp. 220–22 and 271–72. When Muhammed Emin was deposed, Ivan granted him Serpukhov, Khotun, and Koshira, with all their revenues; see Pelenski, *Conquest and Imperial Ideology*, p. 30.

13. *PSRL*, vol. 8 (1859), p. 269; Pelenski, *Conquest and Imperial Ideology*, p. 35.

14. Bazilevich, *Vneshniaia politika*, pp. 63–64; A. Bennigsen and Chantal Lemercier-Quelquejay, "Le Khanat de Crimée du XVIe siècle de la tradition mongole à

la suzeraineté ottomane d'après un document inédit des archives ottomanes," *CMRS* 13 (1972): 323–24; Omeljan Pritsak, "Moscow, the Golden Horde and the Kazan Khanate from a Polycultural Point of View," *SR* 4 (1967): 577–83.

15. M. V. Fekhner, *Torgovlia russkogo gosudarstva so stranami vostoka v XVIv. Trudy gosudarstvennogo istoricheskogo muzeia* (Moscow, 1956), pp. 6, 53–56, 65–66, 81–82, and 94–95.

16. Vasilii III's attempt to create an alternative center of trade on Muscovite territory should be viewed as an attempt to emancipate Muscovy from its commercial dependence on Kazan. Sigismund von Herberstein, *Notes upon Russia*, The Hakluyt Society Works (London, 1851–1852), pp. 67–68 and 72–73.

17. *SIRIO* (St. Petersburg, 1867–1917), vol. 41, pp. 109 and 154 and vol. 95, pp. 27–28, 377, and 386; *PSRL*, vol. 12 (1901/1965), pp. 249 and 256.

18. The importance Ivan IV attached to the conquest of Kazan is also revealed by a less traditional piece of evidence: It is believed that whenever Ivan IV was in a good mood he would have songs about the fall of Kazan and Astrakhan recited to him by the minstrel-entertainers (*skomorokhi*). Russel Zguta, "Skomorokhi: The Russian Minstrel Entertainers," *SR* 2 (1972): 304.

19. Nolde, *La formation de l'empire russe*, pp. 3–5.

20. *PSRL*, vol. 20 (1910), p. 403; Khalikov, "Kazanskoe khanstvo," p. 28; G. I. Peretiatkovich, *Povolzh'e v XV i XVI vekakh (Ocherki iz istorii kraia i ego kolonizatsii)* (Moscow, 1877), pp. 117–18 and 123–26.

21. Analyzing the issue of selection of the khan, Nolde discusses both Mongol and Islamic law and their contributions to the Kazani legal system. Nolde, *La formation de l'empire russe*, p. 6.

22. Khalikov, "Kazanskoe khanstvo," p. 32; Peretiatkovich, *Povolzh'e v XV i XVI vekakh*, p. 126; Veliaminov-Zernov, *Izsledovanie o Kasimovskikh tsariakh i tsarevichakh*, vol. 2, pp. 410–11.

23. Khudiakov, *Ocherki po istorii*, pp. 167–238.

24. Pelenski, *Conquest and Imperial Ideology*, pp. 54–57.

25. *PSRL*, vol. 8 (1859), pp. 271, 273, and 282, and vol. 20 (1910), pp. 416, 451, and 466; *SIRIO*, vol. 41, p. 114.

26. Khudiakov, *Ocherki po istorii*, p. 198.

27. Pelenski, *Conquest and Imperial Ideology*, p. 58.

28. Khalikov, "Kazanskoe khanstvo," p. 32; Nolde, *La formation de l'empire russe*, p. 7.

29. Herberstein, *Notes Upon Russia*, p. 105; Peretiatkovich, *Povolzh'e v XV i XVI vekakh*, p. 117.

30. S. G. Vakhidov, "Iarlyk khana Sakhib-Gireiia," in *Vestnik Nauchnogo Obshchestva Tatarovedeniia*, no. 1–2 (Kazan, 1925), pp. 29–37; Nolde, *La formation de l'empire russe*, p. 13.

31. Sh. F. Mukhamed'iarov, "Tarkhannyi iarlyk Kazanskogo khana Sakhib Gireia 1523g.," in *Novoe o proshlom nashei strany: Pamiati akademika M. N. Tikhomirova*

(Moscow, 1967), pp. 104–8; see also his "K voprosu o polozhenii krestianstva v Kazanskom khanstve," in *Iz istorii klassovoi bor'by i obshchestvennoi mysli v Povolzh'e i Priural'e. Sbornik statei. Uchenye zapiski Kazanskogo gosudarstvennogo universiteta im. V. I. Ul'ianova Lenina* 122, no. 2 (Kazan, 1962), pp. 150–53.

32. T. Halasi-Kun, "Philologica III. Kazan Türkçesine ait dil yadigârları," *Ankara Üniversitesi Dil ve Tarih-Coğrafya Fakültesi Dergisi* 4 (1949): 603–44.

33. A. Rorlich, "Acculturation in Tatarstan: The Case of the Sabantui Festival," *SR* 2 (1982): 316–22.

34. In 1505 alone, 15,000 Russian merchants traveled to Kazan. At the time of the 1552 siege, 5,000 foreign merchants took refuge in the fortress. Of these, the Russians and the Armenians were the most numerous, and they lived in separate quarters of the city. Khalikov, "Kazanskoe khanstvo," pp. 30–31; S. Alishev, "Tarikhtän ber sakhifä," *KU* 3 (1977): 166.

35. *ITASSR*, vol. 1 (Kazan, 1955), pp. 99–113.

36. Kalinin, *Kazan. Istoricheskii ocherk*, p. 30.

37. Ahmet Temir, "Kuzey Türk edebiyatı," in *Türk Dünyası El Kitabı*, vol. 1, p. 507; Kurat, *Uluğ Muhammet hanın yarlığı* and *Yarlık ve bitikler*; T. Halasi-Kun, "Monuments de la langue tatare de Kazan," in *Analecta orientalia memoriae Alexandri Csoma de Körös dicata* (Bibliotheca Orientalis Hungarica, 1942).

38. G. Rakhim and G. Gaziz, *Tatar ädäbiyatï tarikhï. Burïngï dävir*, vol. 1, parts 1 (Kazan, 1924) and 2 (Kazan, 1925); A. Rakhim, *Tatarskie epigraficheskie pamiatniki* (Kazan, 1930); Temir, "Kuzey Türk edebiyatı," p. 508; Ia. G. Abdullin, Ä. Khäyrullin, "Märjani mirasïn öyränu yulïnda," *KU* 10 (1976): 150–60.

39. Temir, "Kuzey Türk edebiyatı," p. 508; Kalinin, *Kazan. Istoricheskii ocherk*, p. 30. The Nur Ali mosque was probably built by the *karachi* (clan leader) Nur Ali, whose name often appears in Russian sources as Muralei. Alishev, "Tarikhtän ber sakhifä," p. 165; T. Bobchenko, A. Garzavina, and K. Sinitsina, *Kazan. Putevoditel'* (Kazan, 1970), p. 112. On the traditions of Kazan Tatar architecture, see N. Khalitov, "Kazan Tatarlarï arkhitekturasïnda milli üzenchäleklär," *KU* 9 (1980): 167–71.

40. Kalinin, *Kazan. Istoricheskii ocherk*, p. 30.

41. Khalikov, "Kazanskoe khanstvo," p. 36; Alishev, "Tarikhtän ber sakhifä," p. 167; Temir, "Kuzey Türk edebiyatı," p. 508.

42. I. Ševčenko, "Muscovy's Conquest of Kazan: Two Views Reconciled," *SR* 4 (1967): 541–47. Although during the past two decades new studies have been added to the existing scholarship on early Tatar history in general and the Bulgar period in particular, the period of the khanate seems to have been bypassed by Soviet as well as Western scholars. As a result, general Tatar histories are still the standard sources for study of the khanate. Among those still useful are the histories written at the beginning of this century: A. Battal, *Tatar tarihi. Qazan Türkleri. Tarihi ve siyasi görüshler* (Istanbul, 1925); G. Gubaidullin, *Tatar tarihi* (Kazan, 1924); and A. Zeki Velidi-Togan, *Türk ve Tatar tarihi* (Kazan, 1912).

43. Pelenski, *Conquest and Imperial Ideology*, p. 8.

CHAPTER 5

1. E. A. Mozharovskii, *Izlozhenie khoda missionerskogo dela po prosveshcheniiu inorodtsev s 1552 po 1867*, in *Chteniia v Imperatorskom Obshchestve Istorii i Drevnostei Rossiiskikh pri Moskovskom Universitete*, book 1, part 2 (Moscow, 1880), as quoted from *Istoriia Gosudarstva Rossiiskogo* 8: 133.

2. The antipodal comparison belongs to J. Pelenski, who employed the principle of binary opposition and relied on structural anthropology for charting the characteristics of the two ethnic groups. See J. Pelenski, *Russia and Kazan; Conquest and Imperial Ideology (1438–1560s)* (The Hague, 1974), p. 303; see also pp. 92–136 and 177 of the same work for his discussion of the justifications for the conquest of Kazan.

3. Cited in Mozharovskii, *Izlozhenie khoda*, p. 13.

4. Ibid., p. 17.

5. The population registers and tax records of Kazan for 1565–1568 indicate that only 43 of the 1,853 houses within the walls of the fortress belonged to Tatars. They were either new converts to Christianity, service Tatars, merchants, craftsmen, or (probably) interpreters. Outside the fortress, there were some 150 houses in the new district founded by Muslim Tatars. Each was the home of at least ten families. I. P. Ermolaev, "Gorod Kazan' po pistsovoi knige 1565–1568 godov," in *Stranitsy istorii goroda Kazani* (Kazan, 1981), pp. 10–11.

6. Frank McCarthy, "The Kazan Missionary Congress," *CMRS* 3 (1973): 310.

7. Mozharovskii, *Izlozhenie khoda*, pp. 24–25.

8. Chantal Lemercier-Quelquejay, "Les missions orthodoxes en pays musulmans de moyenne et basse Volga, 1552–1865," *CMRS* 3 (1967): 369–404; and Mozharovskii, *Izlozhenie khoda*, p. 33.

9. M. V. Kazanskii, *Putevoditel' po Kazani* (Kazan, 1899), p. 45. For government measures aimed at converting Muslims to Christianity, see Ivan Katetov, "Obzor pravitel'stvennykh i tserkovnykh rasporiazhenii kasaiushchikhsia obrashcheniia v Khristianstvo Tatar-Mukhamedan," *Strannik* 8 (1886): 565–91.

10. A. Bennigsen and Chantal Lemercier-Quelquejay, *Islam in the Soviet Union* (New York, 1967), pp. 6–12.

11. McCarthy, "Kazan Missionary Congress," p. 311.

12. Mozharovskii, *Izlozhenie khoda*, p. 57. For detailed information on conversions according to *guberniias* (provinces), see E. A. Malov, *Statisticheskie svedeniia o kreshchennykh Tatarakh* (Ecole Pratique des Hautes Etudes, Paris, n.d., microfilm #653, incomplete), pp. 321–87.

13. Malov, *Statisticheskie svedeniia*, pp. 34–35, 50–51, and 521.

14. Ibid., pp. 61–62, and McCarthy, "Kazan Missionary Congress," pp. 312–13.

15. Mozharovskii, *Izlozhenie khoda*, p. 78.

16. Ibid., pp. 89–90, and Kazanskii, *Putevoditel' po Kazani*, p. 58.

17. Mozharovskii, *Izlozhenie khoda*, pp. 94–95.

18. Ibid., p. 85.

19. For a survey of the schools for new converts, see A. F. Efirov, "Russifikatorskie novokreshchenskie shkoly," *Prosveshchenie natsional'nostei* 4 (1934): 51–58.

20. On June 9, 1767, during her visit to Kazan, Catherine wrote to Voltaire. Commenting on the variety of peoples who lived in Kazan, she stressed the need to find some general principles of administration suitable to all. But how? And she further commented: "C'est presque un monde à créer, à unir, à conserver." W. F. Reddaway, ed., *Documents of Catherine the Great* (Cambridge, England, 1931), p. 18. For her comments on Tatars, see pp. 173–74 and 315 of that same work. For her comments on economic and cultural aspects of life in Kazan, see E. Belov, *Kul'turnye sokrovishcha Rossii: Kazan, N. Novgorod, Kostroma* (Moscow, 1913), pp. 26–35, and Kazanskii, *Putevoditel' po Kazani*, pp. 76–77.

21. M. de Voltaire, "Of the Alcoran and Mohametan Law," in *The Works of M. de Voltaire*, vol. 30 (London, 1763), pp. 43–44.

22. G. Ibragimov pointed out that political and economic imperatives, such as the annexation of the Crimea and the need to expand into the Central Asian markets, determined the more tolerant attitudes of Catherine II toward the Muslims and prompted her to officially sanction the organization of the muftiat (Muslim Ecclesiastical Council); G. Ibragimov, *Tatary v revoliutsii 1905 goda* (Kazan, 1926), p. 9.

23. A. Battal, *Tatar tarihi. Qazan Türkleri. Tarihi ve siyasi görüshler* (Istanbul, 1925), p. 624.

24. At the time of its creation, the Muslim Ecclesiastical Council was called the muftiat of Orenburg because at that time Ufa belonged to the Orenburg guberniia. S. Bobrovnikoff, too, sees the muftiat as a source of unity and strength for the Russian Muslims. See S. Bobrovnikoff, "Moslems in Russia," in *The Moslem World* 1 (1911), p. 15. For the institutional development of the muftiat, see S. Rybakov, *Ustroistvo i nuzhdy upravleniia dukhovnymi delami Musul'man v Rossii* (St. Petersburg, 1917), pp. 1–39. For details on *mufti* (the head of the Muslim Ecclesiastical Council), see Y. R. Walsh's article in H. A. R. Gibb, ed., *The Encyclopedia of Islam*, vol. 2 (Leiden and London, 1965), pp. 866–67.

25. A. Ishaki also saw the organization of the muftiat as a political move on the part of Catherine II, but he pointed out that, although theoretically the Ecclesiastical Council was supposed to be an elected body, the Muslims never elected its members; they were nominated by the Russian government. Often the mufti was merely a civil servant who lacked religious expertise and whose activity was limited to administering examinations for mullahs and keeping the records of civil acts. Ishaki's dissatisfaction with the last mufti before 1917 was even more profound, and he accused A. Baiazitov of unsatisfactory knowledge of the Arabic script. A. Ishaki, *Idel-Oural* (Paris, 1933), pp. 13–14 and 18. There seems to be, however, a contradiction between this opinion expressed by Ishaki in 1933 and his defense of the newly appointed mufti Baiazitov in 1915. See *Yulduz*, August 21, 1915, p. 1. On the other hand, his claim that muftis were merely Russian civil servants performing bureaucratic duties and often failing their leadership responsibilities is substantiated by a document (circular no. 372)

issued by mufti S. Tevkelev on February 20, 1874, concerning the duties of mullahs to report the number of Muslim youths eligible to be drafted. See *Sbornik tsirkuliarov i inykh rukovodiashchikh rasporiazhenii po okrugu Orenburgskogo Magometanskogo Dukhovnogo Sobraniia 1836–1903* (Ufa, 1905), p. 13. The mufti also presided over the Russian language examinations to which mullahs were subjected as a condition for appointment. A fourteen-point statement of examination rules was published in a Kazan newspaper in 1891. See *Kazanskii birzhevoi listok*, January 23, 1891, p. 1.

26. McCarthy, "Kazan Missionary Congress," p. 314. For a discussion of the evolution of Russian nationalism from the cultural reaction stimulated by the war of 1812 to a more doctrinaire formulation, see Hugh Seaton-Watson, *The Russian Empire, 1801–1917* (Oxford, 1967), pp. 267–68.

27. *SRMNP*, vol. 1 (St. Petersburg, 1866–1917), pp. 115–201 and 910.

28. *PSZRI*, vol. 24 (St. Petersburg, 1850), part 1, no. 23423, p. 623.

29. In 1866, 11,000 Tatars of the Kazan guberniia returned to Islam. McCarthy, "Kazan Missionary Congress," p. 315.

30. *PSZRI*, no. 23259, p. 284.

31. Mozharovskii, *Izlozhenie khoda*, pp. 243–52. Kazanskii, *Putevoditel' po Kazani*, p. 61.

32. Il'minskii pointed out that for any missionary it was imperative to learn Islam in detail, in the Islamic centers of the East. E. N. Medynskii, *Istoriia Russkoi pedagogiki* (Moscow, 1938), p. 352. This idea of Il'minskii is strikingly similar to the idea developed in a recent article by the Soviet scholar Vagabov. The only difference is that Vagabov regards knowledge of Islam as valuable only in the context of the campaign for atheism. He argues that the section on atheism at the Institute of Philosophy of the Academy of Science of the USSR could not fulfill its educational task because it lacked specialists on Islam. M. V. Vagabov, "Bol'she vnimaniia Sovetskomu Islamovedeniiu," *Voprosy Filosofii* 12 (1966): 172–75.

33. For details, see S. V. Chicherina, *O Privolzhskikh inorodtsakh i sovremennom znachenii sistemy N. I. Il'minskogo* (St. Petersburg, 1906), p. 16. S. Chicherina married N. Bobrovnikov, the son of Il'minskii's closest friend. Bobrovnikov, who lost his father at the age of ten, was educated by Il'minskii and took up the missionary work at Il'minskii's death in 1891. See Sophy Bobrovnikoff (née Tchitcherine), "Moslems in Russia," pp. 9 and 31.

34. A. F. Efirov, *Nerusskie shkoly Povolzh'ia Priural'ia i Sibiri* (Moscow, 1948), pp. 26–30.

35. Ibid., p. 36. Medynskii gives slightly different figures: He notes that 4,449 boys and 1,887 girls studied between 1863 and 1913 and that 635 men and 260 women became grade-school teachers. Medynskii, *Istoriia Russkoi pedagogiki*, p. 355.

36. Medynskii, *Istoriia Russkoi pedagogiki*, p. 353.

37. McCarthy, "Kazan Missionary Congress," p. 317. Seaton-Watson, *The Russian Empire*, p. 502, as quoted from A. A. Vozkresensky, *O sisteme prosveshcheniia inorodtsev* (Kazan, 1913), pp. 38–40.

38. These measures were prepared at the February 2, 1870, meeting of the Council of the Ministry of Public Instruction. *SRMNP*, vol. 4, pp. 842–44.

39. For details about the evolution of the concept of umma from the politico-religious community founded by Muhammad at Medina to an umma of all Muslims, see R. Paret's article on umma in Gibb, *Encyclopedia of Islam*, vol. 4, pp. 1015–16.

CHAPTER 6

1. For discussions of the most important Islamic reformers of the nineteenth century, see H. A. R. Gibb, *Modern Trends in Islam* (Chicago, 1947), pp. 29 and 56–58; and *Mohammedanism* (London, 1972), p. 120; and Caesar E. Farah, *Islam* (New York, 1970), pp. 236–39.

2. A. Bennigsen has attributed much of the originality of Tatar reformism to the influence of Christian culture, which he has characterized as being more dynamic. A. Bennigsen and Chantal Lemercier-Quelquejay, *Les mouvements nationaux chez les musulmans de Russie. Le "sultangalievisme" au Tatarstan* (Paris, 1960), p. 37. The Tanzimat edicts of 1839 and 1856 marked a period of reform from above in the Ottoman state and laid the path for the confrontation of Islamism and Westernism that eventually led to the birth of Turkism and Turkish nationalism. See Niyazi Berkes, ed., *Turkish Nationalism and Western Civilization. Selected Essays of Ziya Gökalp* (London, 1959), pp. 16–20.

3. Ia. G. Abdullin has produced an excellent study of the reform movement among the Tatars, which he has entitled "Tatar Enlightened Thought." Despite the fact that significant space is given to minor reformers, while others, such as M. Bigi and R. Fahreddin, are treated with silence, Abdullin's monograph is a scholarly presentation of the complex phenomenon of reform. See Ia. G. Abdullin, *Tatarskaia prosvetitel'skaia mysl' (Sotsial'naia priroda i osnovnye problemy)* (Kazan, 1976); for the background and philosophical foundations of the reform movement, see particularly pp. 14–15.

4. Abu-Nasr was born in 1776 in the village of Kursa in the Kazan uezd and died of cholera in 1813 in Istanbul while on his way to Mecca. He began his education at the Mechkere medrese in the Malmyzh uezd and, shortly after the completion of his studies there, left to further his education in Bukhara. Akdes Nimet Kurat, "Kazan Türklerinin medeni uyanış devri," *Ankara Üniversitesi Dil ve Tarih-Coğrafya Fakültesi Dergisi* 3–4 (1966): 101.

5. *Kalam*, the science of Islamic dialectics, developed during the Middle Ages as a reaction against the philosophers (followers of Plato and Aristotle) and against such sects as the Shiites (followers of the fourth Caliph, Ali) and the Mutazilites (rationalists of the ninth century, champions of free will). Sunni (orthodox) Muslims engaged in a deep analysis of their faith in an effort to combat the philosophers; this effort, however, was so intensive that they themselves became philosophers—the kalamists. See Farah, *Islam*, pp. 175–78 and 203–5, and J. Validov, *Ocherki istorii obrazovannosti i literatury Tatar* (Moscow and Petrograd, 1923), p. 27.

6. Validov, *Ocherki istorii obrazovannosti*, pp. 32–33. Ia. G. Abdullin and Ä. Khäyrullin, "Mag"rifätchelek khäräkäte karligachï," *KU* 1 (1977): 144–45.

7. A. Saadi, *Tatar ädäbiyatï tarihi* (Kazan, 1926), p. 66.

8. Merjani was born in the village of Yapanchï, into the family of a Bukhara-educated medrese teacher. His father was his first teacher, and the progress Merjani had made in the study of Arabic and Persian by the age of sixteen earned him the position of substitute teacher at his father's medrese in the village of Tashkichu, where the family had moved. Kurat, "Kazan Türklerinin medeni uyanış devri," pp. 102–3. Validov, *Ocherki istorii obrazovannosti*, p. 34. *Zaman kalendarï* (Orenburg, 1909), p. 33.

9. See Nadir Devlet, "Kazanli tarihçi ve islahatçı din adamı Şihabeddin Mercani," *Kazan* 6 (1971–1972): 10–11, and *Zaman kalendarï* (Orenburg, 1909), p. 33.

10. Devlet, "Şihabeddin Mercani," pp. 10–11, and *Zaman kalendarï*, p. 33. The first mosque was located in the district where the wealthy merchant Yunusov lived. The relationship between Merjani and Yunusov was always tense, a situation that negatively affected the welfare of the medrese; Yunusov never assisted the school, and Merjani had to struggle with adverse teaching conditions. Validov, *Ocherki istorii obrazovannosti*, p. 35.

11. Kurat, "Kazan Türklerinin medeni uyanış devri," pp. 104–5.

12. The journal Merjani kept during his trip to the Middle East was published in Kazan in 1897 by Rizaeddin Fahreddin under the title *Rihalet-al-Merjani*. *Zaman kalendarï* (Orenburg, 1909), p. 33.

13. For a list of Merjani's works and the major sources used by him, as well as a discussion of his influence on Muslim, Russian, and Western European scholars, see Devlet's "Şihabeddin Mercani," *Kazan* 6 (1971–1972): 8–19, and 7–8 (1972): 64–79.

14. On Merjani's religious views, see A. L. Karan, *Şehabettin Mercani turmuşu hem eserleri*, Suyumbike Cultural Society Series, no. 4 (Istanbul, 1964), pp. 38–42. For a recent evaluation of Merjani's contribution, see Ia. G. Abdullin and Ä. Khäyrullin, "Märjani mirasïn öyränu yulïnda," *KU* 10 (1976): 150–60.

15. Validov, *Ocherki istorii obrazovannosti*, p. 38.

16. Karan, *Şehabettin Mercani*, pp. 36–37. For a review of the main theses of Merjani's religious reforms, see Saadi, *Tatar ädäbiyatï tarihi*, p. 67; and A. Battal, *Qazan Türkleri. Tarihi ve siyasi görüshler* (Istanbul, 1925), pp. 177–81. For a discussion of a Merjani manuscript discovered in 1973, see Sh. Safin, "Shihabettin Märjani kul' yazmasï," *KU* 4 (1982): 171–75.

17. Gibb, *Mohammedanism*, pp. 50–51.

18. Validov, *Ocherki istorii obrazovannosti*, p. 40. This first volume containing some 411 pages is the only one that was published. See Devlet, "Şihabeddin Mercani," *Kazan* 6 (1972): 10.

19. Merjani was not a pioneer in advocating the importance of the Russian language for Tatars. It was mullah Gabdarrahman (b. 1754) from the village of Utiz Iman (Chistay uezd, Kazan region) who first urged the people to become involved in solving practical questions related to their daily life rather than wasting their energies on sterile philosophical questions. A new manuscript by U. Imani was discovered in 1973 in Bashkiria; see Gaisa Khösäenov, "Utïz Imäni Bashkortstanda," *KU* 1 (1977): 152–56. On Merjani's ideas concerning the importance of the Russian language for Tatars, see also Karan, *Şehabettin Mercani*, pp. 28–32.

20. A. Arsharuni and Kh. Gabidullin, *Ocherki panislamizma i pantiurkizma v Rossii* (Moscow, 1934), pp. 10–11; Validov, *Ocherki istorii obrazovannosti*, pp. 35–36.

21. For details on Al-Ghazali, and for a partial French translation of his work *Al Munqidh min ad-Dalal*, see F. Jabre, *La notion de certitude selon Ghazali dans ses origines psychologiques et historiques* (Paris, 1958), pp. 393–456. In *Al-Munqidh*, Al-Ghazali actually states that the path to God cannot be intellectually delineated but rests in a mystical experience. Also see W. M. Watt, *The Faith and Practice of Al-Ghazali* (London, 1953).

22. R. Fahreddin was born into a family of mullahs in the village of Kichuchani, Bugulme uezd, Samara guberniia. His first teacher was his father. Later he entered the medrese of Chelchli, where he gained a solid knowledge of Arabic and Persian. This training enabled him to receive an appointment as imam in the Bugulme uezd in 1889 and to become a member of the Ecclesiastical Council in 1891. Fahreddin chose not to emigrate after the 1917 revolutions, and in 1921, on the death of mufti Alimjan Barudi, Fahreddin was appointed mufti, a position he held until his death in 1936. It is believed that Fahreddin is buried in Ufa. *Zaman kalendari* (Orenburg, 1909), p. 37. For a monographic study, see A. Battal, *Rizaeddin Fahreddinoğlu* (Istanbul, 1958).

23. Muhammad Abduh developed the basic principles of his theology in his work entitled *Risalat al-Tawhid* (translated under the title *The Theology of Unity* by Ishaq Musa'ad and Kenneth Cragg [London, 1966]), in which he reassessed Al-Ghazali's ideas regarding the unity of God. In the same work, however, Abduh stressed the need to purge Islam of superstition, to correct misconceptions concerning the articles of faith, and to eliminate errors that had crept into Islam because of misinterpretations of religious texts. See Fazlur Rahman, *Islam* (New York, 1968), pp. 267–68, and Majid Fakhri, *A History of Islamic Philosophy* (New York, 1970), pp. 376–85.

24. Karan, *Şehabettin Mercani*, p. 52.

25. In May 1906, R. Fahreddin resigned his position as kazi to dedicate himself to writing and journalism. The newspaper *Vaqt* was published by the wealthy Tatar industrialist Rameev, who also sponsored publication of the journal *Shura*, which appeared between 1908 and 1915. Validov, *Ocherki istorii obrazovannosti*, pp. 167–68.

26. Rizaeddin Fahreddin, *Ahmed Bay* (Orenburg, 1911), p. 28.

27. Ibn Khallikan was a descendant of the Barmakid family in Khorasan. He studied in Syria, and in 1261, was appointed judge there. In 1271, he became a professor at the Fakhriya college in Cairo. During his professorship, he compiled *Wafiat-al-Ayan*, which contains biographies of Muslim celebrities from the second century of the Islamic period to the first years of his own life. Najib Ullah, *Islamic Literature* (New York, 1963), p. 101.

28. Fahreddin, *Ahmed Bay*, pp. 2–6.

29. For a complete listing of his works, see *Zaman kalendari* (Orenburg, 1909), p. 37.

30. Fahreddin's *Asar* was published in two volumes. Volume 1, contianing eight parts, appeared between 1900 and 1904; and volume 2, composed of six parts, was printed between 1904 and 1908. Among the Volga Tatars depicted in *Asar* are Kursavi

and such representatives of ulama as Nigmetulla al-Avtari, Habibulla Husein, Rahim Mechkeri, Fahrettin Subhankul, and Seyfettin Al-Shinkari. See all parts of R. Fahreddin's *Asar* (Orenburg, 1904–1908) in microfilm no. 1168, Ecole Pratique des Hautes Etudes, Paris.

31. Validov, *Ocherki istorii obrazovannosti*, pp. 32–35.

32. For more information on Ibn-Taymiya, see Rahman, *Islam*, pp. 131–36 and 177–79, and Farah, *Islam*, pp. 223–24.

33. Berkes, *Turkish Nationalism*, p. 50.

34. Ahmed Midhat, an Ottoman reformer, was a prolific writer. Among his unpublished works, there is a voluminous commentary on the Qur'an, written in collaboration with Sheik-ul-Islam, Musa Kazim. Entitled *Kur'an-i Kerim'in felsefesi*, it was the result of seven years of work. The commentary was banned by Abdul-Hamid because the authors envisaged a republic as the most suitable form of government for an Islamic state. Hakkı Tarık Us, ed., *Ahmed Midhat'ı anıyoruz* (Istanbul, 1955), p. 171. For a chronology of A. Midhat's life, and for a listing of his works, see pp. 14–21 and 169–72 of the same work.

35. Gibb, *Modern Trends in Islam*, pp. 27–32.

36. Even before 1905, Nicholas II moved toward granting more religious rights to inorodtsy. On February 26, 1903, he issued a manifesto on religious tolerance, which was followed on December 21, 1904, by an ukaz that further lifted some of the religious restrictions imposed on inorodtsy. See *Za pervyi god veroispovednoi svobody v Rossii* (St. Petersburg, 1907), pp. 6–7, 12, and 15. Fahreddin himself pointed out that publication of the essay of grievances was possible only because of the relaxation of censorship. R. Fahreddin, *Rusya Muslumanlariniñg ihtiyachlari ve anlar haqinda intiqad* (Orenburg, 1906), p. 2.

37. Fahreddin, *Rusya Muslumanlariniñg ihtiyachlari*, pp. 14–15 and 17.

38. For a well-documented account of I. Gasprali's life and work, see the biography by Cafer Seydahmet, *Gaspirali Ismail Bey* (Istanbul, 1934).

39. Kurat, "Kazan Türklerinin medeni uyanış devri," p. 126, and I. Gasprinskii, *Russkoe Musul'manstvo. Mysli, zametki i nabliudeniia Musul'manina* (Simferopol, 1881), p. 25.

40. "Autour du monde musulman," *RMM* 9 (1909): 158.

41. The historians of Tatar cultural and political life are indebted to Musa Jarulla Bigi for the record of all major Muslim congresses held in Russia until 1917. A friend of Fahreddin, and an active reformer himself, Bigi took part as a secretary in all but the ulama congress. He published the records in 1917 in St. Petersburg, in an impressive volume entitled *Islahat esaslari* (Petrograd, 1917).

42. Ibid., p. 50.

43. Ibid., pp. 53–55 and 58–59.

44. Ibid.

45. Ibid., pp. 58–59. Even when the movement of reform resulted in significant changes in the religious thinking and social behavior of Muslims, Russians remained oblivious to these changes because they were misled by missionary writings that

attacked Islam as a religion totally incompatible with modern life. For a presentation of these views, see A. Bennigsen and Chantal Lemercier-Quelquejay, "Musulmans et missions orthodoxes en Russie orientale avant 1917. Essai de bibliographie critique," *CMRS* 1 (1972): 98–106, and M. N. P. Ostroumov's two pamphlets, *Chto takoe Koran?* (Tashkent, 1883) and *Koran i progress* (Tashkent, 1901).

46. Bigi, *Islahat esaslari*, pp. 55–56. For accounts of the situation of Muslim teachers, see *Kazan mukhbiri* 135 (1906): 4 and G. Alisov, "Musul'manskii vopros v Rossii," *Russkaia mysl'* 7 (1909): 54.

47. S. Rybakov, *Ustroistvo i nuzhdy upravleniia dukhovnymi delami Musul'man v Rossii* (St. Petersburg, 1917), p. 39.

48. Ibid., p. 4. The full title of the conference and, therefore, its minutes was *Osoboe soveshchanie po vyrabotke mer dlia protivodeistviia Tatarsko-Musul'manskomu vliianiiu v Privolzhskom krae v 1910 godu i o preobrazovanii Orenburgskogo Magometanskogo Dukhovnogo Sobraniia.*

49. Rybakov, *Ustroistvo i nuzhdy upravleniia dukhovnymi delami Musul'man v Rossii*, pp. 41–42 and 48. For an evaluation of the muftis appointed by the government, see Battal, *Qazan Turkleri*, pp. 173–77.

50. S. Bobrovnikoff, "Moslems in Russia," *The Moslem World*, 1 (1911): 15. The mistakes most Russian missionaries made stemmed from their ignorance, both of Islam and of the traditions of the Muslim inorodtsy. They considered Islam to be the major force in hindering progress but failed to see its inner sources of revival. In 1910, an Orenburg correspondent for *Musul'manin* noted: "Religion is, for our people, the first and most important step toward renaissance and enlightenment." *Musul'manin*, April 15, 1910, p. 109.

51. In terms of social background and educational patterns, Musa Jarulla Bigi's biography is very similar to those of earlier reformers. Born in 1870 in Rostov-on-the-Don, into a family of mullahs, his first teacher was his father, and on completion of this first stage of his education, he moved on to the Gölboyu medrese in Kazan. Bigi traveled more extensively and spent more time abroad than any other religious reformer. He returned to Russia in 1904, to leave again after the events of 1917. This time, his trips took him to Finland, Turkey, and India and finally to Egypt, where he died on October 25, 1949. See *Zaman kalendari* (Orenburg, 1910), pp. 35–36; Kurat, "Kazan Türklerinin medeni uyanış devri," pp. 178–79, and Yusuf Uralgiray, ed., *Uzun günlerde oruç* (Ankara, 1975), p. xx.

52. Musa Jarullah Bigi, "Dinimiz, milletimiz kiymeti," *Yulduz* 1493 (1915):2–3.

53. Although Bigi worked for Abdurrashid Ibrahimov's newspaper, *Ulfet*, and for the journal *Tilmid*, the only activity that captivated him entirely was his research and writing on Islamic theology, which involved him to such an extent that he neglected both his family and his duties as imam of the St. Petersburg mosque, a position to which he was appointed in 1910. Instead, Bigi delegated these duties to Imam Lutfi Ishaki. See Kurat, "Kazan Türklerinin medeni uyanış devri," p. 178. For a partial account of the difficulties involved in building the St. Petersburg mosque (inaugurated in 1910), see *Kazanskii birzhevoi listok* 44 (1891): 2; *RMM* 3 (1906–1907): 419–20,

as quoted from *Irshad*, October 16, 1906; *RMM* 3 (1910): 414; and *Musul'manin*, July 15, 1910, pp. 342–43.

54. *Zaman kalendari* (Orenburg, 1910), p. 36, Validov, *Ocherki istorii obrazovannosti*, p. 74, and Musa Jarullah Bigi, *Halq nazarina bir niche mesele* (Kazan, 1912), pp. 79 and 85.

Bigi himself worked on a Tatar translation of the Qur'an. It is conceivable that that translation was among his archives that remained in St. Petersburg when he left Russia in 1917; it was not found among the archives he left in Finland, which were held by his friends until a few years ago, when the Finnish-Tatar community donated them to the Turkish government. This information is based on the author's interview with Osman Ali, president of the Helsinki Tatar community, held on November 3, 1973, in Helsinki. Bigi's controversial work *Uzun kunlerde ruze* was published in 1975 in Ankara as *Uzun günlerde oruç*. It was edited and annotated by Yusuf Uralgiray and is the first publication to use those of Bigi's archives donated by the Finnish Tatars to the Turkish government.

The Helsinki Tatar community numbers some 600 people who are mainly well-to-do fur merchants and professionals. They represent approximately 50 percent of the 1,150 Tatars living in Finland. The Tatars of Helsinki—like those of Turku, Tampere, and other cities—have a strong sense of community and a firm commitment to the preservation of their national heritage. In this preservation effort, they have encountered no opposition or discrimination from the Finnish government. For population data on Finnish Tatars see *Suomen Virallinen Tilasto*, vol. 6 (Helsinki, 1973), part 1, pp. 506–7. Also see Harry Halén, *A Bibliographical Survey of the Publishing Activities of the Turkic Minority in Finland* (Helsinki, 1979), pp. 3–5.

55. Bigi's book was announced in the journal *Shura* 8 (1910). The front page of that issue carried a symbolic drawing. Its symmetry was antithetic: on the right, a mosque and the arts symbolizing the past; on the left, the sciences and a telescope, books, and a globe symbolizing the future. See A. Bennigsen and Chantal Lemercier-Quelquejay, *La presse et le mouvement national chez les musulmans de Russie avant 1920* (Paris, 1964), pp. 76–77, and Validov, *Ocherki istorii obrazovannosti*, p. 75.

56. For Herzen, see A. Slonim, *The Epic of Russian Literature from Its Origins Through Tolstoy* (New York, 1964), p. 156. The reformists advocated secularism and secularization, but not to the point of totally excluding religion and building a society in which "people do not believe in the commandments of a higher power, but assume that man can find the answers to the questions of his personal and social life in his own autonomous thinking." Edward Heiman, *Reason and Faith in Modern Society: Liberalism, Marxism, and Democracy* (Middletown, 1961), p. 5.

57. On Al-Ma'ari, see Ullah, *Islamic Literature*, pp. 59–60.

58. *Musul'manin*, January 14, 1910, p. 18. When a Samara correspondent for the Tatar journal *Iqtisad* interviewed Faizkhan Davudov, the editor of *Din ve Magishat*, about his opinion of Musa Bigi, Davudov replied that, had Bigi continued his ijtihad at Huseiniye medrese, "he would have ruined all of us." See "Samara ahvalati," *Iqtisad* 7 (1910): 224.

59. See Musa Jarullah Bigi, *Büyük mevzularda ufak fikirler* (St. Petersburg, 1914), p. 66. In his essays, Bigi commented on some 23 issues, but the tariqat and the miracles were by far the matters that interested him most. He had a special chapter (chapter 17) on the value of miracles in Islam. Ibid., pp. 70–78.

60. This number is a relative estimate of the tariqa membership as indicated by A. Ishaki, *Idel-Oural* (Paris, 1933), pp. 29–30. The last prominent leader (*ishan*) of the Middle Volga Naqshbandi seems to have been Zeinulla Rasulov of Troitsk, who died in 1917. See Abdullin, *Tatarskaia prosvetitel'skaia mysl'*, p. 63.

61. "Le mouvement social en Russie," *RMM* 7 (1907): 389.

62. The confrontation between the Shiites and Sunnis in Bukhara was not purely religious, however. In fact, the revival of the old animosity had deep social overtones. According to Suleiman Zhanaev, who reported from Bukhara, the emir appointed a Shiite as administrator over an overwhelmingly Sunni population. S. Zhanaev, "Staraia Bukhara," *Musul'manin* 2 (1910): 48–49. For another account of the Sunni and Shiite clashes in Bukhara, see "Bukhara fitnesi," *Iqtisad* 1 (1910): 94–95 and *Musul'manin*, January 14, 1910, p. 23.

63. The Vaisites called themselves *Naqshbandi*, but they were a totally different group from the Naqshbandis of Kazan. Chantal Quelquejay, "Le Vaisisme à Kazan," *Le monde d'Islam* 1–2 (1959): 95.

64. M. Sagidullin, *K istorii Vaisovskogo dvizheniia* (Kazan, 1930), p. 20. It is conceivable that the extreme nationalism of the Vaisites, and their hope for the restoration of the land of Bulgar, were in response to their economic and social situation rather than an expression of a clearly defined religious doctrine.

65. The Vaisites were really swimming against the current because the number of Muslim mullahs who learned Russian had registered a steady increase. The law of July 16, 1888, concerning the educational census of Muslim clerics was enforced on January 1, 1891. On that date, 31 mullahs successfully passed the Russian-language examination (according to the information provided by the governor-general of Kazan). Also, one-third of the medrese students were learning Russian. N. N. Firsov, *Proshloe Tatarii* (Kazan, 1926), p. 34. At the same time, the Tatars had become more and more interested in zemstvo activities, although they were seldom elected to the zemstvo boards. See B. Veselovskii, *Istoriia zemstva za sorok let*, vol. 1 (St. Petersburg, 1909–1911), pp. 213–14.

66. The anarchism of the Vaisites closely resembles that of the Russian Old Believer sects, with whom they might have been acquainted. See Chantal Quelquejay, "Le Vaisisme à Kazan," p. 100. For another account of the Vaisite sect, see E. V. Molostvova, "Vaisov Bozhii polk," *Mir Islama* 2 (1912): 143–52.

67. "Posledovatel' Vaisova," *Kazanskii birzhevoi listok* 130 (1891): 2.

68. For a detailed account of this incident and some of the practices of the Vaisites, see N. O. Katanov, *Novye dannye o Musul'manskoi sekte Vaisovtsev* (Kazan, 1909), pp. 7–16.

69. The Bolsheviks, in fact, armed the Vaisites in September 1917, a month before the October coup, and thus the Vaisites became the only Tatar group to fight alongside

the Russian workers and soldiers in October. A rather embarrassed explanation of this cooperation has been provided by Sagidullin in *K istorii Vaisovskogo dvizheniia*, p. 13.

70. The staunchest defender of the veil was the Ottoman government, and Ismail Bey Gasprali criticized equally the policies of Abdul Hamid and the antifeminist stand of the Young Turks after their seizure of power. Ismail Bey appealed to the ulama throughout the Islamic world to discuss the question of the veil and formulate its opinion in a fatwa. L. M., "La question du voile," *RMM* 11 (1910): 463–65.

71. The main thesis developed by Soviet historians on this issue is their contention that interest in the status of Tatar women and the struggle for their emancipation started only under the influence of the 1905 revolution. This is another example of attempts to view the 1905 revolution as a sui generis deus ex machina that caused every major change and development in the life of the Tatars at the beginning of the twentieth century. The events of 1905 did play an important role, but they were only a catalyzing agent in the evolutionary changes that Tatar society had begun to experience during the nineteenth century. For a Soviet view of the issue, see A. Kh. Makhmutova and V. N. Smirnova, "Zhenskii vopros v Tatarskoi istoriografii 1917–27 godov," in *Obshchestvenno-politicheskoe dvizhenie i klassovaia bor'ba na Srednei Volge* (Kazan, 1972), pp. 72–75.

72. "La presse musulmane," *RMM* 11 (1910): 459–60. Imam Muhammed Sabir Hasan's stand represented the opinion of the progressive ulama and came in direct response to a request from Ismail Bey Gasprali to clarify the veil issue. Ismail Bey had received a letter from a certain Baroness von Rosen of Austria, who was interested in Islam and wanted to clarify some of the social aspects of religious dogma and rituals. Although the fact that the Baroness sent him the letter is indicative of Ismail Bey's authority outside the Islamic world, he referred the question to the religious leaders of the community. L. B., "La presse musulmane. Russie," *RMM* 1 (1910): 355.

73. The article was entitled "Evropeizatsiia Musul'man" and was probably published in one of the August 1907 issues of *Penzenskiie vedomosti*. The exact date is not indicated on the pages of the newspaper clipping that contains the article. The clipping is part of a larger collection of uncataloged Russian regional newspapers, clippings, and pamphlets at the Helsinki University Library, a collection that belonged to Professor N. Il'in and is referred to as the Il'in Collection.

74. For instance, Zeineb Abdurrahmanov, a woman medical doctor, participated in a feminist meeting held in St. Petersburg in 1908. In preparation, she publicized the meeting and, with the support of the Tatar press, submitted to the public a questionnaire aimed at identifying means to improve the status of women. "Autour du monde musulman," *RMM* 12 (1908): 675. On May 18, 1907, a delegation of women calling themselves the Society for the Defense of the Rights of Women presented their grievances to the Muslim delegation in the Duma. See *Ulfet* 81 (1907): 2. A group of women from Orenburg expressed similar grievances in a letter sent to the Muslim Duma deputies; it contained a warning: "If men do not change their attitude toward us, they should know that the day will come when they themselves will be slaves, and then the entire Muslim race will perish." See "L'éducation des femmes et la civilization musulmane," *RMM* 3 (1908): 800–802.

75. The plight of women attracted the attention of many Tatar writers: Z. Bigiev, *Ölüf, yäki güzäl kïz Khädichä* (Kazan, 1887); M. Ak'ägätzade, *Khisametdin menla* (Kazan, 1886); F. Khalidi, *Mäkhrüsä khanïm* (Kazan, 1906); Sh. Kültäsi, *Mäktäp balasï yahut Säkhilä äbi* (Kazan, 1909). Also on F. Amirkhan's contribution to the issue, see G. Khantemirova, "Fätikh Ämirkhan ijatïnda khatïn-kïzlar azatlïgï temasï," *KU* 8 (1977): 155–59.

76. The exceptionally advanced status of Tatar women, who were generally better educated and much more vocal than other Muslim women, was discussed at various times by A. Vambery; see his "Die Kulturbestrebungen der Tataren," *Deutsche Rundschau* 132 (1907): 88–89, and "The Emancipation of Women in Islam," *The International* 2 (1908): 14. For an account of the status of Turkish women, see Sabine Dirks, *La famille musulmane turque* (Paris, 1969). It is perhaps due to their higher educational level and competence in social and political issues that Tatar women could not become a surrogate proletariat and be used by the Soviets to impose social change, as was done in more conservative Central Asia. For a complete account of this alternative in accomplishing social change, see Gregory J. Massell, *The Surrogate Proletariat: Moslem Women and Revolutionary Strategies in Soviet Central Asia, 1919–1920* (Princeton, 1974).

77. For Muhlise Bobi's election as kazi, see A. Battal, *Qazan Türkleri*, pp. 220–22. This is also discussed in the memoirs of Ahmet Veli Menger, as read on a tape recorded in Ankara in 1975 by Mahmut Tahir, one of the editors of the journal *Kazan*, who has generously provided the author with a copy.

CHAPTER 7

1. Nasiri's secrecy was a measure of caution, because one of the legacies of missionary policies was the tendency of the Tatars to equate any contact with Russian culture and society with russification. Nasiri's realization that knowledge of Russian would rid the Tatars at least of an economic handicap came from the experience of his own family. His father, who was a merchant in the Volga region, and his brother, who was engaged in candle and soap manufacturing in Moscow, had pointed out to him the economic importance of learning the Russian language. For Nasiri's early biography, see J. Validov, *Ocherki istorii obrazovannosti i literatury Tatar* (Moscow and Petrograd, 1923), p. 41. A. N. Kurat, "Kazan Türklerinin medeni uyanış devri," in *Ankara Üniversitesi Dil ve Tarih-Coğrafya Fakültesi Dergisi* 3–4 (1966): 107; A. Saadi, *Tatar ädäbiyatï tarihi* (Kazan, 1926), p. 42. On the importance of learning Russian, also see "Koe chto o Tatarakh," *Kamsko-Volzhskaia rech'* 206 (1914): 6.

2. N. P. Zagoskin, who was known among the Kazan University faculty for his liberal ideas, was also the publisher of the newspaper *Volzhskii listok*. Faseev emphasized the special role played by *Volzhskii listok* in alerting Nasiri to Russian realities. K. F. Faseev, *Iz istorii Tatarskoi peredovoi obshchestvennoi mysli (vtoraia polovina XIX–nachalo XX veka)* (Kazan, 1955), p. 43.

3. Kurat, "Kazan Türklerinin medeni uyanış devri," p. 107; *Zaman kalendarï* (Orenburg, 1909), p. 32.

4. Validov, *Ocherki istorii obrazovannosti*, p. 42.

5. The intellectual milieu of the University of Kazan enabled Nasiri to acquire a knowledge of Russian intellectual life as a whole. Hence, it is conceivable that he wrote his essay on *The Functions of Human Organs*, which emphasized the unity of the human body and soul, under the influence of N. G. Chernyshevskii's *Anthropological Principle in Philosophy*. See Faseev, *Iz istorii Tatarskoi peredovoi obshchestvennoi mysli*, p. 46.

6. The study was entitled "Poveriia i obriady Kazanskikh Tatar" and was published in *Zapiski Imperatorskogo Russkogo Geograficheskogo Obshchestva*, vol. 6 (St. Petersburg, 1880), as quoted in Faseev, *Iz istorii Tatarskoi peredovoi obshchestvennoi mysli*, p. 44.

7. Although Saadi argues that the Europeanization (i.e., Westernization) of Nasiri's thought began with his activity as a member of the archeological society, it would be more correct to assume that this gradual process began much earlier. Perhaps its roots can be traced to Nasiri's decision to learn Russian in the first place. See Saadi, *Tatar ädäbiyatï tarihi*, p. 43.

8. Kurat, "Kazan Türklerinin medeni uyanış devri," p. 108.

9. Nasiri's calendar failed to appear both in 1886 and between 1895 and 1897. In 23 years, the calendar totaled 5,228 printed pages and contained information on all aspects of life. See Saadi, *Tatar ädäbiyatï tarihi*, p. 44. Two contemporaries of Nasiri, Fatih Halitov and Shihabeddin Rahmatullin, published wall calendars in which they printed original stories along with translations from Ottoman, Arabic, and Persian literature. Rahmatullin also wrote a teach-yourself-Russian textbook and a geography text. See Validov, *Ocherki istorii obrazovannosti*, p. 43.

10. *Zaman kalendarï* (Orenburg, 1909), pp. 44–46.

11. Ibid., pp. 33–40. Russian calendars were as much a barometer of changing times as Tatar calendars. For instance, the 1915 issue of the Kazan zemstvo calendar included a Muslim calendar in its pages. This inclusion could be indicative of the fact that the Tatars had become more vocal on the national scene, but it could also suggest a more careful attitude toward Muslims during the war. See *Kazanskii zemskii kalendar' na 1915 god* (Kazan, 1915), p. 15.

12. "Kazanskaia khronika," *Kazanskie vesti* 586 (1892): 2.

13. *Türk ili* (Istanbul, 1928), p. 627.

14. S. A. Zenkovsky, "A Century of Tatar Revival," *American Slavic and East European Review* 10 (1953): 316; A. Vambery, "Die Kulturbestrebungen der Tataren," *Deutsche Rundschau* 132 (1907): 91.

15. For debates on the role of the native language in the educational process, see Musa Jarullah Bigi, ed., *1906 sene 16–21 Avgustda ichtimag itmish Rusya Musulmanlarïnïng nedvesi* (Kazan, 1906), p. 60. For the reaction of the Tatars to the debates in the Duma on the bill concerning the use of native languages in elementary schools, see "Musul'manskaia zhizn' v 1910 godu," *Permskie vedomosti* 27 (1911): 2. See also points 118 and 119 of the regulations in *IV Musul'manskii s'ezd., S. Petersburg. 15–25 iiunia. 1914.* (St. Petersburg, 1914), p. 17.

During the Soviet period, G. Ibragimov emerged as the most vocal defender of

Tatarism. As he stated in 1911 in the pages of *Shura*, and quoted by M. Kh. Khasanov in *Galimdzhan Ibragimov* (Kazan, 1969), p. 39: "We are Tatars. Our language is Tatar, all we do is Tatar, and our future culture will be Tatar." For Ibragimov's thesis of Tatarization as developed during the Soviet period, see his essay *Tatar mädäniyeti ñindi yul belän barajaq?* (Kazan, 1927), pp. 6–7 and 23–24. G. Ibragimov remained an admirer and disciple of Nasiri all his life. He wrote two essays for the 1922 commemorative volume that was published on the twentieth anniversary of Nasiri's death. See *Kayyum Nasiri mäjmugasï* (Kazan, 1922).

16. As quoted by Vambery, "Die Kulturbestrebungen der Tataren," p. 90. The well-to-do Orenburg merchant Gani Bay Huseinov had voiced similar concerns in letters written to mullahs as early as February 1898. See Z. I. Ahsen Böre, ed., *Gani Bay* (Helsinki, 1945), pp. 42–43 and 46.

The periodical press took an active part in support of the vernacular. In 1909, the editors of *Shura* sponsored a language contest for the best article written in the vernacular. The winner was Hadi Atlasi. See A. N. Kurat, "Kazan Türklerinin tanınmış tarihçi ve milliyetçilerinden Hadi Atlas," *Kazan* 16 (1975): 6.

17. N. P. Zagoskin, ed., *Za sto let; biograficheskii slovar' professorov i prepodavatelei Imperatorskogo Kazanskogo Universiteta 1804–1904* (Kazan, 1904), p. 193.

18. Faseev, *Iz istorii Tatarskoi peredovoi obshchestvennoi mysli*, pp. 33–34; and Saviya Mikhailova, "Tatar khalkïnïng mag'rifetche ulï," *KU* 2 (1980): 121–74.

19. Zagoskin, *Za sto let*, p. 194. Khalfin also wrote the first books to popularize medical knowledge in Tatar. Kurat, "Kazan Türklerinin medeni uyanış devri," p. 110.

20. Faseev, *Iz istorii Tatarskoi peredovoi obshchestvennoi mysli*, pp. 34 and 53. Zagoskin, *Za sto let*, p. 234.

21. Z. Bigiev, *Ölüf yäki güzäl kïz Khädichä* (Kazan, 1887).

22. Kurat, "Kazan Türklerinin medeni uyanış devri," p. 111.

23. Faseev, *Iz istorii Tatarskoi peredovoi obshchestvennoi mysli*, p. 34; Zenkovsky, "Century of Tatar Revival," p. 312; Ia. G. Abdullin, *Tatarskaia prosvetitel'skaia mysl' (Sotsial'naia priroda i osnovnye problemy)* (Kazan, 1976), pp. 199–202.

24. Although, by 1904, the Volga Tatars had numerous printing presses of their own, they continued to buy a considerable number of books printed in various Islamic countries. For instance, the introduction to R. Fahreddin's *Asar* featured an advertisement for books from Cairo and other places in Egypt. These books were not only on religion; there were science, history, and geography books as well, and mail orders were available for them all. R. Fahreddin, *Asar*, vol. 1, part 5 (Orenburg, 1904).

25. Arabic printing was introduced in Russia at the beginning of the eighteenth century because of the practical needs of Peter I's government. The first document in Arabic characters printed in Russia was Peter I's *Manifesto* to his Muslim subjects. It was produced on July 15, 1722, by the printing press that had been set up at Astrakhan during the Persian campaign. At the end of the Persian campaign, the printing press was moved to Moscow, where it was idle until the 1770s when its activity was revived. In 1786, the government opened a new printing shop in St. Petersburg; there, materials could be published in Arabic, Persian, Turkish, and Tatar. That year, the print shop produced two volumes in Tatar—one concerning the police code and the other

concerning the organization of the guberniias. Only one year later, in 1787, the first Qur'an was printed in St. Petersburg. See A. Kh. Rafikov, *Ocherki istorii knigopechataniia v Turtsii* (Leningrad, 1975), pp. 59–60 and 101. For information on D. Kantemir, the exiled Moldavian prince who headed Peter I's Arabic printing press, see Al. Piru, *Literatura Română veche* (Bucharest, 1961), pp. 364–409; and G. Călinescu, *Istoria literaturii Române (compendiu)* (Bucharest, 1968), pp. 28–31.

26. K. F. Fuks, *Kazanskie Tatary* (Kazan, 1844), p. 121.

27. N. I. Vorob'ev, *Tatary srednego Povolzh'ia i Priural'ia* (Moscow, 1947), p. 384. In 1902, the same press printed 250 titles, totaling 2.5 million copies. See Vincent Monteuil, *Les musulmans soviétiques* (Paris, 1957), p. 21. Chicherina indicates the same figures, but for the year 1903. See S. B. Chicherina, *O Privolzhskikh inorodtsakh i sovremennom znachenii sistemy N. I. Il'minskogo* (St. Petersburg, 1906), p. 21. Recognition of the typographical quality of the books put out by the university press came when the press was awarded a silver medal at the Kazan Exhibition of 1885 and a gold medal at the Ekaterinburg Exhibition of 1889. The Kazan Exhibition of 1900 included the press on its list of honor. See Sh. Äkhmär, *Matbaachelek tarikhi* (Kazan, 1909), p. 56.

28. Fuks, *Kazanskie Tatary*, p. 20.

29. First investigations of Tatar book printing belong to Rizaeddin Fahreddin, *Qor'än vä tabagät* (Kazan, 1900); Äkhmär, *Matbaachelek tarikhi*; and A. Battal, *Tatar tarihi. Qazan Turkleri. Tarihi ve siyasi görüshler* (Istanbul, 1925), pp. 149–50. Among Soviet scholars, A. G. Karimullin has dedicated most of his efforts to the study of book printing and publishing among the Tatars. See his *Kitap dön'yäsina säyäkhät* (Kazan, 1979) and *Tatarskaia kniga nachala XX veka* (Kazan, 1974), both of which are outstanding. For a discussion of the Kazan university press see pp. 84–87 of the latter.

30. Vambery, "Die Kulturbestrebungen der Tataren," p. 76.

31. Karimullin, *Tatarskaia kniga*, pp. 177–79.

32. Ibid., pp. 56–74.

33. Ibid., pp. 47, 55, and 123. For more on the contributions of Kharitonov's printing activity to the cultural development of the Tatars, see "La presse musulmane," *RMM* 4 (1910): 581; Sh. Äkhmär's *Matbaachelek tarikhi*, which was dedicated to the celebration of Kharitnov's fortieth year in the business of printing, and "Livres et revues," *RMM* 6 (1909): 309.

34. Karimullin, *Tatarskaia kniga*, pp. 22 and 31.

35. Battal, *Qazan Türkleri*, pp. 216–17; "La presse musulmane. Analyses et extraits," *RMM* 2 (1911): 382. In 1912, the number of Muslim printing shops in Russia was 23; that of bookstores, 194. See R. Majerczak, "Une nouvelle statistique de la population musulmane," *RMM* 9 (1914): 272.

36. Äkhmär, *Matbaachelek tarihi*, pp. 58 and 67–70; S. Bagin, *Propaganda Islama putem pechati* (Kazan, 1909), pp. 9–11.

37. For an analysis of the trends in Muslim book publishing in Russia in 1912, see L. B., "Statistiques des publications musulmanes de Russie," *RMM* 4 (1914): 218–20.

38. R. Fahreddin, *Ahmed Bay* (Orenburg, 1911), p. 52.

39. Bagin, *Propaganda Islama*, p. 8.

40. The only Muslim deputy who took the issue to the Duma was the Tatar leader of the Muslim Trudoviki, Kalimulla Hasanov. Sadri Maksudi, the leading Constitutional Democrat, was widely criticized for his silence. This information is based on an essay written by Mansurov and on reports to the Okhrana by such Tatar informers as H. Kaibyshev (code name, Teoretik), who worked for the Kazan Okhrana from 1911 to 1917. See G. Mansurov, *Tatar pravakatrlari* (Moscow, 1927), p. 25.

41. One such work was M. Ak'ägätzade's *Khisametdin menla (Khisametdin Mullah)* (Kazan, 1886).

42. Apparently in 1910 alone, some 20,290 Tatars made use of the services offered by the Kazan Muslim library, Islamiye. This figure is significant because, in 1910, the Muslim population of Kazan amounted to 30,486 people, as compared with 149,060 Russians. See *Garoda Rosii v 1910 godu* (St. Petersburg, 1914), p. 224, and "La presse musulmane," *RMM* 2 (1910): 381.

43. *Malmïzhda Muslumanlar kïraathanesïnïng ustafï (ustav bezplatnoi biblioteki-chital'ni dlia Musul'man v g. Malmyzhe, Viatskoi gubernii)* (Kazan, 1907), p. 3; and *Viatka gubirnasï Malmïzh uiazï Tuntar kariasïndegï "Shems" kitabhanesïnïng ustafï (ustav bezplatnoi biblioteki-chital'ni "Shams" dlia Musul'man v der. Tiunteri Arbarskoi volosti, Malmyzhskogo uezda, Viatskoi gubernii)* (Kazan, 1908), pp. 3 and 10. In addition to books on all areas of life, the catalog of the holdings of the Tatar library from Chelebi contained Muslim newspapers and journals published in Russia, as well as some published in Egypt and Istanbul. See *Asami-al-kutub. Chelebi shehrinde ujretsïz Musul-man kutubhane-kiraathanesïnïng Tatar, Türk ve Arab tïllerïnde bulgan kitaplarena mahsus* (Urnek and Kazan, 1910), pp. 61–62.

44. See "Samara ahvalatï," *Iqtisad* 11–12 (1911): 359.

45. *Asami-al-Kutub* (Kazan: Karimov, 1897), pp. 14–15, 28–29, and 31.

46. *Asami-al-Kutub* (Kazan: Sharif, 1899).

47. *Asami-al-Kutub* (Kazan: Karimov, 1903).

48. *Asami-al-Kutub* (Kazan: Sabah, 1906).

49. *Asami-al-Kutub* (Kazan: Karimov, 1907).

50. *Asami-al-Kutub* (Kazan: Idrisov and Galiev, 1907–1919), pp. 12–13. The emphasis on textbooks continued to increase, as is evident in another book catalog that was published two years later by the bookstore Urnek. See *Asami-al-Kutub* (Kazan: Urnek, 1909).

51. *Asami-al-Kutub* (Orenburg: Ahmed-al-Ishaqi, 1907) and *Asami-al-Kutub* (Kazan: Iqbal, 1907), p. 13.

52. *Asami-al-Kutub* (Orsk: 1910), p. 10.

53. *Asami-al-Kutub* (Orenburg and Ufa: Karimov and Huseinov, 1910–1911). The advancement of book printing, the increase in the book trade, and the growing interest in education and learning are illustrated indirectly by articles on the craft of making bookcases and building libraries, as well as on the art of collecting books. For example, see "Kitap tuplamaq," *Iqtisad* 5 (1910): 141.

54. The Samara courthouse refused to transfer the gift to the community until

appropriate taxes had been paid. But as a result of a petition made by Akhund Meniushev from Saratov, and on the basis of decision no. 767 of the Ministry of the Interior, dated February 14, 1895, the Saratov court issued a circular on November 25, 1895, freeing the community from this taxation. *Sbornik tsirkuliarov i inykh rukovodiashchikh rasporiazhenii po okrugu Orenburgskogo Magometanskogo Dukhovnogo Sobraniia 1836–1903* (Ufa, 1905), pp. 115–16.

55. M. V. Kazanskii, *Putevoditel' po Kazani* (Kazan, 1899), p. 229. The orphanage founded by Ibrahim and Ishak Iunusov was supported financially by a waqf in which merchants from some fourteen stores in the vicinity of the mosque participated. The orphanage accommodated between 20 and 25 children and had a school where they received a bilingual education. This school was also attended by a dozen children from the city. "Autour du monde Musulman," *RMM* 6 (1909): 242, as reported from *Terjuman*, June 1, 1909.

56. Validov, *Ocherki istorii obrazovannosti*, p. 68.

57. A. Bobi, *Haqiqat yahud tughrïlïq* (Kazan, 1904), p. 16.

58. Validov, *Ocherki istorii obrazovannosti*, p. 68, and Bobi, *Haqiqat*, pp. 17–19.

59. Vambery, "Die Kulturbestrebungen der Tataren," p. 76.

60. These figures were reported by Ismail Bey Gasprali at a conference held in Cairo in 1907. "Les musulmans de Russie," *RMM* 28 (1914): 241.

61. For information on the Society Against Polygamy, see *RMM* 1 (1908): 148–49. For the Society for the Assistance of New Muslims, see A. Chatelier, "Les musulmans russes," *RMM* 2 (1907): 162, as based on information extracted from *Ikdam* of June 2, 1906. Also, see S. Bobrovnikoff, "Moslems in Russia," *The Moslem World* 1 (1911): 77 and 13. For accounts of individual or group conversions to Islam, see also *RMM* 7 (1907): 393, *RMM* 5 (1908): 161–62, *RMM* 8 (1908): 715, *RMM* 10 (1909): 294, *RMM* 1 (1910): 104, *RMM* 3 (1910): 413, and M. Mashanov, *Sovremennoe sostoianie Tatar-Mukhamedan i ikh otnoshenie k drugim inorodtsam* (Kazan, 1910), p. 6.

62. The ulamas of the village of Qarghalï (Ufa guberniia) founded a Muslim society called *Musulman Jemiyeti*. See "Autour du monde musulman," *RMM* 11 (1908): 512. For the Society of Kazan Ulama, see A. Chatelier, "Les musulmans russes," *RMM* 2 (1907): 163. In this article, Chatelier states that Muslim societies had different names—calling themselves local unions, circles, or benevolent societies—but that they all had the goal of opening schools, libraries, and reading rooms.

63. See *Goroda Rossii v 1910 godu* (St. Petersburg, 1914), pp. 195, 224, and 276. In 1897, the total population of Kazan was 129,959. See *Naselenie gorodov*, p. 9. In 1911, the Muslims represented 28 percent of the total population of the entire Kazan guberniia. See *Permskie vedomosti*, February 4, 1911, p. 2.

64. As reported in *RMM* 5 (1907): 57.

65. A. Chatelier, "Les musulmans russes," *RMM* 2 (1907): 163, as based on information reported by *Kazan mukhbiri*, August 7, 1906, and *Ikdam*, July 4, 1906.

66. *Musul'manin*, July 15, 1910, p. 398.

67. *Goroda Rossii v 1910 godu*, pp. 705 and 736. In 1897, Orenburg had a population of 37,813. *Naselenie gorodov*, p. 15.

68. *Permskie vedomosti*, February 4, 1911, p. 2.

69. A. Chatelier, "Les musulmans russes," *RMM* 2 (1907): 163, as based on information published in *Kazan mukhbiri*, July 5, 1906.

70. "Les musulmans de Russie," *RMM* 11–12 (1907): 549.

71. The name of this museum became a controversial issue. There was a proposal for naming it after the governor-general, but the intervention of two members of the Orenburg Muslim Society, Timur Shakhsalenev and Abdurrahman Shemsuddinov, prevented it. *RMM* 11–12 (1907): 550.

72. Information according to correspondence from Astrakhan dated July 10, 1910; see *Musul'manin*, August 15, 1910, p. 441.

73. A. Chatelier, "Les musulmans russes," *RMM* 2 (1907): 165.

74. "Les musulmans de Russie," *RMM* 11–12 (1907): 552, as based on information reported in *Terjuman*, September 25, 1907.

75. "Autour du monde musulman," *RMM* 10 (1909): 296.

76. "La presse musulmane," *RMM* 5 (1910): 144. The president of the society, Mustafa Lutfi Ismailov, had been arrested and briefly imprisoned in 1908 following a search of his house. "Autour du monde musulman," *RMM* 5 (1908): 162.

77. *Musul'manin*, August 15, 1910, p. 442.

78. The new society published its statutes in 1909 in a 32-page pamphlet entitled *Khan-Istafkesi Musulmanlarining terakki ve medeniyete yardim jemgiyetining nizam-namesi* (Astrakhan, 1909). For a discussion of this society, see *RMM* 1 (1910): 106–7; and *RMM* 4 (1910): 556.

79. "La presse musulmane. Analyses et extraits," *RMM* 2 (1911): 381.

80. The Missionary Committee of Perm reported that, in 1815, there were 1,517,326 Christians, 108,478 Muslims, and 22,100 animists in the entire guberniia. The figures for 1916 were 1,517,335, 108,476, and 22,100, respectively. See *Permskie vedomosti* 40 (February 11, 1915): 3, and *Permskie vedomosti* 43 (February 25, 1916): 3.

81. *Musul'manin*, June 10, 1910, p. 297.

82. *V mire musul'manstva* 23 (September 23–October 6, 1911): 3–4. *V mire musul'manstva* was a weekly of the Russian Muslims published in Russian in St. Petersburg. Its editors were M. Hajetlashe (also the editor of *Musul'manin*, published in Paris from 1908 to 1914) and A. Datiev. In October 1911, *V mire musul'manstva* also began to publish an edition in the Kazan Tatar language.

83. "Revue de la presse musulmane," *RMM* 12 (1913): 347.

84. "La presse musulmane russe," *RMM* 7–8 (1911): 135.

85. This information is contained in an essay entitled "Pan Turkizmning tuuvi," which was submitted as a report to the Kazan Okhrana by one of its most active agents, Tuhfatulla Mamaliev. Mamaliev was a Tatar teacher from Ufa who had been a member of the Socialist Revolutionary Tangchi group between 1905 and 1906 and who had become an Okhrana informer in 1910, working under the code name of Zhitel'. For Mamaliev's essay and other documents related to Okhrana activities among Tatars, see Mansurov, *Tatar pravakatrlari*, pp. 44, 55–56, and 60.

86. On Lithuanian Tatars, see Leon Bohdanowicz, "Moslems in Poland: Their Origin, History, and Cultural Life," *Journal of the Royal Asiatic Society of Great Britain* (October 1942): 163–80.

87. See *Kuyash* (a Tatar daily published in Kazan from 1912 to 1917), August 25, 1915, p. 3, and September 11, 1915, p. 3.

88. *Han-Istafkesi Musulmanlarïnïng terakki ve medeniyete yardïm jemgiyetïnïng nizamnamesi* (Astrakhan, 1909), pp. 2–4; *Imankul aulïnïng medeniyet ve iqtisad jemgiyet jeriyasïnïng ustafï* (Orenburg, 1911), pp. 2–3; *Timr (Qaraqamïsh) Musulman jemgiyet hayriyesïnïng ustafï (Uralsk oblast)* (Orenburg, 1909), pp. 2–3.

89. Often, Volga Tatars who were employed as civil servants in the Russian bureaucracy and were members of various Russian professional organizations were able to assist Muslim benevolent societies by influencing the decisions of the Russian organizations in matters concerning the Tatars. For instance, Hafiz Akchurin, a member of the Kazan petty bourgeois society (*meshchanskoe gorodskoe obshchestvo*) was instrumental in securing scholarships from this organization for two Tatar students, one of whom attended the Lazarev Institute for Oriental Languages. Similarly, Yusuf Osmanov, who was a member of the Petropavlovsk municipal administration (*gorodskoe samoupravlenie*) and a bank employee, included Tatar books and newspapers in the orders he filled for the city library. These books and newspapers were used by the local benevolent society. The above information is based on information from the memoirs of Ahmet Veli Menger, recorded on tape in 1975 in Ankara by Mahmut Tahir, who has provided the author with a copy.

90. *Timr (Qaraqamïsh)*, p. 3.

91. A. N. Kurat, "Kazan Türklerinin medeni uyanış devri," p. 174.

92. See *Zauralskii krai*, March 15, 1914, p. 2; June 22, 1914, p. 5; and March 10, 1916, p. 3. Cooperatives were also becoming popular among the Kirghiz. See *Sibirskaia zhizn'*, November 26, 1916, p. 3, and December 8, 1916, p. 4. The existence in 1918 of a special journal dedicated to problems of cooperation indicates that this form of response to the economic needs of the Tatars had become widespread in less than one decade. See *Ufa kaoperativere* 1 (1918): 26–29.

93. A testimony to the increased Tatar interest in credit associations is the fact that they translated two sample statutes for this type of organization into Tatar. See *Aullarda volostlarda häm istanitsalarda yasala turghan abshistvinni issuda-isbirigatilni (yani aqcha saqli turghan kassalar) nïng abrazsavi ustafï (Obraztsovyi ustav sel'skikh, volostnykh i stanichnykh obshchestvennykh ssudosberegatel'nykh kass)* (Kazan, 1904) and *Kriditni tavarishstvanïng abrazsavi ustafï (Ustav kreditnogo tovarishchestva)* (Kazan, 1907). On the need to open a Muslim bank in order to provide the Muslims with an adequate financial institution, see "Musulman banqasï," *Iqtisad* 8 (August 1910): 236, and "Kriditni tavarishstva nichun ichärga?" and "Vaq burch jemgiyetlerïnïng ishleri," *Iqtisad* 2 (February 1911): 54–55 and 55–56.

94. See Kurat, "Kazan Türklerinin medeni uyanış devri," pp. 174–75, and the statute of the Chistopolsk association of shareholders: *Chistaydaghï putribitiller jemgiyetïnïng ustafï (Ustav Chistopol'skogo obshchestva potrebitelei)* (Kazan, 1910), pp. 1–3.

95. In this project, they received technical assistance from the Astrakhan Society of Gardeners and from B. Svetlin, the Astrakhan representative of the guberniia agricultural department. See "Yana tamat zavudu," *Iqtisad* 6 (June 1912): 170–71.

96. See "Jemagat tgrmäni," and "Jemagat itifaqï," *Iqtisad* 7 (July, 1910): 195 and 216–17.

97. Kurat, "Kazan Türklerinin medeni uyanış devri," p. 174. According to A. V. Menger's memoirs, Karamshakov felt it suitable that an amount representing payment of the initial credit be sent to St. Petersburg as a contribution to the building of the mosque, which was encountering financial difficulties. Found in the author's copy of A. V. Menger's memoirs, recorded on tape by M. Tahir in Ankara in 1975.

CHAPTER 8

1. K. F. Fuks, *Kazanskie Tatary* (Kazan, 1844), p. 113. For discussions of the high incidence of literacy among the Tatars, also see Ia. D. Koblov, *Konfessional'nye shkoly Kazanskikh Tatar* (Kazan, 1916), pp. 3–4 and 9, A. I. Anastasiev, "O Tatarskikh dukhovnykh shkolakh. Nabliudeniia i zametki inspektora uchilishch," *Russkaia shkola* (December 1893): 126–30, and *ITDM* (Moscow, 1937), pp. 351–52, as based on an account quoted from *Opisanie vsekh v Rossiiskom gosudarstve obitaiushchikh narodov* (St. Petersburg, 1799), part 2, pp. 11–12.

2. For a discussion of the authority wielded by the mullahs, and for a definition of their duties as given by the Department of Ecclesiastical Affairs of the Ministry of Interior, see M. N. A. Bobrovnikov, "Russko-tuzemnye uchilishcha, mekteby i medresy v Srednei Azii," *ZMNP* (May–June 1913): 228; "Kazanskaia khronika," *Kazanskie vesti*, August 18, 1893, p. 3; *O Magometanskikh mullakh. Religiozno-bytovoi ocherk* (Kazan, 1907), pp. 9–10; Koblov, *Konfessional'nye shkoly Kazanskikh Tatar*, p. 50; and *Sbornik tsirkuliarov i inykh rukovodiashchikh rasporiazhenii po okrugu Orenburgskogo Magometanskogo Dukhovnogo Sobraniia 1830–1903* (Ufa, 1905), pp. 42–43. For a discussion of mektebs and medreses, see M. N. P. Ostroumov, "Musul'manskie maktaby i Russko tuzemnye shkoly v Turkestanskom Krae," *ZMNP* 1–2 (1906): 115–26.

3. Koblov, *Konfessional'nye shkoly Kazanskikh Tatar*, pp. 24, 28, and 31–34, and *Zaman kalendarï* (Orenburg, 1909), p. 45.

4. For a presentation of medrese life, see J. Validov, *Ocherki istorii obrazovannosti i literatury Tatar* (Moscow and Petrograd, 1923), pp. 13–32; A. N. Kurat, "Kazan Türklerinin medeni uyanış devri," *Ankara Üniversitesi Dil ve Tarih-Coğrafya Fakültesi Dergisi* 3–4 (1966): 98; *Tatary Srednego Povolzh'ia i Priural'ia* (Moscow, 1967), pp. 379–80; Fuks, *Kazanskie Tatary*, p. 114; and Ia. D. Koblov, *O Magometanskikh mullakh. Religiozno-bytovoi ocherk* (Kazan, 1907), p. 14.

5. Koblov, *Konfessional'nye shkoly Kazanskikh Tatar*, pp. 36–39, and 48–49.

6. Of these, 39 schools were for Christian Tatars, 10 for Chuvash, 11 for Mari, 1 for Udmurts, and 1 for Russians. See A. F. Efirov, *Nerusskie shkoly Povolzh'ia, Priural'ia i Sibiri* (Moscow, 1948), pp. 11 and 17.

7. For details on Il'minskii's schools and his role in preparing cadra for the inorodtsy, see E. N. Medynskii, *Istoriia Russkoi pedagogiki* (Moscow, 1938), p. 355; and D. Zelenin, "N. I. Il'minskii i prosveshchenie inorodtsev," *Russkaia shkola* 3 (1902): 175–94.

8. Efirov, *Nerusskie shkoly*, p. 13.

9. Ibid., pp. 29–30; O. V. Kaidanova, *Ocherki po istorii narodnogo obrazovaniia v Rossii i SSSR na osnove lichnogo opyta i nabliudenii*, vol. 1 (Berlin, 1938), pp. 100–108. For figures on schools sponsored by the Ministry of Education for Tatars, see *Permskie vedomosti*, October 1, 1910, p. 4; and N. I. Vorob'ev, *Kazanskie Tatary. Etnograficheskoe issledovanie material'noi kul'tury dooktiabr'skogo perioda* (Kazan, 1953), pp. 53–54.

10. Mahmudov, one of the Tatar deputies to the Third Duma, addressed the issue of linguistic Russification in one of his speeches. See *Stenograficheskie otchety Gosudarstvennoi Dumy 3-go sozyva* (St. Petersburg, 1907), p. 671. Government efforts aimed at promoting the Russian language even led to the closing down of some mektebs under the pretext that students who attended them in addition to attending Russo-Tatar schools became exhausted and their health was in danger. See circular no. 6453 of the Ministry of the Interior, issued on December 4, 1893, in *Sbornik tsirkuliarov Dukhovnogo Sobraniia* (Ufa, 1905), p. 101.

11. See *SRMNP*, vol. 4 (St. Petersburg, 1876), pp. 832–35. See also M. A. Miropiev, "K voprosu o prosveshchenii nashikh inorodtsev," *Russkaia shkola* 5–6 (1901): 121–36; D. A. A., "Vopros o prosveshchenii Tatar," *Russkaia shkola* 7–8 (1905): 237–57; G. Gasilov, "Osnovnye voprosy natsional'noi shkoly," *Revoliutsiia i kul'tura* 2 (1928): 26–27; and *Rezoliutsii kursov-konferentsii perepodgotovki natsional'nykh pedtekhnikumov* (Kazan, 1925), p. 9.

12. M. V. Kazanskii, *Putevoditel' po Kazani* (Kazan, 1899), pp. 177 and 193, and Shirinskii-Shakhmatov, "Materialy dlia istorii i statistiki nashikh gimnazii," *ZMNP* 1 (1864): 129–71.

13. *SRMNP*, vol. 2, pp. 305–8.

14. Ibid., p. 690.

15. Ibid., vol. 5, pp. 476, 773, and 776.

16. This assumption is based on a figure that indicates that, between 1801 and 1917, only 20 to 30 Tatars graduated from Kazan University. The data excludes the number of eventual gymnasia graduates who never entered a university or who received a degree from universities other than that of Kazan. See *Tatary Srednego Povolzh'ia Priural'ia*, p. 406. On Tatars who studied in Russian schools, also see "Les musulmans de Russie," *RMM* 11–12 (1907): 545. Tatar gymnasium students were still rare in 1911, and as a result, they remained among the newsmakers. For instance, a Samara newspaper reported that, in 1911, two Tatar youths had entered the gymnasium and one, the *real'noe uchilishche*. See "Samara ahvalatï," *Iqtisad* 6 (1912): 188. In the same year, however, 378 students graduated from the Samara medrese. See "Samara ahvalatï," *Iqtisad* 4 (1912): 128.

17. Bobrovnikov, "Russko-tuzemnye uchilishcha," p. 228; G. Ibragimov, *Tatary v revoliutsii 1905 goda* (Kazan, 1926), p. 30.

18. A. Vambery, "The Awakening of the Tatars," *The Nineteenth Century* 54 (February 1905): 222.

19. G. Alisov, "Musul'manskii vopros v Rossii," *Russkaia mysl'* 7 (1909): 60. Abdullin advanced the idea that Russia and Russian culture were not the only channels that acquainted the Tatars with Western culture. The cultures of Ottoman Turkey and the Middle East performed the same function, and books were always an important part of the luggage of the Tatar pilgrim and merchant. See Ia. G. Abdullin, *Tatarskaia prosvetitel'skaia mysl' (Sotsial'naia priroda i osnovnye problemy)* (Kazan, 1976), p. 38. Also see "Arap mekteplerïnïng hali," *Mektep*, Dec. 24, 1911, p. 36.

20. The Soviet leadership was aware of the role of mektebs in the life of Tatars, and until the end of the Civil War, it made concessions to the religious feelings of the Muslims in order to gain their support. The Tatar newspaper *Chulpan*, for instance, which was published in Moscow by Muskom (Muslim commissariat), announced in the fall of 1918 that children could begin signing up for the Muslim (sic) schools. In Moscow, such a school was to open in the building adjacent to the mosque. See *Chulpan*, Oct. 17, 1918, p. 3.

21. See Y. Akchura, "Turklerïnïng büyük muallim ve muhariri Ismail Bey Gasprinskii," *Il*, Sept. 25, 1913, p. 2, and Ibragimov, *Tatary v revoliutsii 1905 goda*, p. 31.

22. I. Gasprinskii, *Rehber-i muallimin yani muallimlere yuldash* (Bakhchesarai, 1898), pp. 12–13. For a Soviet account of jadid schools in the Crimea, see M. Bunegin, "Tatarskaia shkola v Krymu," *Prosveshchenie natsional'nostei* 1 (1931): 52–54.

23. Koblov, *Konfessional'nye shkoly Kazanskikh Tatar*, pp. 68–72.

24. For a full account of the interview, see "Samara ahvalatï," *Iqtisad* 7 (1910): 223.

25. For an integral text of the resolution, see "Shkol'nyi vopros v Russkom musul'manstve," *Mir Islama* 5 (1913): 3 and 290–92.

26. On the growing secularization of the medrese curriculum, see "Mufti hazretnïng yadigarï," *Iqtisad* 12 (1910): 374–75, and "Dini gali Dar-ul-Funun," *Iqtisad* 8–10 (1911): 229–30.

27. By 1908, the Muslim press employed the term *muderris* almost exclusively when referring to teachers. For an example, see "Musulmanlarda teraqi eserleri," *Iqtisad* 3 (1908): 95. For point 27 of the resolution see "Shkol'nyi vopros v Russkom musul'manstve," *Mir Islama* 5 (1913): 292.

28. The Tatars of Orenburg published Gani Bay's letters in 1912, as a tribute to him on the tenth anniversary of his death. The original 1912 edition, in Arabic script, is not available in Western libraries, and I was not able to find it in private collections. For this study, I used a reprint in Latin script (from the original edition), published by the Volga Tatar community of Helsinki. See Z. I. Ahsen Böre, ed., *Gani Bay* (Helsinki, 1945), p. 38. The Helsinki edition contains only 67 letters but features accounts by those who knew Gani Bay.

29. M. Aminov, "Le progrès de l'instruction chez les musulmans russes," *RMM* 10 (1909): 261–63.

30. "Mestnaia khronika. O Tatarskom obrazovanii." *Orenburgskii krai*, December 11, 1908, p. 3.

31. "Musulman mekteplerine program," *Iqtisad* 3 (1911): 95–96.

32. Koblov, *Konfessional'nye shkoly Kazanskikh Tatar*, pp. 76–79. The community of Samara was one of the few to petition the city for full financing to open a Russo-Tatar school. "Samara ahvalatï," *Iqtisad* 11–12 (1911): 358.

33. "La presse musulmane. Extraits et analyses," *RMM* 12 (1912): 667.

34. "Mektepler meselesi," *Iqtisad* 5–6 (1911): 186–87.

35. Menulla Sabirjan (b. 1866) was an enlightened village teacher from Mamadysh uezd who was unhappy with the old system and wrote textbooks to improve the quality of teaching. See *Zaman kalendarï* (Orenburg, 1910), p. 39.

36. For an example of notes on, and reviews of, textbooks, see *Yulduz*, June 6, 1915, p. 2. In Orsk, the Shark bookstore listed geography atlases in addition to textbooks. See "Livres et revues. Publications russes," *RMM* 2 (1911): 403.

37. "Autour du monde musulman," *RMM* 8 (1908): 715. For titles of other textbooks, see Bobrovnikov, "Russko-tuzemnye uchilishcha," p. 232; S. Bobrovnikoff, "Moslems in Russia," *The Moslem World* 1 (1911): 15; and "Livres et Revues en Russie," *RMM* 12 (1910): 728–30.

38. See Koblov, *Konfessional'nye shkoly Kazanskikh Tatar*, pp. 82–83, and *Tatary Srednego Povolzh'ia Priural'ia*, p. 390.

39. See "Magarif," *Iqtisad* 5 (1910): 130–31.

40. For a breakdown of the weekly hours of medrese instruction devoted to particular disciplines, see Bobrovnikoff, "Moslems in Russia," pp. 16–17; Y. Akchura, *L'Etat actuel et les aspirations des turco-tatares musulmans en Russie* (Lausanne, 1916), p. 12; and A. Ishaki, *Idel-Oural* (Paris, 1933), p. 19.

41. For a list of requirements for the examinations held in Ufa between September 27 and September 29, 1910, see L. B., "La presse musulmane. Russie," *RMM* 10 (1910): 356–57.

42. At times, such double standards led to comical situations. For instance, in the excitement that followed the arrival of one inspector, the students forgot to remove a geography map from the wall. When asked about the purpose of the map a student explained that it was needed to follow the journeys of the prophet Muhammad. See A. Kh. Makhmutova, "Vozniknovenie svetskikh zhenskikh shkol u Tatar," in Iu. I. Smykov, ed., *Ocherki istorii narodov Povolzh'ia i Priural'ia* (Kazan, 1967), p. 181.

43. "Mahkeme-i-Shariye ve medreselernï teftish," *Iqtisad* 11 (1910): 348, and "La presse musulmane. Extraits et analyses," *RMM* 1 (1911): 167.

44. Abdullin, *Tatarskaia prosvetiteliskaia mysl'*, p. 209. Among the medreses of the Kazan guberniia, some of the largest were Chistai, Kïzlau, Menger, Satïsh, Uri, Mechkere, and Kishkar (which was famous for its excellence in teaching logic and dialectics). See "Shkol'nyi vopros v Russkom musul'manstve," *Mir Islama* 2 (1913): 453–54.

45. Abdullah Battal-Taymas, *Ben bir ışık arıyordum* (Istanbul, 1962), pp. 14–15; *Zaman kalendarï* (Orenburg, 1910), pp. 34–35; and Kurat, "Kazan Turklerinin medeni uyanış devri," p. 177.

46. The entrance examination requirements were published in *Vaqt*, July 26, 1913. See "Shkol'nyi vopros v Russkom musul'manstve," *Mir Islama* 2 (1913): 452.

47. These figures are based on a program Koblov attributed to medrese Galiye of Kazan. Because his data are based on information published by A. Barudi in *Al-din-wa-l-Adab* in 1913, it is most likely he had Muhammediye in mind. See Koblov, *Konfessional'nye shkoly Kazanskikh Tatar*, pp. 96–102.

48. Battal-Taymas, *Ben bir ışık arıyordum*, pp. 17–20.

49. A. Saadi, *Tatar ädäbiyatï tarihi* (Kazan, 1926), pp. 73–74.

50. The Islahists did not have a well-defined program; they adhered to the general ideas of cultural reform, but receptiveness to socialist ideas placed them at the radical end of the jadid intellectuals. See Ibragimov, *Tatary v revoliutsii 1905 goda*, pp. 192–94.

51. See Kh. Kh. Khasanov, *Revoliutsiia 1905–1907g. v Tatarii* (Moscow, 1965), pp. 313–19; "Shkol'nyi vopros v Russkom musul'manstve," *Mir Islama* 2 (1913): 442–43 and 446–49; and Efirov, *Nerusskie shkoly*, pp. 47 and 68.

52. *Mir Islama* 2 (1913): 450–51. On responses to the economic hardships of both Osmaniye and Muhammediye medreses, see R. Fahreddin, *Ahmed Bay* (Orenburg, 1911), pp. 30–31.

53. For the program of the Muhammediye medrese of Troitsk, see Bobrovnikov, "Russko-tuzemnye uchilishcha," pp. 239–41.

54. Fahreddin, *Ahmed Bay*, pp. 31–32.

55. Interview with Osman and Haider Ali brothers, fur merchants, and leaders of the 350-member Helsinki Tatar community, conducted by the author on January 14, 1974, in Helsinki.

56. Fahreddin, *Ahmed Bay*, pp. 31–32.

57. See Mahmut Tahir, "Kazan Türklerinde tahsil-bilim (Medrese-i-Hüseiniye)," *Kazan* 3 (1971): 54.

58. On the village medrese, see Koblov, *Konfessional'nye shkoly Kazanskikh Tatar*, p. 60; and Fahreddin, *Ahmed Bay*, p. 39.

59. See A. V. Menger, "Bubi medresesi ve Bubi kardeşler," *Kazan* 3 (1971): 33–34.

60. Validov, *Ocherki istorii obrazovannosti*, p. 67.

61. Kaibyshev's report noted that Feyzulla Muhammed, a son of a Russian Muslim from Viatka guberniia who had emigrated to Turkey and one of the teachers at Bobi, had been a member of pan-Turkist circles in Istanbul before his return to Russia to take a position at Bobi. G. Mansurov, *Tatar pravakatrlarï* (Moscow, 1927), pp. 28–30 and 68.

62. Krivonogov served a prison sentence for having warned the teachers about the raid. He was denounced by the teacher Faiz Davudov, who was also an Okhrana agent. See Mansurov, *Tatar pravakatrlarï*, p. 72.

63. Qur'an, 3: 32.

64. For details on the Bobi affair, see Mansurov, *Tatar pravakatrlarï*, pp. 36–37, 69, and 70–76, and Menger, "Bubi medresesi," pp. 35 and 37–38.

65. *ITASSR*, vol. 1 (Kazan, 1955), p. 471. As a result of the December 1910 measures to counteract Tatar-Muslim influence in the Volga area, many other schools or private residences of Tatars were searched, three teachers of Muhammediye medrese were fired, and schools throughout the Volga area were closed for various periods of time. See *V mire Musul'manstva*, October 14, 1911, p. 3; and "La presse musulmane. Extraits et analyses," *RMM* 4 (1911): 144–45. The Muslim press alerted Tatar public opinion to the fact that communities should become involved in finding employment for teachers from the medreses that were being closed by the government. See *V mire Musul'manstva*, October 7, 1911, p. 3.

66. *RMM* 1 (1908): 149.

67. "Statistika uchashchikhsia Kazani," *Kazanskie vesti*, December 10, 1892, p. 3. Priority was given to poor villages, in which case the merchants also paid the salaries of the teachers. See Ahsen Böre, *Gani Bay*, pp. 16, 23, 25, 28, 48, 64, and 68, and Saadi, *Tatar ädäbiyatï tarihi*, pp. 74–75.

68. Between 1908 and 1910, 168 male and 106 female teachers attended summer courses at Bobi. In 1908, there were 20 men and 6 women; in 1909, 64 men and 42 women; and in 1910, 84 men and 58 women. Menger, "Bubi medresesi," p. 33.

69. See "Musul'manskaia zhizn'," *Kamsko-Volzhskaia rech'*, May 21, 1909, p. 3.

70. "Dar-ul-Muallimin nik kirek," *Iqtisad* 4 (1911): 187–88; "Imamlarnïng hallerini islah," *Iqtisad* 4 (1911): 98–100; "Autour du monde musulman," *RMM* 1–2 (1909): 140; and "Bibliographie musulmane russe," *RMM* 2 (1906–1907): 297.

71. "Imamlarïmïznïng kuzden tüshmekï," *Iqtisad* 3 (1911): 67–68.

72. In a letter of 1898, Gani Bay mentioned that some 150 abïstays were engaged in teaching girls. Their monthly salary was only about 5 rubles. See Ahsen Böre, *Gani Bay*, p. 17.

73. Ibid., pp. 19, 34–35, and 70–73; *Zaman kalendarï* (Orenburg, 1909), p. 45; "Autour du monde musulman," *RMM* 3 (1909): 320.

74. On Huseinova's school, see A. Kh. Makhmutova, "Shkola Liabiby Khusainovoi v Kazani," in *Stranitsy istorii goroda Kazani* (Kazan, 1981), pp. 55–65.

75. "Autour du monde musulman," *RMM* 11 (1908): 513.

76. "Autour du monde musulman," *RMM* 10 (1908): 235, and "La presse musulmane. Analyses et extraits," *RMM* 2 (1911): 381. In 1908, the same year that Baghbestan Khalaf opened her school in Orenburg, the Tatars of the Sukonnaia quarter of Kazan petitioned for permission to open a school. The authorities agreed, on the condition that Russian be included in the curriculum. See *Volzhsko-Kamskaia rech'*, February 16, 1908, p. 3.

77. For more on the campaign for girls' schools in the Tatar press, see "La presse musulmane. Russie," *RMM* 10 (1910): 356.

78. See Makhmutova, "Vozniknovenie svetskikh zhenskikh shkol u Tatar," pp. 176–77; the letter to the author from Osman Ali, dated July 14, 1975, Helsinki; and the author's interview of January 14, 1975, with Reyhane Apa, a former graduate of the Bobi girls' school. Reyhane Apa spoke with pride about the multilateral education she received at Bobi, an education that included the French language. She also stressed

that the name of the Bobi girls' school, alone, was often sufficient to determine the appreciation a graduate received from any community. Reyhane Apa began her teaching career in the village of Yanapar and continued it in Finland, where she moved with her merchant husband shortly before 1917. The respect she enjoyed as a teacher of many generations of youth was reflected in the number of people who came to Helsinki from all parts of Finland to pay their final respects when she died in 1975.

79. Menger, "Bubi medresesi," p. 40.

80. *Yulduz* reported the opening of a new girls' school in Troitsk and listed the subjects of the curriculum, which were overwhelmingly secular. See *Yulduz*, June 14, 1915, p. 2.

81. Makhmutova, "Vozniknovenie svetskikh zhenskikh shkol u Tatar," pp. 182–84. Besides a genuine interest in better education for girls, the interest in a gymnasium for girls might have been prompted by other reasons. In 1910, *Vaqt* of Orenburg reported that five Muslim girls had been admitted to Orsk's Russian gymnasium. In 1910, *Musul'manin* alerted its readers about an increase in the suicide rate among the Tatar youths, most of the deaths caused by unhappy romances between Russian students and Tatar girls. A Tatar gymnasium for girls would have prevented close contact between the young Russians and Tatar girls and thus decreased the possibility of romances and their unhappy consequences. See "Autour du monde musulman," *RMM* 3 (1910): 414, and *Musul'manin*, June 10, 1910, p. 296.

82. An article in *Iqtisad* stressed that a school of agricultural economy in the Samara guberniia received students of all nationalities. The agricultural schools included, besides subjects related directly to forestry and agriculture, the study of accounting, of Russian laws regarding agriculture, and of veterinary science. See "Selski haziaistva mektebï," *Iqtisad* 2 (1911): 52–53.

83. "Rusyada tijaret mekteplerï," *Iqtisad* 9 (1910): 266–67; "Tijaret mekteplerï," *Iqtisad* 12 (1909): 361–62; *Iqtisad* 8 (1910): 233–34.

84. "Musulman shakirdler," *Iqtisad* 11 (1909): 334.

85. "Sevdegar balalarïnïng terbiyesï," *Iqtisad* 3 (1908): 73–74, and "Gazitelerden," *Iqtisad* 11–12 (1911): 313.

86. "Uqu urïnlarï," *Iqtisad* 8–10 (1911): 230–33. *Iqtisad* published numerous articles on crafts, describing some and listing the economic advantages of others. Here are some examples: "Bizde sanagat," *Iqtisad* 2 (1908): 47–48; "Musulman qariyelerinde sanaat" and "Bizim hunerjiler," *Iqtisad* 8 (1909): 238–39 and 239–40; "Quyan aulïnïng sanaat mektebï," *Iqtisad* 5–6 (1911): 155–56.

87. "Kimler itishdiremiz," *Iqtisad* 56 (1911): 138–39; "Sanaatnï qutlandïrmak lazim," *Iqtisad* 3 (1908): 77–78.

88. "Turmalarda sanaat," *Iqtisad* 12 (1909): 367. This article welcomes the prison craft shops as a first step toward rehabilitating delinquents and preventing crime.

89. Many Tatar youths chose the medical profession; the inclination they showed toward that field seems to have had its origin in the fact that medical studies were the only branch of higher education into which Tatars were welcomed in the nineteenth century. *Polnoe sobranie zakonov Rossiiskoi imperii, Sobranie 2, 1949,* vol. 24 (St. Petersburg, 1850), section 2, p. 42.

90. In the Middle East, Medina and Cairo apparently were centers exclusively for higher Islamic studies. In 1907, for instance, the Muslim pilgrims from Russia visited the Kazan students in Medina. See *RMM* 6 (1907): 223, as reported from *Terjuman* of March 23, 1907. Beirut, however, was becoming increasingly popular as a higher education center because, besides Islamic theology, it offered the advantages of colleges and universities sponsored by Western European countries, among which the French and American medical schools were most popular. See A. Krymskii, *Musul'manstvo i ego budushchnost'* (Moscow, 1899), pp. 92–93 and 95. The highest concentration of Russian Muslim students (including Tatars) seems to have been in Istanbul, where they prepared mainly for teaching careers. See *RMM* 1 (1908): 152. In Western Europe, Russian Muslims favored Paris and Geneva over other university centers. See "La presse musulmane. Extraits et analyses," *RMM* 4 (1911): 145. In 1911, a Tatar youth had ventured as far as the Pacific Coast of the United States to study chemistry at the University of San Francisco. His name was Habibula Baibulatov, and he was a former medrese student. To assist those who wanted to make inquiries about American universities, *V mire Musul'manstva* published his address. See *V mire Musul'manstva*, September 23, 1911, p. 3.

91. These women were apparently only auditing the courses offered by the medical schools, since they do not appear in the records the Geneva Medical School kept for its regular students. Letter to the author from William Geisendorf, dean of the Faculty of Medicine, University of Geneva, dated June 26, 1975.

92. On the relationship between the Tatars and the Kazakh steppes or Turkestan, as well as on the impact of the Tatars on the education of the Muslims in these areas, see Frank McCarthy, "The Kazan Missionary Congress," *CMRS* 3 (1973): 321–24; Violet Connolly, "The Nationalities Question in the Last Phase of Tsardom," in E. Oberländer, ed., *Russia Enters the Twentieth Century, 1894–1917* (New York, 1971), p. 179; Vambery, *Awakening of the Tatars*, p. 78; P. Znamenskii, "Sistema inorodcheskogo obrazovaniia v Turkestanskom krae pri generale-gubernatore K. P. Fon-Kaufmane," *Russkaia shkola* 7–8 (1902): 79–84 and 90–97; and S. Farforovskii, "Narodnoe obrazovanie u Turkmen," *Russkaia shkola* 2 (1911): 64–65. The Tatars wielded considerable influence among the Muslims of the steppes and Turkestan; they also maintained a close interest in the life of the Muslims in both regions and defended the rights of the Kazakhs against the government policies designed to resettle Russians into the steppes. See "Turkestan muslumanlarïnïng pravasï," *Ulfet*, May 23, 1907, p. 1; "Autour du monde musulman," *RMM* 9 (1909): 160. The March 31, 1906, rules concerning the education of Eastern inorodtsy (*Pravila o nachal'nykh uchilishchakh dlia inorodstev zhivushchikh v vostochnoi i iugo-vostochnoi Rossii*) were aimed at terminating the influence of the Tatars on the education of other Russian Muslims. The rules provided that the teachers must be either of the same nationality as their students or Russian. See I. Levin, "Materialy k politike tsarizma v oblasti pis'mennosti inorodtsev," *Kul'tura i pismennost' Vostoka* 6 (1930): 8–9.

93. A. K. Ilkul, an Ottoman jadid teacher who in 1913 traveled through Russia on his journey to Kashgar, noted in his memoirs a meeting with two young Tatar teachers who had traveled on the same train bound for Tashkent, where they were to teach at jadid schools. Ilkul met other Tatar teachers throughout his travels in Turkestan and

China. See A. K. Ilkul, *Türkistan ve Çin yollarında unutulmayan hatıralar* (Istanbul, 1955), pp. 31–34.

94. In 1911, there were 32 mosques and 12 mektebs, with a total of 1,200 students in Pekin. Due to the efforts of A. Riza and S. Tahir, the reforms that had changed the Volga Tatar schools reached the Pekin mekteb as well. See A. Ahmedi, "Qïtay muslumanlari," *Iqtisad* 8–10 (1911): 294. There is still other evidence of the Tatar influence on the Muslim schools of the Far East: Their curriculum was similar, if not identical, to that of the mektebs and medreses of the Volga-Ural area. The account of M. Tahir, who himself attended such a school in Harbin, indicates that even the emphasis on Russian language remained unchanged. See letter from M. Tahir to the author, dated September 22, 1975.

CHAPTER 9

1. As quoted in Kh. Kh. Khasanov, *Revoliutsiia 1905–1907g. v Tatarii* (Moscow, 1965), p. 133.

2. G. Alisov, "Musul'manskii vopros v Rossii," *Russkaia mysl'* 7 (1909): 45.

3. Mamaliev had previously joined the Okhrana under the code name of Zhitel'. Mansurov published Mamaliev's essay in its entirety in his work on the Tatar informers and agents-provocateurs for the Okhrana. See G. Mansurov, *Tatar pravakatrlari* (Moscow, 1927), p. 44.

4. Ibid., pp. 56–57. In his work entitled *Sibir timir yuli yani ahvali millet*, the Tatar poet Majid Gafuri (1880–1934) praised the achievements of Western European civilization in science, technology, education, and culture and invited the Tatars to follow the Western European example. For discussions of M. Gafuri and his place in Tatar literature, see Ahmet Temir, "Tukay deviri Kazan şairleri," *Kazan* 3 (1971): 13; *Istoriia Tatarskoi Sovetskoi literatury* (Moscow, 1965), pp. 171–92; and A. Biniiatullina, *Pisateli Sovetskogo Tatarstana* (Kazan, 1970), pp. 129–34.

5. *Sharkirdlik* is actually a collective noun. Although its exact English translation as "student life" is rather awkward, there is a Russian equivalent, *studenchestvo*, that renders the meaning exactly. A. Ishaki claimed that the membership of Shakirdlik went beyond the confines of the Volga-Ural region and encompassed students from the Crimea and even Turkestan. I have not been able, however, to find any evidence that proves his contention. See A. Ishaki, *Idel-Oural* (Paris, 1933), pp. 32–33.

My search for details concerning the nature, or the program, of the party Hurriyet yielded no positive results. The newspaper under the same name is listed as being the organ of a revolutionary group. See A. Bennigsen and Chantal Lemercier-Quelquejay, *La presse et le mouvement national chez les musulmans de Russie avant 1920* (Paris, 1964), pp. 25 and 84.

6. See Khasanov, *Revoliutsiia 1905–1907g.*, pp. 131 and 174–75.

7. Ibid., p. 315. A. Bennigsen indicates that Brek was organized in the spring of 1906. See A. Bennigsen and Chantal Lemercier-Quelquejay, *Les mouvements na-*

tionaux chez les musulmans de Russie. Le "sultangalievisme au Tatarstan" (Paris, 1960), p. 53.

8. The Volga Tatars had a preference for the name *Tang Yulduzï*. In 1896, Nasyri applied for permission to publish a newspaper under that name, but the authorities denied it. Bennigsen and Lemercier-Quelquejay, *La presse*, pp. 84–85, and S. A. Zenkovsky, *Pan-Turkism and Islam in Russia* (Cambridge, Mass., 1960), p. 37.

9. The only biography of Yamashev is still Kh. Kh. Khasanov's work in Tatar: *Husain Yamashev* (Kazan, 1954). For the history of the Social Democratic party in Kazan, see N. G. Anisimov, *Kazanskii l'nokombinat* (Kazan, 1960); T. Iu. Burmistrova, *Natsional'naia politika bol'shevikov v pervoi Russkoi revoliutsii 1905–1907g.* (Leningrad, 1962); S. Livshits, *Kazan' v gody pervoi Russkoi revoliutsii (1905–1907)* (Kazan, 1930); and Kh. Kh. Khasanov, "Kazanskie sotsial-demokraty v period bor'by za sozdaniie marksistkoi partii v Rossii (1894–1904)," in *Ocherki istorii partiinoi organizatsii Tatarii* (Kazan, 1962).

10. Bennigsen and Lemercier-Quelquejay, *La presse*, p. 56.

11. The best work on the Yamashev group is G. Ibragimov's *Ural häm Uralchïlar* (Kazan, 1926). Mamaliev, in his report to the Okhrana, argued that Yamashev pressed the Social-Democrats to publish a paper of their own, and as a result, *Ural* was born. See Mansurov, *Tatar pravakatrlarï*, p. 58, and G. Ibragimov, *Tatary v revoliutsii 1905 goda* (Kazan, 1926), pp. 88–92. Unfortunately, *Ural* is not available in any library outside the Soviet Union and is even beyond the reach of the Western scholar whose access to archival materials and library holdings in the USSR excludes access to special collections.

12. Khasanov, *Revoliutsiia 1905–1907g.*, p. 297; for a discussion of *Ural*, see pp. 298–302.

13. The strength of the Tatar social democracy was indicated by the size of their delegation to the Fifth Congress of the Russian Social Democratic Labor Party in 1907. Only one Tatar, probably Yamashev, attended the congress. See D. Lane, *The Roots of Russian Communism: A Social and Historical Study of Russian Social Democracy* (Assen, 1969), p. 44, and J. Validov, *Ocherki istorii obrazovannosti i literatury Tatar* (Moscow and Petrograd, 1923), p. 65.

14. A. Ibrahimov was born in 1853 in the Siberian town of Tara, into a family whose ancestors had come to the Ural region from Bukhara. Upon his graduation from the medrese in 1871, he left for Mecca, where he studied for eight years before going to Istanbul in 1879. In 1882, at the insistence of his countryman Abdurrashid Bey, Ibrahimov returned to Russia, where he became involved in the jadid schools. In 1892, he was elected a member of the muftiat in the capacity of judge, but personal problems caused him to leave again for Istanbul in 1895. In 1896, he traveled from Istanbul to Switzerland, where a meeting with novelist A. V. Amfiteatrov introduced him to the Russian revolutionary circles in Switzerland. See A. N. Kurat, "Kazan Türklerinin medeni uyanış devri," *Ankara Üniversitesi Dil ve Tarih-Coğrafya Fakültesi Dergisi 3–4* (1966): 123–24. For Amfiteatrov, see Ettore Lo Gato, *Histoire de la littérature russe des origines à nos jours* (Tournai, Belgium: Desclée de Brouwer, 1965), pp. 493–94. Hans Bräker's contention that Ibrahimov believed in a Muslim renaissance without any

contacts with the West is incorrect. See Hans Bräker, "The Muslim Revival in Russia," in E. Oberländer, ed., *Russia Enters the Twentieth Century, 1894–1917* (New York, 1971), p. 193.

15. Actually, Abdurrashid Bey had returned to Russia first in 1900 and even published the newspaper *Mir'at* in St. Petersburg from 1900 to 1902. Between 1902 and 1903, he was in Japan, where he is believed to have been involved in anti-Russian propaganda that led to his deportation at the request of the Russian consul. There is some evidence pointing to the fact that Abdurrashid Bey's Japanese connection began prior to his trip in 1902 and 1903 and lasted until his death in Japan in September 1944. See U.S. Office of Strategic Services Research and Analysis Branch, R. & A. no. 890.2, *Japanese Attempts at Infiltration Among Muslims in Russia and Her Borderlands* (Washington, D.C., 1944), pp. 9, 15–16, 25–27, 30, 32, 52, 56, 58, 79–81, and 84–85.

16. A. Arsharuni and Kh. Gabidullin, *Ocherki panislamizma i pantiurkizma v Rossii* (Moscow, 1934), pp. 23–24.

17. He discussed the concepts of extraterritorial autonomy in a work published in 1905 and entitled *Idare-i muhtariyet*; see G. Ibragimov, *Tatary v revoliutsii 1905 goda*, pp. 235–36. For a comparison of the components of territorial and extraterritorial autonomy, see *Ulfet*, May 11, 1906, p. 21.

18. Musa Jarullah Bigi, *Islahat esaslarï* (Petrograd, 1917), pp. 3–4.

19. Khasanov, *Revoliutsiia 1905–1907g.*, pp. 80–83.

20. Bigi, *Islahat esaslarï*. For a discussion of the ulama congress and its daily sessions, see pp. 15–79; for the memoir of the students, see pp. 79–82; for individual and village petitions, see pp. 82–111; and for the proposal drafted by the congress, and the public reaction to it, see pp. 112–51.

21. Y. Akchura was born in 1876 to a wealthy family in Simbirsk. His father died when Akchura was two years old, and his mother, Bibi-Kamer Banu Yunusov, moved with her son to Istanbul when Yusuf was only seven years old. There, he entered the military school in 1887, and after graduation, entered the military academy. As a student at the academy, Akchura was imprisoned several times for his affiliation with the circles of the Young Turks. After his release from prison in 1900, he left for Paris, where he attended the Ecole Libre des Sciences Politiques, from which he graduated in 1903. Because of Akchura's association with the Young Turk circles in Paris, the borders of the Ottoman empire were closed to him. In 1903, he returned to Russia, where he lived until 1908, when he moved to Istanbul. In 1904, Akchura wrote his major political essay *Uch-tarz-i-siyaset*. He wrote his essay in Russia but published it in Cairo in the May and June 1904 issues of the newspaper *Turk*. See Abdullah Battal-Taymas, *Ben bir ışık arıyordum* (Istanbul, 1962), pp. 114–117 and 127. For a monograph on Akchura, see M. F. Tugay, *Yusuf Akçura. Hayatı ve eserleri* (Istanbul, 1944).

22. A delegation of students participated in these first meetings of the Kazan community. During the third gathering at the Saydashev residence, there was some opposition to the presence of the students, but it was disregarded by the majority. See Bigi, *Islahat esaslarï*, pp. 5–6.

23. Bigi indicated that there were four or five students present at the meeting, but he

did not give their names, except for that of B. Ahtamov. See *Islahat esaslari*, pp. 162–65.

24. Ibid., p. 167.

25. In March 1905, the Kazan Committee of the Russian Social Democratic Party announced that it had intensified its propaganda among the local Muslim population by translating political pamphlets into Tatar and by inviting Tatars to its meetings. One of the bilingual pamphlets distributed by that committee in the spring of 1905 was entitled *Comrade Tatars*. See R. Nafigov, *Formirovanie i razvitie peredovoi Tatarskoi obshchestvenno-politicheskoi mysli. Ocherk istorii 1895–1917* (Kazan, 1967), p. 105.

26. Bigi, *Islahat esaslari*, pp. 167–69.

27. Arsharuni and Gabidullin, *Ocherki panislamizma*, p. 24, indicated that the total number of participants at the first congress was 150 but failed to mention the source of their information. Musa Bigi's account is more reliable because he drafted the documents of the congress and because his presentation contained a breakdown of the total number of participants by regions: 28 of the delegates were from the Caucasus; the remaining 80, from the Volga-Ural region and the Crimea. See Bigi, *Islahat esaslari*, pp. 172–73.

28. The text of the resolutions, in Tatar and Russian, was published in Bigi, *Islahat esaslari*, pp. 175–77.

29. Ibid., p. 174.

30. Ibid., pp. 201–2.

31. The election of Akchura, as well as the rapprochement between the Kadets and the Muslims, was just a tactical move; this fact is reflected in Miliukov's own assessment of the nationalities question. See P. N. Miliukov, *Natsional'nyi vopros (proiskhozhdenie natsional'nosti i natsional'nye voprosy v Rossii)* (Paris, 1925), pp. 170–71.

32. This essay, entitled *Uch-tarz-i-siyaset*, contains Akchura's doctrine of Turkish nationalism, wherein he advocates the idea of a Turkish national state as the best form of political organization for Turks. See Y. Akchura, *Uch-tarz-i-siyaset* (Istanbul, 1909), pp. 2–3, 11–14, and 29–31. On Y. Akchura's political philosophy, see also Von Gerhard Mende, "Yusuf Akchura bin Vorkamper des Turkismus," *Osteuropa* 10 (1934–1935): 564–68; and "Les courants politiques dans la Turquie. Origine du panturquisme ou pantouranisme," *RMM* 12 (1912): 174–75.

33. Bigi, *Islahat esaslari*, pp. 217–18; for the program, see pp. 220–33; for the resolutions of the congress see pp. 237–38.

34. Zenkovsky, *Pan-Turkism and Islam*, pp. 42–43.

35. Bigi, *Islahat esaslari*, pp. 178–81; Bennigsen and Lemercier-Quelquejay, *Le "sultangalievisme au Tatarstan,"* pp. 58–59.

36. Kurat, "Kazan Türklerinin medeni uyanış devri," p. 138.

37. Bigi, *Islahat esaslari*, pp. 214–15 and 240–41.

38. A. Chatelier, "Les musulmans russes," *RMM* 1 (1907): 199 and 151–52, as reported from *Muayyad*, April 21, 1906, and *Kazan mukhbiri*, July 23 and August 6, 1906.

39. *1906 sene 16–21 Augustda ichtimag itmish Rusya Muslumanlariniñg nedvesi* (Kazan, 1906), pp. 3–10. The third congress was also the first one to receive press coverage, as some eleven Muslim newspapers, most of which had been established in the spring of 1906, sent their reporters to N. Novgorod. There were also correspondents from Russian newspapers, such as *Rech'* and *Orenburgskii krai*. See Arsharuni and Gabidullin, *Ocherki panislamizma*, pp. 2 and 28.

40. The fifteen members of the Commission for Political Affairs were A. Topchibashi from the Caucasus; M. Davidovich, the Crimea; Sh. Koshchegulov, the steppes; and H. Maksudov, S. Maksudov, J. Baiburin, M. Bigi, Iu. Bikboev, A. Ashurov, Sh. Syrtlanov, L. Ishakov, J. Huramshin, A. Apanaev, A. Nigmetullin, and G. Galiev from the Volga-Ural region. The Commission for School Reform consisted of M. Salihov and A. Ahundov from the Caucasus; M. Davidovich, the Crimea; M. Jaferov, Turkestan; and F. Sadykov, A. Albetov, H. Maksudov, A. Bobi, A. Mustafin, K. Kanafiev, A. Hairullin, and N. Suleimanov from the Volga-Ural region. Members of the Commission for Religious Affairs were Sh. Salihov, the Caucasus; I. Zakiev, the Crimea; and G. Galiev, G. Hajiev, I. Zakiev, K. Tarjimanov, H. Masudov, A. Saiundukov, M. Mansurov, A. Rasulev, S. Ishakov, Sh. Shafigullin, J. Allaunggarov, J. Akchura, S. Urmanov, and A. Mametov from the Volga-Ural. See *Rusya Musulmanlariniñg nedvesi*, pp. 19–22.

41. It is difficult to ascertain what exactly Ismail Bey had in mind—whether it was possible resistance or just perseverance in carrying on cultural reforms. The exact phrase he used was, "Hukukumuznï tevil ile degil, gayret ile alalïm. *Gayret* could be translated as "patience, perseverance, hard and intensive work as well." See *Rusya Musulmanlariniñg nedvesi*, pp. 32 and 36.

42. Ibid., p. 16. It is interesting that even the leading Kadet politician, P. Miliukov, considered that the Muslims' demands were moderate. See Miliukov, *Natsional'nyi vopros*, p. 171.

The Russian authorities were distrustful of all Muslim intellectuals, whom they suspected of pan-Turkist designs, but were particularly wary of socialists such as Ishaki, who in 1907 was exiled to Arkhangelsk for three years. See Hoover Institution, *Okhrana Archives*, Box 233, File XIIIf (1)5, Bibliographical card #11643, and *RMM* 1 (1908): 186, as reported from *Yulduz* and *Terjuman* of November 16, 1907.

43. As a historian, Hadi Atlasi was perhaps more receptive to the idea of a nation-state than to one of cultural autonomy because he was aware of the independent political entities the Vogla Muslims had enjoyed in the past. For his speech, see *Rusya Musulmanlariniñg nedvesi*, p. 32.

44. For speeches of Ishaki, Tuktarov, Alkin, Syrtlanov, and Akchura, see *Rusya Musulmanlariniñg nedvesi*, pp. 33–34 and 39–41. For the Ishaki-Tuktarov debate, see Y. Akchura, *L'État actuel et les aspirations des turco-tatares musulmans en Russie* (Lausanne, 1916), p. 13, and G. Alisov, "Musul'manskii vopros v Rossii," p. 47.

45. On Apanaev's involvement in politics and his problems with the Russian authorities, see "Autour du monde musulman," *RMM* 10 (1909): 296–97.

46. *Rusya Musulmanlariniñg nedvesi*, pp. 101–10.

47. Ibid., Appendix, pp. 5–10.

48. See Arsharuni and Gabidullin, *Ocherki panislamizma*, p. 31; *Tatary Srednego Povolzh'ia i Priuralia* (Moscow, 1967), p. 402; and Nafigov, *Formirovanie i razvitie*, p. 71.

49. The Central Committee of Ittifak consisted of the following members: Abdur-rashid Ibrahimov (editor of the St. Petersburg newspaper *Ulfet*), Yusuf Akchura (editor of *Kazan muhbiri* and member of the Central Committee of the Kadet party), Said Giray Alkin (lawyer, Duma member, and owner of the newspaper *Kazan muhbiri*), Ismail Bey Gasprali (owner and editor of the Bakhchesarai newspaper *Terjuman*), Alimardan Topchibashi (lawyer and owner of the Baku newspaper *Kaspii*), Abdullah Apanaev (Kazan muderris), A. Barudi (muderris and prominent Kazan ulama), Sadreddin Maksudov (editor and owner of the Kazan newspaper *Yulduz*), Mustafa Davidovich (mayor of Bakhchesarai), Shahmardan Koshchegulov (Kirghiz mullah), and Selim Giray Janturin (Ufa zemstvo member and Duma deputy). Five more members were later added to the Central Committee; they came from Baku, Elizavet-pol, Orenburg, Erevan, and Turkestan, areas that had not been represented at the congress. See *Rusya Musulmanlariniñ nedvesi*, pp. 167–69.

50. E. Oberländer, "The Role of the Political Parties," in Oberländer, *Russia Enters the Twentieth Century*, p. 76. For a detailed presentation of the Russian political parties in the dumas, see Warren B. Walsh, "Political Parties in the Russian Dumas," *Journal of Modern History* 1 (1950): 144–50. For the social composition of the dumas, see Walsh's "The Composition of the Dumas," *The Russian Review* 2 (1949): 111–15. For profiles of Duma deputies, see M. M. Boiovich, *Chleny gosudarstvennoi Dumy (Portrety i biografii). Pervyi sozyv. 1906–1911. Sessiia 27 IV–9 VII 1906* (Moscow, 1906), pp. 26, 109–10, 116, 212, 214, 368, 371, and 373; *Chleny pervoi gosudarstvennoi Dumy s portretami* (Moscow, 1906), pp. 20, 28, 43, and 65–66; and N. Pruzhanskii, ed., *Pervaia Rossiiskaia gosudarstvennaia duma* (St. Petersburg, 1906), pp. 46–47, 53, 57–58, 60–62, 64, 67–68, 129, 133, 139, and 146–47.

51. Alisov, "Musul'manskii vopros v Rossii," p. 46; and *Gosudarstvennaia Duma. Ukazatel' k stenograficheskim otchetam. 1906 god. Sessiia pervaia. Zasedaniia 1–38 (27 IV–4 VIII 1906)* (St. Petersburg, 1907), pp. 28, 82, and 118. Even the peasant-mullah deputies of the Duma were more receptive to religious and cultural issues than to economic problems. For instance, in an interview with the American journalist Samuel Harper, Husainov spoke extensively of the cultural concerns of the Tatars, complain-ing that Tatars were not able to enter universities and that election laws, as they related to Tatars, were unjust; he also criticized the land policies of the government, which allowed the estate owners to get by without paying taxes. See University of Chicago archives, *Samuel Harper Papers*, Box 24, Folder 19. Harper did not name his interview subject in his notes, indicating only that the Duma member being interviewed was a Tatar school teacher from Viatka who had been elected on the Kadet ticket. Sh. Husainov was the only schoolteacher from Viatka in the First Duma.

52. Kurat, "Kazan Türklerinin medeni uyanış devri," p. 147, *RMM* 2 (1908): 413–14, and *RMM* 10 (1908): 233.

53. Oberländer, "Role of Political Parties," p. 79. For a contemporary analysis of the elections to the Second Duma, see *Samuel Harper Papers*, Box 24, Folder 25. In preparation for the elections to the Second Duma, the authorities took measures to

prevent the participation of Yusuf Akchura, whose involvement in politics they probably considered harmful. Akchura was imprisoned for 43 days without any explanation from the authorities. In a journal he kept, Akchura noted that most of the sixteen prisoners with whom he shared a cell were students. See Y. Akchura, *Mevküfiyet hatïralarï* (Orenburg, 1907), p. 44.

54. For a list of the Muslim deputies, see *Chleny 2-oi gosudarstvennoi Dumy. Biografii. Sravnitel'naia kharakteristika chlenov 1-oi i 2-oi dumy. Alfavitnyi ukazatel'* (St. Petersburg, 1907), pp. 1, 3–4, 16, 18, 27, 29–30, 59, 75, 91, 94, 98, 104, 108–10, and 115; and "Les députés Musulmans à la duma," *RMM* 5 (1907): 79–80.

55. The March 31, 1907, issue of *Terjuman* reported the defection of the six deputies to the Left and considered it a betrayal of the Muslim cause. See *RMM* 6 (1907): 224.

56. The first issue of *Duma* appeared on April 21, 1907, in St. Petersburg. Edited by K. Khasanov, it published only six issues. Benningsen and Lemercier-Quelquejay, *La presse*, p. 88.

57. On H. Atlasi, see Battal-Taymas, *Ben bir ışık arıyordum*, pp. 74–77.

58. *Gosudarstvennaia Duma. Ukazatel' k stenograficheskim otchetam. Vtoroi sozyv 1907 god. Zasedaniia 1–53 (20 fevralia–2 iiunia 1907)* (St. Petersburg, 1907), pp. 4, 7, 9, 19–20, and 24; see also Khasanov, *Revoliutsiia 1905–1907g.*, p. 289.

59. For the program of the Dumachïlar see *Programma Musul'manskoi fraktsii v Gosudarstvennoi Dume* (St. Petersburg, 1907), and *ITASSR*, vol. 1 (Kazan, 1955), p. 458.

60. *Gosudarstvennaia Duma. Vtoroi sozyv. Stenograficheskie otchety. 1907. Sessiia vtoraia*, 2 vols. (St. Petersburg, 1907), vol. 1, pp. 163, 165, 183, and 185, and vol. 2, pp. 641 and 923; V. A. Maksimov, ed., *Sbornik rechei deputatov Gosudarstvennoi Dumy I i II sozyva. Kniga pervaia* (St. Petersburg, 1908), p. 498; and *RMM* 7 (1907): 388.

61. Oberländer, "Role of Political Parties," p. 80, and "The Duma Elections," *The Times* (London), November 1, 1907, p. 9.

62. *Gosudarstvennaia Duma. Ukazatel' k stenograficheskim otchetam. Chasti I–III. Tretii sozyv. Sessiia I. 1907–8* (St. Petersburg, 1908), pp. 63, 99, 128, 187, 193, 262, 264, and 275. For profiles of Muslim deputies see also *RMM* 4 (1911): 143–44.

63. See "The Third Duma. Opening ceremony," *The Times* (London), November 15, 1907, p. 7.

64. *ITASSR*, vol. 1, p. 470.

65. For comments on issues raised by Muslim deputies see *RMM* 1 (1910): 106, *RMM* 12 (1910): 667, *RMM* 1 (1911): 166–67, and S. Bagin, *Ob otpadenii v Magometanstvo kreshchennykh inorodtsev Kazanskoi eparkhii i o prichinakh etogo pechal'nogo iavleniia* (Kazan, 1910), p. 17.

66. See *Natsionalisty v 3-ei gosudarstvennoi Dume* (St. Petersburg, 1912), pp. 263–65.

67. For Maksudov's speech as quoted from *Rossiia*, May 3, 1908, see *RMM* 6 (1908): 353–56. For other speeches see *RMM* 4 (1909): 437–42.

68. "Deputat Maksudov o tret'ei Dume," *Kazanskii vecher*, December 31, 1907, p. 2; and "Okolo Dumy," *Sibirskaia zhizn'*, December, 1906, p. 5. Foreign observers also commented on the efforts of the liberals to unite and noted that, without a coalition, the Duma would scarcely yield any results. See "Opposition Parties in the Dumas," *The Times* (London), November 9, 1907, p. 5.

69. See *RMM* 9 (1909): 158 and *RMM* 5 (1910): 143.

70. For comments by the foreign press on the Fourth Duma elections, see *Samuel Harper Papers*, Box 26, Folder 40. For listings and profiles of Fourth Duma Muslim deputies, see *Adres-kalendar' na 1916 god* (St. Petersburg, 1916), pp. 114 and 126; and *Gosudarstvennaia Duma. Ukazatel' k stenograficheskim otchetam. Chasti I–III. Chetvertyi sozyv. Sessiia I. 1912–13* (St. Petersburg, 1913), pp. 22, 65–66, 97, 103–4, 149, and 198. Also see N. N. Olshanskii, ed., *Chetvertaia Gosudarstvennaia Duma. Portrety i biografii* (St. Petersburg, 1913), pp. 17, 19, 60, 66, 127, and 193.

71. Kurat, "Kazan Türklerinin medeni uyanış devri," pp. 151–52.

72. *RMM* 6 (1914): 255.

73. See "Fraktsiaga yardïm kirek," *Yulduz*, August 19, 1915, p. 1.

74. Arsharuni and Gabidullin, *Ocherki panislamizma*, p. 45, as quoted from an article of Tuktarov published in the March 29, 1914, issue of *Il*. By 1914, A. Ishaki, too, seems to have shifted from the Left to the ideals of unity outlined in the philosophy of Ittifak. He called for unity in an article published in issue 32 of the same newspaper, *Il*, for 1914. See Kurat, "Kazan Türklerinin medeni uyanış devri," p. 154.

75. *Millet* appeared in Tatar and Russian. Its publication was announced in Russian newspapers as well. See "Musul'manskaia politicheskaia gazeta," *Kamsko-Volzhskaia rech'*, December 19, 1913, p. 2. The owner of *Millet* was S. Janturin; its editor, I. Lobanov; and the most frequent contributor, A. Ahtamov. See Bennigsen and Lemercier-Quelquejay, *La presse*, p. 82.

76. The fourth congress had been planned for August 10, 1907, but the years of reaction hindered its organization. See *Rusya Musulmanlarïnïng nedvesi*, p. 140. For the ten-chapter plan of religious reform drafted by the congress, and for a list of its participants, see *IV Musul'manskii s'ezd. S. Petersburg, 15–25 iiunia. 1914.* (St. Petersburg, 1914), pp. 1–15. The sessions of the fourth congress were held behind closed doors, and no representatives of the Muslim press were allowed to attend.

77. On Akchura's activities after his departure from Russia, see J. Gabrys, *L'indépendence lituanienne. Faits, impressions, souvenirs. 1907–1920*, n.p., n.d., pp. 277–82; *Revendications des nationalités opprimées. Recueil des memoirs, rapports, et documents présentés à la III-me conférence des nationalités. Lausanne 27–29 Juin 1916* (Lausanne, 1917), pp. 140–44; and Hoover Institution, *Okhrana Archives*, Box 121, 1910, File XIIIb(1), folder 1E, documents 699, 735, 770; Box 127, 1917, folder 1A, document 33.

CHAPTER 10

1. *Shura*, March 6, 1917, p. 1.

2. M. K. Mukhariamov, *Oktiabr' i natsional'no-gosudarstvennoe stroitel'stvo v Tatarii (Oktiabr' 1917g.–1920g.)* (Moscow, 1969), pp. 16–17.

3. T. Davletshin, *Sovetskii Tatarstan. Teoriia i praktika Leninskoi natsional'noi politiki* (London, 1974), p. 58.

4. I. Ionenko and I. Tagirov, *Oktiabr' v Kazani* (Kazan, 1967), pp. 90–95. The Kazan Socialist Committee had a special impact upon the Union of Tatar Women Workers led by G. Tazetdinova and A. Saifi. M. K. Mukhariamov, "Bor'ba za ustanovlenie i uprochenie Sovetskoi vlasti v Tatarii," in *ITASSR* (Kazan, 1973), p. 121.

5. The Central Provisional Bureau for the Muslims of Russia was created on March 15, 1917, at the initiative of the Muslim deputies of the Fourth Duma and was chaired by the Menshevik A. Tsalikov. The text of the appeal is reproduced in S. M. Dimanshtein, *Revoliutsiia i natsional'nyi vopros*, vol. 3 (Moscow, 1930), pp. 293–94.

6. *ITASSR*, vol. 2 (Kazan, 1956), p. 11.

7. The composition of the presidium of the congress was as follows: I. Akhtiamov, A. Ishaki, A. Tsalikov, A. Topchibashev, F. Karimi, G. Khodzhaev, Kh. Gabashi, Kh. Dusmukhamedov, S. Iakubova, I. Alkin, M. Bigi, and D. Saidakhmetov. See Davletshin, *Sovetskii Tatarstan*, pp. 64–65.

8. *Bütün Rüsiyä Müsülmanlarïnïng 1917 nchï yïlda 1–11 mayda Maskauda bulghan 'umumi isiyizdïnïng prutaqullarï* (Petrograd, 1917), pp. 305–12, 431–32, and 450.

9. Ibid., pp. 423–29.

10. Ibid., pp. 344–47, 354–58, and 373–81.

11. Ibid., pp. 80–121, 178–84, and 227–28.

12. Ibid., p. 408.

13. Milli Shura was chaired by Tsalikov and had its headquarters in Moscow; the Petrograd ISKOMUS was chaired by Ishaki.

14. Davletshin, *Sovetskii Tatarstan*, p. 112.

15. Dimanshtein, *Revoliutsiia i natsional'nyi vopros*, pp. 317–18; A. Bennigsen and Chantal Lemercier-Quelquejay, *Islam in the Soviet Union* (New York, 1967), p. 80; Kh. Kh. Khasanov, *Formirovanie Tatarskoi burzhuaznoi natsii* (Kazan, 1977), pp. 277–79.

16. As quoted from *Kamsko-Volzhskaia rech'* of July 29, 1917, in Mukhariamov, "Bor'ba za ustanovlenie i uprochenie Sovetskoi vlasti v Tatarii," p. 27. Harbi Shura published its own paper entitled *Bezneng Tavïsh*; see Davletshin, *Sovetskii Tatarstan*, p. 116.

17. S. Maksudi became the president of the Milli Idare collegium. Ufa was the choice for Milli Idare headquarters because its location facilitated contacts with the Bashkirs while also rendering the collegium less vulnerable to the political tensions of Kazan. Last, but not least, Ufa was the seat of the muftiat, and the role a progressive mufti, such as G. Barudi, could play as a bridge builder could hardly be overlooked. Dimanshtein, *Revoliutsiia i natsional'nyi vopros*, p. 317.

One of the most outspoken critics of Harbi Shura and Milli Idare, and even of the self-determination right of the peoples of Russia, was K. Grasis, a member of the Kazan Soviet. K. Grasis, *K natsional'nomu voprosu* (Kazan, 1918), pp. 6 and 13. Also see M. Korbut, "Natsional'nye dvizheniia v Volzhsko-Kamskom krae v 1917," *Revoliutsionnyi Vostok* 7 (1929): 178.

18. Mukhariamov, "Bor'ba za ustanovlenie i uprochenie Sovetskoi vlasti v Tatarii," pp. 22–23.

19. For the full text of the appeal, see *Dekrety Sovetskoi vlasti*, vol. 1 (Moscow, 1957), pp. 113–15.

20. Davletshin, *Sovetskii Tatarstan*, pp. 140–41; for Stalin's comments, see M. Abdullin, "Protiv fal'sifikatsii istorii Tatarskoi avtonomii," *Kommunist Tatarii* 3 (1972): 44.

21. All twenty members of the Kazan Revolutionary Committee were Russians, and of the eleven members of the Kazan Soviet of People's Commissars, only one—Mirsaid Sultangaliev—was a Tatar.

22. The Idel-Ural state was to include the Kazan and Ufa guberniias in their entirety, along with parts of the Perm, Viatka, Simbirsk, and Samara guberniias. See *Obrazovanie Bashkirskoi ASSR. Sbornik dokumentov i materialov* (Ufa, 1959), pp. 126–27.

23. Davletshin, *Sovetskii Tatarstan*, p. 155.

24. *Dekrety Sovetskoi vlasti*, p. 317. On Narkomnats, see E. I. Pesikina, *Narodnyi komissariat po delam natsional'nostei i ego deiatel'nost' v 1917–1918g.* (Moscow, 1950); on Vakhitov, see R. I. Nafigov, *Mullanur Vakhitov: Istoriko-biograficheskii ocherk* (Kazan, 1975).

25. Both were jadids and nationalists. Whereas Ibragimov (Tatar) was a Socialist Revolutionary, Manatov (Bashkir) had no clear political convictions. On Ibragimov, see M. Kh. Khasanov, *Galimdzhan Ibragimov* (Kazan, 1969).

26. I. M. Klimov, *Obrazovanie i razvitie Tatarskoi ASSR* (Kazan, 1960), p. 26.

27. Klimov, *Obrazovanie*, p. 28; Mukhariamov, "Bor'ba za ustanovlenie i uprochenie Sovetskoi vlasti v Tatarii," p. 39. On the Trans-Bulak republic episode, also see A. Tarasov, *Razgrom kontrrevoliutsionnoi avantiury Tatarskoi burzhuazii v nachale 1918g.* (Kazan, 1940).

28. R. G. Khairutdinov, *Na putiakh k Sovetskoi avtonomii: provedenie Leninskoi natsional'noi politiki tsentral'nym Tataro-Bashkirskim kommisariatom v 1918–1919g.* (Kazan, 1972), p. 32.

29. I. G. Gizatullin, *Zashchishchaia zavoevaniia Oktiabria. Tsentral'naia Musul'manskaia voennaia kollegiia. 1918–20* (Moscow, 1979), pp. 21 and 25.

30. Ibid., pp. 30–36.

31. Ibid., p. 58.

32. Ibid., pp. 53–55, 58, 64, 68, and 74–75.

33. Ibid., p. 55.

34. E. B. Genkina, *Obrazovanie SSSR. Sbornik dokumentov. 1917–1924g.* (Moscow and Leningrad, 1947), p. 38.

35. Pesikina, *Narodnyi kommissariat*, pp. 117–19. The secretary of the Ural Bureau of the Central Committee of the Russian Communist (Bolshevik) Party, I. Tuntul, even sent a letter to the Central Committee of the Russian Communist (Bolshevik) Party challenging its national policy. M. A. Saidasheva, *Lenin i sotsialisticheskoe stroitel'stvo v Tatarii, 1918–1923* (Moscow, 1963), pp. 64–65.

36. *Obrazovanie TASSR. Sbornik dokumentov i materialov* (Kazan, 1963), p. 174.

37. Mukhariamov, "Bor'ba za ustanovlenie i uprochenie Sovetskoi vlasti v Tatarii," pp. 171–77, 180–83, and 191–95; Richard Pipes, *The Formation of the Soviet Union: Communism and Nationalism, 1917–1923* (Cambridge, Mass., 1964), pp. 260–63. Relevant monographs on the formation of TASSR are I. M. Klimov, *Natsional'nye momenty v gosudarstvennom i partiinom stroitel'stve v Tatarii. Vosstanovitel'nyi period* (Kazan, 1960), and R. G. Khairutdinov, *Osushchestvlenie kommunisticheskoi partiei Leninskoi programmy po natsional'nomy voprosu 1917–1920* (Kazan, 1976). Some of the Tatar nationalist leaders were never reconciled to the demise of the project for an Idel-Ural state. A. Ishaki pursued the dream in emigration and, in 1928, organized in Warsaw an Idel-Ural Independence Committee. A. Akiş, *Idel-Ural davası ve Sovyet emperyalizmi* (Yenişehir and Ankara, 1963), p. 29.

38. F. Saifi, *Trudy Doma Tatarskoi kul'tury*, vol. 1 (Kazan, 1930), p. 194; Mukhariamov, "Bor'ba za ustanovlenie i uprochenie Sovetskoi vlasti v Tatarii," p. 196; Ahmet Temir, "Idil-Ural ve Yöresi," in *Türk Dünyası El Kitabı*, vol. 2 (Ankara, 1976), pp. 1260–62.

CHAPTER 11

1. Soviet scholarship is particularly sensitive to bourgeois interpretations of the issue of national autonomy and spares no effort to criticize them. One such effort belongs to the Tatar scholar M. Abdullin, who took issue with the analyses of S. Zenkovsky, R. Pipes, E. H. Carr, S. von Mende, B. Spuler, and M. Rodinson. See M. Abdullin, "Protiv fal'sifikatsii istorii Tatarskoi avtonomii," *Kommunist Tatarii* 3 (1972): 43–49.

2. S. B., "Soltanghälief Kem?" in Gh. Qushay, ed., *Kontr-rivolütsion Soltanghäliefchelkkä qarshï* (Kazan, 1929), p. 85. Born in 1880 to a teacher's family in the village of Qmrsqalï in Bashkiria, Sultangaliev studied first in the village mektep and then in the Russian-Tatar Teachers' school of Kazan. He worked as a teacher in his native village, then as a librarian in the first zemstvo library that opened in Ufa. It was at this time that he became actively involved in jadid secularism and advocated the transformation of zemstvo schools into national schools. By 1911, he had already made his journalistic debut, contributing many articles to the zemstvo organ *Ufimskii Vestnik*. Sultangaliev's journalistic activity expanded over the years, as he contributed to many Russian and Tatar periodicals, such as *Russkii Uchitel'*, *Musul'manskaia Gazeta*, *Kavkazskoe Slovo*, *Baku*, *Bakinskaia Kopeika*, and *Tormysh*, under pseudonyms as diverse as Karmaskalinis, Khalïq ughlï, Mirsayit, Tatar maghallime, and Kolke bashï. He took part in the May and July 1917 Muslim congresses and became one of the most prominent figures of the Muslim Socialist Committee of Kazan. He joined the Russian Communist Party (Bolshevik) in November 1917 and soon became chairman of the Central Muskom; member of the Inner Collegium of Narkomnats; editor of the official organ of Narkomnats, *Zhizn' Natsional'nostei*; president of the Muslim Military Collegium; and member of the Central Executive

Committee of the TASSR. He was first arrested in 1923, when he was accused of nationalist deviation and excluded from the Communist party. Soon, however, he was released and allowed to work in Georgia and Moscow, where he was employed at the RSFSR state publishing agency. After his second arrest in 1928, he was tried, convicted, and sentenced to ten years of hard labor in the Solovki camp, where he was last seen in 1939. See Qushay, *Kontr-rivolütsion*, pp. 84–86, and A. Bennigsen and S. Enders Wimbush, *Muslim National Communism in the Soviet Union. A Revolutionary Strategy for the Colonial World* (Chicago, 1979), pp. 207–8.

3. From a speech published first in *Znamia revoliutsii* 44 (1918), as quoted in A. Arsharuni and Kh. Gabidullin, *Ocherki panislamizma i pantiurkizma v Rossii* (Moscow, 1934), p. 78. The validity of Sultangaliev's analysis seems to have been vindicated by Muslim socialists of the Third World, who years later echoed his ideas. The Pakistani A. M. Malik argued: "Muslim socialists represent a third road to human progress, which is neither the dictatorship of the proletariat nor capitalist exploitation. It is a harmonious combination of the contradictory interests of society." A. M. Malik, *Labor Problems and Policy of Pakistan* (Karachi, 1954), pp. 32–33.

4. Bennigsen and Wimbush, *Muslim National Communism*, p. 42.

5. For Ibragimov's biographic profile, see A. Rorlich, "G. Ibragimov," in Joseph L. Wieczynski, ed., *Modern Encyclopedia of Russian and Soviet History*, vol. 14 (Lexington, 1976–84), pp. 113–17.

6. *Stenograficheskii otchet IX oblastnoi konferentsii Tatarskoi organizatsii RKP(b)* (Kazan, 1924), p. 109 (hereafter cited as *Stenograficheskii otchet*).

7. S. Atnaghulïf, "Soltanghäliefchelkneng tarikhi tamrlarï," in Qushay, *Kontr-rivolütsion*, p. 38.

8. K. Tobolef, "Sotsializm höchüme häm burzhua ilimintlarïnïng aktiflashularï," in Qushay, *Kontr-rivolütsion*, p. 14. In his criticism of national Communists, Kasymov summarized their program as "not the struggle of all working people against the exploiting classes but the struggle of all Tatars against all Russians." G. Kasymov, *Pantiurkistskaia kontrrevoliutsiia i ee agentura-Sultangalievshchina* (Kazan, 1930), p. 79.

9. See Gimranov's report to the fifth session (May 15, 1924) of the Ninth Tatar Party Conference. *Stenograficheskii otchet*, p. 130.

10. Kasymov, *Pantiurkistskaia kontrrevoliutsiia*, p. 89.

11. One of the criticisms leveled against Sultangaliev after his purge was that he conceived his party as a mass party, open to peasants, workers, and intellectuals (i.e., bourgeois jadid intellectuals) alike. M. Bochakov, "Milli Firka i Sultangalievshchina," *Prosveshchenie natsional'nostei* 6 (1930): 21.

12. Party membership, although only open to Muslims, did not discriminate against foreign Muslims. Turks and Turkey in general, and Turkish Communists in particular, were at the center of attention of the Tatar leadership and the press, at least until 1921. Tatar periodicals feature numerous articles about Turkish Communists and their leader, M. Subhi, as well as about M. Kemal (Atatürk), who was characterized as a "Red commander" leading his nation's fight for freedom. There is even an almost apologetic note in one article that justifies why M. Kemal was not a party

member. It seems that only his pasha status prevented the Tatar Communists from offering him membership in their party. *Azad Seber* 12 (May 12, 1921): 1; *Kommunist* 46 (December 12, 1920): 3; and Ahraba [pseud.], "Askeri güchümüz häm Mustafa Kemal," *Azad Seber* 2 (February 3, 1921): 1. The pseudonym Ahraba, which the author of this article chose to use, is interesting. It can be translated as "relative" or "kinfolk"—still another indication of the sentiment of Muslim-Turkic unity that prevailed among the Muslims of Russia during those years.

13. As quoted in Bennigsen and Wimbush, *Muslim National Communism*, p. 62.

14. The national Communists, who represented the majority in the Tatar party organization, prevailed, however, and by June 1921, they succeeded in removing Said-Galiev from the post of president of the Tatar Council of People's Commissariat (Sovnarkom), appointing K. Mukhtarov in his place. To soften the blow of his political downfall in Tatarstan and reward Said-Galiev for his orthodoxy, however, Moscow appointed him president of the Crimean Sovnarkom. See T. Davletshin, *Sovetskii Tatarstan. Teoriia i praktika Leninskoi natsional'noi politiki* (London, 1974), pp. 187–88, as quoted from M. G. Roshal', "O politicheskom polozhenii v Tatarskoi respublike v 1920g.," *Istoricheskii arkhiv* 2 (1961): 162.

15. Davletshin, *Sovetskii Tatarstan*, pp. 184–87.

16. *Pervyi s'ezd narodov Vostoka. Baku, 1–8 sent. 1920. Stenograficheskie otchety* (Petrograd, 1920), pp. 144–50 and 179–80, and G. Z. Sorokin, *I s'ezd narodov Vostoka* (Moscow, 1961), pp. 32–33.

17. M. Parsin, "Yäshler arasnda Soltanghäliefchelkneng yoghntïsï," in Qushay, *Kontr-rivolütsion*, pp. 73–76.

18. G. Kasymov, who provided one of the most detailed and critical analyses of Sultangalievism, held the jadid background of the national Communists directly responsible for their nationalist deviation. For him, the simple fact that K. Mukhtarov, G. Mansurov, G. Enbaev, M. Burundukov, and V. Iskhakov were graduates of the Galiye, Bobi, and Muhammediye medreses was sufficient proof of their sins, and Sultangaliev's contribution to *Mir Islama* was a valid evidence of his reactionary views. Kasymov, *Pantiurkistskaia kontrrevoliutsiia*, p. 80.

19. M. Sultangaliev, *Metody antireligioznoi propagandy sredi musul'man* (Moscow, 1922), pp. 2–6.

20. M. Kobetskii, "Sultangalievshchina kak apologiia Islama," *Antireligioznik* 1 (1930): 12–14; A. Arsharuni, "Ideologiia Sultangalievshchiny," *Antireligioznik* 5 (1930): 22–25.

21. Tobolef, "Sotsializm höchüme," pp. 12–17.

22. Arsharuni and Gabidullin, *Ocherki panislamizma*, p. 23. Discussing the attachment of the Muslims to their religion, Sultangaliev compared the Tatars, who had one mosque for every 700 inhabitants, with the Russians, who had one church for 10,000 believers. M. Khucheyef, "Islam häm Soltanghäliefchelek," in Qushay, *Kontr-rivolütsion*, p. 70.

23. B. Szczesniak, ed., *The Russian Revolution and Religion. A Collection of Documents Concerning the Suppression of Religion by the Communists, 1917–1925* (Notre

Dame, Indiana, 1959), pp. 34–35; M. I. Shakhnovich, *Lenin i problemy ateizma* (Moscow and Leningrad, 1961), p. 604.

24. N. Ashirov, *Evoliutsiia Islama v SSSR* (Moscow, 1972), p. 15.

25. Kasymov, *Pantiurkistskaia kontrrevoliutsiia*, p. 88.

26. M. Kh. Khasanov, *Galimdzhan Ibragimov* (Kazan, 1969), p. 311.

27. See *Stenograficheskii otchet. Pervyi vsesoiuznyi tiurkologicheskii s'ezd. 26 II–5 III 1926* (Baku, 1926), pp. 277–80.

28. Ibid., p. 230.

29. There was little time for the Tatars to adjust to the use of the new alphabet, for in 1937, still another decree discarded the Latin alphabet and replaced it with the Cyrillic. Adoption of the Cyrillic alphabet was only the cultural ramification of the battle against Islam that had been launched in 1917, and it was a major weapon in the effort aimed at achieving the final goal of russification under the banner of *sblizhenie* (drawing together) of the peoples of the Soviet Union.

30. For a detailed analysis of Ibragimov's essay, see A. Rorlich, "'Which Way Will Tatar Culture Go?' A Controversial Essay by G. Ibragimov," *CMRS* 3–4 (1974): 363–71.

31. S. Atnagulov was a left-wing Tatar Communist who overestimated the weight and class consciousness of the Tatar proletariat. Criticism of his view was voiced in the pages of *Qzïl Tatarstan* in 1922 and was led by Sultangaliev's companions. That same year, Atnagulov participated in the campaign against Sultangalievism by articulating his criticism in an essay entitled "Soltanghäliefchelkneng tarikhi tamrlarï." See Qushay, *Kontr-rivolütsion*, pp. 35–40.

32. G. Ibragimov, *Tatar mädäniyeti nindi yul belan barajaq?* (Kazan, 1927), pp. 33 and 35.

33. *Stenograficheskii otchet*, pp. 19, 96, 115, 119, and 121–22.

34. Kasymov, *Pantiurkistskaia kontrrevoliutsiia*, p. 86.

35. *Stenograficheskii otchet*, pp. 21–22, 51, 114, and 121–22.

36. In fact, indirect sources indicate that Sultangaliev and several other national Communists founded a secret group, called Ittihad ve Tarakki (Union and progress), in Moscow as early as 1921. This group seems to have included Z. Validi (Bashkir), A. Baytursun, and A. Bukeyhanov, and T. Ryskulov (Kazakhs), V. Ibrahimov (Crimean Tatar), and N. Khodzhaev and F. Khodzhaev (Uzbek). See Bennigsen and Wimbush, *Muslim National Communism*, p. 87, as based on *Pravda Vostoka* (Tashkent) of December 18, 1934. Kasymov contends that G. Mansurov, K. Mukhtarov, and G. Enbaev belonged to the Moscow underground center, while M. Burundukov, V. Iskhakov, G. Maksudov, and M. Budaili belonged to the Kazan center. Kasymov, *Pantiurkistskaia kontrrevoliutsiia*, p. 95.

37. Tobelef, "Sotsializm höchüme"; Y. Chanïshïf, "Soltanghäliefchelkneng jimerelie"; and S. Borhan, "Gruppachïlïq chghshlarï Soltanghäliefchelkke qarshï koreshke qomachaulïylar"—all essays in Qushay, *Kontr-rivolütsion*, pp. 14–15, 52–55, and 56–57, respectively.

38. A Central Asian Communist, A. Ikramov, who was purged and tried in 1938,

claims he was the leader of the Central Asian organization Milli Istiklal (National Independence). This information is based on R. C. Tucker and S. F. Cohen, eds., *The Great Purge Trial: Transcript of the Moscow Trial of the anti-Soviet Bloc of Rightists and Trotskyites* (New York, 1965), pp. 297 and 304–5.

39. As early as 1925, antireligious activity received direction and coherence through Soiuz Voinstvuiushchikh Bezbozhnikov (The union of militant godless), 1925–1947 and its corollaries among the Tatars: Allahsïzlar (The godless) and Dinsizler (The faithless). The assorted collection of antireligious organizations launched a media campaign aimed at awakening the believers and converting them to atheism. The publication of the first issue of the journal *Fen häm Din* (Science and Religion) in September 1925 marked the beginning of the organized antireligious press campaign in Tatar. The relatively evenhanded *Fen häm Din* was replaced in 1928 with the more militant *Sugïshchan Allasïz* (The militant godless), thus bringing to the field of antireligious propaganda the intolerance and ruthlessness that, in 1928, characterized the campaign against national Communists. For a discussion of *Fen häm Din*'s antireligious campaign, see S. Said-Galiev, "Pervyi god raboty. Iz otcheta zhurnala *Fän häm Din* za 1925–26g.," *Antireligioznik* 4 (1927): 26–34.

40. "V. K. P(b) Üzäk Kontrol' Komisiaseneng Mokhtarïf, Mansurïf, Yanbayïf, Sabirïf, Drän Ayrlï häm firdäislär turndaghï qararï," in Qushay, *Kontr-rivolütsion*, p. 87.

41. "Tatarstan partia Olkä Komiteteneng ochnje plinumi rizolitsiasnnan," in Qushay, *Kontr-rivolütsion*, pp. 92–94.

42. Qushay, *Kontr-rivolütsion*, p. 87.

43. Davletshin, *Sovetskii Tatarstan*, p. 197, as quoted from *Qzïl Tatarstan* of April 20, 1930. The increase in the percentage of Tatars in the party organization from 28.5 in 1922 to 37.3 in 1930 was undoubtedly eliminated by the effect of these purges. M. K. Mukhariamov, "My nash, my novyi mir postroim," *ITASSR* (Kazan, 1955), p. 141.

44. When the nationalization of the Tatar-owned printing presses and polygraphic enterprises—and there were 26 in Kazan alone—was completed in 1921, the government viewed the event as a major victory over reactionaries and nationalists, who had been deprived of a major weapon. Judging from the fate of Tatgosizdat, however, nationalization was apparently not enough to shield book publishing from nationalist influences. For a detailed discussion of the nationalization of businesses and industry in Tatarstan, see K. A. Nazipova, *Natsionalizatsiia promyshlennosti v Tatarii (1917–1921)* (Moscow, 1976), pp. 125, 147, and 161–64.

CHAPTER 12

1. Shirin Akiner, *Islamic Peoples of the Soviet Union* (London, Boston, Melbourne, and Henley, 1983), pp. 62 and 80.

2. G. Ibragimov, *Tatar mädäniyeti nindi yul belän barajaq?* (Kazan, 1927), pp. 22–23.

3. Hélène Carrère d'Encausse, *L'Empire éclaté. La révolte des nations en URSS* (Paris, 1978), pp. 255–71.

4. Iu. V. Arutiunian and L. M. Drobizheva, "Sovetskii obraz zhizni: Obshchee i natsional'no osobennoe," *SE* 3 (1976): 10–23.

5. V. I. Kozlov, *Natsional'nosti SSSR. Etnodemograficheskii obzor* (Moscow, 1975), pp. 84, 92, 200, 211, and 224–25; P. G. Pod'iachikh, *Naselenie SSSR* (Moscow, 1961), pp. 51–53 and 77–79.

6. N. A. Tomilov, "Sovremennye etnicheskie protsessy u Tatar gorodov zapadnoi Sibiri," *SE* 6 (1972): 87–97.

7. "1981–82 uku yïlïna Tatar mektepleri öchïn ukïtu planï," *Sovet Mektebe* 7 (1981): 5.

8. According to a 1958 analysis by the minister of education of Tatarstan, M. Makhmutov, 27 percent of all students in the institutions of higher education of Tatarstan were Tatars. In 1966, their number grew to 35 percent, and in 1972, it reached 42 percent. See *KU* 4 (1973): 158–59. In his discussion, Makhmutov addresses the issue of the crisis of Tatar education in the 1950s. For more on this question, see S. Romanyshyn, "School Reform and the Language Question in the USSR," *Problems of the Peoples of the USSR* 2 (1959): 17–21; *Naselenie SSSR, 1973. Statisticheskii sbornik* (Moscow, 1975), p. 37; A. Prauda, "Vliianie bilingvizma na nekotorye iavleniia narodnoi kul'tury," *SE* 2 (1972): 17–26; M. N. Guboglo, "Sotsial'no-etnicheskie posledstviia dvuiazychiia," *SE* 2 (1972): 26–37.

9. *ITASSR* (Kazan, 1973), p. 221; Kozlov, *Natsional'nosti SSSR. Etnodemograficheskii obzor*, pp. 108–9.

10. Kh. Mingnegulov, "Däreslek häm programma," *KU* 6 (1976): 170–74. The textbook discussed in his article is M. Gainullin and M. Mähdiev's *Tatar ädäbiyatï. Urta mäktäpneng 8 nche klassï öchen däreslek* (Kazan, 1975).

11. Sh. Galiev, "Tugan tel," *KU* 10 (1982): 55. The publication of the *Anthology of Children's Literature* in 1980 was followed by several volumes of children's poetry. See *Tatar balalar poeziase antologiyase* (Kazan, 1980); G. Rakhim, *Chächäk takïya* (Kazan, 1981); A. Rashitov, *Koyashlï il-bakhet ile* (Kazan, 1981); and M. Galiev, *Jingäsem kilde* (Kazan, 1981).

12. G. Burbiel, "Tatar Literature," in G. S. N. Luckyi, ed., *Discordant Voices in the non-Russian Soviet Literatures, 1953–1973* (Oakville, Ontario, 1975), p. 117.

13. N. Fattakh, "Erak gasïrlar avazï," *KU* 9 (1976): 152–71 (8 essays), *KU* 10 (1976): 127–50 (11 essays), and *KU* 11 (1976): 156–71 (8 essays).

14. Ibid., 9 (1976): 152.

15. A. M. Orlov, "Opyt issledovaniia protsessa sekuliarizatsii v Tatarskikh selakh," *Voprosy nauchnogo ateizma* 16 (1974): 100.

16. L. M. Drobizheva, "Sotsial'no kul'turnye osobennosti lichnosti i natsional'nye ustanovki," *SE* 3 (1971): 5–14; I. O. Shkaratan, "Etnosotsial'naia struktura gorodskogo naseleniia Tatarskoi ASSR (po materialam sotsiologicheskogo obsledovaniia)," *SE* 3 (1970): 13.

17. *RN* 3 (1930): 9.

18. N. Ashirov, *Evoliutsiia Islama v SSSR* (Moscow, 1972), p. 123.

19. On data for political socialization of women, see T. Bobchenko, A. Garzavina, and K. Sinitsina, *Kazan. Putevoditel'* (Kazan, 1970), p. 48.

20. Ashirov, *Evoliutsiia Islama v SSSR*, p. 91.

21. Ibid., p. 22.

22. A. Inkeles, *Social Change in Soviet Russia* (Cambridge, Mass., 1968), p. 228.

23. S. Savoskul, "Sotsial'no-etnicheskie aspekty dukhovnoi kul'tury sel'skogo naseleniia Tatarskoi ASSR," *SE* 1 (1971): 12. Also see Iu. G. Petrash and R. N. Khamitova, "K kharakteristike protsessa modernizatsii sovremennogo Islama v SSSR," *Voprosy nauchnogo ateizma* 2 (1966): 107 and 331. One of the ethnosociological studies of the rural population of Tatarstan revealed that 50.9 percent of the Tatars had undergone circumcision, compared with only 35.8 percent of the Russian population who had received the Christian baptism.

24. R. Sadri, "Resurgence of the Interest in Islam Among the Tatar Intelligentsia," *RLRB*, January 11, 1983, pp. 1–5. Equally interesting is A. Akhmedov's book *Sotsial'naia doktrina Islama*. In this study, Akhmedov departs from Ashirov's analysis and no longer accuses the Muslim clergy of hypocrisy in trying to reconcile Islam and communism. Instead, he explains their positive attitude toward communism and their loyalty to the Soviet state on the basis of their adoption of the ideals of socialism as their own. A. Akhmedov, *Sotsial'naia doktrina Islama* (Moscow, 1982), pp. 131–32.

25. A. Kalganov, "Ideologiia esheneng möhim buinï," *Tatarstan Kommunisty* 1 (1983): 71–77, as quoted by R. Sadri in "Anti-Islamic Propaganda in the TASSR," *RLRB*, Feb. 21, 1983, p. 1.

26. Z. A. Ishmukhametov, *Sotsial'naia rol' i evoliutsiia Islama v Tatarii* (Kazan, 1979).

27. M. Zarif, *Ishannar-därvishlär* (Kazan, 1931), as quoted by Ishmukhametov in *Sotsial'naia rol'*, p. 44.

28. Ishmukhametov, *Sotsial'naia rol'*, p. 49.

29. M. Gosmanov, "Miraska ikhtiram," *KU* 12 (1979): 168–69.

30. *Istoriia Tatarskoi ASSR (S drevneishikh vremen do nashikh dnei)* (Kazan, 1960); *Istoriia Tatarskoi Sovetskoi literatury* (Moscow, 1965); *Tatar teleneng anglatmalï süzlege*, 3 vols. (Kazan, 1977–1981). On the dictionary, see F. Safiullina, "Khazinädä nilär bar?" *KU* 1 (1983): 171–78.

31. P. N. Starostin and P. K. Urazmanov, "Pervoe Povolzhskoe arkheologo-etnograficheskoe soveshchanie," *SE* 4 (1975): 145–48; N. V. Bikbulatov and L. I. Nagaeva, "Vtoroe Povolzhsko-Uralskoe arkheologo-etnograficheskoe soveshchanie," *SE* 5 (1977): 139–42.

32. V. N. Vasilov and T. I. Sultanov, "Vsesoiuznaia tiurkologicheskaia konferentsiia," *SE* 3 (1977): 142–43.

33. Änäs Khälid, "Abu-Khämid el-Garnatyinïng Bolgarga Säyakhäte. Säyakhätche häm anïng äsärläre," *KU* 6 (1976): 148–58.

34. A. Kh. Khalikov, *Volgo-Kam'e v nachale epokhi rannego zheleza. VIII–VI v.v. do*

n.e. (Moscow, 1977); F. Kh. Valeev, *Drevnee i srednevekovoe iskusstvo Srednego Povolzh'ia* (Ioshkar-Ola, 1975); Mirkassyim Gosmanov, "Tarikhlïk Fänneng zaruri taläbe," *KU* 4 (1976): 178–83; Dinä Välieva, "Bolgar sängate sakhifälärennän," *KU* 1 (1977): 139–44.

34. See E. J. Lazzerini, "Tatarovedenie and the 'New Historiography' in the Soviet Union: Revising the Interpretation of the Tatar-Russian Relationship," *SR* 4 (1981): 625–36; also his "Ethnicity and the Uses of History: The Case of the Volga Tatars and Jadidism," *Central Asian Survey* (November 1982): 61–69. The gaps in Tatar historiography and the areas that needed particular attention were discussed by M. K. Mukhariamov, "Za glubokoe issledovanie istorii Tatarii," *Kommunist Tatarii* 4 (1972): 37–42.

35. S. Alishev, "Prisoedinenie narodov Srednego Povolzh'ia k Russkomu gosurdarstvu," in *Tatariia v proshlom i nastoiashchem. Sbornik statei* (Kazan, 1975), pp. 172–85; Kh. G. Gimadi, "Ob istoricheskom znachenii prisoedineniia Tatarii k Russkomu gosudarstvu," in *Izvestiia Kazanskogo filiala Akademii Nauk SSSR*, no. 3, 1955.

36. A. G. Karimullin, *Tatarskaia kniga nachala XX veka* (Kazan, 1974); also his *Kitap don'yäsïna säyäkhät* (Kazan, 1979); and Kh. Kh. Khasanov, *Formirovanie Tatarskoi burzhuaznoi natsii* (Kazan, 1977), pp. 116–41.

37. Ia. G. Abdullin, *Tatarskaia prosvetitel'skaia mysl'. (Sotsial'naia priroda i osnovnye problemy)* (Kazan, 1976), and his "Obshchee i osobennoe v Tatarskom prosvetitel'stve," *Kommunist Tatarii* 5 (1978): 75–80.

38. M. Usmanov, *Zavetnaia mechta Khusaina Faizkhanova* (Kazan, 1980), p. 189.

39. A. Kh. Khalikov, "Kazan kaychan häm kaydan bashlagan kitken," *KU* 8 (1978): 137–46; S. Alishev, "Tarikhtän ber sakhifä," *KU* 3 (1977): 165–69.

40. M. Gainullin, *Tatar ädipläre* (Kazan, 1978), p. 171.

41. R. Mustafin, "Obogoshchaiushchie traditsii (O sovremennoi Tatarskoi literature)," *Volga* 3 (1973): 180–82.

42. R. Mustafin, "Polnovodnye pritoki (Obzor molodoi poezii Tatarii)," *Volga* 8 (1974): 168–76.

43. Zöl'fät, *KU* 8 (1982): 44–45.

44. Mustafin, "Obogoshchaiushchie traditsii," p. 182.

45. F. Musin, "Zemlia i chelovek na nei. Derevnia v sovremennoi Tatarskoi proze," *Oktiabr'* 6 (1972): 207–13.

46. *Arkhiv samizdata. Materialy samizdata*, January 6, 1978, document no. 3086, p. 6.

47. Ibid., document no. 3086, p. 7.

48. The language behavior data are based on the information contained in the ethnosociological survey of the TASSR conducted by Iu. V. Arutiunian and his associates. See Iu. V. Arutiunian, L. M. Drobizheva, and O. I. Shkaratan, *Sotsial'noe i natsional'noe: Opyt etnosotsiologicheskikh issledovanii po materialam Tatarskoi ASSR*

(Moscow, 1973), p. 258, and Guboglo, "Sotsial'no-etnicheskie posledstviia dvuiazychiia," p. 34.

49. *Arkhiv samizdata*, document no. 3087, p. 3.

50. Ibid., document no. 3085, p. 4; and A. Novitskii, "Okhrana i ispol'zovanie pamiatnikov istorii i kul'tury," *Kommunist Tatarii* 8 (1980): 86–88.

51. G. Rakhim, "Teleknameler," *KU* 8 (1976): 178–79.

Bibliography

Abduh, Muhammad. *The Theology of Unity.* Translated by Ishaq Musa'ad and Kenneth Cragg. London, 1966.

Abdullin, Ia. G. "Obshchee i osobennoe v Tatarskom prosvetitel'stve." *Kommunist Tatarii* 5 (1978): 75–80.

———. "Rukhi asïlïbïz" [Our spiritual foundation]. *KU* 6 (1980): 150–56.

———. *Tatarskaia prosvetitel'skaia mysl'.* (*Sotsial'naia priroda i osnovnye problemy*). Kazan, 1976

Abdullin, Ia. G., and Khäyrullin, Ä. "Märjani mirasïn öyränu yulïnda" [On the road to studying Merjani's heritage]. *KU* 10 (1976): 150–60.

Abdullin, H. "Protiv fal'sifikatsii istorii tatarskoi avtonomii." *Kommunist Tatarii* 3 (1972): 43–49.

Adres-kalendar' na 1916 god. St. Petersburg, 1916.

Ahmedi, A. "Qïtay muslumanlarï" [Chinese Muslims]. *Iqtisad* 8–10 (1911): 294.

Ähmerov, A. *Kazan tarihi* [Kazan history] (in Tatar, Arabic script). (Kazan, 1909).

Ahraba [pseud.]. "Askeri güchümüz häm Mustafa Kemal" [Our military might and Mustafa Kemal]. *Azad Seber* 2 (1921) 1.

Ahsen Böre, Z. I., ed. *Gani Bay* (in Arabic script). Orenburg, 1912. Reprint. Helsinki, 1945.

Ak'ägätzade, M. *Khisametdin menla* (*Khisametdin Mullah*) (in Tatar, Arabic script). Kazan, 1886.

Akchura, Y. *L'État actuel et les aspirations des turco-tatares musulmans en Russie.* Lausanne, 1916.

————. *Mevküfiyet hatïralarï* [Prison memoirs] (in Tatar, Arabic script). Orenburg, 1907.

————. *Uch-tarz-i-siyaset* [Three political systems] (in Ottoman Turkish, Arabic script). Istanbul, 1909.

Äkhmär, Sh. *Matbaachelek tarikhï* [A history of book printing] (in Tatar, Arabic script). Kazan, 1909.

Akhmarov, G. N. *O iazyke narodnosti Misharei.* Kazan, 1903.

————. "Teptiari i ikh proiskhozhdenie." *Izvestiia obshchestva arkheologii, istorii i etnografii pri Kazanskom universitete* 28 (1908): 340–64.

Akhmedov, A. *Sotsial'naia doktrina Islama.* Moscow, 1982.

Akiner, Shirin. *Islamic Peoples of the Soviet Union.* London, Boston, Melbourne, and Henley, 1983.

Akiş, A. *Idil-Ural davası ve Sovyet emperyalizmi* [The Idil-Ural question and Soviet imperialism]. Yenişehir and Ankara, 1963.

Al-Ghazali, Abu Hamid. *Al Munqidh min ad-Dalal* [Guide for the errants]. Edited by Mahmud 'Abd al-Halīm. Cairo, 1964.

Alishev, S. "Gaziz Gubaidullin kak istorik." In *Issledovaniia po istoriografii Tatarii.* Kazan, 1978, pp. 46–54.

————. "Prisoedinenie narodov Srednego Povolzh'ia k russkomu gosudarstvu." In *Tatariia v proshlom i nastoiashchem. Sbornik statei.* Kazan, 1975, pp. 172–85.

————. "Tarikhtän ber sakhifä" [A page from history]. *KU* 3 (1977): 165–69.

Alisov, G. "Musul'manskii vopros v Rossii." *Russkaia mysl'* 7 (1909): 34–55.

Allworth, E., ed. *Soviet Nationality Problems.* New York, 1971.

————. *Nationalities of the Soviet East: Publications and Writing Systems.* New York, 1971.

Amalrik, Giuzel'. *Vospominaniia o moem detstve.* Amsterdam, 1976.

Aminov, M. "Les progres de l'instruction chez les musulmans russes." *RMM* 10 (1909): 261–63.

Anastasiev, A. I. "O Tatarskikh dukhovnykh shkolakh. Nabliudeniia i zametki inspektora uchilishch." *Russkaia shkola* (December 1893): 126–30.

Anisimov, N. G. *Kazanskii l'nokombinat.* Kazan, 1960.

Ankara Üniversitesi Dil ve Tarih-Coğrafya Fakültesi Dergisi [Publication of the faculties of language and history-geography at Ankara University]. Ankara.

Arat, R. R. "Kasım Hanlığı" [The Kasimov khanate]. In *Islam Ansiklopedisi* [Islamic encyclopedia]. Vol. 7. Istanbul, 1955, pp. 380–86.

Arkheologiia i etnografiia Bashkirii. Ufa, 1971.

Arkheologiia i etnografiia Tatarstana. Kazan, 1976.

Arkhiv samizdata. Materialy samizdata. January 6, 1978, no. 3085, 3086, 3087.

Arsharuni, A. "Ideologiia Sultangalievshchiny." *Antireligioznik* 5 (1930): 22–25.

Arsharuni, A., and Gabidullin, Kh. *Ocherki panislamizma i pantiurkizma v Rossii.* Moscow, 1934.

Arutiunian, Iu. V., and Drobizheva, L. M. "Sovetskii obraz zhizni: Obshchee i natsional'no osobennoe." *SE* 3 (1976): 10–23.

Arutiunian, Iu. V.; Drobizheva, L. M.; and Shkaratan, O. I. *Sotsial'noe i natsional'noe: Opyt etnosotsiologicheskikh issledovanii po materialam Tatarskoi ASSR.* Moscow, 1973.

Asami-al-kutub [Names of books] (in Tatar, Arabic script). Kazan: Karimov, 1897.

Asami-al-kutub (in Tatar, Arabic script). Kazan: Sharif, 1899.

Asami-al-kutub (in Tatar, Arabic script). Kazan: Karimov, 1903.

Asami-al-kutub (in Tatar, Arabic script). Kazan: Idrisov and Galiev, 1906–1907.

Asami-al-kutub (in Tatar, Arabic script). Orenburg: Ahmed-al-Ishaqi, 1907.

Asami-al-kutub (in Tatar, Arabic script). Kazan: Iqbal, 1907.

Asami-al-kutub (in Tatar, Arabic script). Kazan: Karimov, 1907.

Asami-al-kutub (in Tatar, Arabic script). Kazan: Sabah, 1907.

Asami-al-kutub (in Tatar, Arabic script). Kazan: Urnek, 1909.

Asami-al-kutub (in Tatar, Arabic script). Orenburg and Ufa: Karimov and Huseinov, 1910–1911.

Asami-al-kutub (in Tatar, Arabic script). Orsk (1), 1910.

Asami-al-kutub. Chelebi shehrinde ujretsïz Musluman kutubhane-kïraathanesïnïng Tatar, Türk ve Arab tïllerïnde bulgan kitaplarena mahsus [Names of books. Referring to books in Tatar, Turkish, and Arabic at the Free Muslim Library reading room in the town of Chelebi] (in Tatar, Arabic script). Kazan: Urnek, 1910.

Ashirov, N. *Evoliutsiia Islama v SSSR.* Moscow, 1972.

Ashmarin, N. I. *Bolgary i Chuvashi.* Kazan, 1902.

Asim, N. *Türk tarihi* [Turkish history]. Istanbul, 1898.

Atlasi, H. *Qazan Hanlïgï* [The Kazan khanate]. (Kazan, 1913 and 1920).

Atnaghulïf, Sälakh. "Soltanghäliefchelkneng tarikhi tamrlarï" [The historic roots of Sultangalievism]. In Gh. Qushay, ed., *Kontr-rivolütsion Soltanghaliefchelkkä garshï* [Against counterrevolutionary Sultangalievism]. Kazan, 1929, pp. 35–40.

Aullarda volostlarda häm istanitsalarda yasala turghan abshistvinni issuda-isbirigatilni (yani aqcha saqli turghan kassalar) nïng abrazsavi ustafi. (Obraztsovyi ustav sel'skikh, volostnykh i stanichnykh obshchestvennykh ssudosberegatel'nykh kass) (in Tatar, Arabic script, and Russian text). Kazan, 1907.

Azad Seber [Free Siberia]. 1921.

Bagin, S. *Ob otpadenii v Magometsanstvo kreshchennykh inorodtsev Kazanskoi eparkhii i o prichinakh etogo pechal'nogo iavleniia.* Kazan, 1910.

———. *Propaganda Islama putem pechati.* Kazan, 1909.

Bahadir Han, Ebulgazi. *Histoire des Mongols et des Tatares.* St. Petersburg, 1871–1874. Reprint. St. Leonards, 1970.

Barthold, W. "Tatar." In *Enzyklopedie des Islam.* Vol. 4 (Leiden and Leipzig, 1934): 759–61.

Bartol'd, V. V. *Raboty po istorii filologii tiurkskikh i mongol'skikh narodov. Sochineniia.* 6 vols., Moscow, 1963–1968.

Battal, A. [Abdullah Battal-Taymas] *Tatar tarihi. Qazan Türkleri. Tarihi ve siyasi görushler* [Tatar history. The Kazan Turks. A historical and political approach] (in Turkish, Arabic script). Istanbul, 1925.

——. *Rizaeddin Fahreddinoğlu.* Istanbul, 1958.

——. "Qazan Türkleri" [Kazan Turks] (in Turkish, Arabic script). In *Türk Ili.* Istanbul, 1928, pp. 616–47.

——. *Ben bir ışık arıyordum* [I was in search of light]. Istanbul, 1962.

——. *Kazan Türkleri: Türk tarihinin hazin yaprakları.* [The Kazan Turks: The sad pages of Turkish history]. Ankara, 1966.

Bazilevich, K. V. *Vneshniaia politika russkogo tsentralizovannogo gosudarstva.* Moscow, 1952.

Belov, E., *Kul'turnye sokrovishcha Rossii: Kazan, N. Novgorod, Kostroma.* Moscow, 1913.

Bennigsen, A., and Lemercier-Quelquejay, Chantal. *Islam in the Soviet Union.* New York, 1967.

——. *La presse et le mouvement national chez les musulmans de Russie avant 1920.* Paris, 1964.

——. "Le khanate de Crimée du XVIe siècle de la tradition mongole à la suzeraineté ottomane d'après un document inédit des archives ottomanes. *CMRS* 13 (1972): 321–37.

——. *Les mouvements nationaux chez les musulmans de Russie. Le "sultangalievisme" au Tatarstan.* Paris, 1960.

——. *Les musulmans oubliés. L'Islam en Union Soviétique.* Paris, 1981.

——. "Musulmans et missions orthodoxes en Russie orientale avant 1917. Essai de bibliographie critique." *CMRS* 1 (1972): 98–106.

Bennigsen, A., and Wimbush, S. Enders. *Muslim National Communism in the Soviet Union: A Revolutionary Strategy for the Colonial World.* Chicago, 1979.

Berezin, I. "Bulgary na Volge. S risunkami Bulgarskikh drevnostei i nadpisei." In *Uchenye zapiski Imperatorskogo Kazanskogo Universiteta.* Vol. 3. Kazan, 1853, pp. 74–160.

——. "Ocherk vnutrennego ustroistva Ulusa Dzhuchieva." In *Trudy Otdeleniia Imperatorskogo Russkogo Arkheologicheskogo Obshchestva.* St. Petersburg, 1864, pp. 387–494.

Berkes, Niyazi, ed. *Turkish Nationalism and Western Civilization. Selected Essays of Ziya Gökalp.* London, 1959.

Bigi, Musa Jarullah. *Büyük mevzularda ufak fikirler* [Small thoughts on big issues] (in Tatar, Arabic script). St. Petersburg, 1914.

——. "Dininiz milletimiz kıymeti" [The value of our religion and nation]. *Yulduz* 1493 (1915): 2–3.

———. *Halq nazarïna bir niche mesele* [A few problems for people's attention] (in Tatar, Arabic script). Kazan, 1912.

———. *Islahat esaslarï* [Foundations of reform] (in Tatar, Arabic script). Petrograd, 1917.

———, ed. *1906 sene 16–21 Avgustda ichtimag itmish Rusya Musulmanlarïnïng nedvesi* [The congress of the Russian Muslims held on August 16–21, 1906] (in Tatar, Arabic script). Kazan, 1906.

Bigiev, Z. *Ölüf, yäki güzäl kïz Khädichä* [Ölüf, or The beautiful girl Khädichä] (in Tatar, Arabic script). Kazan, 1887.

Bikbulatov, N. V., and Nagaeva, L. I. "Vtoroe Povolzhsko-Uralskoe arkheologo-etnograficheskoe soveshchanie." *SE* 5 (1977): 139–42.

Biniiatullina, A. *Pisateli Sovetskogo Tatarstana.* Kazan, 1970.

Bobi, A. *Haqiqat yahud tughrïliq* [Truth or justice] (in Tatar, Arabic script). Kazan, 1904.

Bobrovnikov, M. N. A. "Russko-tuzemnye uchilishcha, mekteby i medresy v Srednei Azii." *ZMNP* (May–June 1913): 189–241.

Bobrovnikoff, S. "Moslems in Russia." *Moslem World* 1 (1911).

Bohdanowicz, Leon. *Les musulmans en Pologne; Origine, histoire, et vie culturelle.* Jerusalem, 1947.

———. "Moslems in Poland: Their Origin, History, and Cultural Life." *Journal of the Royal Asiatic Society of Great Britain* (October 1942): 163–80.

Boiovich, M. M. *Chleny gosudarstvennoi Dumy (Portrety i biografii). Pervyi sozyv. 1906–1911. Sessiia 27 IV–9 VIII.* Moscow, 1906.

Bolshakov, O. G., and Mongait, A. L., eds. *Puteshestvie Abu Khamida al-Garnati v Vostochnuiu i Tsentral'nuiu Evropu (1131–1153).* Moscow, 1971.

Bräker, Hans. "The Muslim Revival in Russia." In E. Oberländer, ed., *Russia Enters the Twentieth Century, 1894–1917.* New York, 1971, pp. 182–99.

Brockelmann, Carl. *History of the Islamic Peoples.* London, 1979.

Bunegin, M. "Tatarskaia shkola v Krymu." *Prosveshchenie natsional'nostei* 1 (1931): 52–54.

Burbiel, G. "Tatar Literature." In G. S. N. Lukyi, ed., *Discordant Voices in the non-Russian Soviet Literatures, 1953–1973.* Oakville, Ontario, 1975, p. 117.

Burmistrova, T. Iu. *Natsional'naia politika bol'shevikov v pervoi russkoi revoliutsii 1905–1907g.* Leningrad, 1962.

Bütün Rüsiyä Müsülmanlarïnïng 1917 nchï yïlda 1–11 mayda Maskauda bulghan 'umumi isiyizdïnïng prutaqullarï [The protocols of the All-Russian Congress of Muslims held in Moscow on May 1–11, 1917] (in Tatar, Arabic script). Petrograd, 1917.

Călinescu, G. *Istoriia literaturii Române (compendiu).* Bucharest, 1968.

Carrère d'Encausse, Hélène. *L'Empire éclaté. La revolte des nations en URSS.* Paris, 1978.

Chicherina, S. V. *O Privolzhskikh inorodtsakh i sovremennom znachenii sistemy N. I. Il'minskogo.* St. Petersburg, 1906.

Chistaydagï putribitiller jemgiyetïnïng ustafï *(Ustav Chistopol'skogo obshchestva potrebitelei).* Kazan, 1910.

Chleny 2-oi gosudarstvennoi Dumy. Biografii. *Sravnitel'naia kharakteristika chlenov 1-oi i 2-oi Dumy. Alfavitnyi ukazatel'.* St. Petersburg, 1907.

Chleny pervoi gosudarstvennoi Dumy s portretami. Moscow, 1906.

Chteniia v Imperatorskom Obshchestve Istorii i Drevnostei Rossiiskikh pri Moskovskom Universitete. Moscow, 1846–1918.

Chulpan. 1918.

CMRS [Cahiers du monde russe et soviétique]. Paris, 1960–.

Connolly, Violet. "The Nationalities Question in the Last Phase of Tsardom." In E. Oberländer, ed., *Russia Enters the Twentieth Century, 1894–1917.* New York, 1971.

D. A. A. "Vopros o prosveshchenii Tatar." *Russkaia shkola* 7–8 (1905): 237–57.

Davletshin, T. *Cultural Life in the Tatar Autonomous Republic.* New York, 1953.

———. *Sovetskii Tatarstan. Teoriia i praktika Leninskoi natsional'noi politiki.* London, 1974.

Deiatel'nost' partiinoi organizatsii Tatarii po osushchestvleniiu Leninskoi idei stroitel'stva sotsialisticheskogo obshchestva. Kazan, 1971.

Dekrety sovetskoi vlasti. 2 vols. Moscow, 1957 and 1959.

Dimanshtein, S. M. "Ideologicheskaia bor'ba v natsional'nom voprose." In S. M. Dimanshtein, *Revoliutsiia i natsional'nosti.* Vol. 3. Moscow, 1930, pp. 2–7.

———. *Revoliutsiia i natsional'nyi vopros.* 3 vols. Moscow, 1930.

Dingelstadt, V. "The Musulman Subjects of Russia." *The Scottish Geographical Magazine* 1 (1903): 1–8.

Dirks, Sabina. *La famille musulmane Turque.* Paris, 1969.

Efirov, A. F. *Nerusskie shkoly Povolzh'ia, Priural'ia i Sibiri.* Moscow, 1948.

———. "Russifikatorskie novokreshchenskie shkoly." *Prosveshchenie natsional'nostei* 4 (1934): 51–58.

Ezhov, N. *Voennaia Kazan' v 1917 godu.* Kazan, 1957.

Fahreddin, Rizaeddin. *Ahmed Bay* (in Tatar, Arabic script). Orenburg, 1911.

———. *Asar* (in Tatar, Arabic script). 2 vols. Orenburg, 1904–1908.

———. *Qor'än vä tabagät* [The Qur'an and the art of book printing] (in Tatar, Arabic script). Kazan, 1900.

———. *Rihalet-al-Merjani* [The voyage of Merjani] (in Tatar, Arabic script). Kazan, 1897.

———. *Rusya Muslumanlarïnïng ihtiyachlarï ve anlar haqïnda intiqad* [The needs of the Muslims and a criticism regarding them] (in Tatar, Arabic script). Orenburg, 1906.

Fakhri, Majid. *A History of Islamic Philosophy.* New York, 1970.

Fakhrutdinov, R. G. *Arkheologicheskie pamiatniki Volzhsko-Kamskoi Bulgarii i ee territorii.* Kazan, 1975.

Farah, Caesar E. *Islam*. New York, 1970.

Faseev, K. F. *Iz istorii Tatarskoi peredovoi obshchestvennoi mysli (vtoraia polovina XIX-nachalo XX veka)*. Kazan, 1955.

Fedorov-Davydov, G. A. *Kochevniki Vostochnoi Evropy pod vlast'iu zoloto-ordynskikh khanov. Arkheologicheskie pamiatniki*. Moscow, 1966.

———. *Obshchestvennyi stroi Zolotoi Ordy.* Moscow, 1973.

Fekhner, M. V. *Torgovlia russkogo gosudarstva so stranami vostoka v XVIv. Trudy gosudarstvennogo istoricheskogo muzeia*. Moscow, 1956.

———. *Velikie Bulgary. Kazan'. Sviazhsk*. Moscow, 1978.

Ferrand, G., ed. *Le Tukfat al-albāb de Abū Hamid al-Andalusī al-Garnatī édité d'après les Mss. 2167, 2168, 2170 de la bibliothèque nationale et le Ms. d'Alger*. Paris, 1925.

Firsov, N. N. "Nekotorye cherty iz istorii torgovo-promyshlennoi zhizni Povolzh'ia (s drevneishikh vremen do osmotra etogo kraia imperatritsei Ekaterinoi II-oi)." In *Izvestiia Obshchestva Arkheologii, Istorii i Etnografii pri Imperatorskom Kazanskom Universitete*. Vol. 14. Kazan, 1897, pp. 478–94.

———. *Proshloe Tatarii*. Kazan, 1926.

Fisher, A. W. *Crimean Tatars*. Stanford, 1978.

IV Musul'manskii s'ezd. S. Petersburg. 15–25 iiunia 1914. St. Petersburg, 1914.

IV–XVIII yuzyıllarında Karadenizin kuzeyindeki Türk kavimleri ve devletleri [Turkish states and tribes north of the Black Sea during the fourth through eighteenth centuries]. Ankara, 1972.

Fuks, K. F. *Kratkaia istoriia goroda Kazani*. Kazan, 1817.

———. *Kazanskie Tatary*. Kazan, 1844.

Gabrys, J. [pseud.]. *L'independence lituanienne. Faits, impressions, souvenirs, 1907–1920*. n.p., n.d.

Gainullin, M. *Tatar ädipläre* [Tatar writers]. Kazan, 1978.

Gainullin, M., and Mähdiev, M. *Tatar ädäbiyatï. Urta Mäktäpneng 8 nche klassï öchen däreslek* [Tatar literature textbook for the eighth grade of middle school]. Kazan, 1975.

Galiev, M. *Jingäsem kilde* [My sister-in-law arrived]. Kazan, 1981.

Gasilov, G. "Osnovnye voprosy natsional'noi shkoly." *Revoliutsiia i kul'tura* 2 (1928): 26–27.

Gasprinskii, I. *Rehber-i muallimin yani muallimlere yuldash* [A guide for teachers, or A teacher's companion] (in Tatar, Arabic script). Bakhchesarai, 1898.

———. *Russkoe Musul'manstvo, Mysli, zametki i nabliudeniia Musul'manina*. Simferopol, 1881.

Gazizullin, F. G. *Dorogoi k pravde*. Kazan, 1979.

Genkina, E. B. *Obrazovanie SSSR. Sbornik dokumentov. 1917–1924g*. Moscow and Leningrad, 1947.

Genning, V. F. *Rannie Bolgary na Volge; Bol'she Tarkhanskii mogil'nik*. Moscow, 1964.

Gibb, H. A. R. *The Encyclopedia of Islam*. 4 vols. to date. Leiden and London, 1960–.

————. *Modern Trends in Islam*. Chicago, 1947.

————. *Mohammedanism*. London, 1972.

Giniiatullina, A. *Pisateli Sovetskogo Tatarstana*. Kazan, 1970.

Gizatullin, I. G. *Zashchishchaia zavoevaniia Oktiabria. Tsentral'naia Musul'manskaia voennaia kollegiia. 1918–20*. Moscow, 1979.

Glazatyi, Ioan. *Skazanie o tsarstve Kazanskom*. Moscow, 1959.

Gökalp, Z. *Türkçülüğün esasları*. Istanbul, 1970.

Gol'strem, V. *Musul'manskaia pechat' v Rossii v 1910 godu*. St. Petersburg, 1911.

Golubovskii, P. V. *Pechenegi, polovtsy i tiurki do nashestviia tatar.* Kiev, 1884.

Gordlevskii, V. A. *Elementy kul'tury u Kasimovskikh Tatar. Trudy Obshchestva Issledovaniia Riazanskogo kraia*. Riazan, 1927.

Goroda Rossii v 1910 godu. St. Petersburg, 1914.

Gorokhov, G. M. *Reaktsionnaia shkol'naia politika tsarizma v otnoshenii Tatar Povolzh'ia*. Kazan, 1941.

Gosmanov, Mirkassyim. "Tarikhlïk fänneng zaruri taläbe" [The necessary requirement of the historical science]. *KU* (1976): 178–83.

Gosudarstvennaia Duma. Ukazatel' k stenograficheskim otchetam. Chasti I–III. Chetvertyi sozyv. Sessiia I. 1912–13. St. Petersburg, 1913.

Gosudarstvennaia Duma. Ukazatel' k stenograficheskim otchetam. Chasti I–III. Tretii sozyv. Sessiia I. 1907–8. St. Petersburg, 1908.

Gosudarstvennaia Duma. Ukazatel' k stenograficheskim otchetam. 1906 god. Sessiia pervaia. Zasedaniia 1–38 (27 IV–4 VIII 1906). St. Petersburg, 1907.

Gosudarstvennaia Duma. Ukazatel' k stenograficheskim otchetam. Vtoroi sozyv 1907 god. Zasedaniia 1–53 (20 fevralia–2 iiunia 1907) St. Petersburg, 1907.

Gosudarstvennaia Duma. Vtoroi sozyv. Stenograficheskie otchety. 1907. Sessiia vtoraia. 2 vols. St. Petersburg, 1907.

Grasis, K. *K natsional'nomu voprosu*. Kazan, 1918.

Grekov, B. D. "Volzhskie Bolgary v IX–X vekakh." In *Istoricheskie zapiski*. Vol. 14. Moscow, 1945, pp. 3–37.

Grekov, B. D., and Iakubovskii, A. Iu. *Zolotaia Orda i ee padenie*. Moscow and Leningrad, 1950.

Grekov, B. D., and Kalinin, N. F. "Bulgarskoe gosudarstvo do mongol'skogo zavoevaniia." In *Materialy po istorii Tatarii*. Kazan, 1948, pp. 97–184.

Grousset, René. *L'empire des steppes*. Paris, 1952.

Gubaidullin, G. *Burungu Bulgharlar* [Ancient Bulgars] (in Tatar, Arabic script). Kazan, 1927.

————. "Iz proshlogo Tatar." In *Materialy po izucheniiu Tatarstana*. Vol. 2. Kazan, 1925, pp. 71–111.

————. *Tatarlarnïng kilep chiguvï häm Altïn Urda* [The origin of the Tatars and the Golden Horde] (in Tatar, Arabic script). Kazan, 1924.

————. *Tatar tarihi* [Tatar history] (in Tatar, Arabic script). Kazan, 1923.

Guboglo, M. N. "Sotsial'no-etnicheskie posledstviia dvuiazychiia." *SE* 2 (1972): 26–37.

Gumilev, L. N. "Udel'no-lestvichnaia sistema u tiurok v VI–VII vekakh. K voprosu o rannikh formakh gosudarstvennosti." *SE* 3 (1959): 11–16.

Halasi-Kun, T. "Monuments de la langue tatare de Kazan." *Analecta orientalia memoriae Alexandri Csoma de Köros dicata.* Biblioteca Orientalis Hungarica, 1942.

——. "Philologica III. Kazan Türkçesine ait dil yadigârları [Monuments of the Kazan Turkish language]. *Ankara Üniversitesi Dil ve Tarih Coğrafya Fakültesi Dergisi* 4 (1949): 603–44.

Halén, Harry. *A Bibliographical Survey of the Publishing Activities of the Turkic Minority in Finland.* Helsinki, 1979.

Han-Istafkesi Muslumanlarïnïng terakki ve medeniyete yardïm jemgiyetïnïng nizamnamesi [The statutes of the Han-Stavka Moslem Society for Assistance to Progress and Culture] (in Tatar, Arabic script). Astrakhan, 1909.

Harper, S. *Papers.* University of Chicago Archives.

Heiman, E. *Reason and Faith in Modern Society: Liberalism, Marxism, and Democracy.* Middletown, 1961.

Herberstein, Sigmund (von). *Notes upon Russia.* London, 1851–52.

Iakubovskii, A. Iu. "K voprosy ob istoricheskoi topografii Itilia i Bolgar v IX i X vekakh." *SA* 10 (1948): 225–70.

Ibragimov, G. *Kayyum Nasiri mäjmugasï* [The Kayyum Nasiri Journal]. Kazan, 1922.

——. *Tatar mädäniyeti nindi yul belän barajaq?* [Which way will Tatar culture go?] (in Tatar, Arabic script). Kazan, 1927.

——. *Tatary v revoliutsii 1905 goda.* Kazan, 1926.

——. *Ural häm Uralchïlar.* [Ural and the Uralists] (in Tatar, Arabic script). 1926.

Il. St. Petersburg, 1913.

Ilkul, A. K. *Türkistan ve Çin yollarında unutulmayan hatıralar* [Unforgettable memoirs of China and Turkestan]. Istanbul, 1955.

Imankul aulïnïng medeniyet ve iqtisad jemgiyet jeriyasïnïng ustafï [The status of the economic and cultural society of the Imankul village] (in Tatar, Arabic script). Orenburg, 1911.

Imeretinska, F., and Lykoshin, P. I. *Blagotvoritel'naia Rossiia.* St. Petersburg, 1901.

Inkeles, A. *Social Change in Soviet Russia.* Cambridge, Mass., 1968.

Inorodetz [pseud. of Juozas Gabrys]. *La Russie et les peuples allogènes.* Berne, 1918.

Ionenko, I., and Tagirov, I. *Oktiabr' v Kazani.* Kazan, 1967.

Iqtisad [Economics]. Samara, 1908–1912.

Ishaki, A. *Idel-Oural.* Paris, 1933.

Ishmukhametov, Z. A. *Sotsial'naia rol' i evoliutsiia Islama v Tatarii.* Kazan, 1979.

Issledovaniia po istoriografii Tatarii. Kazan, 1978.

Istoriia Tatarii v dokumentakh i materialakh. Moscow, 1937.

Istoriia tatarskoi sovetskoi literatury. Moscow, 1965.

Istoriko-arkheologicheskii sbornik k 60-letiiu A. V. Artsikhovskogo. Moscow, 1962.

ITASSR [*Istoriia tatarskoi avtonomnoi sovetskoi sotsialisticheskoi respubliki*]. 2 vols. Kazan, 1955–1956.

ITASSR. Kazan, 1960.

ITASSR. Kazan, 1973.

Iusupov, G. V. *Vvedenie v bulgaro-tatarskuiu epigrafiku.* Moscow and Leningrad, 1960.

Iz istorii klassovoi bor'by i obshchestvennoi mysli v Povolzh'e i Priural'e. Sbornik statei. Uchenye zapiski Kazanskogo gosudarstvennogo universiteta im. V. I. Ul'ianova Lenina. Kazan, 1962.

Izvestiia kazanskogo filiala Akademii Nauk SSSR, no. 3. Kazan, 1955.

Izvestiia Obshchestva Arkheologii, Istorii i Etnografii pri Imperatorskom Kazanskom Universitete. Vol. 4. Kazan, 1897, part 1.

Jabre, F. *La notion de certitude selon Ghazali dans ses origines psychologiques et historiques.* Paris, 1958.

Kaidanova, O. V. *Ocherki po istorii narodnogo obrazovaniia v Rossii i SSSR na osnove lichnogo opyta i nabliudenii.* 2 vols. Berlin, 1938.

Kalganov, A. "Ideologiia esheneng möhim buini" [An important aspect of ideological work]. *Tatarstan Kommunisty* [The communist of Tatarstan] 1 (1983): 71–77.

Kalinin, N. F. *Kazan. Istoricheskii ocherk.* Kazan, 1952.

Kamsko-Volzhskaia rech'. Kazan, May–December, 1913.

Kappeler, Andreas. *Russlands Erste Nationalitäten: Das Zarenreich und die Völker der Mittleren Wolga vom 16 bis 19 Jahrhundert.* Vienna, 1982.

Karan, A. L. *Şehabettin Mercani turmuşu hem eserleri* [The life and works of Shihabeddin Merjani]. Suyumbike Cultural Society Series, no. 4. Istanbul, 1964.

Karimullin, A. G. *Kitap dön'yäsina säyäkhat* [A journey to the world of books]. Kazan, 1979.

———. *Tatarskaia kniga nachala XX veka.* Kazan, 1974.

———. *U istokov Tatarskoi knigi.* Kazan, 1971.

Kasymov, G. *Pantiurkistskaia kontrrevoliutsiia i ee agentura-Sultangalievshchina.* Kazan, 1930.

Katanov, N. O. *Novye dannye o Musul'manskoi sekte Vaisovtsev.* Kazan, 1909.

Katetov, Ivan. "Obzor pravitel'stvennykh i tserkovnykh rasporiazhenii kasaiushchikhsia obrashcheniia v Khristianstvo Tatar-Mukhamedan." *Strannik* 8 (1886): 565–91.

Kayyum Nasiri mäjmugasi [The K. Nasiri Journal]. Kazan, 1922.

Kazakov, I. *Pamiatniki Bolgarskogo vremeni v vostochnykh raionakh Tatarii.* Moscow, 1978.

Kazan. Ankara, 1970–1981.

Kazanskie vesti. Kazan, January–October 1892.

Kazanskii, M. V. *Putevoditel' po Kazani.* Kazan, 1899.

Kazanskii birzhevoi listok. Kazan, January–June 1891.

Kazanskii telegraf. Kazan, January–November 1915.

Kazanskii vecher. Kazan, January–December 1907.

Kazanskii zemskii kalendar' na 1915 god. Kazan, 1915.

Khairutdinov, R. G. *Na putiakh k sovetskoi avtonomii: Provedenie Leninskoi natsional'noi politiki tsentral'nym Tataro-Bashkirskim kommissariatom v 1918–1919g.* Kazan, 1972.

———. *Osushchestvlenie kommunisticheskoi partiei Leninskoi programmy po natsional'nomy voprosu 1917–1920.* Kazan, 1976.

Khakov, V. "Katlaulï mäs'älälärne khal itu yulïnda" [Toward solving important problems]. *KU* 11 (1978): 169–74.

Khälid, Änäs. "Äbu Khämid el-Garnatyinïng Bolgarga säyakhäte. Säyakhätche häm anïng äsärläre [Abu Hamid al-Garnati's voyage to Bulgar. The traveler and his works]. *KU* 6 (1976): 148–58.

Khalidi, F. *Mäkhrüsä khanïm* [Lady Mäkhrüsä] (in Tatar, Arabic script). Kazan, 1906.

Khalikov, A. Kh. *Arkheologiia i etnografiia Tatarstana.* Kazan, 1976.

———. "K voprosu o nachale tiurkizatsii naseleniia Provolzh'ia i Priural'ia." *SE* 1 (1972): 100–110.

———. "Obshchie protsessy v etnogeneze Bashkir i Tatar Povolzh'ia i Priural'ia." In *Arkheologiia i etnografiia Bashkirii.* Vol. 4. Ufa, 1971, pp. 30–37.

———. *Proiskhozhdenie Tatar Povolzh'ia i Priural'ia.* Kazan, 1978.

———. *Tatar khalkïnïng kilep chïgïshï* [The origin of the Tatar people]. Kazan, 1974.

———. *Volgo-Kam'e v nachale epokhi rannego zheleza. VIII–VI v.v. do n.e.* Moscow, 1977.

Khalikov, A. Kh., and Genning, V. F. *Rannie Bolgary na Volge: Bol'she Tarkhanskii mogil'nik.* Moscow, 1964.

Khan-Istafkesi Musulmanlarïnïng terakki ve medeniyete yardïm jemgiyetinïng nizamnamesi [The Khanskaia-Stavka Society for Assistance to Muslim Progress and Culture]. Astrakhan, 1909.

Khantemirova, G. "Fätikh Ämirkhan ijatïnda khatïn-kïzlar azatlïgï temasï" [The theme of the freedom of girls/women in Fatikh Amirkhan's works]. *KU* 8 (1977): 155–59.

Khasanov, Kh. Kh. *Formirovanie Tatarskoi burzhuaznoi natsii.* Kazan, 1977.

———. *Husain Yamashev.* Kazan, 1954.

———. *Makhmud Kashghariy. (Khaeti vä geografik merasi).* [Makhmud Kashghariy. (His life and geographic heritage)]. Tashkent, 1963.

———. *Revoliutsiia 1905–1907g. v Tatarii.* Moscow, 1965.

Khasanov, M. Kh. *Galimdzhan Ibragimov.* Kazan, 1969.

Khisamov, Nurmokhammat. "Ädäbiyatka tarikhi karash" [A historical approach to literature]. *KU* 1 (1981): 183–86.

———. *"Kyssa-i Yusuf" Kul' Ali. Analiz istoricheskogo siuzheta i avtorskogo tvorchestva.* Moscow, 1979.

Khösäenov, Gaisa. "Utïz Imäni Bashkortstanda" (Utïz Imäni in Bashkiria). *KU* 1 (1977): 152–56.

Khudiakov, M. *Ocherki po istorii Kazanskogo khanstva.* Kazan, 1923.

Khvol'son, D. A., ed. *Izvestiia o Khozarakh, Burtashakh, Bolgarakh, Mad'iarakh, Slavianakh i Russakh Abu-Ali Akhmeda Ben Omar Ibn-Dasta, neizvestnogo dosele arabskogo pisatelia nachala X veka, po rukopisi Britanskogo Muzeia v pervyi raz izdal, perevel i ob'iasnil D. A. Khvol'son.* St. Petersburg, 1896.

Kilisli, Rifat Bilge. "Divanu Lugat it-Turk ve Emir Efendi" [Divanu Lugat it-Turk and Emir Efendi]. *Türk Kültürü* 8, no. 88 (1970): 253–70.

Klimov, I. M. *Natsional'nye momenty v gosudarstvennom i partiinom stroitel'stve v Tatarii. Vosstanovitel'nyi period.* Kazan, 1960.

———. *Obrazovanie i razvitie Tatarskoi ASSR.* Kazan, 1960.

Klimovich, L. "Religioznoe dvizhenie v Tatarskoi respublike." *Antireligioznik* 4 (1927): 57–58.

Kobetskii, M. "Sultangalievshchina kak apologiia Islama." *Antireligioznik* 1 (1930): 2–14.

Koblov, Ia. D. *Konfessional'nye shkoly Kazanskikh Tatar.* Kazan, 1916.

———. *O Magometanskikh mullakh. Religiozno-bytovoi ocherk.* Kazan, 1907.

Korbut, M. "Natsional'nye dvizheniia v Volzhsko-Kamskom krae v 1917." *Revoliutsionnyi Vostok* 7 (1929): 178.

Kovalevskii, A. P. *Chuvashi i bulgary po dannym Akhmeda Ibn-Fadlana.* Cheboksary, 1954.

———. *Kniga Akhmeda Ibn-Fadlana i ego puteshestvie na Volgu v 921–922 g. Stat'i, perevody i kommentarii.* Kharkov, 1956.

Koyash. Orenburg, August–September 1915.

Kozlov, V. I. *Natsional'nosti SSSR. Etnodemograficheskii obzor.* Moscow, 1975.

Krachkovskii, I. Iu., ed. *Puteshestvie Ibn-Fadlana na Volgu.* Moscow and Leningrad, 1939.

Kriditni tavarishstvanïng abrazsavi ustafi (Ustav kreditnogo tovarishchestva). Kazan, 1907.

Krymskii, A. *Musul'manstvo i ego budushchnost'.* Moscow, 1899.

KU [*Kazan Utlarï* (The fires of Kazan)]. Kazan, 1922–.

Kültäsi, Sh. *Mäktäp balasï yahut Säkhilä äbi* [The schoolboy or Grandmother Säkhilä] (in Tatar, Arabic script). Kazan, 1909.

Kuntsevich, G. Z. *Istoriia o Kazanskom khanstve ili Kazanskii letopisets.* St. Petersburg, 1905.

Kurat, Akdes Nimet. "Altın Ordu devleti" [The Golden Horde state]. In *Türk Dünyası El Kitabı* [A handbook of the Turkic world]. Vol. 2. Ankara, 1976, pp. 926–33.

———. "Altın Ordu kağanlığı" [The Golden Horde khanate]. In *IV–XVIII yüzyıllarında Karadenizin kuzeyindeki Türk kavimleri ve devletleri* [Turkish states and tribes north of the Black Sea during the fourth through the eighteenth centuries]. Ankara, 1972, pp. 119–52.

———. "Kazan Hanlığı" [The Kazan khanate]. *Ankara Üniversitesi Dil, Tarih-Coğrafya Fakültesi Dergisi* 12 (1954): 227–46.

———. *Kazan Hanlığını kuran Uluğ Muhammed Han yarlığı* [The yarlyk of Ulu Muhammed, founder of the Kazan khanate]. Istanbul, 1937.

———. "Kazan Türklerinin medeni uyanış devri" [The era of the Kazan Turks' cultural awakening]. *Ankara Üniversitesi Dil ve Tarih-Coğrafya Fakültesi Dergisi* 3–4 (1966): 94–196.

———. "Kazan Türklerinin tanınmış tarihçi ve milliyetçilerinden Hadi Atlas (1875–1940)" [The well-known historian and nationalist of the Kazan Turks, Hadi Atlas (1875–1940)]. *Kazan* 16 (1975): 4–5.

———. "Malazgirt zaferi sıralarında Idil boyu ve Karadeniz'in kuzeyindeki Türk kavimleri [Turkish tribes north of the Black Sea and along the Volga River at the time of the Malazgirt victory]. *Kazan* 7–8 (1972): 2.

———. *Topkapı Sarayı müzesi arşivindeki Altın Ordu, Kırım ve Türkistan hanlıklarına ait yarlık ve bitikler* [Yarlyks and documents of the Golden Horde, the Crimean and Turkestan khanates in the Topkapı palace museum]. Istanbul and Ankara, 1940.

Kurbatov, Kh. R. *Tatar alfavity häm orfografiyäse tarikhï* [The history of the Tatar alphabet and orthography]. Kazan, 1960.

Kuzeev, R. G. *Istoricheskaia etnografiia Bashkirskogo naroda.* Ufa, 1978.

———. *Proiskhozhdenie Bashkirskogo naroda. Etnicheskii sostav. Istoriia rasseleniia.* Moscow, 1974.

Lane, D. *The Roots of Russian Communism: A Social and Historical Study of Russian Social Democracy.* Assen, 1969.

L'assistance publique et privée en Russie. St. Petersburg, 1906.

Lazzerini, E. J. "Ethnicity and the Uses of History: The Case of the Volga Tatars and Jadidism." *Central Asian Survey* (November 1982): 61–69.

———. "Tatarovedenie and the 'New Historiography' in the Soviet Union: Revising the Interpretation of the Tatar-Russian Relationship." *SR* 4 (1981): 625–36.

Livshits, S. *Kazan' v gody pervoi russkoi revoliutsii (1905–1907).* Kazan, 1930.

Lo Gato, Ettore. *Histoire de la littérature russe des origines à nos jours.* Desclée de Brouwer, Belgium, 1965.

Luckyi, G. S. N., ed. *Discordant Voices in the non-Russian Soviet Literatures, 1953–1973.* Oakville, Ontario, 1975.

Lunacharsky, A. V. "Problemy obrazovaniia v avtonomnykh respublikakh i oblastiakh." *Zhizn' natsional'nostei* 1 (1924): 31–32.

McCarthy, Frank. "The Kazan Missionary Congress." *CMRS* 3 (1973): 308–33.

Mähdiev, Mokhammät. "Rus orientalistlarïnïng eshchänlege häm tatar vakïtlï mat-bugatï" [Russian orientalists and the Tatar periodical press]. *KU* 3 (1980): 173–74.

Makhmutova, A. Kh. "Shkola Liabiby Khusainovoi v Kazani." In *Stranitsy istorii goroda Kazani.* Kazan, 1981, pp. 55–66.

_____. "Vozniknovenie svetskikh zhenskikh shkol u Tatar." In Iu. I. Smykov, ed., *Ocherki istorii narodov Povolzh'ia i Priural'ia*. Kazan, 1967, pp. 174–87.

Makhmutova, A. Kh., and Smirnova, V. N. "Zhenskii vopros v Tatarskoi istoriografii 1917–27 godov." In *Obshchestvenno-politicheskoe dvizhenie i klassovaia bor'ba na Srednei Volge*. Kazan, 1972, pp. 72–75.

Maksimov, A. V., ed. *Sbornik rechei deputatov gosudarstvennoi dumy I i II sozyva. Kniga pervaia*. St. Petersburg, 1908.

Malik, A. M. *Labor Problems and Policy of Pakistan*. Karachi, 1954.

Malmïzhda Muslumanlar kïraathanesïnïng ustafï (ustav bezplatnoi biblioteki-chital'ni dlia Musul'man v g. Malmyzhe, Viatskoi gubernii). Kazan, 1907.

Malov, E. A. *O novokreshchenskoi kontore*. Kazan, 1873.

_____. *Statisticheskie svedeniia o kreshchennykh Tatarakh*. n.d. (Ecole Pratique des Hautes Etudes, Paris, microfilm #653, incomplete.)

Mansurov, G. *Tatar pravakatrlarï* [Tatar provocateurs] (in Tatar, Arabic script). Moscow, 1927.

Mashanov, M. *Sovremennoe sostoianie Tatar-Mukhamedan i ikh otnoshenie k drugim inorodtsam*. Kazan, 1910.

Massell, Gregory J. *The Surrogate Proletariat: Moslem Women and Revolutionary Strategies in Soviet Central Asia. 1919–1920*. Princeton, 1974.

Materialy po istorii Tatarii. Kazan, 1948.

Materialy po izucheniiu Tatarstana. 2 vols. Kazan, 1925.

Mathews, R. H. *A Chinese-English Dictionary, Compiled for the China Inland Mission*. Shanghai and Cambridge, England, 1969.

Medynskii, E. N. *Istoriia russkoi pedagogiki*. Moscow, 1938.

Men-da bei lu (Polnoe opisanie mongolo-tatar). Moscow, 1975.

Mende, Gerhard (Von). "Yusuf Akchura bin Vorkamper des Turkismus." *Osteuropa* 10 (1934–1935): 564–68.

Menger, A. V. "Bubi medresesi ve Bubi kardeşler" [The Bubi medrese and the Bubi brothers]. *Kazan* 3 (1971): 33–41.

Merjani, Sh. *Mustafad al-Akhbar fi-l-Ahwal Qazan wa Bulgar* [Select information on the situation of Kazan and Bulgar]. Part 1, Kazan, 1897; part 2, Kazan, 1900.

Mezhdunarodnye otnosheniia, politika, diplomatiia. (Sbornik statei k 80-letiiu akademika I. M. Maiskogo. Moscow, 1964.

Miliukov, P. N. *Natsional'nyi vopros (proiskhozhdenie natsional'nosti i natsional'nye voprosy v Rossii)*. Paris, 1925.

Mingnegulov, Kh. "Däreslek häm programma" [Textbooks and programs]. *KU* 6 (1976): 170–74.

Miropiev, M. A. "K voprosu o prosveshchenii nashikh inorodtsev." *Russkaia shkola* 5–6 (1901): 121–36.

Mirsky, D. S., and Whitfield, F. J., eds. *A History of Russian Literature from Its Beginning to 1960*. New York, 1968.

Moiseeva, G. N., ed. *Kazanskaia istoriia.* Moscow and Leningrad, 1954.

Mokhammed'iarov, Sh. F. *Osnovnye etapy proiskhozhdeniia i etnicheskoi istorii tatarskoi narodnosti.* Moscow, 1968.

Molostvova, E. V. "Vaisov Bozhii polk." *Mir Islama* 2 (1912): 143–52.

Monteuil, Vincent. *Les musulmans soviétiques.* Paris, 1957.

Mozharovskii, E. A. *Izlozhenie khoda missionerskogo dela po prosveshcheniiu inorodstvev s 1552 po 1867. Chteniia v Imperatorskom Obschchestve Istorii i Drevnostei Rossiiskikh pri Moskovskom Universitete,* book 1, part 2. Moscow, 1880.

Mukhamadiev, A. G. "Bulgaro-Tatarskaia monetnaia sistema serediny 13v." In *Issledovaniia po istoriografii Tatarii.* Kazan, 1978, pp. 126–40.

Mukhamed'iarov, Sh. F. "K voprosu o polozhenii krestianstva v Kazanskom khanstve." *Iz istorii klassovoi bor'by obshchestvennoi mysli v Povolzh'e i Priural'e. Sbornik statei. Uchenye zapiski Kazanskogo gosudarstvennogo universitete im. V. I. Ul'ianova Lenina* 122, no. 2 (1962): 150–53.

———. "Tarkhannyi iarlyk Kazanskogo khana Sakhib Gireia 1523g." In *Novoe o proshlom nashei strany: Pamiati akademika M. N. Tikhomirova.* Moscow, 1967, pp. 104–108.

Mukhamedova, R. G. *Tatary-Mishari: Istoriko-etnograficheskoe issledovanie.* Moscow, 1972.

Mukhariamov, M. K. *Oktiabr' i natsional'no-gosudarstvennoe stroitel'stvo v Tatarii (Oktiabr' 1917g.–1920g.)* Moscow, 1969.

———. "Za glubokoe issledovanie istorii Tatarii." *Kommunist Tatarii* 4 (1972): 37–42.

Musin, F. "Zemlia i chelovek na nei. Derevnia v sovremennoi Tatarskoi proze." *Oktiabr'* 6 (1972): 207–13.

Mustafin, R. "Obogoshchaiushchie traditsii (O sovremennoi tatarskoi literature)." *Volga* 3 (1973): 180–82.

———. "Polnovodnye pritoki (Obzor molodoi poezii Tatarii)." *Volga* 8 (1974): 168–76.

Musul'manin. Paris, 1910.

IV Musul'manskii s'ezd. S. Petersburg. 15–25 iiunia. 1914.

Mutallibov, S. M., ed. *Mahmud Kashghariy: Türkiy süzler devani (Devanu lughat it-Turk)* [Mahmud Kashghariy: A dictionary of Turkish words (Devanu lughat it-Turk)]. Tashkent, 1960.

Nafigov, R. *Formirovanie i razvitie peredovoi tatarskoi obshchestvenno-politicheskoi mysli. Ocherk istorii 1895–1917.* Kazan, 1967.

———. *Mullanur Vakhitov: Istoriko-biograficheskii ocherk.* Kazan, 1975.

Naselenie gorodov po perepisi 28-go ianvar'ia 1897 goda. St. Petersburg, 1897.

Naselenie SSSR (Chislennost', sostav i dvizhenie naseleniia). 1973. Statisticheskii Sbornik. Moscow, 1973.

Naselenie SSSR, 1973. Statisticheskii sbornik. Moscow, 1975.

Naselenie SSSR. Po dannym vsesoiuznoi perepisi naseleniia 1979 goda. Moscow, 1980.

Natsionalisty v 3-ei gosudarstvennoi Dume. St. Petersburg, 1912.

Nazipova, K. A. *Natsionalizatsiia promyshlennosti v Tatarii (1917–1921).* Moscow, 1976

Nolde, B. *La formation de l'empire russe. Etudes, notes et documents.* 2 vols. Paris, 1952–1953.

Novitskii, A. "Okhrana i ispol'zovanie pamiatnikov istorii i kultury." *Kommunist Tatarii* 8 (1980): 86–88.

Novoe o proshlom nashei strany: Pamiati akademika M. N. Tikhomirova. Moscow, 1976.

Oberländer, I., ed. *Russia Enters the Twentieth Century, 1894–1917.* New York, 1971.

Obrazovanie Bashkirskoi ASSR. Sbornik dokumentov i materialov. Ufa, 1959.

Obrazovanie TASSR. Sbornik dokumentov i materialov. Kazan, 1963.

Obshchestvenno-politicheskoe dvizhenie i klassovaia bor'ba na Srednei Volge. Kazan, 1972.

Ocherki istorii partiinoi organizatsii Tatarii. Kazan, 1962.

Ocherki po izucheniiu mestnogo kraia. Kazan, 1930.

Olshanskii, N. N., ed. *Chetvertaia gosudarstvennaia Duma. Portrety i biografii.* St. Petersburg, 1913.

O Magometanskikh mullakh. Religiozno-bytovoi ocherk. Kazan, 1907.

Opisanie vsekh v Rossiiskom gosudarstve obitaiushchikh narodov. St. Petersburg, 1799.

Orenburgskii krai. Orenburg, 1908.

Orenburgskoe slovo. Orenburg, 1916.

Osoboe soveshchanie po vyrabotke mer dlia protivodeistviia tatarsko-musul'manskomu vliianiiu v Privolzhskom krae v 1910 godu i o preobrazovanii Orenburgskogo Magometanskogo Dukhovnogo sobraniia. Kazan, 1910.

Ostroumov, M. N. P. *Chto takoe Koran?* Tashkent, 1883.

——. *Koran i progress.* Tashkent, 1901.

——. "Musul'manskaia vysshaia shkola (madrasa)." *ZMNP* 5 (1906): 113–67.

Pelenski, Jaroslaw. *Russia and Kazan: Conquest and Imperial Ideology (1438–1560s).* The Hague, 1974.

Peretiatkovich, G. I. *Povolzh'e v XV i XVI vekakh (Ocherki iz istorii kraia i ego kolonizatsii).* Moscow, 1877.

Permskaia zhizn'. Perm, 1916.

Permskie vedomosti. Perm, 1910–1916.

Pervyi s'ezd narodov Vostoka. Baku, 1–8 sent. 1920. Stenograficheskie otchety. Petrograd, 1920.

Pesikina, E. I. *Narodnyi komissariat po delam natsional'nostei i ego deiatel'nost' v 1917–1918g.* Moscow, 1950.

Petrash, Iu. G., and Khamitova, R. N. "Kharakteristike protsessa modernizatsii sovremennogo Islama v SSSR." *Voprosy nauchnogo ateizma* 4 (1967).

Petrushevskii, I. P. "K istorii soiurgala." *SV* 6 (1949): 227–46.

Pinegin, M. *Kazan' v eia proshlom i nastoiashchem.* Kazan, 1890.

Pipes, Richard. *The Formation of the Soviet Union: Communism and Nationalism, 1917–1923.* Cambridge, Mass., 1964.

Piru, Al. *Literatura Română veche.* Bucharest, 1961.

Pod'iachikh, P. G. *Naselenie SSSR.* Moscow, 1961.

Polivanov, E. D. *Foneticheskie osobennosti kasimovskogo dialekta.* Moscow, 1923.

Prauda, A. "Vliianie bilingvizma na nekotorye iavleniia narodnoi kul'tury." *Sovetskaia etnografiia* 2 (1972): 17–26.

Primernye programmy predmetov prepodavaemykh v nachal'nykh narodnykh uchilishchakh vedomstva Ministerstva Narodnogo Prosveshcheniia. St. Petersburg, 1897.

Programma Musul'manskoi fraktsii v gosudarstvennoi Dume. St. Petersburg, 1907.

Pruzhanskii, N., ed. *Pervaia Rossiiskaia gosudarstvennaia Duma.* St. Petersburg, 1906.

PSRL [Polnoe sobranie russkikh letopisei]. 39 vols. St. Petersburg, Moscow, and Leningrad, 1846–1980.

PSZRI [Polnoe sobranie zakonov rossiiskoi imperii]. St. Petersburg, 1830–1917.

Quelquejay, Ch. "Le Vaisisme à Kazan." *Le monde d'Islam* 1–2 (1959): 90–95.

Qushay, Gh., ed. *Kontr-rivolütsion Soltanghäliefchelkkä qarshï* [Against counterrevolutionary Sultangalievism]. Kazan, 1929.

Rafikov, A. Kh. *Ocherki istorii knigopechataniia v Turtsii.* Leningrad, 1975.

Rahman, Fazlur. *Islam.* New York, 1968.

Rakhim, A. *Materialy dlia bibliografii po tatarovedeniiu (1918–1930).* Kazan, 1930.

———. *Tatarskie epigraficheskie pamiatniki.* Kazan, 1930.

Rakhim, G. *Chächäk takïya* [The flower hat]. Kazan, 1981.

Rakhim, G., and Gaziz, G. *Tatar ädäbiyatï tarikhï. Burïngï dävir* [A history of Tatar literature. The ancient period] (in Tatar, Arabic script). 2 vols. Kazan, 1924–1925.

Rakowska-Harmstone, T. *Russia and Nationalism in Central Asia. The Case of Tadzhikistan.* Baltimore and London, 1970.

Rashitov, A. *Koyashlï il-bakhet ile* [Sunny land—land of happiness]. Kazan, 1981.

Raspredelenie naseleniia imperii po glavnym veroispovedaniiam. St. Petersburg, 1901.

Reddaway, W. F., ed. *Documents of Catherine the Great.* Cambridge, England, 1931.

Revendications des nationalités opprimées. Recueil des mémoires, rapports, et documents présentés à la III-me conférence des nationalités. Lausanne 27–29 Juin 1916. Lausanne, 1917.

Rezoliutsii kursov-konferentsii perepodgotovki natsional'nykh pedtekhnikumov. Kazan, 1925.

Rieber, A. J. *Merchants and Entrepreneurs in Imperial Russia.* Chapel Hill, 1982.

RLRB [Radio Liberty Research Bulletin]. Washington, D.C., 1976–.

RMM [Revue du monde musulman]. Paris, 1906–1914.

RN [Revoliutsiia i natsional'nosti]. 1930.

Romanyshyn, S. "School Reform and the Language Question in the USSR." *Problems of the Peoples of the USSR* 2 (1959): 17–21.

Rorlich, A. "Acculturation in Tatarstan: The Case of the Sabantui Festival." *SR* 2 (1982): 316–22.

———. "G. Ibragimov." In *Modern Encyclopedia of Russian and Soviet History.* Vol. 14. Lexington, 1976–1984, pp. 113–17.

———. " 'Which Way Will Tatar Culture Go?' A Controversial Essay by G. Ibragimov." *CMRS* 3–4 (1974): 363–71.

Roshal', M. G. "O politicheskom polozhenii v Tatarskoi respublike v 1920g." *Istoricheskii arkhiv* 2 (1961): 156–65.

R-ov. "O nachal'nom obrazovanii inorodtsev." *Inorodcheskoe obrazovanie* 3 (1915): 738–52.

Rozhkova, M. K. *Ekonomicheskaia politika tsarskogo pravitel'stva na Srednem Vostoke vo vtoroi chetverti XIX veka i russkaia burzhuaziia.* Moscow, 1949.

———. *Ekonomicheskie sviazi Rossii so Srednei Aziei. 46-60-e gody XIX veka.* Moscow, 1963.

Rybakov, S. *Ustroistvo i nuzhdy upravleniia dukhovnymi delami Musul'man v Rossii.* St. Petersburg, 1917.

Rywkin, Michael. *Moscow's Muslim Challenge: Soviet Central Asia.* New York, 1982.

SA [*Sovetskaia arkheologiia*]. Moscow and Leningrad, 1936–.

Saadi, A. *Tatar ädäbiyatï tarihi.* [A history of Tatar literature] (in Tatar, Arabic script). Kazan, 1926.

Sadri, R. "Resurgence of the Interest in Islam Among the Tatar intelligentsia." *RLRB,* January 11, 1983, pp. 1–5.

Safargaliev, M. G. *Raspad Zolotoi Ordy. Uchenye zapiski Mordovskogo Gosudarstvennogo Universiteta. Vypusk XI.* Saransk, 1960.

Safin, Sh. "Shihabettin Märjani kul yazmasï." *KU* 4 (1982); 171–75.

Safiullina, F. "Khazinädä nilär bar?" [What does the treasure house hold?]. *KU* 1 (1983): 171–78.

Sagidullin, M. *K istorii Vaisovskogo dvizheniia.* Kazan, 1930.

Saidasheva, M. A. *Lenin i sotsialisticheskoe stroitel'stvo v Tatarii, 1918–1923.* Moscow, 1963.

Said-Galiev, S. "Pervyi god raboty. Iz otcheta zhurnala Fän häm Din za 1925–26g." *Antireligioznik* 4 (1927): 26–34.

Saifi, F. *Trudy doma tatarskoi kul'tury.* 3 vols. Kazan, 1930.

Sbornik materialov po voprosam o smeshannykh brakakh i o veroispovedanii detei ot sikh brakov proiskhodiashchikh. St. Petersburg, 1906.

Sbornik rechei deputatov gosudarstvennoi Dumy I i II sozyva. Kniga pervaia. St. Petersburg, 1907.

Sbornik tsirkuliarov i inykh rukovodiashchikh rasporiazhenii po okrugu Orenburgskogo Magometanskogo Dukhovnogo Sobraniia 1836–1903. Ufa, 1905.

SE [Sovetskaia etnografiia]. Moscow, 1926–.

Seton-Watson, H. *The Russian Empire, 1801–1917*. Oxford, 1967.

Serbina, K. N., ed. *Ustiuzhskii letopisnyi svod*. Moscow and Leningrad, 1950.

Seydahmet, Cafer. *Gaspirali Ismail Bey*. Istanbul, 1934.

Shaknovich, M. I. *Lenin i problemy ateizma*. Moscow and Leningrad, 1961.

Shastina, N. P. *Puteshestvie na vostok Plano Karpini i Gil'oma Rubruka*. Moscow, 1957.

Sheehy, A. "Data from the Census of 1979 on the Tatars and the Bashkirs." *RLRB*, July 15, 1980, pp. 2–4.

Shirinskii-Shakhmatov. "Materialy dlia istorii i statistiki nashikh gimnazii." *ZMNP* (1864) 1: 129–71.

Shishkin, N. I. *Istoriia goroda Kasimova s drevneishikh vremen*. Riazan, 1891.

"Shkol'nyi vopros v Russkom musul'manstve." *Mir Islama* 2 (1913): 433–67 and 5 (1913): 3 and 290–92.

Singalevich, S. P. *Staraia i novaia Kazan'*. Kazan, 1927.

SIRIO [Sbornik imperatorskogo russkogo istoricheskogo obshchestva]. 148 vols. St. Petersburg, 1867–1917.

Slonim, A. *The Epic of Russian Literature from Its Origins Through Tolstoy*. New York, 1964.

Smirnov, K. A. *Velikie Bolgary*. Moscow, 1969.

Smirnov, A. P. "K voprosu o proiskhozhdenii Kazanskikh Tatar po dannym etnografii." *SE* 3 (1946): 75–86.

———. "K voprosu o proiskhozhdenii Tatar Povolzh'ia." *SE* 3 (1946): 43.

———. *Nekotorye voprosy srednevekovoi istorii Povolzh'ia*. Kazan, 1957.

———. *Volzhskie Bolgary*. Moscow, 1951.

Smolin, V. F. *K voprosu o proiskhozhdenii Kamsko-Volzhskikh Bolgar. Razbor drevneishikh teorii*. Kazan, 1921.

Smykov, Iu. I., ed. *Ocherki istorii narodov Povolzh'ia i Priural'ia*. Kazan, 1967.

Solov'ev, S. M. *Istoriia Rossii s drevneishikh vremen*. 15 vols. Moscow, 1959–1965.

Sorokin, G. Z. *I s'ezd narodov Vostoka*. Moscow, 1961.

Spuler, B. *The Muslim World. The Mongol Period*. Leiden, 1960.

———, ed. *History of the Mongols Based on Eastern and Western Accounts of the Thirteenth and Fourteenth Centuries*. Berkeley and Los Angeles, 1972.

SR [Slavic Review]. 1961–.

SRMNP [Sbornik rasporiazhenii po Ministerstvu Narodnogo Prosveshcheniia]. 9 vols. St. Petersburg, 1866–1917.

Stal'nyi, V. *Kadety*. Moscow, 1930.

Stenograficheskii otchet IX oblastnoi konferentsii Tatarskoi organizatsii RKP(b). Kazan, 1924.

Stenograficheskii otchet. Pervyi vsesoiuznyi tiurkologicheskii s'ezd. 26 II–5 III 1926. Baku, 1926.

Stenograficheskie otchety gosudarstvennoi Dumy 3-go sozyva. St. Petersburg, 1907.

Sultangaliev, M. *Metody antireligioznoi propagandy sredi musul'man.* Moscow, 1922.

Suomen Virallinen Tilasto. Helsinki, 1973.

SV [*Sovetskoe vostokovedenie*] Moscow, 1940–.

Szczesniak, B., ed. *The Russian Revolution and Religion. A Collection of Documents Concerning the Suppression of Religion by the Communists, 1917–1925.* Notre Dame, Indiana, 1959.

Tahir, Mahmut. "Kazan Türklerinde tahsil-bilim (Medrese-i-Hüseiniye)" [Education—knowledge among Kazan Turks. Hüseiniye medresse]. *Kazan* 3 (1971): 54–57.

Tarasov, A. *Razgrom kontrrevoliutsionnoi avantiury tatarskoi burzhuazii v nachale 1918g.* Kazan, 1940.

Tarık Us, Hakkı, ed. *Ahmed Midhat'ı anıyoruz* [Remembering Ahmed Midhat]. Istanbul, 1955.

Tatar balalar poeziase antologiyase [An anthology of poetry for Tatar children]. Kazan, 1980.

Tatar teleneng anglatmalï süzlege [The explicative dictionary of the Tatar language]. 3 vols. Kazan. 1977–1981.

Tatariia v proshlom i nastoiashchem. Sbornik statei. Kazan, 1975.

Tatary Srednego Povolzh'ia i Priural'ia. Moscow, 1967.

Tatary Srednego Povolzh'ia v Pugachevskom vosstanii. Kazan, 1973.

Temir, Ahmet. "Tatar sözünün menşei hakkında" [On the origins of the term *Tatar*]. *Kazan* 3 (1971): 41–45.

———. "Tukay deviri Kazan şairleri" [Kazan writers of the Tukay era]. *Kazan* 3 (1971): 13.

———. "Türk-moğol imparatorluğu devrinde askeri teşkilat" [Military organization during the Mongol-Turkish empire]. *Kazan* 7–8 (1972): 7–24.

Tevfikoğlu, M. "Ali Emir Efendi." *Türk Kültürü* 8 (1970): 244–52.

Thomsen, V. *Inscriptions de l'Orkhon.* Helsingfors, 1896.

Tikhomirov, M. N. *Rossiia v XVI stoletii.* Moscow, 1962.

Timar (Qaraqamïsh) Musulman jemgiyet hayriyesiniñ ustafï (Uralsk oblast) [The statutes of the Timr-Qaramïsh Muslim Benevolent Society of the Uralsk region] (in Tatar, Arabic script). Orenburg, 1909.

Tizengauzen [Tiesenhausen], V. G., ed. *Sbornik materialov otnosiashchikhsia k istorii Zolotoi Ordy.* 2 vols. Moscow and Leningrad, 1941.

Tokarev, S. A. *Etnografiia narodov SSSR. Istoricheskie osnovy byta i kul'tury.* Moscow, 1958.

Tomilov, N. A. "Sovremennye etnicheskie protsessy u Tatar gorodov zapadnoi Sibiri." *SE* 6 (1972): 87–97.

Tretii vserossiiskii Musul'manskii s'ezd. Kazan, 1906.

Trofimova, T. A. *Etnogenez Tatar Srednego Povolzh'ia v svete dannykh antropologii.* Moscow and Leningrad, 1949.

Trudovaia pomoshch v guberniiakh Kazanskoi, Viatskoi, i Simbirskoi. Otchet po trudovoi pomoshchi v 1899. St. Petersburg, 1900.

Trudy Otdeleniia Imperatorskogo Russkogo Arkheologicheskogo Obshchestva. Part 8. St. Petersburg, 1964.

Tucker, R. C., and Cohen, S. F., eds. *The Great Purge Trial: Transcript of the Moscow Trial of the Anti-Soviet Bloc of Rightists and Trotskyites.* New York, 1965.

Tugay, M. F. *Yusuf Akçura. Hayatı ve eserleri* [Yusuf Akchura. His life and works]. Istanbul, 1944.

Türk Dünyası El Kitabı [A handbook of the Turkic world]. 2 vols. Ankara, 1976.

Türk ili (in Turkish, Arabic script). Istanbul, 1928.

Uchenye zapiski Imperatorskogo Kazanskogo Universiteta. Part 3. Kazan, 1852.

Ukazatel' dlia puteshestviia ego Imperatorskago Vysochestva Nikolaia Maksimilianovicha kniazia Romanovskogo, gertsoga Leikhtenbergskago na Ural'skii khrebet. 1866. 2 vols. St. Petersburg, 1866. Manuscript, University of Wisconsin Manuscript Collection: MS 115.

Ulkutasir, M. Şakir. *Kaşgarlı Mahmut.* Istanbul, 1946.

Ullah, Najib. *Islamic Literature.* New York, 1963.

Unat, Faik Reşit. *Hicri tarihleri miladi tarihe çevirme kılavuzu* [Guide for converting dates of the Muslim calendar to their Christian calendar equivalents]. Ankara, 1959.

U.S. Office of Strategic Services, Research and Analysis Branch, R. & A. no. 890.2. *Japanese Attempts at Infiltration Among Muslims in Russia and Her Borderlands.* Washington, D.C., 1944.

Uralgiray, Yusuf, ed. *Uzun günlerde oruç* [Fasting during long days]. Ankara, 1975.

Usmanov, M. *Zavetnaia mechta Khusaina Faizkhanova.* Kazan, 1980.

Vagabov, M. V. "Bol'she vnimaniia sovetskomu islamovedeniiu." *Voprosy filosofii* 12 (1966): 172–75.

Vakhidov, S. G. "Iarlyk khana Sakhib-Gireiia." In *Vestnik Nauchnogo Obshchestva Tatarovedeniia,* no. 1–2. Kazan, 1925, pp. 29–37.

Valeev, F. Kh. *Drevnee i srednevekovoe iskusstvo Srednego Povolzh'ia.* Ioshkar-Ola, 1975.

Validov, J. *Ocherki istorii obrazovannosti i literatury Tatar.* Moscow and Petrograd, 1923.

Välieva, "Bolgar sängate säkhifälärennän [From the pages of Bulgar art]. *KU* 1 (1977): 139–44.

Vambery, A. "The Awakening of the Tatars." *The Nineteenth Century* 54 (February 1905): 217–27.

———. "Die Kulturbestrebungen der Tataren." *Deutsche Rundschau* 132 (1907): 72–92.

———. "The Emancipation of Women in Islam." *The International* 2 (1908): 14.

Vaqt (in Tatar, Arabic script). Orenburg, 1913.

Vasilov, V. N., and Sultanov, T. I. "Vsesoiuznaia tiurkologicheskaia konferentsiia." *SE* 3 (1977).

Veliaminov-Zernov, V. *Issledovanie o Kasimovskikh tsariakh i tsarevichakh.* 2 vols. St. Petersburg, 1863.

Velidi-Togan, A. Zeki. *Türk ve Tatar tarihi* [Turkish and Tatar history] (in Tatar, Arabic script). Kazan, 1912.

Vernadsky, G. V. *Zolotaia Orda. Egipet i Vizantiia v ikh vzaimootnosheniiakh v tsarstvovanie Mikhaila Paleologa.* Prague, 1927.

Veselovskii, B. *Istoriia zemstva za sorok let.* 2 vols. St. Petersburg, 1909–1911.

Vestnik Nauchnogo Obshchestva Tatarovedeniia. Kazan, 1925.

Viatka gubirnasï Malmïzh uiazï Tuntar kariasïndegï "Shems" kitabhanesïnïng ustafï (ustav bezplatnoi biblioteki-chital'ni "Shams" dlia Musul'man v der. Tiunteri Arbarskoi volosti, Malmyzhskogo uezda, Viatskoi gubernii. Kazan, 1908.

Volgo-Kam'e v nachale epokhi rannego zheleza VIII–VI v.v. do n.e. Moscow, 1977.

Voprosy etnogeneza tiurkoiazychnykh narodov Srednego Povolzh'ia i Priural'ia. Kazan, 1971.

Vorob'ev, N. I. *Kazanskie Tatary. Etnograficheskoe issledovanie material'noi kul'tury dooktiabr'skogo perioda.* Kazan, 1953.

———. *Tatary srednego Povolzh'ia i Priural'ia.* Moscow, 1947.

Vozkresensky, A. A. *O sisteme prosveshcheniia inorodtsev.* Kazan, 1913.

Walsh, Warren B. "The Composition of the Dumas." *Russian Review* 2 (1949): 111–16.

———. "Political Parties in the Russian Dumas." *Journal of Modern History* 1 (1950): 144–50.

Watt, W. M. *The Faith and Practice of Al-Ghazali.* London, 1953.

Wieczynski, Joseph L., ed. *Modern Encyclopedia of Russian and Soviet History.* 40 vols. Lexington, 1976.

Yulduz. Orenburg, 1915.

Zabiri, A. *Kïskacha tarih-i Bolghar* [Brief history of Bulgar] (in Tatar, Arabic script). Kazan, 1907.

Zagoskin, N. P., ed. *Za sto let: Biograficheskii slovar' professorov i prepodavatelei Imperatorskogo Kazanskogo Universiteta 1804–1904.* Kazan, 1904.

Zäkiev, M. Z. *Tatar khalïk teleneng barlïkka kilue* [The emergence of the Tatar vernacular]. Kazan, 1977.

Zaliai, L. Z. "K voprosu o proiskhozhdenii Tatar Povolzh'ia (po materialam iazyka)." *SE* 3 (1946): 87–91.

Zaman kalendarï [Calendar]. Orenburg, 1909, 1910, and 1912.

Za pervyi god veroispovednoi svobody v Rossii. St. Petersburg, 1907.

Zarif, M. *Ishannar-därvishlär* [Ishans-dervishes]. Kazan, 1931.

Zauralskii krai. Orenburg, 1914–1916.

Zelenin, D. "N. I. Il'minskii i prosveshchenie inorodtsev." *Russkaia shkola* 3 (1902): 175–94.

Zenkovsky, S. A. "A Century of Tatar Revival." *American Slavic and East European Review* 10 (1953): 303–19.

———. *Pan-Turkism and Islam in Russia.* Cambridge, Mass., 1960.

Zguta, Russel. "Skomorokhi: The Russian Minstrel Entertainers." *SR* 2 (1972): 297–314.

Zhanaev, S. "Staraia Bukhara." *Musul'manin* 2 (1910): 48–49.

Zimin, A. A. *Rossiia na poroge novogo vremeni.* Moscow, 1972.

ZMNP [*Zhurnal Ministerstva Narodnogo Prosveshcheniia*]. St. Petersburg, 1834–1917.

Znamenskii, P. "Sistema inorodcheskogo obrazovaniia v Turkestanskom krae pri generale-gubernatore K. P. Fon-Kaufmane." *Russkaia shkola* 7–8 (1902): 79–97.

Index